Organizational decision making

McGraw-Hill Series In Management

Keith Davis, CONSULTING EDITOR

organizational

decision

making

Fremont A. Shull, Jr.

RESEARCH PROFESSOR OF
MANAGEMENT AND SOCIOLOGY
UNIVERSITY OF GEORGIA

André L. Delbecq

GRADUATE SCHOOL OF BUSINESS AND INDUSTRIAL RELATIONS
RESEARCH INSTITUTE
UNIVERSITY OF WISCONSIN

L. L. Cummings

GRADUATE SCHOOL OF BUSINESS AND INDUSTRIAL RELATIONS
RESEARCH INSTITUTE
UNIVERSITY OF WISCONSIN

McGraw-Hill Book Company
New York St. Louis San Francisco Düsseldorf London Mexico
Panama Sydney Toronto

organizational decision making

Library of Congress Catalog Card Number 76-119829

57182

1 2 3 4 5 6 7 8 9 0   MAMM   7 9 8 7 6 5 4 3 2 1 0

This book was set in Caledonia by The Maple
Press Company, and printed on permanent paper
and bound by The Maple Press Company. The
drawings were done by John Cordes, J. & R.
Technical Services, Inc. The editor was Sally
Mobley. Stuart Levine supervised the production.

foreword

All life is adaptive. Even the single-celled amoeba reacts to environmental changes in such a way as to preserve life-sustaining constant states—to reduce tensions. We could say that it reacts in such a way as to achieve something worthwhile, something of value. In man, this adaptation has become self-conscious, and we speak of this self-conscious adaptation as "mind." By virtue of his mastery of symbols, man can react to symbolic representation of the environment; he does not have to await direct contact with it. Consequently, he can react to a good deal more than what is immediately and directly present. As George Herbert Mead said, the past and the future are always with him in the present.

Man's freedom from the immediate environment, his ability to create tentative environments symbolically, provides him with the opportunity (and the necessity) to exercise choice, to reason. Nonconscious action, action without symbolizing, as Leslie White would have called it, can be depicted as a sequence of events from environmental change, to tension in the living organism, to random action until the tension is reduced. Tension-reducing actions are defined as successful. They tend to be learned and subsequently repeated when the same stimulus appears, thereby eliminating the wasteful period of random activity.

In lower animals, many of these successful action patterns are acquired genetically; they are instinctive. When action becomes conscious, it can be depicted as a sequence of events from problem (environmental stimulus), to choice of means (action), to goal (reduction of tension). That is to say, parallel to events in the environment and the organism are symbolic events—problem, means, and ends. The theory of choice, decision making as it is currently called, is concerned with these symbolic events. The parallelism between these two sets of events, the organismic and the symbolic, is assumed.

Man's curiosity knows no bounds. He is even curious about his curiosity. In the past hundred years or so he has become increasingly curious about his mental processes, including how he makes his choices or decides. The literature on this subject has become voluminous, indeed. It can be divided, roughly, into two types, the normative and the descriptive. With a few exceptions, both types see the individual as the center of decision. The first type, the normative, has been dominated by economists (lately also statisticians) and has been concerned with the rules of rational choice. The second type has been dominated by those psychologists who have used a decision-making approach to try to explain individual behavior.

Since both economizing and individual behavior are matters of concern to the managements of organizations, decision-making literature has become a part of management literature. In addition, a few people have tried to study organizations by studying a few specific decisions made by organizations, especially investment decisions. Some modest success has been achieved in this endeavor so that decision-making literature is now frequently classified in that amorphous catch-all called "organization theory." Literacy in this subject presumes some familiarity with research and writing in the field of decision making.

For the student of organization, the situation with regard to material on decision making is unsatisfactory in two respects. First, most of it is not obviously relevant to the study of organizations. Trying to understand organizations from this perspective is like trying to understand life using the sciences of chemistry and physics but not biology. It is just too difficult. In the second place, the literature is too voluminous, scattered, eclectic, fugitive. As far as I know it has not yet been summarized in textbook form.

This book by Professors Shull, Delbecq, and Cummings will go far toward eliminating these difficulties for the general student of organization and administration. This book is a treatise on decision making. Furthermore, in their conception of the subject the authors go beyond individual choices in various small unnatural situations (the ingenuity of psychology professors in imposing unusual choices upon their student subjects in the laboratory leaves one a little dizzy) and discuss the impact of both informal and large formal organization structures upon choice behavior.

Although they also tackle the problem of the norms of rationality, the authors' primary orientation is descriptive and predictive. They summarize a large amount of material on this subject, but they also add a good deal of fruitful theorizing and reconstructing of their own. This book will help to fill a big gap in our textual material for education in administration and to do it at a high level of intelligence.

Victor A. Thompson

The University of Illinois
Urbana, Illinois

preface

This book focuses on several perspectives relevant to the understanding and improvement of decision making within formally structured and administered organizations. Our colleagues and students who have attempted to teach and learn about organizational decision making are well aware of the complexity of the issues involved.

Our strategy for dealing with this complexity is reflected in a specific approach to the study of decision making. *First,* we treat decision making within the organization as a major dependent variable in administration. Events occur and behaviors exhibit themselves as decisions (and their implementations) within the organization. Decisions are, therefore, subject to norms of efficiency and effectiveness.

Second, the processes through which decisions are made, implemented, and evaluated are complex and frequently opaque. This implies that the study of decision making must be multilevel (individual, interpersonal, organizational, and environmental) and attend multiple variables within each level.

In order to introduce the student of decision making to this complexity, we have in the past typically sent him to several bodies of literature, each reflecting a different perspective on decision making within the organization. Usually these would be psychology, sociology, economics, administration, political science, mathematics, and logic. We have traditionally viewed this survey of related areas of theory as necessary for a comprehensive knowledge of decision making. On the other hand, it possessed several weaknesses: (1) it segmented, artificially, our understanding of the wholeness and unity of organizational decision making, (2) it assumed unrealistically high levels of mathematical and behavioral competence on the part of the consumers of such material, and (3) it did not necessarily provide a unifying theme centering on the relevance of these approaches to understanding and improving decision making within the organization.

Third, as a result of these problems, in the present effort we have sifted several perspectives from several disciplines in an attempt to capture the flavor and dimensions of decision making but in a fashion which, we hope, provides easier entrance into these multiple disciplines.

Fourth, such a generic overview implies that our strategy is intentionally somewhat abstract and eclectic. We assume this posture because our aim is to sketch out the field and to provide several perspectives from which decision making may be viewed.

Fifth, we have purposely attempted to minimize prescriptive and normative positions. This means that in the material to follow, the reader will find concepts and propositions with which he may feel uncomfortable. Our reaction to these probable feelings is that this work purposefully offers perspectives that raise questions as well as suggest insights.

Two tactics are employed in implementing the total plan. First, the chapters of the book are sequenced as building from a microperspective to a macroperspective. We begin by examining the individual as a perceiving and learning organism attempting to adapt to and change its environment through effective decision making. Next we examine this decision maker in his interpersonal (small-group) situations. Finally, we expand our perspective to include organizational and environmental influences on decision making. Thus, in terms of discipline-oriented perspectives, we move across selected areas of psychology, social psychology, sociology, economics, and general administration. Second, we include in the chapters technical, speculative, and applied illustrations. These serve varying purposes: In most cases they extend a topic beyond the hard, empirical evidence bearing on that topic. In a few cases, they generalize the contents of the chapter by exploring several administrative implications of the topic. In both cases, the illustrations provide a more specific, narrowing focus.

The authors owe a special debt of gratitude to many individuals who have influenced their thinking concerning the field of decision making and have provided special help, stimulation, or criticism at strategic stages in the development of the book.

For Professor Shull's contribution, he is primarily obligated to the many discussions on decision making which he has had with graduate students at Indiana University, Southern Illinois University, and the University of Wisconsin. The logic and structure of this work owe much to that of Herbert Simon and Victor Thompson. He would like to acknowledge, also, the editors at McGraw-Hill, especially Robert Locke and Keith Davis, who offered constant encouragement and aided in developing initially the approach of this book. Junior Feild also deserves his thanks for editorial help. Finally, he is indebted to Southern Illinois University for allowing him to allocate a significant proportion of his time to this endeavor.

Professor Delbecq wishes to acknowledge, in particular, the special role which George Psathas and Sheldon Stryker played in introducing him to the nexus between small-group theory and decision-making behavior as a graduate student; and, likewise, the sage tutorage of James Thompson, whose theories of decision strategies within organizations provided a transition into the macro-organizational linkage. He also acknowledges the unique contribution of two colleagues, Alan Leader and Thomas Klein, who throughout the subsequent six years in the development of his thinking have been extraordinary colleagues whose generous criticism and dialogue have constantly forced him to reexamine his perspectives.

Professor Cummings wishes to acknowledge the encouragement and insight provided by several colleagues: James D. Thompson of Vanderbilt University and Donald L. Harnett of Indiana University, John O'Shaughnessy and William H. Newman of Columbia University, and, most importantly, his two co-authors, as do his co-authors acknowledge his contributions.

All three authors owe particular gratitude to the following, who offered major parts of published works or written materials: Jay Dalal, William Gore, Delbert Miller, and Richard Newman; and *Administrative Science Quarterly, Behavioral Science, Business Perspectives, Free Press of Glencoe,* and *Journal of Purchasing.*

Fremont A. Shull, Jr.

Andre L. Delbecq

L. L. Cummings

contents

Organizational Perspectives

Econological Perspectives

part

INTRODUCTION

one

one

BASIC CONCERNS AND CONTEXT

Man's life is an ongoing stream of decisions, a continuum of choice-making imperatives. He is constantly confronted with situations where he more or less consciously selects among alternative courses of action or states of existence. Whether he acts as a part of an administered organization, a member of a small, closely knit group, or independently, this exigency is not altered. As scientist or layman, vocationally or domestically, he constantly exercises his preferences.

His choices may be trivial or significant, personally or organizationally related. They may involve foresight and logic or manifest shortsightedness and limited rationality. His decisions may entail careful deliberation or only fleeting attention. A significant part of man's life reflects the decision process—even some habitual behavior can be viewed as automatic responses to choices previously made. For this reason alone, decision making merits study and evaluation. Its significance becomes doubly important, though, to the student of management because of the growing emphasis on decision making as a central dimension of administrative and organizational theory.

Evolving Concern in Administrative Science

An interesting and necessary management concern is occasioned by the current emphasis on decision making in administrative theory. Decisions, McCammy argued in 1947, are ". . . at the very center of the process of administration and the discussion of administration will be more systematic if we accept a framework for the analysis of decision making." More recently, Braybrooke (1963, p. 536) has contended that: "It is worth investigating the notion that the essential contribution of the man in power . . . is to make decisions, for this is a better description of his activities than many others and perhaps is closer to being a distinctive description than most." Injunctions such as these have compelled a greater and more sophisticated concern with decision making in administered systems.

This increasing attention stems, in part, from rather subtle changes in attitudes toward and knowledge about man as he operates in an organizational environment. These changes have been reinforced by a cultural modification of members' expectations and competencies relative to participation in organizations.

Concurrent with these developments, a third evolvement, originating largely in the physical and biological sciences, has shed new light on the administrator's role, especially as it pertains to specialization in regulating organizational decision making. The nature and implications of this latter development, now generally subsumed under the caption "cybernetics,"[1] are worthy of brief comment.

CONCERNS WITH DECISION MAKING IN MANAGEMENT

A major and traditional *raison d'être* for organized behavior has been the need to exploit the advantages of task specialization and division of labor (cf. Simon, 1947). While not always recognized, vertical specialization can occur in organizations, as between decision making and operations. Although this distinction between "thinking" and "doing" may

---

[1] A detailed recounting of the evolution of the concept is not offered; only implications for our purposes will be discussed here. For a more complete discussion, see Wiener, 1948.

be more academic than real, it provides a basic justification historically for leadership in group behavior. In this regard, the notion of cybernetics has added insight into managerial behavior.[2] To this concept we turn our attention.

For survival in an environment which is less than fully benevolent and within which other entities compete for scarce resources, some foresight and deliberation would seem to have positive value. Managerial theory assumes that some specialization in steerage or directional activity is required if more than random, reflexive accommodation to the environment is to be made by an organization. Accordingly, where processing activities are performed by nonmanagers, control is required in order to ensure direction and coordination. If self-contained, then, such an organization can be seen as a self-regulating system, attempting to modify its environment in some way, with management functioning as the regulator or homeostatic agency.

This simile suggests that human organizations are composed of selected members who perform instrumental acts in an attempt to act upon the environment. More important to our concern with complex organizations, efficient "modification" of the environment requires, in addition, coordination as well as directional decisions, given interdependence among the operational activities. We can, therefore, define *administration* as strategic decision making about the external environment and the regulation of instrumental decisions internal to the organization. The functions of administration can be seen from this perspective as similar to those of the mind and nervous system of the human being.

Cybernetics, in this sense, has become a normative model for administrative behavior (cf. Nagel, 1952).[3] Admittedly, propagation and elaboration of this analog for social organizations has resulted in a growing emphasis upon the structure and function of the system rather than upon the role of a particular manager. As such the cybernetic model is simplistic. Nonetheless, it provides insight into administered systems. (See, for example, Optner, 1960.)[4]

This approach may be viewed as depicted in Figure 1-1. From this

---

[2] Webster shows that cybernetics comes from the Greek word, *Kybernetes,* meaning "helmsman." Thus, it would appear to be similar in connotation to *supervision.*

[3] At the same time, the reader should be aware of the limitations and possible misdirection offered by cybernetics as an isomorphism of human organizations. Unless, for example, a second-level program is imputed to the regulator, the system is purely adaptive, while man as a regulator can learn to act strategically. Moreover, human information channels tend to break down because, in the hierarchy, an incumbent becomes both receptor and affector. In fact, as contrasted to closed-loop control, many authorities refer to open-control systems wherein man is involved.

[4] The approach centers attention on communication and decision networks imposed upon the operating units, rather than on microcosmic supervisory (face-to-face) functions which may or may not relate to the total system.

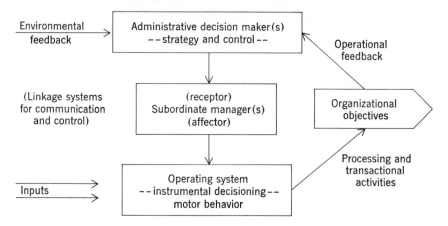

FIGURE 1-1   COMPLEX ORGANIZATIONS AS SELF-REGULATING SYSTEMS

vantage point, we can see that each incumbent of a managerial position—each role receptor—acts as an affector within the system as well; that is, as well as receiving messages from the system, he decides and transmits.

Decision making, of course, cannot be examined merely in terms of the aggregate system. Since each managerial incumbent has certain discretionary powers, particularly in the light of current tendencies toward decentralization, each management position—and, in truth, each operational position—becomes a decision center itself. In addition, given the organizational hierarchy, each decision center can be conceived as being more or less linked with some higher decision center. From all of this, we can see decision-making theory as having three concerns in the administration of organized systems:

1. As a conceptual vantage point for the development of models to gain insight into and improve the administrator's decisions as he operates as a responsible agent within the total administrative system;

2. As a conceptual framework for understanding, influencing, and predicting interaction between other actors holding positions in the organization; and

3. As a first approximation for understanding the organization as a system manifesting decisions in its struggle for survival and growth within a dynamic and competitive environment.

Conceptual Evolution of the Decision Unit

As stated above, the orientation and posture toward man and the states of knowledge and norms of his behavior have tremendous impact upon the conceptualization and implementation of an administered system. In this light, then, it seems appropriate to examine, briefly, the changing view of man in an organizational context. This evolution is especially worthy of elaboration since it illustrates further the cause of increasing focus on decision making as a concern of administration. In addition, such an account demonstrates how man and his knowledge and attitudes about himself are functions of his own heritage as well as products of his times. Finally, this discussion helps form the conceptual base for the perspectives on man taken in this work.

Early management theory drew working assumptions from the classical "economic man," which depicted him as generally malleable—in fact, a passive agent of the organization. This point of view held, for example, that organizations are ". . . controlled by natural persons, but these 'officers' act for the organization and not as individuals" (Knight, 1951, p. 29). Man was considered a homogeneous resource responding, for relevant predictive (theoretical) purposes, rather singly and exclusively to economic stimuli. Within this conception, interest in decision making was evidenced by normatively stated economic prescriptions for the decision unit—the firm. The assumptions were made that knowledge and information were nearly perfect, and that sensitivity and identification with the organization were almost complete. In this way, we could speak of the *firm's* decision.

However, with the advent of growing aggregations, implying large scale employment and extensive bureaucratic superstructures, organizations could be typified more accurately as complex decision networks. In emerging *bureaucracy*, largely associated with governmental administration, concern (for example, by Weber, 1947) was directed to this network in terms of intra-organizational, rather than only external, market, behavior. Here, attention was largely on structuring and defining positions to enhance organizationally rational decisions made by incumbents within the hierarchy. In this conception, man was considered malleable but was allowed to exercise discretion according to delegated authority, as within constraints of formal organizational rules.[5] While largely holding to the assumptions of organizational commitment and identification, the concept of homogeneous man was waived through the proposition of expertise; that is, the differential capacities among members can be assigned so as to make better organizational decisions, and candidates should be selected and hired accordingly. Attending injunctions, then, stemmed from formally structuring roles and their

[5] What is being described is generally true of both "bureaucratic" and "organization management" theory. The major distinction is that bureaucracy treats instrumental decisions made by subordinates in dealing with clients (distributive activities), while organization management tends to concentrate on internal coordinating activities. For the latter, which was an historical progeny, see Mooney and Reiley and Urwick.

relationships so as to maximize incumbents' potential, especially in matching "expert" man to formal role requirements.

Somewhat coincidental with this body of thought, another "school" evolved: *scientific management*. While still viewed as generally malleable and most responsive to economic stimuli, man had lost his attribute of homogeneity, as in bureaucracy, through the proposition of technical specialization.[6] As analogous to perceptions of physical resources, man required and was subject, however, to "purification" and refinement; that is, his behavior could be made more organizationally rational through training and indoctrination.

This latter perspective on man, scientific management, coming shortly after the industrial revolution, is largely attributable to the prevailing economic environment and business philosophy. Its conceptualizations and practices are culture-bound, which can be suggested as follows: In order to achieve mass distribution of the products of mass production, with price the major competitive weapon, and with efforts to maintain unit margins, there was a tremendous downward pressure on wages; but, as Commons argued, unions formed a bulwark against this pressure.[7] Since a reduction in the numerator of the fraction:

$$\frac{\text{Wages per hour}}{\text{Output per hour}} = \text{unit labor cost}$$

was restrained because of unionization, managers would turn to attempts to increase the denominator of the fraction in order to decrease the costs of these increasingly competitive products. This, then, was an impetus to scientific management.[8] Such an approach was amplified by the engineering backgrounds of many practitioners prominent in the "scientific management" movement.

Although scientific management was limited to thinking in terms of machine analogs, its thrust had a considerable impact upon developing propositions for organizational decision making. By 1910, it was acknowledged that: (1) organizational decisions were made by incumbents of

[6] See Taylor's (1911) concepts of "specialization" and "best" man. Also, see Fayol's principles of "centralization" and "selection."

[7] This is an oversimplification of the "extension of the market theory," as proposed by Commons (1936), of the union movement.

[8] Bureaucracy was a culturally directed phenomenon as well. The concept gained publicity as societies in Western Europe emerged from what Riesman has called a "tradition-directed" state. As a route to avoiding "anomie" and social disorganization, rationally patterned interaction was seen as a substitute for such social controls as mysticism, charisma, and hereditary privileges. Through specialization, bureaucratization not only offered precision and efficiency, but also presented vocational security and the elimination of personalized hostilities and power.

positions, that is, people; (2) decision makers might be influenced by the structural design of the system; and (3) since decision makers were modifiable, they could be indoctrinated (cf. Gantt, 1910, pp. 147–150). These historical elaborations on the conception of man paved the way for what seem to be, now, far-reaching implications.[9]

While thinkers in the field were still holding to the machine analogy, but with this new awareness, they explored two additional aspects of man: the facts that (1) since he is a precious resource whose energies can be dissipated, certain maintenance costs can pay high dividends, for example, in the way of rest periods to overcome fatigue; and that (2) he is only limitedly malleable, that is, he has certain physical limitations for which certain equipment adjustments are required. Therefore, physiological study should be made of him. Physiological knowledge could be used to maximize the output of the man-machine combination, rather than that of the machine alone (cf. Gilbreth, 1913). While explorations of "physiological" man did not pertain directly to decision making, the attending paternalistic attitude did influence decision premises of the manager and did facilitate development of a point of view that had both tactical and ethical considerations more directly useful for our purposes.

The recognition of man as a physical being suggests that he might respond to changes in the physical environment, such as to changes in heat, light, and noise. The testing of this hypothesis resulted in the unveiling of another dimension of man: that he is a sensitive social creature, although acting in terms of his vocational pursuits.[10] The acceptance of these findings, as compared to earlier conceptions, suggests that man is not a simple, econotechnical stimulus response mechanism, but that he intrudes mediation between a change in the stimulus field and his actions. Moreover, relevant and viable aspects of the stimulus field are social in nature, while the mediation process itself is influenced by social forces. With recognition given to the socio-emotional nature of man, and since not all social forces are necessarily congruent with formal dictates of the organization, it can be said that these forces can become organizationally dysfunctional.[11] Indeed, organizations, as social

[9] Let us admit, however, that each and all of these conceptions can be traced into antiquity.

[10] The reference to the now famous Hawthorne studies is apparent. See, for example, Roethlishberger and Dickson (1948). At about this same time, *Gestalt* psychology arose as a reaction to earlier, simple stimulus-response or behavioral psychology, which amplified concern with man's social predilections.

[11] Many of these conclusions were formulated only for operative (nonmanager) employees. However, they are now accepted by most authorities as relating to administrative behavior itself. For early recognition of this fact, see Miller and Form, 1951, esp. pp. 217–218.

artifacts, can have dysfunctions for their members and to their own performance.

Whether innate or acquired, these social tendencies were discovered as intervening variables between "organizational" inducements and membership behavior. For example, we asume that aspirations and contentment are partially socially directed. Then, we can note that where D = lack of satisfaction, R = reward (wages), A = aspiration level, S = satisfaction, P = performance, and C = contentment, the organizational practice (for example, $+ \Delta R$) may not have a predictably singular and linear effect upon behavior (cf. Asch, 1960, pp. 18–22, and Vroom, 1964). As implied in the following diagram, rewards, satisfaction, and performance may interact in complex ways. Furthermore, Porter and Lawler (1968) have offered evidence and a theoretical model suggesting that the direction of causality may flow from performance to satisfaction.

$$D \to \uparrow Rw \to \uparrow S \underset{\longrightarrow}{\overset{\displaystyle \downarrow A \to \downarrow P(?)}{\underset{\displaystyle \uparrow C \to \downarrow P(?)}{\rightleftarrows \uparrow P(?)}}}$$

Reinforcing this social conceptualization of the employee, the "group mind" thesis in psychology prevailed in certain quarters.[12] This view held that the group takes on the characteristics of an individual and, in fact, is more important than the individual, especially for predictive purposes (cf. Asch, 1952, pp. 142–144). Implications of this view are that, for example, organizational structure and leadership posture should be focused upon the "group" and, by doing so, grossly abstract from individual personalities. The belief was also held that, as a social being, the major "motivational" medium for the actor is through his direct social contact with the organization, his immediate supervisor.

These conceptualizations have been criticized on both moral and empirical grounds. The ability to program or train supervisors in "good human relations" has met with but limited success and has been severely questioned. Further, many authorities criticize the "manipulative" role of supervisors on ethical grounds (Roethlisberger, 1948, pp. 11–19). Another consequence of the application of this concept has been some tendency to concentrate on the negative features of man—on his ignorance, apathy, and contrariness. Thus, we find themes espousing "motivation through training," "motivation through indoctrination," and "motivation through communication." Attending programs have been

---

[12] In fact, social determinism seemed to hold sway. Here, the individual was assumed to have no volition, identity, or self-direction of his own as he operated in a social system, that is, man was totally social situation oriented.

criticized for their intent as well as their empirical naïveté and, accordingly, their operational effectiveness.

Such criticisms of the early "school of *human relations*" have shifted much of the concern with administrative science to organization theory and to "behavioral" decision theory. Many dysfunctional acts of employees, for example, are now attributed to practices relating to technological design, such as routinization and standardization of task, while rigid and autocratic authority structures are seen to elicit poor supervisory behavior and underdeveloped subordinates (cf. Argyris, 1958, pp. 107–116). Structural design and leadership posture are recognized as significant variables in a subordinate's decision. Thus, the relevant field has come to include (1) man's subjective perceptions of the decision area; (2) his values and expectations; and (3) his cognitive and computational abilities (March and Simon, 1958, p. 33).[13]

These shifts in attention and emphasis have had far-reaching effects upon management thought and practice, for example, implications of the "social responsibleness" of business and the nature and purpose of executive development. But of major concern here is the fact that, as perceptions of the administrator have broadened and as his knowledge about the "whole" man has increased, he has begun to learn more about himself and the behavior of others in dealing with organizational problems.

Not only have awareness and attitudes changed, but also complexities and sizes of contemporary organizations have grown. Thus, while cognizance, itself, has enlarged and deepened, reality has changed. Soujanen (1955, p. 17), in describing these changes on the business scene as related to the decision-making process, has said that hierarchy and supervisory control still dominate, but that

> . . . other decision-making processes have become important. In the control of the operating divisions of the large corporation, the price system is replacing hierarchy at very rapid pace. Similarly, voting, or control by the led, is being increasingly incorporated into the decision-making structure of the progressive organization. Finally, bargaining or control (influence) of leaders by leaders (e.g., within committees), has shown a phenomenal growth in recent years.

Each of these aspects of cognizance and reality bears investigation, and it is in this way that each becomes a topical area in this work.[14]

[13] Compare these areas of concern to Emerson's statement (1912, p. 74) that: "The differences between groups of men lie almost wholly in their ideals, organization, equipment and supervision."

[14] Although, substantively, each dimension will be treated as largely an independent variable, we subscribe to the idea that man must be considered in terms of his whole being, whose behavior arises from an interlocking set of functions which makes him one organism and not a set of discrete organs (Allport, 1954, pp. 28–29).

Thus far we have attempted to: (1) suggest how a general systems approach to management has disclosed new necessities for administrative decision making; and (2) describe personal and social realities of administrative decision fields. Now let us turn our attention to requirements for the operational dimensions of management decisions.

Effective Decision Making

Whatever the system surrounding him or whatever his idiosyncratic orientation, the focus of the decision maker is on accommodation or control. In this light, two considerations are immediately apparent: (1) Since decisions ultimately find their utility in implementation, (2) decisions must be action oriented—that is, directed toward relevant and controllable aspects of the environment.[15] Indeed, Griffiths (1958, p. 123) asserts: "Decisions are totally pragmatic in nature; that is, their value is dependent upon the success of the action which follows."

ACTION ORIENTATION

As organizationally rewarded, the employment contract requires that members ultimately *do* something or cause something to be done that will favorably affect or reduce the impact of unfavorable events upon the organization's fortunes.

While the member reminisces and reflects upon the past, as a constituent of an organization, he meets his contractual obligations only by his contributions to organizational purposes.[16]

Within our concept of an executive, the decision maker, as a non-operator who is removed from immediate instrumental action on the system's output, through his decisions has an impact upon organizational goals, evaluation of which is, at best, a difficult task, especially in the short run.[17] Nonetheless, while administrative performance is viewed

[15] This is not to imply there are not certain intrinsic satisfactions to decision making itself.

[16] Reminiscing may well have some influence on effective decision making in the way that such ruminations affect the frame of reference, influence the cognitive set, and suggest novel alternatives.

[17] Both the "structural" and the "process" approach to management are insightful. Loosely, they may be called: (1) organization theory and (2) decision theory. In the former, the organization structure is seen as the primary, if not the single, agent constraining and influencing decision processes. This approach concentrates upon the environmentally structured determinants of choice, "the institutional bases of events." In this regard, Thompson (1961, p. 7) states: "An organization is not merely the chance result of a number of decisions made by a number of rational decision-makers. Only decisions of decision-makers already *in* the organization, and only their organizational decisions, are relevant. The organization, therefore, must first be accounted for, or decision-making theory never gets beyond individual psychology." Yet we

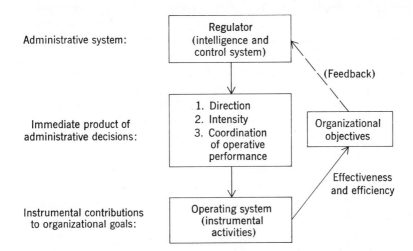

FIGURE 1-2   PRODUCTS OF ADMINISTRATIVE DECISIONS

as an indirect determinant of operative performance, it is at the same time a major determinant of operations, as shown in Figure 1-2.[18] Accordingly, managerial decisions must be judged ultimately in terms of their impact upon organizational goal achievement, if only through the effectiveness and efficiency they impart to operational performance.[19] Therefore, even administrative decisions are action oriented. In this light, then, "the term 'decision' is to be applied to all *judgments which directly affect a course of action*" (Griffiths, 1958, p. 122). This course of action, however, may be implemented by one's own behavior or by that of others in the organization.

GOAL-DIRECTED BEHAVIOR

Organizations are goal directed. In fact, it is difficult to conceive of or describe any particular class of organizations without referring to

---

hold rather firmly to an individualistic point of view. For certain purposes, this is a most fruitful perspective. However, in Chap. 6 we examine formally patterned structure, through the concept of matrix organization theory. In a sense, then, we think of decision making as a *causal* force, in and of organizations, as well as a consequence elicited by organizations (cf. Gore, 1962, p. 50).

[18] It should be noted that administration contributes to organizational survival in ways other than instrumental efficiency, for example, by directly enhancing the organization's legitimacy in the containing environment.

[19] Measures of the immediate product of management are, as yet, very crude; but various measures of "cohesion" might well reflect coordination and morale, which, in turn, could relate to identification with the organization.

the nature of the goal for which it strives, symbolizing its *raison d'être*.[20] When we assume rationality, we are positing that action-oriented decisions are concluded in the light of one or more given ends or values.[21]

Nonetheless, each and every decision in the organization need not lead directly to organizational accomplishment—any specific choice may be made in pursuit of personal, private goals of the individual, which may or may not coincide with organizational purpose. When this distinction is made, we mean by *organizational decisions* those choices made according to the consequences of the proposed act upon the attainment of organizational goals. Since a formal enterprise purpose may not be the sole or even dominant value determining the choices made by a member, where his personal values dominate, we will speak of *personal rationality* (cf. Simon, 1947, esp. pp. 76–77).[22] However, the member's decisions may serve both ends or compromise between them.

We may conclude that decision-making behavior is rational to the extent that it chooses a solution that promotes the achievement of one or a given set of goals, personal or organizational. Naturally, the value of a decision and the associated action relates to the dispatch with which this goal is attained and the efficiency of its implementation. However, because of our concern with ex ante behavior and, therefore, of ignorance imposed by the existence of future unknowns, we will be most concerned with subjective rationality. We are concerned with decisions made before the fact rather than with judgments concerning past events, and we are as much if not more concerned with subjective perceptions and personal values of the decision maker than we are with objective facts and organizational goals.

While the value of a decision is dependent upon the attainment of a given goal or set of goals, such accomplishment is a function of both the accuracy of the decision and its implementation. In evaluating a decision, then, a distinction must be made between the effects of goal accomplishment brought about by better decisions and those attainments

---

[20] We speak, for example, of *religious, economic,* or *political* organizations, when identifying the basic purposes of the organization. Katz and Kahn (1966, pp. 111–115) give an insightful discussion of "genotype functions" as a means for understanding organizations.

[21] In the case of gaming, random behavior itself may be a strategy, and even in this case the means may be deliberately random but the ends are not.

[22] Many different dimensions and classifications of decision making exist, most of which will be treated in some detail in this work. Drucker (1954, pp. 357–358), for example, has classified decisions upon the basis of the futurity of the decision, that is, upon the time span for which it commits the business to a course of action, and the speed with which the decision can be reversed. Tannenbaum (1950, pp. 24–25) makes a distinction between decisions pertaining to an ultimate end versus an immediate means. Dale (1953, p. 2) classifies decisions upon the basis of the uncertainty involved.

arising directly from execution. Skilled behavior can fail in the light of a poorly conceived course of action; likewise, a decision brilliantly conceived can prove worthless without effective implementation.

We find direct costs associated with decision making, as: (1) establishing relevant solution criteria; (2) obtaining knowledge about causation; (3) selecting an appropriate solution strategy; and (4) processing (or mediating) the decision itself. But the efficacy of a decision is dependent upon the viability of a wide range of factors, such as the level of acceptance that will be given to the proposal and the enthusiasm with which it will be implemented, as well as the appropriateness of the prescribed action itself. In this sense, then, we have at least a threefold problem in evaluating the "goodness" of a decision: (1) the viability of the ex ante decision; (2) the degree of congruency between the prediction and the reality or validity[23] of the solution as it occurs; and (3) the enthusiasm and skill with which the proposal is pursued—the attractiveness of the venture.

To take the second of these, there is the "risk" that our perceptions of reality at any moment are invalid, which is then compounded by our inability to symbolize our perceptions of reality accurately. Such risks become even greater as we attempt to anticipate the future. But, as discussed later, payoff can accrue more to forward-looking decisions, as contrasted to accommodating behavior, and often the manager's decisions are actually designed to create uncertainty in an already uncertain future. In fact, Drucker (1959, pp. 25–26) objects to the idea that business managers minimize risk, asserting that their task is to create risk.[24] Whatever the case, we "search" for information and techniques to reduce or avoid the uncertain aspects of our own futures through forward-looking behavior.

Distinguishing between unplanned behavior and forward-looking action, we can see the relevancy of a "second-level" decision. Here the concern is with the value-cost relationship of decision making itself, that is, with the problem of equating increasing costs of an improved decision to the higher payoff from improving that decision. The possibil-

[23] Here we are using validity in a peculiar statistical sense, i.e., the efficacy potential of an ex ante decision according to the actual state of affairs as it evolves during execution.

[24] To quote Long (1966): "At this point, the truly fundamental and troublesome issue could be raised as to how far management should go in attempting to remove possible adverse consequences of events whose outcomes are not certain, when such removal is costly."

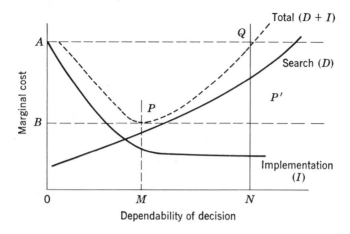

FIGURE 1-3 MARGINAL COSTS OF SEARCH AND IMPLEMENT-
ING DECISIONS

ity exists that a "poorer" decision, for example, one based upon less
reliable forecasts, associated with lower second-level costs may be, on
the net, more economical than more dependable decisions when decision-making costs are added to costs of implementation.[25]

Under the conditions depicted in Figure 1-3, with minimum marginal
total cost as the decision rule, *OM* is the optimum decision dependability
where cost of search is positively related to dependability. In this situation, *OM* may be considerably below the maximum reliability that might
be sought.

While conventional tools of marginal analysis may be employed in
conceptually resolving this problem, assessing the cost and the value
of second-level decisions is a very complex task. In the first place, decision making is process-like and not a single event, even where the
conclusion may come from prodigious computer effort. Moreover, decision making has temporal dimensions, not only of a sequential nature,
but also in the way of revisions of the action program.[26] Thus, while

---

[25] An insistence on a high degree of reliability may result in the expenditure of
costly effort in rumination, reasoning, and search which may increase not only the
direct costs of decision making but also certain indirect costs because of unemployment of assets during the delay thus incurred. (Cf. Hart, 1951, especially pp. 46–60.
This proposition explains the positive slope to *OD* in Figure 1-3).

[26] Simon (1947, pp. 1–4) suggests that managerial actions following a decision are
resolvable into still more problems which call for further choice.

insightful, the cost curves depicted above are difficult, if not impossible, to ascertain with much accuracy.

A second problem of determining the net value of a second-level decision has to do with the fact that its contribution rests partially upon its intrinsic worth, as in confidence afforded the actor: Uncertainty is multidimensional, that is, uncertainty exists with respect to the future state of affairs as well as concerning the internal worth of the decision. Therefore, the decision rule for second-level decisions may reflect subjective dispositions toward the validity of the decision itself. In the above diagram, the minimum level of certainty acceptable might be ON. If such is the case, we are concerning ourselves with the desirability of certainty versus uncertainty as a commodity of its own. In the case just cited, ex ante desires for ON certainty, an increase of MN, dictates an increased cost of NQ minus MP. From this, we may conclude that the disposition (risk aversion) on the part of the decision maker must be taken into account when analyzing second-level decisions (cf. Friedman, 1953, pp. 303–304).

In order to illustrate the relationship between information available and the disposition of the decision maker, we can hypothesize three knowledge situations, with associated responses. (See Luce and Raiffa, 1957, pp. 275–327.) In the first of these, because of ignorance of the variables involved, the individual may not be disposed to obtain more information or to concern himself further with the problem. The crystallization of this disposition, in itself, constitutes a decision or forms a behavioral choice as well. Secondly, a decision maker may recognize that sufficient information is not at hand to arrive at any decision but that more data can be made available—he has sufficient knowledge concerning the action potentials to act toward the decision but not enough to resolve the problem itself. Therefore, he "decides" to get more information, that is, to search. Thirdly, and perhaps more realistic in an administered setting, a decision maker may feel that the information is inadequate; that is, at best he can only approximate the probability distribution, but he is forced to arrive at a decision—he has to take a chance that some intelligent but uncertain action is better than none at all.

The explication of formal directives in an organization designed to preclude irrationality on the part of members gives rise to another complexity of evaluating second-level decisions. This has to do with side effects of communicating decisions which establish decision premises for others and henceforth give precedent for similar decisions. Generally, then, the internal worth of the decision is related to the desire to predict a subordinate's behavior by increasing the "routineness" of his actions through implanting a particular choice configuration on his decision mechanism. While such practices obtain their value from eliciting predictable behavior, they may create inflexible and inappropriate behavior in the course of what may be universally changing conditions.

Nonetheless, time and energies exploited in the identification, evaluation, and resolution of a problem do "net" decision makers more than random or unplanned behavior. In fact, we intend to imply that the selected course of action "nets" an actor more than the costs of (1) implementing and executing the action *plus* (2) evaluating and choosing the available alternatives.

Thus far, then, we have considered goal-directed and action-oriented behavior in our conception of effective decision making; but to these we must add certain environmental conditions. The requirements that we hold for "effective" decisioning presuppose that the actor perceives a real choice opportunity. Essentially, this requires that (1) he feel that a real set of alternative actions exist; (2) certain relevant variables be under his control; and (3) there be some payoff to deliberate and foresightful action. In this sense, then, the features of the environment that contain the problem require analysis.

A mature, highly complex society requires certain constraints on individual behavior and groups—that is, social controls. One way of viewing the necessity for social controls is observing their functioning in any particular subculture or organization.

In order to benefit from creative social interaction, foresightfully patterned coordination is required (cf. Knight, 1951, pp. 15–22, and Schneider, 1957, pp. 77–81). Individuals, thus, are not free to exercise unlimited choice; they relate themselves in some predictable fashion to others in the system. Where group effort is involved—in society, family, or business—cooperation is obtained by imposing, and policing, a system of norms and rules which specify for the individual behavior as well as necessary interrelationships. Eventually, man becomes conditioned to the notion that rules and actions necessary to enforce them are right and proper, that is, rules and their enforcement become legitimate in their own right (cf. Parsons, 1951, pp. 36–45). From such "learning," the individual perceives that certain alternatives will be judged acceptable whereas other activities will be deemed illegitimate and inappropriate.

In our culture, most "rules of the game" are presented in negative fashion: we are told what we cannot do—not what we must do. Such prescriptions permit individual discretion. Rules expressed in positive,

```
           Legal restrictions
 ─────────────────────────────────────────
  s
  n
  a        Moral and ethical norms
  e
  m
 ─────────────────────────────────────────
  e
  v
  i        Formal policies and rules
  t
  a
  n
 ─────────────────────────────────────────
  r
  e
  t        Unofficial social norms
  l
  A
 ─────────────────────────────────────────
```

//
////////////// Discretionary area ////////
////////// (acceptable choices of action) //////
//

FIGURE 1-4   THE NOTION OF BOUNDED DISCRETION IN DECI-
SION MAKING

as opposed to negative, fashion rigidly prescribe behavior, with associated judgments relating only to the applicability of the rule. In Figure
1-4, as relates to our culture, an actor is surrounded by legal and ethical
curbs on discretion. In addition, the exigencies attending the goal requirements of a formalized organization impose additional constraints
on behavior; and symbiotic relations in particularized social groupings
within an organization will further inhibit individual differences. Nonetheless, our conception of decision making assumes real choice, that
is, the availability of at least one alternative course of action.

VIABLE ALTERNATIVES

A second requirement of our environmental condition is that, in some
sense, goal contributions can be identified with one or more alternative
means,[27] and that one or more essential variables in the problem field
are under control; in effect the decision maker can do something about
the problem: He perceives a favorable impact of action following his
decision on the problem area.

Note, however, the basic assumption underlying this position: that
the decision maker can manipulate or influence some future state of
affairs or, at the very least, intelligently prepare for the future. This

[27] This contribution may actually be a positive payoff or only a reduction in negative effects in terms of the prescribed goal(s). In this latter case, the problem solver
is said to be faced with a "Hobson's choice." (Cf. Koontz, 1958, p. 52.)

premise implies more than merely expediently accommodating to future conditions as they become imminent. The implication is that managerial decision making may be forward-looking and positive, involving more than a passive, ad hoc accommodation to prevailing states of affairs.

It may be argued that the future cannot be "controlled," but any action has its historical consequences. These consequences may find their source in their impact upon the decision maker—for example, in his experiences and, thus, predisposition—or in their impact upon the realities of the environment, upon competitors' perceptions and, thus, behaviors, for instance. Such antecedents to later decisions and outcomes are real and viable. Therefore, and at least in this one dimension, man "manipulates" his future.

Problem situations have different susceptibilities to change; thus, the decision maker's impact on various parts of the environment both is limited and varies from situation to situation. In some measure, individual or organizational influences on the environment are negligible, such as on the gross national product. In this case, the decision maker is confronted with a tactical or accommodation problem. In others, as in competitive behavior in duopoly situations, the impact of individual action may be strong. In the first example, the decision maker is confronted with an adaptation or nonstrategic problem, although still subjected to future uncertainties (cf. Hicks, 1950, esp. chap. 2). A problem which encompasses conditions where the fortunes of actors are interdependent is strategic (cf. Fellner, 1949, pp. 71–77). In either case, we assume that before-the-fact mediation can contribute to the fortunes of the actor.

One of the major attributes of anticipatory decisions is the impact upon the decision maker himself. Given our conditions of foresightful mediation, the decision maker enters the (future) arena with prior knowledge, especially as compared to those who do not act in any ex ante fashion—that is, those who do not, before the fact, assess and anticipate while choosing and elaborating upon a particular course of action.[28] Anticipatory behavior has two functions. One arises from the exploration of historical events necessary for intelligent predictions of the future. A knowledge of history finds most of its value in its predictive potential. History, in this sense, is causal and can be scrutinized for appropriate analogies and isomorphisms. While complete replicas may never occur in all their detail, general trends and configurations do

---

[28] This preconceived course of action, or plan, may have certain dysfunctional repercussions. It may create a given "set" (or predisposition) that precludes flexibility and intelligent adjustment to the realities of the situation which were not anticipated. (See Bush and Mosteller, 1957.)

repeat over time. Therefore, historical appraisals, with their generated predictions of future conditions, make it possible to create a sense of, and commitment to, direction that otherwise might not be had.

Not only do forward-looking assessments make for more reliable decisions, but also they permit more intelligent adjustments in case conditions encountered are not as anticipated.[29] Previous explorations of alternative solutions may reduce delay during execution where realignment or readjustment is required, that is, an intelligent prediction of future affairs may permit the actor to behave across several alternative courses of action in an enlightened manner.[30]

A second function of anticipatory behavior arises from noninvolvement with actual performance of the act; ex ante behavior can be only simulated at most. A frame of reference may thus be elicited where relationships are seen and associations made. The repetitiveness of events, for example, can be more clearly perceived. Such associations may reduce the cost of the actor's change in "set" between what otherwise might be perceived as dissimilar acts (cf. Deese, 1958, pp. 74–98). From the above, then, we can see two basic advantages of foresightful decision making: (1) a carefully developed *modus operandi* prepared for some anticipated state of affairs; and (2) a favorable and efficient psychological set which may reduce delay in execution.

Intellection

As Homo sapiens, we feel, perhaps prejudicially, that man is uniquely proficient in perceiving and conceptualizing the environment so as to better manipulate it and accommodate to it. Moreover, we like to think that we are more proficient in problem solving than most, if not all, of our kindred in the animal world.[31] For the lower animal, behavior appears to be circumscribed by rather strict stimulus-response relationships, with the absence of the complex mediation processes usually attributed to man. On the other hand, some animals appear to be able

---

[29] This presupposes that relevant alternatives were surveyed before being discarded for the original choice.

[30] This ability depends upon the degree of commitment of resources for a particular action that cannot be withdrawn or diverted to the new act. (Cf. Hart, 1951, pp. 46–60, and Koontz, 1958, p. 55.)

[31] While the porpoise's environment may be simpler for it than man finds his, further investigation of the former's behavior may dispel the accepted differential superiority of man in many dimensions, especially in his sensory abilities and affiliative tendencies.

to rise above mere trial and error in problem solving, perhaps employing both insight and foresight (Deese, 1959, pp. 273–274).[32]

We contend, however, that man's behavior is generally more systematic and characterized less by trial and error than is the behavior of the brute animal. In fact, he symbolizes and, in turn, adapts to nonexisting environments. But we may not conclude that he always chooses an objectively, or even subjectively, ideal solution to his problems. Indeed, the conditions that we establish later suggest that reduction in cognitive trial and error may lead to a less than ideal solution. The mere abstraction of the problem field, for example, may reduce the range of search for alternative solutions so that optimal solutions are not disclosed. In addition, inordinate delays may occur either because of inordinate search efforts or from indulgence in the satisfactions of decision making itself. Finally, gross irregularities among choices may occur over time and among individuals because of differential use of decision criteria and solution strategies. Nonetheless, man does anticipate his own behavior and treats problems in a foresightful and cognitive fashion—an individual does not have to undergo physical punishment in order to behave so as to avoid it.

SCIENTIFIC METHOD

The desire to understand, predict, and control forces in the environment suggests an open and inquiring mind, a major aspect of which is the attempt to conceive of reality as it truly exists and not as someone tells us that it is or as we would wish that it be. Since ultimately we want knowledge about our environment in order to exert control, we must first discern this environment and define it in terms of its actual dimensions. In order to gain this understanding, however, we must be willing to accept it as it really exists, attributing to reality its own order and configuration. The demand for this type of explanation results from a desire to answer such questions as: "What is it?" and "Why is it?"—that is, from man's scientific search into causality.

According to Bross (1953, p. 6), man's evolution from "ooze to Oak Ridge" has shown a continuous movement toward greater use of "scientific" technologies. One might argue that such an evolution is a measure of his growth and maturity, reflecting one or more of the following criteria: (1) the ability to conceptualize and reason on causalities in reality outside one's own direct experiences, or abstract thought; (2) the propensity to follow thought patterns prescribed by ends other than

---

[32] Caution should be exercised in arriving at such conclusions, since what appears to be foresightful behavior may be instinctive, that is, an unlearned, delayed, and complex adaptive response.

those associated with the immediate and private self, or objectivity; and (3) the willingness to subject inferences or deductions to tests of logical consistency and empirical validity, or scientific method. Whether or not these dimensions of man's behavior mirror his growth as the most cogent and viable measures, such behavior carries considerable value in our culture.

As well as can be documented historically, the decision behavior of man has shown several changes in context over recorded history.[33] Bross (pp. 6–17) suggests the following classification of modes of decision making:

I. From a simple *Biological Mechanism* operating through:
   A. Innate needs by means of a direct motor response to an external stimulus, and
   B. Acquired, thus habitual, behavioral responses to sensory experiences without conscious mediation;
II. Through a set of *Cultural Refinements,* as the employment of:
   A. Differentiated roles in the way of decision-making specialists (e.g., priests, kings, and witch doctors), and
   B. Explanations of causality in terms of anthropomorphic devils and gods;
III. To Logical and *Scientific Philosophy* of proof, based upon standardized rules of:
   A. Logic of inference from accepted deductive processes, and
   B. Validity tests of judgments made about events in reality.

While this evolution may or may not be judged as advancement toward man's ultimate attainments, it does exemplify growing sophistication in man's dealing with his environment. Nonetheless, we do not mean to imply that all of man's decision behavior does, or should, lie within the classification that we will label "scientific method." In some cases, especially where extreme sensory stimuli are present or where the physiological tolerance of the individual is low, his biological mechanism may, and perhaps should, dominate.

Although scientific method may have greatest appeal in dilemmas resolved through tests of causality, the acceptance given to profundities of legitimated authorities or to the franchise of public consensus may carry more weight on questions of values or norms. Our society, confounded with the choice between the credence given to democracy and the reliance placed on expertise, aggressively seeks certainty through both means.[34] The typical conception of a pyramidal organization and

[33] For a historical review of psychological theories of thinking, see Vinacke, 1952, pp. 9–19.

[34] One wonders whether the drive for "professionalism" among certain groups, for example, personnel managers and statisticians, is motivated by a desire to screen membership for expertise or to provide a source of appeal to "authorities" in decision making.

the role of the bureaucratic specialist—the expert—suggests certain cultural mechanisms supporting authoritative dominance in our society today. Finally, the tenacity of habit in holding to our beliefs is important in decision making, and much propaganda is still directed to our sentiments in the way of direct appeals to our intuition and emotions by statements about what is "self-evident" and "obviously true." (See, for example, Cohen and Nagel, 1934, p. 195.) Whatever the case, man's increasing ability to control or accommodate to his environment is a function of the consistency and reliability of his reasoning and the extent that scientific method sways him on questions of fact.[35]

Now, given our conditions on foresight and scientific reasoning, we wish to examine certain structural elements of the choice-making mechanism itself. For introductory purposes, our immediate discussions are constrained by a fairly restrictive and mechanistic model. The following limitations are held: (1) So-called "sudden insight," that behavior which spontaneously and instantaneously results in a solution, is excluded from our analysis. (2) Decision making is treated as a rather static, fixed event by ignoring the possibility of changes in learning and evocation during the reasoning process. (3) For the perceived set of alternative actions, which are assumed to be limited, only risk and not uncertainty is associated with anticipated outcomes, that is, at least subjective probabilities can be assigned to the alternative future states. The purpose of imposing these restrictions is to make for greater manageability of the constructs which are developed here.

Within this limited model, three underlying assumptions govern the direction of our explorations. They can be enumerated as follows: First, the decision maker perceives, accurately or inaccurately, a problem (real or fancied) which he judges to be of concern in some way to him, that is, a problem exists which he believes to rest in the province of effective decision making as defined above. Second, the decision maker treats the problem in its first-level dimensions, that is, the question of concern is how best to deal with the problem in some positive, behavioral sense, as the underlying question of whether or not to deal with the problem has already been affirmed. Third, the decision maker is involved in some conscious, cognitive manner with selecting a specific course

[35] This is not to say that the scientific method is to become the final attainment of a culture in its search for new methods of discoving knowledge. Man's resources may be relatively untapped and new technologies may well develop in his quest for understanding.

of action, that is, neither habit nor pure trial-and-error behavior is considered to be his mode of problem solving.

Because the decision as defined by us is ex ante, both action and resultant outcomes occur at some future date. This being the case, evaluations of possible alternative states are based upon *estimates* concerning the likelihood of the consequences occurring and the level of satisfaction, that is, utility, associated with them.

But, since effective decision making implies futurity, the data with which the decision maker deals are not real, ex post facts concerning conditions prevailing at execution date. The "stuff" of the decision is at best an intelligent anticipation concerning some future state of affairs. In retrospect, should actual results coincide exactly with anticipated results, it could be argued that one of two situations had been achieved: (1) The problem solver had full knowledge of all relevant causalities, or (2) he made a chance estimate which coincided exactly with the actual conditions (for example, errors in expectations counterbalanced each other, whereby the net result occurred as anticipated). Because the latter explanation lies outside our purview, we assume that the decision maker attempts to increase the reliability with which anticipated conditions will coincide with the real state of affairs.[36] The degree of accuracy with which such predictions can be made depends upon how well past, or present, phenomena can be extrapolated to fit the future state of affairs. A strict and simple causal relationship is not likely to exist between a given alternative course of action and its consequences, that is, some risk exists as to the nature of the outcome. Thus, the outcome must be predicted or some probability distribution of possible outcomes determined for each act.[37]

Moreover, a single outcome has more than one possible value consequence, having perhaps both positive and negative elements—for example, advertising may increase sales but may have differing quantities of "positive" net value—and a "desirability" evaluation must be made relating them, that is, a preference scale established which orders the outcomes according to their desirability. (Cf. Vail, 1954, p. 90; and Debreu, 1954, pp. 159–166.)

These concepts are illustrated in Table 1-1. From such desirability and probability evaluations as columns (2) and (3) an actuarial value

---

[36] Note the tremendous number and often immeasurability of the variables involved, as in the difficulties of defining and measuring the productivity of advertising. Add then the problems of anticipating changing wants, technology, natural resources, law, and institutions and the difficulty of forecasting wars and acts of God.

[37] Probability is the numerical value expressing the likelihood that an outcome will occur. The theoretical limit of this likelihood—that is, complete certainty that the event will occur—is 100 percent. Risk is a measure of the departure from this theoretical limit. Cf. Lange, 1952, pp. 20–31.

Table 1-1   Computations of actuarial value

(1) ALTERNATIVE STATES	(2) SUBJECTIVE NET VALUE (U) (E.G., DOLLARS)	(3) PROBABILITY OF OCCURRENCE (P) (PERCENT)	(4) ACTUARIAL VALUE (E) (P × U)
I	250	60	150
II	240	75	180
III	240	80	192
IV	220	85	187
V	200	90	180

can be determined. According to Hicks (1950, esp. chap. 2), the economically rational man should choose the maximum actuarial value[38] state III, with value of 192.

However, the decision maker may impose other decision rules upon a given set of alternatives in making his final choice.[39] To exemplify, we offer the following possibilities:

DECISION RULE	CHOICE
(a) Maximize E.	III
(b) Maximize P.	V
(c) Maximize U.	I
(d) Maximize E w/P $\geq$ 0.85.*	IV
(e) Maximize E from first two alternatives.**	II

* For example, desire for high certainty.
** For example, desire to restrict cost of search.

Thus, within this highly mechanistic view, the actuation of choice is brought about by probability judgments, desirability evaluations, and the imposition of a decision rule (Bross, 1953, esp. chap. 3).[40]

[38] He uses the term "expected value." Notice that this choice criterion does not take into account the different shapes of the probability curves (cf. Friedman, 1953, p. 303) or the concept of discounted values (cf. Hart, 1951, pp. 92–95).

[39] See Luce and Raiffa's (1957) discussion of "decision criteria," esp. pp. 278–286.

[40] We have implied that subjective and objective probabilities are equal and that utility is a linear function of our measure, for example, money. To this Scodel, Ratoosh, and Minas say, "If both assumptions are made, it becomes very easy to construct a theoretical formulation for predicting decision making in general. Unfortunately, models utilizing both assumptions are extremely poor in making predictions about the way persons actually behave in risk-taking situations" (1960, p. 37).

The Unit of Decision Making

As implied earlier, the study of decision making requires the analysis of at least three sets of variables: (1) the decision maker, including his subjective perceptions of the problem and his unique frame of reference for his intellectual ruminations; (2) the ends or goals being sought, either those of the organization or his private set of values or some mix of the two; and (3) the environment within which the action is to take place. In the latter case, for example, we have scanned the choice opportunity offered by the environment in the way of discretion and payoff offered. Now, we propose to concern ourselves most specifically with the decision-making unit itself.

On the one hand, the individual is considered the unit of decision making inasmuch as only individuals are capable of making decisions. On the other hand, this proposition, that decision making is a human and individualized activity, does not negate the fact that it has certain social overtones and underpinnings, pointing out only that it is unique to the individual.[41] Although social forces are at play, the associated and necessary mental processes are inherently individual. While man is socialized, the elements shown in Figure 1-5 are nurtured and performed only by the individual. Perception and motivation, for example, can be defined only in terms of the individual personality.

Here, we contend further that the individual responds to all of him

---

[41] While we may speak of consensus in a group and not neurological manifestations of decision making, our central concern is the individual as decision maker.

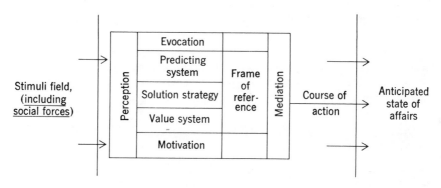

FIGURE 1-5   THE INDIVIDUAL DECISIONING UNIT

that is evoked by the stimulus field, which may include a number of diverse interests as well as psychological mechanisms. These interests vary in importance to him and may conflict with, as well as reinforce, one another. However, it is the character of these differing and nonconstant human elements of decision making which determine the nature and direction of choice. In this sense, we are concerned with, and our decision model must encompass, actual human behavior rather than only those concerns which are derived from a set of normative prescriptions. Thus, we will direct our attention as much, if not more, to the study of how people really act as to reviewing prescriptive rules of conduct. (Cf. Scitovsky, 1952, esp, p. 358.)

SOCIOLOGICAL CONSIDERATIONS

A completely egoistic explanation of man's behavior is not our total point of view. The reader is encouraged to accept the idea that socialization *is* effective—that social forces are at play and social learning may well result in a genuine transformation of man's psychological constitution. In addition, the innate nature of man may include certain viable affiliative tendencies or a "collective unconscious." (See Parsons, 1951, pp. 190–191.) We doubt that individual behavior can be understood and predicted without reflection upon the sociological environment in which he operates or to which he makes reference for his choices. This is not to argue that either social affiliations or personal perceptions are more important, but merely that the former are relevant and significant features of decision making.[42]

All of this is not to say that "the television tube is what makes the picture," but that to study nuclear power without understanding the atom is insufficient. The importance of language in the thought processes of man is not trivial. Thus, while holding to the proposition that decision making finds its essence in the individual, we can elaborate on Figure 1-5 as Figure 1-6. Accordingly, we begin to see the vital nature of social-psychological forces in our study of decision making.

Decision making is a social event to the extent, for example, that facts and values are social phenomena. The validity of a "fact" is often a function of the incidence in society of observation of an event. Values often reflect group norms which have become internalized by the mem-

[42] McCammy (1947, pp. 41–42) takes a rather polar view. He states that: ". . . no single individual alone ever makes a decision in administration. He is always influenced by other persons, whether present in person or in spirit; and his conclusions are a result of advice, affection, hostility, fear, envy, admiration, contempt, or condensation involved in the complex of human relationships that pervade administration."

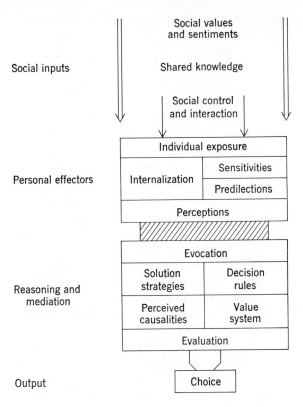

Social inputs

Social values
and sentiments

Shared knowledge

Social control
and interaction

Individual exposure

Personal effectors

Internalization

Sensitivities

Predilections

Perceptions

Evocation

Reasoning and
mediation

Solution
strategies

Decision
rules

Perceived
causalities

Value
system

Evaluation

Output

Choice

FIGURE 1-6   SOCIAL INPUTS TO DECISION MAKING

bers (cf. Arrow, 1951). Moreover, decisions may be shared or made in common settings. The subordinate's decision is typically reviewed by his superordinate in a bureaucracy. In addition, we can identify permanent and ad hoc groups whose very purpose is decision making. The decision process, the concept of the problem, and the variables considered are most often sociological in nature. Here, direct social interaction is of significant concern in our study. (Cf. Bales, 1950.)

Decision Making Defined

We have discussed attributes of an effective decision as goal directed, action oriented, and made according to certain parameters of efficiency. We have said something about the role of intellection in foresightful behavior, but we have not as yet defined decision making itself.

Etymologically, the verb *decide* is derived from the Latin prefix *de-*, meaning "off," and the word *caedo*, meaning "to cut." In this sense, some cognitive process cuts off as preferred, or elects, a particular course of action from among a set of possible alternatives. The process of meeting and resolving choice-making situations is the essence of decision making. (Cf. Tannenbaum, 1950, p. 23.)

This process of meeting and resolving choice-making situations can be viewed as a simple, isolated act, i.e., exclusive attention can be concentrated upon the concluding phase of the process. The selection of a particular pattern of behavior[43] does represent its consummation, but this view may exclude certain concerns with certain highly related, if not inherent, activities of the process. If choice—the act of electing an alternative—is given exclusive attention, many antecedent and associated phenomena are precluded from analysis, for, as we have suggested, other relevant dimensions are: (1) the predisposition of the decision maker; (2) the signal for the decision; and (3) the filters and sequences employed in evaluating the information employed in the decision. Thus, in order to permit discussion of such questions, we will treat decision making as process-like, somewhat analogous to problem solving.

We view the decision-making process as a conscious activity, not as merely an automatic behavioral response. Such a statement is not meant to imply that there are no "unconscious" decisions or that they are not worthy of analysis, but rather that decisions which currently lend themselves to descriptive analyses are those which businessmen consciously make.[44] Yet the totality of man's mind is involved. Therefore, included in our conception of decision making are: (1) *cognition,* those activities of the mind associated with knowledge; (2) *conaton,* the action of the mind implied by such words as "willing," "desire," and "aversion"; and (3) *affectation,* the aspects of the mind identified with emotion, feeling, mood, and temperament.

Finally, decision acts, while not devoid of environmental impingements, are human events. Various types of hardware, such as various types of automatic data-processing equipment, may be employed to aid the decision-making process. Such mechanical devices enhance the speed, capacity, and accuracy of evaluations, and they may replace cer-

---

[43] The behavioral pattern decided upon may be a single act or a series or combination of acts, but each pattern is perceptively, if abstractly, discrete. In actual practice, however, the set of alternatives, at least as perceived, may not be exhaustive of the real situation or mutually exclusive.

[44] We admit that aspects of conscious decision making also may escape observation and analysis.

tain personnel who perform specific acts contributing to administrative decisions. Nonetheless, even the best of the hardware must be programmed by man and the forthcoming computations must be assessed by the responsible person.

From all of this, then, we will define decision making as: *a conscious and human process, involving both individual and social phenomena, based upon factual and value premises, which concludes with a choice of one behavioral activity from among one or more alternatives with the intention of moving toward some desired state of affairs.*

Thus far we have not attempted to delve deeply into any one phase of decision making. But it should be apparent to the reader that the subject area is extremely complex. Because of this seeming complexity and because decision making is an intellectual activity which has, thus far, largely defied direct observation[45] there is much to be learned about the subject and, very likely, much to be discarded of what we now think we now know. Accordingly, the development of a rational and comprehensive system explaining decision making is extremely difficult, if not impossible. Nevertheless, the behavioral sciences, among other disciplines, treat the subject area and considerable literature of a theoretical and empirical nature exists. Therefore, we take current evidence and knowledge and hope to build a model for administrative decision making in some logical and meaningful fashion. The current emphasis on decision making in administrative science gives certain credence, and perhaps urgency, to such an effort.

bibliography

ALLPORT, GORDON W.: "The Historical Background of Modern Social Psychology," in Gardner Lindzey (ed.), *Handbook of Social Psychology*, vol. 1 (Reading, Mass.: Addison-Wesley Publishing Co., 1954), pp. 3–56.

ARGYRIS, CHRIS: "The Organization: What Makes It Healthy?" *Harvard Business Review*, vol. 36, no. 6, November-December, 1958, pp. 107–116.

ARROW, KENNETH J.: "Mathematical Problems in the Social Sciences," in Daniel Lerner and Harold Lasswell (eds.), *The Policy Sciences* (Stanford University Press, 1951), pp. 140, 141.

ASCH, SOLOMON E.: *Social Psychology* (New York: Prentice-Hall, Inc., 1952).

BALES, R. F.: *Interaction Process Analysis* (Cambridge: Addison-Wesley Press, 1950).

[45] Recent studies on the functioning of various aspects and structures of the brain seem to hold promise of more direct observation than that of the past. See Duffy, 1962, esp. pp. 66–73.

BRAYBROOKE, DAVID: *A Strategy of Decision; Policy Evaluation as a Social Process* (New York: Free Press of Glencoe, 1963).

BROSS, IRWIN D. J.: *Design for Decision* (New York: The Macmillan Company, 1953).

BUSH, R. R., FREDERICK MOSTELLER, and G. L. THOMSON: "A Formal Structure for Multiple-Choice Situations," in R. M. Thrall, C. H. Coombs, and R. L. Davis (eds.), *Decision Processes* (New York: John Wiley & Sons, Inc., 1957), pp. 99–126.

COHEN, MORRIS R., and ERNEST NAGEL: *An Introduction to Logic and Scientific Method* (New York: Harcourt, Brace and Company, Inc., 1934).

COMMONS, JOHN R.: *History of Labor in the United States* (New York: The Macmillan Company, 1936).

DALE, ERNEST: "New Perspective in Managerial Decision Making," *Journal of Business*, vol. 26, no. 1, January, 1953, pp. 1–8.

DEBREU, GERARD: "Representation of a Preference Ordering by a Numerical Function," in R. M. Thrall, C. H. Coombs, and R. L. Davis (eds.), *Decision Processes* (New York: John Wiley & Sons, Inc., 1954), pp. 159–166.

DEESE, JAMES: *The Psychology of Learning* (New York: McGraw-Hill Book Company, 1958).

DRUCKER, PETER F.: *The Practice of Management* (New York: Harper & Brothers, 1954).

————: "Thinking Ahead: Potentials of Management Science," *Harvard Business Review*, vol. 37, January-February, 1959, pp. 25–26, 28, 30, 146, 148, 150.

DUFFY, ELIZABETH: *Activation and Behavior* (New York: John Wiley & Sons, Inc., 1962).

FELLNER, WILLIAM: *Competition Among the Few* (New York: Alfred A. Knopf, Inc., 1949).

FLEISHMAN, E. A.: "The Measurement of Leadership Attitudes in Industry," *Journal of Applied Psychology*, vol. 37, 1953, pp. 153–158.

FRIEDMAN, MILTON: *Essays in Positive Economics* (Chicago: University of Chicago Press, 1953).

GANTT, HENRY L.: *Work, Wages and Profits* (New York: The Engineering Magazine Co., 1910).

GILBRETH, FRANK B.: "Units, Methods and Devices of Measurement Under Scientific Management," *Journal of Political Economy*, vol. 21, no. 7, July, 1913, pp. 618–629.

GORE, WILLIAM J.: "Decision-Making Research: Some Prospects and Limitations," in Sidney Malick and Edward H. van Ness (eds.), *Concepts and Issues in Administrative Behavior* (Englewood Cliffs, N.J.: Prentice-Hall, Inc., 1962).

GRIFFITHS, DANIEL E.: "Administration as Decision-Making," in Andrew Halpin (ed.), *Administrative Theory in Education* (Chicago: The Midwest Administration Center, 1958), pp. 119–149.

HART, ALBERT G.: *Anticipations, Uncertainty and Dynamic Planning* (New York: Augustus M. Kelley, Inc., 1951).

HICKS, J. R.: *Value and Capital* (Oxford, England: Oxford University Press, 1950).

KATZ, DANIEL, and ROBERT L. KAHN: *The Social Psychology of Organizations* (New York: John Wiley & Sons, Inc., 1966).

KNIGHT, FRANK H.: *The Economic Organization* (New York: Augustus M. Kelley, Inc., 1951).

KOONTZ, HAROLD: "A Preliminary Statement of Principles of Planning and Control," *The Journal of the Academy of Management*, vol. 1, no. 1, April, 1958, pp. 48–61.

LANGE, OSCAR: *Price, Flexibility and Employment* (Evanston, Ill.: The Principia Press, Inc., 1952).

LONG, JOHN D.: "Problem Definition—A Prelude to Problem Solving," *Annals of Society of CPCU*, vol. 13, Fall, 1966, pp. 97–115.

LUCE, R. DUNCAN, and HOWARD RAIFFA: *Games and Decisions* (New York: John Wiley & Sons, Inc., 1957).

MCCAMMY, JAMES L.: "Analysis of the Process of Decision-Making," *Public Administration Review*, vol. 7, no. 1, 1947, pp. 41–48.

MARCH, JAMES G., and HERBERT A. SIMON: *Organizations* (New York: John Wiley & Sons, Inc., 1958).

MILLER, DELBERT C., and WILLIAM H. FORM: *Industrial Sociology* (New York: Harper & Brothers, 1951).

NAGEL, ERNEST: "Self-Regulation," *Scientific American*, vol. 185, no. 3, September, 1952, pp. 83–96.

OPTNER, STANFORD L.: *Systems Analysis for Business Management* (Englewood Cliffs, N.J.: Prentice-Hall, Inc., 1960).

PARSONS, TALCOTT: *The Social System* (Glencoe, Ill.: The Free Press, 1951).

PORTER, LYMAN W., and E. E. LAWLER III: *Managerial Attitudes and Performance* (Homewood, Ill.: Richard D. Irwin, Inc., 1968).

ROETHLISBERGER, FRITZ J.: "A New Look for Management," *Worker Morale and Productivity*, General Management Series No. 141 (New York: American Management Association, 1948), p. 13.

SCHNEIDER, EUGENE V.: *Industrial Sociology* (New York: McGraw-Hill Book Company, 1957).

SCITOVSKY, T.: "A Note on Profit Maximization and Its Implications," in George J. Stigler and Kenneth E. Boulding (eds.), *Readings in Price Theory* (Chicago: Richard D. Irwin, Inc., 1952), pp. 352–360.

SCODEL, ALVIN, PHILBURN RATOOSH, and J. SAYER MINAS: "Some Personality Correlates of Decision Making Under Conditions of Risk," in Willner (ed.), *Decisions, Values and Groups* (New York: Pergamon Press, 1960).

SIMON, HERBERT A.: *Administrative Behavior* (New York: The Macmillan Company, 1947).

SUOJANEN, WAINO W.: "The Span of Control—Fact or Fable," *Advanced Management*, vol. 20, no. 11, November, 1955.

TANNENBAUM, ROBERT: "Managerial Decision-Making," *Journal of Business*, vol. 22, no. 1, January, 1950, pp. 22–29.

——— and FRED MASSARIK: "Participation by Subordinates in the Managerial Decision-Making Process," *Canadian Journal of Economics and Political Science*, vol. 16, no. 4, August, 1950, pp. 410–413.

TAYLOR, FREDERICK W.: *Shop Management* (New York: Harper & Brothers, 1911).

THOMPSON, VICTOR A.: *Modern Organization* (New York: Alfred A. Knopf, Inc., 1961).

THRALL, R. M., C. H. COOMBS, and R. L. DAVIS (eds.): *Decision Processes* (New York: John Wiley & Sons, Inc., 1954), pp. 19–38.

VAIL, STEFAN: "Alternative Calculi of Subjective Probabilities" in R. M. Thrall, C. H. Coombs, and R. L. Davis (eds.), *Decision Processes* (New York: John Wiley & Sons, Inc., 1954).

VINACKE, W. EDGAR: *The Psychology of Thinking* (New York: McGraw-Hill Book Company, 1952), p. 188.

VROOM, VICTOR: *Work and Motivation* (New York: John Wiley & Sons, Inc., 1964).

WEBER, MAX: *The Theory of Social and Economic Organization*, trans. A. M. Henderson and Talcott Parsons (New York: Oxford University Press, 1947).

WIENER, NORBERT: *Cybernetics* (New York: John Wiley & Sons, Inc., 1948).

part

PSYCHOLOGICAL PERSPECTIVES

two

two

PERCEPTION AND MEDIATION

This chapter, devoted to a partial understanding of the psychological bases of decision making, finds its credence in the fact that decision making is nested uniquely in the individual. As we said in Chapter 1, the individual is considered the unit of decision making, inasmuch as only individuals are capable of making decisions. While we admit that to the individual some or perhaps major parts of the "stimulus surround" are social in nature, here we take a rather egoistic point of view by largely abstracting from socialization and the more immediate social impingements on decision making.

While concern with decision making could logically start with certain normative prescriptions, based upon some notion of economic science, for example, here we are attempting to understand human decision making as empirical investigators have found it. As Scrodel (in Willner, 1960, p. 37) has said:

> Formally inclined investigators begin with normative notions, e.g., maximization of expected utility, and concern themselves principally with attempting to explain why the behavior of experimental subjects deviate from these norms. The principal difficulty involved in making assumptions of this kind is that these assumptions involve a product of subjective probability and utility and that neither the subjectively held probability nor the utility of any choice is usually known.

Therefore, we will concern ourselves with psychological understanding of what Ward Edwards (in Willner, 1960, p. 4) has called "the higher mental processes." In this way we give our attention to how man, first, acquires and organizes information about a problem situation. As Edwards (*ibid.*) suggests, "This means more than perceiving the situation, for it also means recalling relevant information and putting it all, perceived and recalled, together into a structure which might be called an understanding of the situation. Second, is the processing and transformation of the information in such a way as to produce a set of alternative courses of action, one of which the problem-solver must choose." The third process—the final one for us—is the choice of one of these courses of action, whether or not that alternative is implemented as originally conceived. These three phases of information processing will be viewed as the basic cognitive processes underlying decision making. Most of the psychological literature would refer to the role played by *perception* and *mediation* in decision making.

Finally, in order that the reader not be misled by focusing solely on the decision maker to the exclusion of the stimulus surround and in order for us to discuss the interaction between decision making and realities of the problem field, we will examine perception and mediation in terms of abstracting and operationalizing a problem, that is, the way in which a model of the problem is formulated. Such a discussion, however, is more speculatively than empirically founded and more pragmatically than theoretically based.

Three general caveats, moreover, are in order. First, the theoretical and experimental literature cannot be neatly categorized. There is considerable overlap and inner connectedness, in terms of relevance and implications, in the literature. Thus, what particular items of substantive content one chooses to classify as "perception" or "mediation" is largely arbitrary. The primary criterion for such a classification scheme, therefore, becomes its utility for purposes of conceptualization and empirical research. This is generally true in the case of most hypothetical constructs; and both perception and mediation are *hypothetical constructs* which are useful concepts to describe the process by which the stimulus field is converted to meaningful behavior in response to this stimulus field. Secondly, as yet no one has "seen" a percept or has observed mediation in operation. Generally speaking we make an inference from overt activity about some mental processing which seems to "account for" the overt activity which has been observed and measured. The third and final caveat is that we have been referring to some "higher mental process." However, the psychological literature suggests that thinking takes place within an organism but that this organism is not just the "brain." While the organism which may be used directly in thinking processes is the mind, the mind is composed of various physical as well as psychic aspects. We will restrict our major attention to what may be called the "cognitive" processes of the decision maker. In some way, then, we are concerned with the "self" or "person" as it is involved in solving problems. Perception itself has provided a basis for the development of theories of personality. Therefore, it seems appropriate at this time to briefly explain how perception provides a basis for the psychology of decision making.

Perceptual Bases of Personality Theory

The study of personality development and functioning is a well-established field of psychological theory and research. It is concerned with both the functioning and the origins of so-called "normal" personality dimensions and with the causes, functioning, and treatment of various deviations from the norms.

We will restrict our attention in this section to those aspects of personality research and theory which serve as a mechanism to illustrate the processes of perception and mediation, i.e., those constructs most closely related to decision making. The emphasis will be further restricted by considering only the development and operation of the perceptual and mediatory processes of the "normal" personality.

Perception or perceptual activity is conceived of as supplying the raw materials "from which an individual constructs his own personally meaningful environment" (Blake and Ramsey, 1951, p. 1, preface).

Personality theory is necessarily concerned with the origin and development of certain affective, conative, and cognitive constellations of the individual person. This leads personality theorists to consider the sources of such individual attributes and the mechanisms through which they are created and developed. In general, *perceptual processes* enter the domain of personality theory as mechanisms of the organism through which the sources transmit their stimulus properties to the organism.

In our context, the *mediatory processes* become the interpretative mechanisms through which these stimuli are made personally meaningful.

However, the flow between perception and personality theory is not solely unidirectional. The personality constructs of the individual (needs, motives, attitudes, etc.) influence the perceptual process.

Our approach here is to follow the process as a sequence, as described by March and Simon: a concern, first, with perception—an awareness of the stimulus surround; second, certain "internal" variables at play on the choice mechanism; and third, the mediation process itself. However, a word of caution is necessary. The intent here is to examine various approaches to perception and mediation and analyze certain variables involved. This should not be construed as an attempt to build an eclectic model.

The areas of interest might be diagramed as found in Figure 2-1.

As depicted in Figure 2-1, the perceptual response can be conceived

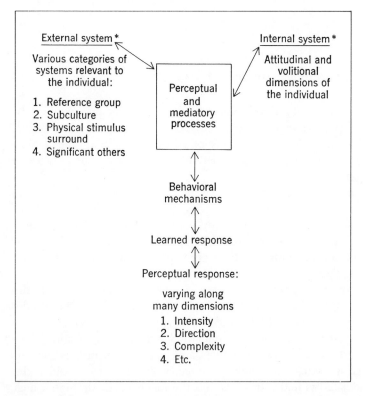

FIGURE 2-1 PERCEPTUAL AND MEDIATORY VARIABLES IN DECISION MAKING. ITEMS NOTED BY ASTERISK REFER TO POSITION RELATIVE TO THE PHYSIOLOGICAL AND ANATOMICAL BOUNDARIES OF A GIVEN INDIVIDUAL

of as a resultant of the interaction between the external and the internal systems. The specific character of the perceptual response is conditioned not only by the perceptual and mediatory processes but also by the abilities, both motor and sensory, and learned responses of the organism. As will be noted in the next chapter, learning probably also plays a significant role in the development of the mediatory processes that characterize an individual personality.[1]

For our purposes—the distinguishing between perception and mediation—the following definitions will be employed:[2]

> *Perception:* This is narrowly described as the receipt of internal (proprioceptive, etc.) and external stimuli which mutually activate the sense organs. The percepts (patterns of neural stimulation) provide the premediation content upon which the mediatory processes act.
>
> *Mediation:* This is conceived of as the process through which the cognitive and affective elements of the human being impinge upon (add to, subtract from, distort, etc.) the percept. Mediation is the process which intervenes between the physical receipt of stimuli (percepts) and the response (behavioral act) by which we identify and "measure" the mediating processes.

Both of these psychological processes underlie managerial and organizational decision making, and an elementary understanding of their nature is essential to an understanding of decision making.

Approaches to the Study of Perception

At least three major approaches to perception can be discerned in the literature: an introspective or analytic approach, a phenomenological or gestalt approach, and behavioristic approaches to perception.[3] Each of these has some relevance to our concern with decision making.

The first of these, predominant until about 1910, is the introspective approach to perception. For this approach, the subject matter was "conscious experience" of the normal adult human mind. The tool used to

---

[1] As can be seen from Figure 2-1, any attempt to categorize a particular subject matter into one or the other of the two segments—perception or mediation—is necessarily arbitrary.

[2] Other definitions might be equally useful. The significant point is that some operational distinction is necessary since these processes are not generally distinguished in psychological literature. Most "theories of perception" are more accurately referred to as "theories of perception and mediation."

[3] One of the reasons for the complexity and contradictory nature of theory and research in the area of perception lies in the tradition of historically "correct" approaches.

study the phenomenon was introspection, and only introspection. The writers dominant in this approach were Wundt, Titchener, Kulpe, and Wertheimer, in his early life.

The purpose of the introspective-analytic approach was to analyze the structure of conscious experience into its irreducible components, for example, sensations, images, and feelings. The philosophy underlying this purpose was that there are certain fundamental "building blocks" in experience, and that one can ascertain these fundamental and irreducible components of perception by means of the introspective analysis of conscious experience. Implied in this purpose and philosophy were two working assumptions: (1) language mirrors experience and in order to use introspective methods to study experience, it is necessary to assume an isomorphic relationship between language and experience; and (2) a subject in normal, ordinary introspections will commit the *stimulus error:* this means that the subject will say he sees an "object" rather than discrete elements of his experience. The task of the psychologist then becomes one of ascertaining these elements from the "perceived" object.

There are certain limitations associated with the approach of the introspectionist. One of these has to do with the ability of a decision maker to analyze his sensations, for example, his ability to analyze "wetness" into its component elements. Nonetheless, there are still a few psychologists searching for the "irreducible elements of conscious experience" today; but there are fewer using this approach than are using the two following approaches.

Gestalt psychology is a major representative of the phenomenological approach in contemporary psychology. Since much more will be said about gestalt psychology, here it is sufficient to merely suggest that the tools of the gestaltist are much the same as those of the introspectionist—namely, introspection. However, the purpose to which such tools are put is greatly different. The purpose is to study the perceptual processes in terms of figure-ground relationships through the study of meaningful wholes rather than of elements like event quality and duration. The contemporary psychologist, utilizing such an approach, studies such phenomena as: transposition, figural aftereffects, and perceptual constancy. Each, as will be seen, has a significant bearing on decision making as we view it.

The third approach, behavioralism, is partially based on the criticism that the phenomenological approach is too "vague." Behaviorists utilize psychophysical methods in studying perceptions. These methods are intended to remove as much subjectivity in ascertaining the decision makers' responses as possible. In this way, a concern is directed toward the study of functional correlations between observable and measurable stimulus-response relationships. Since this approach is in greatest repute and respectability today, it is worthy of elaboration.

Contemporary Theory and Perception

The main contribution of the behavioristic approach to the study of perception is its emphasis on the objective and scientific approach to the study of perception—its methodological contribution. This emphasis is a basic factor in the controversy that is causing the diversity of approaches in current perceptual literature, such as the question of nativism, or congenital concern, versus empiricism, or experiential explanation.

There appear to be two modern theories or schools within the behavioral category: the adaptation level, or accommodational, theory and the directive state, or motivational, theory. We will outline the basic concepts inherent in these two approaches and briefly review evidence which has been marshaled to support their relative validity.

A. THE ADAPTATION LEVEL THEORY[4]

Each individual is hypothesized to have a perceptual norm or frame of reference against or within which a stimulus object can be judged. This norm or frame of reference is established by the individual's past exposure to ranges of magnitudes and intensities of the stimulus. While these scales are *subjective* and *personal* to the individual, they are measurable through his verbal responses.

The proponents of this theory claim the advantage that adaptation level theory is amendable to quantitative formulations through the application of psychophysical methods. The human organism is assumed to establish some *dimensional* or *quantitative* order by which magnitudes can be judged. The individual achieves such an order by establishing some neutral—indifferent or nondiscriminable—range of experience on each dimension of his varied experience. During his past life, he has been exposed to a large range of stimuli magnitudes. He establishes an "average" range of magnitudes as a standard. He then judges incoming stimuli as large or small, heavy or light, and the like, according

---

[4] A thorough review of theorizing in perception is: F. H. Allport, *Theories of Perception and the Concept of Structure* (New York: John Wiley & Sons, Inc., 1955). This section draws extensively upon this work.

to their position relative to the standard; a case in point being a manager's assessment of his current departmental budget in terms of his previous budgets. Note that, since these standards of judgment are primarily related to past perceptual experiences, it should be possible to experimentally manipulate an individual's frame of reference and, therefore, his perceptual responses by varying past experiences. As will be noted subsequently, much of this type of experimental work has been done. Furthermore, evidence collected by researchers, working under different theoretical assumptions, can be interpreted within the adaptation level hypothesis.

The *adaptation level* represents a "centering" of the organism with respect to the stimuli confronting it and has been referred to as the "true zero of functioning." The position of this functional zero or adaptation level is said to determine the structure of the stimulus field as perceived. It is hypothesized that the adaptation level is established from the individual's total array of past and present sensory experiences through a process of *pooling*. Through this process the organism arrives at some kind of "average" of its sensory experiences on each dimension, for example, in perception of distance, and, thus, of the relative height of a single mountain of a range several miles distant. This pooling process is not necessarily conscious. It has both physiological and neurological as well as psychological elements.

The theory hypothesizes that experiences received from three different stimuli sources will have an impact on the adaptation level. These three sources are:

1. The series of stimuli that are presented (e.g., the budget and its presentation);
2. The background series of stimuli (e.g., cues on the financial state of the organization); and
3. The residual effects from earlier stimuli (e.g., historical experience with the budget).

The relative impact of these three kinds of stimuli is hypothesized to be dependent upon their:

1. Relative frequencies;
2. Proximity;
3. Affective value.

Researchers using this approach have been able to devise formulae for assigning weights to such factors and to compute for a given individual in a given experimental situation a weighted average (usually a weighted geometric mean of all the stimuli) that will predict his adaptation level.

Experimentally, it has been found that the perceived magnitude of an identical stimulus can vary depending on the constellation of series, standard, and background stimuli. The experimental methodology and supporting evidence have been summarized by Helson (1947, 1948, 1951). The individual is asked to judge, for example, a weight as heavy or light—not heavier or lighter; in other words, the adaptation level methodology differs from the comparative psychophysical methodology. The individual has to formulate his own system of judgment or frame of reference.

Two research findings are of major interest to us. Helson points out that *social stimulation* influences individual perception and judgment; for instance, social interactions may also "pool." This may take the form of leveling, where individual judgments are brought into line with a consensual norm. *Individual differences* also appear which can be explained by differentials in total stimulus experience and/or by personal differences in the weighting of various parts of the stimulus field. The possibility may be that personality differences are due to differential exposure to stimulating conditions, thereby building up differences of adaptation level.

"Level of aspiration" is an example of another phenomenon acting on a frame of reference in relation to some norm. This phenomenon can be interpreted in terms of the adaptation level theory as follows.

The "level of aspiration" represents an assessment of a prediction by an individual of his future performance in some task. The components of the "pool" might be conceived as knowledge of: (1) own past performance, (2) self-abilities, (3) performance of others, etc. This level of aspiration, in turn, becomes a significant norm in influencing the judged satisfaction to be derived from the consequences of the alternative chosen in making a decision.

As a *transition* to our second contemporary theory of perception, directive state theory, we might note that the adaptation level theory does not adequately incorporate considerations of the need system or affective aspects of human behavior. The emphasis of the adaptation level theory is largely on the structural properties of past and present stimulus fields. Moreover, this theory does not adequately account for the selectivity of perception. The latter limitation means that the adaptation level theory does not present constructs which aid one in explaining why some segments of the total stimulus field are perceived as relevant and others are perceived as ground or not distinguished at all. Thus we are led to a consideration of a theory of perception which is concerned with the question of the directional or selective attributes of the perceptual process, for example, why some decision makers attend to the authority relations and others attend to the task dimension of their roles.

B. THE DIRECTIVE STATE THEORY OF PERCEPTION

In its experimental form this body of theory centers on the motivational dimensions of human behavior as they influence the perception of value-latent stimuli. This perspective means that a directive state theory of perception views the study of perception as interdependent with other subject areas in psychology—with learning, personality, and social development.

The major proponents of the directive state theory of perception have been Bruner, Postman, and Murphy (1943, 1947, 1948, 1950, 1951). Relying mostly on Bruner and Postman, the directive state theory, in its broadest terms, can be described as follows: There are two determinants of any given perception: (1) the autochthonous or structural, and (2) the behavioristic or motivational. The gestaltists and adaptation level theorists tend to overemphasize the former, according to the directive state theorists.

Bruner and Postman claim that two contrasting programs of theory and experiment are needed to explain perception, that is, the *formal,* incorporating the structural determinants, and the *functional,* incorporating the motivational determinants. The autochthonous determinants include the stimulus, the effects of stimulation upon the receptors, the afferent neurons, and the sensory cortical areas. As responses to the stimulus field, these phenomena represent the innate and relatively unchangeable endowment of the individual for the activity of perceiving. Behavioral determinants of perception are related to the "higher-level" mental processes. Included in this category are such concepts as needs, tensions, values, defenses, and emotions of the individual. Taken together these behavioral factors form a *central directive state.* The older, formal theories are said to have neglected such determinants of perception. The experimenter, working within the boundaries of the formal theory, attempted to control for these behavioral determinants while varying the structural elements of the stimulus field. Experimentalists of the directive state approach hold that their task is to systematically vary these behavioral determinants—treating them as independent variables. This makes their work highly relevant for our later concerns with the social and organizational influences upon decision making in the administered setting.

Experimental evidence in support of the directive state theory can be summarized by stating six propositions deduced from directive state theory which have been empirically supported (Allport, 1955, pp. 309–319). Specific relevance to our concern is suggested for each.

1. Bodily needs tend to determine what is perceived; creature comfort may be an organizational concern.

2. Reward and punishment associated with the perceiving of objects tend to determine what is perceived. They also tend to determine its apparent magnitude and its speed of recognition; the formal reward system may influence membership behavior.

3. The values characteristic of the individual tend to determine the speed with which words related to those values are recognized; co-optation may be an effective device in institutionalizing an organization.

4. The value of objects to the individual tends to determine their perceived magnitudes; orientation and ideology may be factors of concern in recruiting.

5. The personality characteristics of the individual predispose him to perceive things in a manner consistent with those characteristics; persons high in authoritarianism may perceive a problem field differently from those low in authoritarianism.

6. Verbal stimuli that are emotionally disturbing or threatening to the individual tend to require a longer recognition time than neutral words, to be so misperceived as radically to alter their form or meaning, and to arouse their characteristic emotional reactions even before they are recognized; for effectiveness in organizational communication, reduction in noise may require deletion of threat-arousing symbols.

It should be noted, however, that there is enough evidence which does not support the directive state theory for one to say that these propositions should be accepted with extreme caution and, as valid, only within the confines of the experimental situations from which the positive evidence was gleaned.

Conceptualization of Perception

The two contemporary approaches presented above suggest, as stated before, the controversy on the question of nativism versus empiricism.

Those theorists favoring the doctrine of nativism tend to emphasize structural determinants of the perceptual experience. "Perception" is interpreted narrowly, and it does not include the cognitive processes which are incorporated in the directive state theory. Perception is seen, not as "insight," but as an immediate, uncontaminated process grounded in physiological laws and present in the human being from birth. The dimensions of the phenomenon of perception are limited to such things as sensory quality, dimensionality of the stimulus surroundings, constancy, and configuration. The physiological phenomena of relevance are relatively simple, that is, cortical excitation set up by receptors and afferent neurons, versus such physiological phenomena as traces, overlays, etc., which are relevant to the empiricist.

The empiricist incorporates a much broader range of phenomena under the label "perception." Particularly, cognitive and mediational processes are considered relevant. This broadened scope is reflected in the interrelatedness of "perception" with learning and personality theory. The origins of the motivational theories of perception are in empiricism. Its use of past experience as relevant data leads to a much broader and more fruitful, even if less operational and less pure, theory of perception. The role of the human behavioral system is seen as interacting with the stimulus field in the determination of "meaningful" percepts. This point of view tends to be emphasized here.

RELEVANT DIMENSIONS

The diversity of conceptualizations and measures of perception gives a variety of insights and interests to the study of decision making. Each of these, while showing a theoretical or empirical bias, will find its application in the work which follows in later chapters.

The first of these areas of relevance might be referred to as *sensory characteristics and dimensions*. The psychologist notes that visual stimuli have qualities, such as hue, and related concepts of quantity, such as intensity or illumination. These sensory qualities and dimensions are the parts or segments which the associationist discusses and the existence of which the gestaltist doubts. For this aspect of perception the perceiving organism is conceived of as purely "passive." In contrast to the gestalt approach, this orientation limits perception to only such stimulus attributes as "dimensions of sensation," such as quality, intensity, duration, clearness, etc. The gestalt psychologist would argue that "quality cannot be fully described in terms of these attributes alone." Nonetheless, except for a physiological approach to the study of perception, the empiricist's approach may be "the purest" in the sense of being the least reducible of those which we have mentioned; that is, these attributions seem most basic to all percepts on any sensory dimension. In addition, they offer insight for our purposes, for example, a concern with clarity of instructions.

The scholar, studying the *perceptual constancy phenomenon*, manipulates physical dimensions of the stimulus field, noting how the perceiver maintains a constancy as to the percept he sees as the surrounding "cues" are varied systematically. An emphasis on the phenomenon of perceptual constancy "explains" how an organism is able to consistently and accurately identify the objects of his environment as his angles and positions of orientation with respect to the stimulus field change. Here we might be concerned with, for example, perceptual constancy of an individual occupying multiple roles.

In the study of *configurations*, the percept is seen as being less determined by the dimensions of the stimulus and environment and more by processes operating within the perceiving organism, i.e., the problem solver. The emphasis of this approach centers on the inner relationships among the parts and between parts and wholes. Parts or segments are never to be perceived separately—the "whole character" of any percept is predominant.[5] In this case we might contend that an instruction cannot be interpreted in isolation from the environment of its receipt, and that both total more than the sum of the isolated parts.

In his concern with a *frame of reference*, the experimenter will tend to require the individual to give an absolute judgment on some sensory dimension where no external standard of reference is given the subject. The individual, thus, is required to form his own series or scale of standards. Helson's "adaptation level," previously mentioned, is a salient illustration of this approach. Such studies could lend insight into the behavior of organizational members making decisions where no policies or rules are available.

The reader should note that, as he has focused on these dimensions of perception, he has been approaching more and more closely the concept of mediation. The last approach to be mentioned here is the *set* or *state* of the perceiver. This particular approach allows more complete attention to the importance of individual differences in the perceptual phenomenon. The role of need states, attitudes, beliefs, prejudices, etc., can be treated in this context—or in "mediation," as will be done in this particular work. The concept of *set* best facilitates, relative to those above, the study of interdependence of motivation, learning, and perception. However, it is possible that "perceptual set" may be primarily based on less complicated intervening variables, like frequency of past exposure or the related concept of familiarity. For example, Johnson (1961, p. 255) tells of one experiment where the decision maker was confronted with the situation where he was asked to match a third object either in type of texture or in general shape. If the problem solver had been working previously with shape, he picked the "shape" solution. In this way, he demonstrated to the experimenter that past experience is a particularly important influence on the perception of ambiguous problems.

Before leaving the concept of "*set*" and moving to the discussion of

[5] This concept is most closely associated with gestalt psychology.

mediation, it seems appropriate to quote Vinacke (1952, p. 178), in his conclusions to the discussions of insight. He states that: "The efficient management of a present situation depends upon the development and application of modes of attack or appropriate set. That is, relationships, principles, attitudes, methods, etc., are more significant than specific content, or specific operations, or specific rules." The significance of the concept of *set* emerges repeatedly in our discussion of decision making. This is particularly true in the case of our later discussions of socialization and bureaucracy.

Mediation: The Role of Volitional and Affective Factors in Perception

In a previous section of this chapter, we noted that there seems to be experimental evidence for a "directive state theory of perception." As noted, this evidence has led to six conclusions (cf. Allport, 1955, pp. 309–319), which can be summarized as follows:

1. Bodily needs tend to determine what is perceived.

2. Reward and punishment tend to determine what is perceived as well as its apparent magnitude and speed of recognition.

3. Values characteristic of the individual tend to determine the speed with which symbols are recognized.

4. The value of objects to the individual tends to determine their perceived magnitude.

5. Personality characteristics of the individual predispose him in perception.

6. Emotionally disturbing stimuli tend to: (1) require a longer recognition time, (2) be misperceived, and (3) arouse emotional reactions before they are recognized.

Each of these confirmed hypotheses incorporates mediatory processes as herein defined. Each of these behavioral responses is interpreted to be a function of something in addition to the physical stimulus field. Theorists and researchers on perception have attempted to "explain" these experimental findings through the use of various hypothetical constructs intervening between neurophysical receipt and overt behavior. We will summarize these volitional and affective "mediatory explanatory constructs" in terms of the concepts used by researchers and theorists in the field.[6]

The essence of mediation, as noted earlier, is that some "mechanism"

---

[6] However, as noted previously, one seldom finds the term "mediation" in the writings of these scholars.

operates between the affective or volitional conditions and the behavioral or perceptual response. (Cf. F. H. Allport, 1955, p. 319.) This hypothetical mechanism has been referred to in various ways—varying across dimensions of complexity, consciousness, salience, or relative importance as one determinant of the perceptual response, etc. A few of these interpretations will be summarized in order to illustrate various possible dimensions of "mediation."

1. AUTISM

This mediatory process has been conceived of as a "wishful perceiving" in the direction of need satisfaction. The mechanisms linking the motivational state of the individual to the perceptual process and its result have not been adequately specified, operationally. Thus, we deal with autism only incidentally.

2. PERCEPTUAL HYPOTHESIS

This function is assumed to be set up by any need or demand internally or externally imposed on the individual. Such forms of reasoning appear to be similar to that conceptualization of an attitude as a "readiness to respond" in a directive and affective manner. The hypothesis, itself, can be confirmed or rewarded by the attainment of a rewarding percept. The hypothesis is said thereby to become "fixated." The result is that those perceptual objects which confirm the hypothesis tend to become selected habitually—and also become more vivid and perceived as greater in size or magnitude. In the specialized language of these researchers, the perceptual objects become "accentuated." There is an obvious interrelation suggested here between perception and learning theory. We will return to this subject in more detail subsequently.

3. SELECTIVE SENSITIZATION, PERCEPTUAL DEFENSE, AND VALUE RESONANCE

Postman, Bruner, and McGinnies (1948) have suggested that through these mediatory processes individualized structures impinge upon perception. While all have general similarity, selective sensitization refers to the process through which value orientations lower the threshold for acceptable stimuli; perceptual defense is the process through which the perceptual threshold for unfavorable stimulus objects is raised; and value resonance is the process by which the perceiver, under conditions of rapid stimulus exposure so that object identification is impossible, is induced to perceive the stimulus object as being within his value area. The description of such phenomena contributes to the understanding of selective focusing and organizationally rational responses. These three mechanisms are often supplemented by numerous other operations in perceptual research and theory, such as "availability," "normalization," "dominance," "assimilation," "compromise formation," "vigilance," "primitivation," "hierarchy of thresholds," "degree of personal relevance," etc.

4. NEED ORGANIZATION

The broad emphasis on the need structure of an individual in the other theories has been complemented by approaches which place great emphasis on individual differences in need organization. This latter approach means that mediation encompasses such concepts as "ego structure," "perceptual attitude," "tolerance for ambiguity and uncertainty," and other non-need factors. These additional dimensions can encompass most nonaffectively oriented attributes of personality. Such variables would influence the decision maker in terms of, for example, his risk propensity.

5. SUBCEPTION

This mechanism was reported by McCleary and Lazarus and refers to autonomic discrimination without awareness (in Bruner and Krech, 1950, pp. 171–179). The unconscious nature of the "subception" process makes it most difficult to study. The theoretical explanations of "subception" have been largely in terms of physiological constructs and interrelations. But the process can be described as follows: Cues from "inimical" or hostile stimuli are evaluated by the central nervous system, even though the impulses from these stimuli do not become fully integrated to the point of recognition. Largely unconsciously, then, avoidance of "further anxiety" results from a subliminal raising of the individual's perceptual threshold, that is, a further screening of external stimuli. In this light, subception becomes a variant of perceptual defense.

Study of the notion of perceptual defense as a mediatory process is hampered by the basic assumption that something is perceived before it can be perceived. This leads one into the trap of conceiving of a "pre-perceiver" which protects the perceiver. Thus, the problem centers on finding some way of relating the autochthonous, or stimulus field, to behavioral factors in perception. But the process of mediation must be conceptualized so as to have consistent, observable referents. It must also be *reliable* and *essential* in the sense that, given need "x" and stimulus field "a," we can always produce the same behavioral or perceptual response, given the same mediatory process. The need, therefore, is for an ex ante rather than an ex post mechanism.

Such a mechanism is found in the directive state theory—or, more specifically, the perceptual defense theory—as "advanced" by Bruner and Postman in their formulation of the "hypothesis theory" (Rohrer and Sherif, 1951, chap. 10). An essential notion of the construct is that an individual perceiver is always *set* to perceive—and to perceive in some particular way, that is, an ex ante hypothesis on the state of the stimulus field. Each perceiver is conceived of as having "perceptual expectancy" hypotheses from past experience which cue him as to what objects to look for and how they will appear in the field. The information provided by the stimulus field takes the form of "cues" or "clues" that serve to confirm or refute the hypotheses or tend to generate new hypotheses.

Within this theory, the mediatory process can be conceptualized as functioning as follows: If the stimulus information confirms the hypothesis, then a stable perceptual organization results. If the stimulus information tends to refute the hypothesis, then a new hypothesis is evoked— from memory—or formulated until one is established that is confirmed. Then a stable perceptual organization results.

Several postulates for testing have been derived from this hypothesis theory (F. H. Allport, 1955, pp. 381–382):

1. The stronger the hypothesis, the greater is the likelihood of its arousal and the less the amount of appropriate and supporting stimulus information that will be required to confirm it.

2. Where the hypothesis is weak, a large amount of appropriate and supporting information is necessary for its confirmation.

3. The stronger an hypothesis, the greater is the amount of contradictory stimulus information necessary to refute it; and the weaker it is, the less contradictory stimulus information is needed to refute it.

Postman, Bruner, and other theorists have used the hypothesis theory to reinterpret some of the results of the directive state theory. The major contribution of such reformulations, especially for us, has been an explicit inclusion of the concept of "set." Given our concerns here, this construct may contribute to our understanding, for example, of innovative problem solving.

In contrast, when this hypothesis theory of mediatory processes is evaluated against the criteria we previously established, it does not appear to hold much advantage over the older directive state theory. The problems of identifying and operationally defining some observable, independent mediatory constructs are only one step removed. We still have no clues as to how these hypotheses, or expectations of certain stimulus objects, are formed, changed, confirmed, or refuted. If we accept the "fact" that something exists which does dynamically mediate between the volitional and affective attributes of the personality and the physical properties of the stimulus input, then we may be forced to measurement on the physiological and neurological level in order to identify and measure this "something."

However, we can speculate on the application of what we do know about the abstraction process, especially if we do no violence to existing evidence. This we do here by examining how a decision maker conceptualizes a problem. Such a discussion is particularly timely; with the increasing academic emphasis on the techniques of problem solving, scholars have tended to lose interest in the configuration and nature of problems in the real world.[7] Our counter-balancing focus is on the conceptualization and operationalization of a problem.

Conceptualization of a Problem

The current attention to problem solving, as an investigation of cognitive processes used in the search for meaningful adaptation to the environment, has many historical antecedents. Logicians and philosophers have studied problem solving in highly theoretical ways for at least as long as recorded history through the concern with "mental philosophy." (Cf. Cofer and Appley, 1964, pp. 19–55.)

Early attention related to man's concern with differentiating himself from his environment and, then, to his abilities in perceiving that environment so as to better accommodate to it. But modern scholarship, dealing with problem solving, seems to have closer historical ties with man's search for means of obtaining greater objectivity, i.e., loosely, the scientific method. (Cf. Berelson and Steiner, 1964, pp. 15–35.) This latter approach appears to stem from dissatisfaction with appeals to intuition and authority for appropriate problem solutions. The intent of the "scientific method" is to provide a more valid concept of reality in order to more effectively control it. (Cohen and Nagel, 1934, pp. 191–196.)

STATEMENT OF CONCERN

Many, if not all, of these earlier conceptualizations of cognitive processes were derived through introspection: (1) Given a personal perception

---

[7] Indeed, Professor Victor A. Thompson, University of Illinois, Urbana (personal correspondence, November, 1968), states: "These prescriptions ignore various human limitations with regard to calculation and ignorance; and Simon, 1959, has shown they assume that a uniquely rational solution ('to maximize') exists in the real world. Furthermore, there is no logically satisfactory rule for terminating search, as Braybrooke and Lindbloom (1963) say; so that one must predict the end of history in order to meet the criteria of classical rationality."

of a problem-related stimulus (Why did I receive this stimulus rather than others?); (2) How did I process this "information"? (How did I infer from these data?); and, finally, (3) What choice of action was made to deal with the problem? (Why did I choose this act rather than others?). Indeed, while in low repute in some circles, there is a modern school of "introspectionism."

Today, however, the literature on administrative problem solving turns away from the insights offered by the introspection of wise practitioners. The trend has been to develop esoteric technologies and highly abstract constructs for normatively guiding decision making. To the extent that this evolvement in highly rationalistic models has become an exclusive concern, the scholar may have "thrown out the baby with the dirty water." He may be ignoring the situational tenor of constructs, propositions, and technologies in dealing with the problem, especially as it is perceived and defined by the human problem solver.[8]

Current emphasis on technology versus situation may be related to a dominant concern with administrative rather than entrepreneural behavior. As Gomberg (1964, p. 54) contends: "The principal work of the entrepreneur is the formulation of what the problem is rather than the determination of a decision. The resulting decision is implicit in the way the problem is formulated. The great emphasis on decision making has obscured this distinction." Nonetheless, many of the current studies find management actually spending a large proportion of time in search, but relatively little time in what is classed as decision making.[9]

Stemming largely from mathematical economics, prescriptive decision rules and algorithmic technologies are offered as guides to the administrator for organizationally optimal decision making. The formulations associated with these contemporary tools take the form: Given an array of alternatives, with a (subjectively known) probability distribution, the application of a given decision rule (e.g., maximization of mathematical expectations) projects a normative choice.

Some of these formalistic deductions have been tested empirically in the concern with solution protocols and the operations of "sudden insight." These studies, however, are conducted generally with "the prob-

[8] Necessarily, experimental design in the physical sciences has dealt with the necessity and sufficiency of relevant variables and their interrelationships. Moreover, for some years, psychologists have studied the perception of relationships of parts of the field attended—*via* measures of, for example, "contrast." Too, gestalt psychologists have hypothesized on part-whole relationships and configuration. Nonetheless, few of these conceptions and findings appear to have found their way into existing literature on administrative decision making.

[9] For a review of studies on the allocation of an executive's time, see Robert Dubin, "Business Behavior Behaviorally Viewed," in George Strother (ed.), *Social Science Approaches to Business Behavior* (Homewood, Illinois: Richard D. Irwin, 1962), pp. 11–55.

lem" highly controlled, abstract, and standardized. In this way, the actor's reflections on the environment containing the problem are treated rather superficially. Such artificial "fields" have tended to dominate the concern of most contemporary management scholars. As a result, much recent literature on managerial decision making abstracts from the stimulus surround that actually contains the problem. Certainly, the unadorned "description" of the problem-solving process does not suffice. This method suggests that one should (1) define the problem, (2) collect the facts, (3) establish alternative behaviors, (4) evaluate alternative choices, and (5) decide upon an act. Nor is the bland, *ceteris paribus*, statement of an algorithmic function, $c = x + by$, insightful for our purposes.

Historical data, but seldom experimental procedures, are used in solving financial problems. Aggregate economic data are found in abundance, but there is a paucity of information on actual behavior of managerial incumbents. Some consideration may be given to reality in the way of feasibility tests on implementing a decision; yet little attention is given to the excitation factor and its surroundings which originally gave rise to the solution process. Our purpose here, therefore, is to study certain dimensions of a problem field and, in a limited way, to review primitive responses of the actor.

PROBLEM SOLVING

The label "problem solving" is used inconsistently in the literature and often interchangeably with decision making. The presumption of effectiveness in decision making and the concept of a problem as discussed here make the notions of decision making and problem solving closely allied. Yet in their fullest meaning the terms are not synonymous. In at least one dimension, for example, problem solving appears to be a more generic concept than decision making, i.e., solving a problem may well involve a set of decisions. In turn, though, the conclusion of a major decision may have involved the solving of several related problems.

Some types of "choice" are not of a problem-solving nature. Previous decisions, for example, may be reviewed with reflections on the historic optimality of that choice, i.e., ex post decisions can be made about the past which may have no immediate bearing on selecting future courses of action. Reminiscing may influence effective decisions, but concern here is with that process of intellection which directly selects a course of action.[10] In contrast, some problems do not involve decision

---

[10] Ex post decisions probably always have an indirect bearing on effective decision making, especially in the way that historical choices and outcomes are used to simulate some aspect of the future or affect the weight given to relevant variables.

making as a deliberative process. Either habitual action or a pure behavioral response may be a mode of problem solving—to remove one's
hand from a hot flame does not require much in the way of higher
mental processes. Moreover, except for some simple cognitive triggering
of behavior, habitual responses do not meet our restricted attention
to mediated action. (Cf. Katona, 1953, pp. 307–318.)

To further clarify our concern with problem solving, we can examine
Whitney's (1950, p. 68) statement that: "The problem comes out of
a situation in which there is a recognition that something is the matter,
that unsolved difficulties exist." To us, then, a problem involves a re-
ciprocal relationship: (1) the relevant environment (2) is observed (or
predicted) as to have come to a state deemed undesirable by the actor,
through chance, adversity, or whatever, and (3) he wishes to act on
it. Thus, for our purposes, a problem can be defined as *a perceived
departure from a desirable state of affairs by an actor who is predisposed
to deal foresightfully with the situation and who has some control over
assignable cause(s).*

DISPOSITION TO DECIDE

Many alternative predictions may be made for the actor who is objectively confronted with a problem. In terms of the actual dimensions
of reality, the departure (or impediment) may not be perceived or
the deviation may not offer a sufficient stimulus to activate the individual. For example, in Figure 2-2, XY (the extent of the deviation)
may not be perceived as sufficiently disquieting to evoke a change in
behavior.[11] Finally, subjective costs of dealing with the problem may
outweigh anticipated benefits of moving state II toward state I.

Correction of deviation, XY, has two dimensions: (1) the value of

[11] This proposition on stimulus-sufficiency is similar to the concept of satisficing
(versus maximizing) behavior. See Chapter 7.

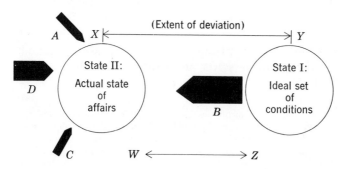

FIGURE 2-2   THE NATURE OF A PROBLEM DIAGRAMMED

the movement toward state I and (2) the cost of the change away from state II. Subjective evaluations of these values are highly complex. Cost, for example, has three elements: (1) the "psychic" cost of decision making, (2) the cost of search and possible unemployment of assets during that period, and (3) the cost of implementing the decision.[12] Nonetheless, we assume that the manager typically is disposed to decide on a course of action so as to reduce the deviation, XY, and to do so directly in terms of state II. In fact, it is inconceivable that most managers, "locked in" a bureaucratic setting, can often evade the taking of action on the state of nature.

This is not to suggest that the actor observes reality correctly or will not be influenced by current fashion (e.g., "good human relations") or early training (e.g., specialization in accounting). Furthermore, it is entirely possible that the actor fails to deal directly with the deviation and merely redefines the problem field so as to "define the problem away."

ESSENTIAL CONTROL

We assume that the problem solver is concerned with varying the environment, whether it be a restoration of previous conditions or "creating" a new state of affairs. On the one hand, as may be the realistic case, he may never feel able to "step into a flowing stream at the same place," especially as he has—or his aspirations have—changed. In this case, he is impelled by dynamic equilibrium: Some optimal balance across the relevant factors must be attained, but to return to a previous state cannot be the goal.

On the other hand, he may desire some restoration of previous order. The process of restoration may be circulated as a closed-loop control system, with the decision maker acting as a regulator of the operating (instrumental) system. If, then, the output of operations is monitored in terms of deviations from standard, the regulator (decision maker) is activated only when deviations occur, i.e., the system is "error controlled." Under these conditions, actual output oscillates constantly about some established standard, and complete restoration may never be found. Whatever the case, the problem solver is viewed as holding control over the problem field.

[12] This movement can be analyzed marginally, i.e., the cost of a given movement toward I can be evaluated against the perceived value of attaining that movement. After the movement has begun, increasing marginal costs or decreasing marginal value of each movement may result in an imperfect restoration of II to I, as WZ in Figure 2-2. However, eventually increasing costs or decreasing productivity does not necessarily set in during the relevant change, for example, because of psychic satisfactions from decision making.

If the problem solver is devoted to treating the disorder (often, in business parlance, "overcome the barrier to a goal"), he must locate and act on the variable(s) causing that departure. His first task, then, is to isolate and define the essential (independent) variables at play in the field, in Figure 2-2, the variables, A, B, C, and D. His second step is to sort from this set those variables which are influencing the deviation, as B or D or both in the above figure. Thirdly, through historical observations or experimental data, he must make certain assumptions about (assign certain probabilities to) the (1) sufficiency of the variables to restore the desired state and (2) his ability to operate upon these variables in such a way that his purpose will be achieved. (In Figure 2-2, for example, he might choose to increase the intensity of D, decrease the intensity of B, or utilize some combination of the two acts.) Finally, he must choose a course of action *on how* to operate upon the vagrant variable.

However, the problem solver may not wish to treat the variables of prime cause. He may, for example, find an array of variables of secondary or tertiary importance which, he feels, in some cumulative fashion are more amenable to his control or, in total, have a more immediate and observable impact upon the deviation. Such a disposition may account for the oft-heard statement that one should move slowly and deal with the minor problems (causes) first. The desire may be to gain some knowledge about, or control of, the minor causes before manipulating those variables expected to be more important for a variety of reasons, including the presence of randomness in the system.

That variable which appears to be random to the problem solver, however, may be within a larger or different system than that conceived by him; his frame of reference, through which he views the problem field, may cloud reality. To him, the relevant version of the field is that part which is conceptually structurable and perhaps quantifiable,[13] or his limitation may lie in a prevailing state of technology, e.g., similar to Heisenberg's "uncertainty principle." Nonetheless, the constraints established above, that the actor can and wants to act on the problem, still hold.

However, the question as to *how* he acts depends upon his assessments of available resources and his own (or his agent's) skills in employing these resources. In this regard, it is important to note that the potential of a choice of action is dependent upon the efficacy of the causal vari-

[13] In fact, there are many scientific orientations which might argue that to "know" is to suppose "measurability." The susceptibility to, and type of, measurement varies rather broadly by discipline. Yet measures of the less tangible and quantifiable can be gained indirectly, albeit loosely and perhaps only intuitively, from those related variables which are measurable, if the degree and direction of the relationship can be at least crudely approximated. (Cf. Shull, 1960, pp. 18–22.)

able—relative and absolute—as well as the actor's own control of the variable. He may find the situation such that the efficacy of D relative to B (in Figure 2-2) is high but his control of B relative to D is more than offsetting. Accordingly, causal control is a matter of degree. Problem solutions are subject to a variety of determinants, such as unwillingness to provide restoration as well as constraints on the ability to do so.

SYMPTOMATIC REMEDIES

Thus far it has been assumed that certain (independent) variables are acting in such a way as to make some segment of the relevant universe deviate from ideal or normal.[14] (Note that the variable is independent in that it can cause the deviation but dependent in that the problem solver or his agent can act upon it.) In contrast, much of what appears to be reality is nothing more than a symbol of inherent property of the field. Yet the actor may take these signs or manifestations "to mean" the real object. In addition, while the actor may want to operate on the causal factor, it may be sensed too late or he may be unable to directly perceive it at all. Accordingly, he may search for cues of the disorder and attend immediately to them.[15]

Often trying, these symptoms of the deviation may act positively for the problem solver. Symptoms may manifest themselves before an organic pathology has developed and, in this way, herald the disorder. Moreover, especially where the cause of the deviation cannot be observed directly, the pattern of these symptoms may give clues as to the source of the problem. (See Figure 2-2, where the intent is to depict a congruence between the symptomatic and causal systems.) Indeed, in terms of priority of action, dealing with the symptom may take precedence over treating the cause: We must live in the short run, or the long run may become irrelevant. In fact, such activities may demand all available resources.

There is no doubt that symptoms may require corrective measures in their own right. The causal system may hold most importance in terms of strategic goals and functioning of the organism (as low morale); but, since the symptomatic system may be dysfunctional on its own, it may require some type of remedy, e.g., fever (symptomatic of pneu-

---

[14] The word *ideal* is differentiated from *normal* so as to imply the presence of aspirations in level of attainment, i.e., to connote target attributes and not to denote feasibility measures, as with efficiency or effectiveness.

[15] Concern with symptoms is referred to as "the short-run problem" in much of the management literature. Yet, while "problem" is commonly intended to mean the manifested departure itself, the distinction between cause and manifestation of deviation is emphasized here.

monia) may require treatment directly. Yet, these symptoms must not be mistaken for a cause of the deviation. Symptomatic remedies may facilitate causal adjustments but not cure the (long-run) problem. Indeed, to the extent that the two solutions are dependent, there is the need for congruency between short and long-run actions, i.e., the effect of the symptom-remedy must not mitigate the long-run solution or vice versa.[16]

Depending upon the complexity of the problem field, highly intricate relationships may require definition and evaluation. Whatever the complexity, however, inferences about significance and judgments about relevance must be made.

Inference is the process of reasoning from (assumed, accepted, "known") premises, perceived from or overlayed upon objective reality, to a logical conclusion. (It can be typified by the syllogistic form "if . . . , then . . .").[17] Thus, an inference is essentially a conclusion on the agreement or disagreement on the relationship of two or more phenomena. The pronouncement of an inference, therefore, is made in the form of a denial or affirmation of some relationship founded on certain cognitive processes. Such a statement suggests a claim of truth or validity.

Over time, man has developed a high sense of the artist (often buttressed by scientific findings) in perceiving the presence of a disorder or attributing a cause to a deviation.[18] We have all had occasions to observe and have been astounded by this talent, e.g., "feeling the pulse of a motor" through vibrations of the automobile fender. We assume that the "expert" has had sufficiently varied experiences and developed a classification scheme so that his cues on symptomatic relationships are reliable and that his inferences about causality (e.g., ignition versus

[16] Often overlooked as well are the side effects of any particular remedy. Certain of these side effects may be dysfunctional to the organism via the attending solution or from its own outcomes. (The use of "wonder drugs" is a case in point.)

[17] Inference, as a province of statistics, has to do with an algorithmic method for establishing significance of dependency. While some scientists do not want to speculate beyond "relationship" (correlation), the sanctity of the .05 confidence level has not been de facto supported. While the method of statistics, itself, is in need of verification, the method of deduction (especially introspection) may leave some scientists most wanting.

[18] Attention, throughout this discussion, pertains more to actual than to predicted deviations, yet control systems for a projected course of action may be geared to symptomatic measures heralding disequilibrium, and ex ante simulations may be evaluated in terms of such symptomatic arousals.

carburetion system) are valid. Certainly, across various professional areas, high credence and legitimacy are given to the knowledge gained from "practical" experience. Whatever his proficiency, as Chipman (1960, p. 70) states: ". . . the individual in everyday life must make inferences about the world about him in order to act intelligently. To use a term suggested to me by Donald T. Campbell, the individual is a 'quasi-scientist'; whether or not it is explicitly formulated, he has a theory about the world he lives in, however crude." But, whether scientist or layman, the validity of the actor's inferences are limited by his awareness of, and ability to make, inferences about causality.

NORMATIVE JUDGMENTS

Problem solving, as the concern with the cause of deviation from some normal or desired state of affairs, involves not only perceptions (predictions) of reality (state II) but also an appropriate set of standards (state I in Figure 2-2). The observance of deviation presupposes a referent or criterion to which perceived reality is compared. The search for deviations involves an assessment of the agreement between reality, as it is perceived, and the set of normative values evoked by both internal and external stimuli.

These values may be specific operating criteria or vague rules of social decorum but they are related, in some way, to the ideal that the individual has set for himself. They are partially associated with policies, ethical concepts, and mythical injunctions which surround the actor as yardsticks or comparatives of normalcy and which he has internalized. Many of these rules or guidelines are so deeply imbedded in culture that he accepts them unquestioningly.

The normative model imposed on the problem field by the actor partially determines his perception of reality and, thus, helps frame the definition of the problem. The world is filtered through this value-laden model. Furthermore, as this normative set operates on choice, it influences both the capacity and the nature of the solution process. The criteria which give direction to behavior indirectly determine the capacity of man to control the environment in which he finds himself. Since function, reciprocally, determines structure and since—to the extent rationality dominates—ends dictate means,[19] this normative set determines capacity as well as influences choice. Where the property of money is high as a "medium of exchange" but unimportant as a "store of value,"

[19] Here, decision making is viewed as rational to the extent that it promotes a solution that results in the achievement of a goal. In contrast, Professor Larry Tarpey, University of Kentucky, contends that in our society rationality is judged by choice of goals, and not achievement (personal correspondence, February, 1968).

its function is single-purposed and its capacity is narrower than its potential.

The development of such normative systems may sanctify the mystic of many cults and often the legitimate fees of business consultants. The (outside) consultant is used for many reasons by a decision maker, but common to his services is his more generalized conception of situations. He is often employed because of what may be the absence of situational bias[20] that gives to him perceptions of a larger array of alternative solutions as well as different values. Whatever the case, however, problem conceptualization is value laden.

Much of the efficacy of man's cerebral behavior is attributed to the capacities which permit or enhance cognitive behavior and foresightful problem solving.[21] A requisite to such behavior and one which empowers his systematic, intellectual behavior presupposes an ability to develop abstract symbols of reality. That is, the decision maker can conceive of the real world in symbolic form. A second supposition is related to his ability to manipulate these symbols cognitively rather than directly treat objects in the field itself.

Operating as part of this behavior is the "concept" which is a partially preconditioned mental representation of some (set of) phenomenon, that representation of an event or idea that man holds in his mind. These concepts may be representative of his senses—for example, loud, hot, or high; or they may represent the intangible and immaterial, as error, unknown, or infinite. Whatever these concepts, they provide a bridge into reality for the individual. A concept is the mental link between objective reality and his subjective being. His conceptual system is the means for mentally penetrating the realities of the problem field. As Harvey et al. (1961, p. 1) contend,

> An individual interacts with his environment by breaking it down and organizing it into meaningful patterns congruent with his own needs and psychological make-up. [Thus, concepts provide a connecting link between the individual and his environment. They act as] . . . a system of ordering that serves as the mediating linkage between the input side (stimulus) and the output side (response) [and] . . . may be viewed as a categorical system, an intervening medium, or program through which impinging stimuli are coded, passed, or evaluated on their way to response evocation.

[20] It might also be asked whether or not practitioners define problems in terms of traditional ("comfortable") guidelines so that habitual ways ("pat" solutions) may appear appropriate.

[21] This is not to imply that all, or even most, of human decision making is of this type.

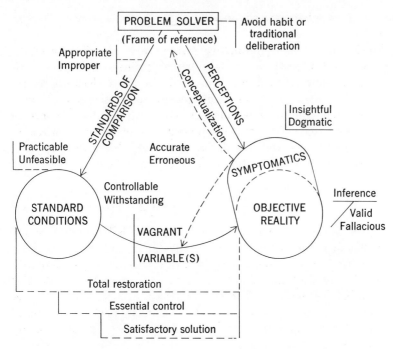

FIGURE 2-3   MAJOR ELEMENTS OF INTERACTION BETWEEN PROBLEM OBSERVER
AND STIMULI FIELD

In this way, the decision maker does not approach each new problem field with a clean slate. He bears with him a conceptual frame of reference which is endemic to him. He carries with him a memory set, and within this storage drum, the various items have differing susceptibilities to evocation from the external stimuli. Thus, with stimuli of the problem field and, bilaterally with this memory set, a particular conception will be activated. To the extent that the actor has sensed and conceived and that he has stored relevant experiences and images, it can be expected that only selected aspects of his memory will be activated by particular dimensions of the problem field.[22] Even a decision maker's conclusion of the novelty of a problem suggests mental scanning of his repertoire, especially that part associated with the stimuli field. In turn, his scanning scope will have determined the variables and interrelationships which he attends in the problem situation. Those concepts,

[22] We can note here two psychological operations which can be exemplified by differentiating between "fix" and "fixity." The first relates to the focus that the decision maker takes on the stimuli field—largely that to which he attends in the problem, i.e., his "fix." The second, "fixity," has to do with the constancy with which he attends to the same (original) dimensions and variables in different stimulus fields.

which are made operational through his disposition and sensitivities, determine his definition of the problem.

Thus, we have operationally discussed man's ability to (1) perceptively conceive of objective reality, which involves the creation of ideas and images, and (2) mediate on these conceptions, involving judgments on significance and relevancy and inferences on relatedness among variables.

Obviously, our discussion of these "psychological mechanisms" thus far does not exhaust the subject of "mediation." The following section on perception and learning, therefore, is intended to further illustrate the mediatory side of the overall perceptual process.

Learning and Perception: Interdependent Processes

As will be noted in the next chapter, learning, in both theory and research, is a complicated phenomenon which cannot be understood by simply relating it to perception. However, not only are perception and learning conceptually related as fields of study within psychology, but they are also interdependent in terms of an explanation of decision making.

Here we briefly consider this interdependence. In the next chapter, we look more specifically and thoroughly at the theoretical issues, research methodology, and substantive findings of the literature on learning.

OPERATIONAL DISTINCTIONS

In contrasting learning and perception, we must add an additional variable to our discussion, reward-punishment systems. Then in terms of reward-punishment systems vis-à-vis stimulus fields, learning studies can be conceived of as holding the stimulus input constant while systematically varying the reward system. Research on perception would be characterized as holding the reward parameters constant while varying the physicalistic stimulus input or the relevant components of the internal personality system, that is, of motive strength through relative incentive-object deprivation. In both cases, selected behavior responses are systematically observed and measured. In the case of learning, the relevant response is some persistent change in behavior which cannot be attributed to maturation processes or the evocation of unconscious habits. In the study of perception, the relevant behavioral response is some verbal or motor response which is preselected by the experimenter and which usually relates to some more or less specific referent.

The real difficulty in attempting to operationally define and study either perception or learning is that:

1. One process, either learning or perception, cannot be held in a steady state while the researcher investigates the other;

2. The net behavioral response of either is a resultant of the interdependence of all psychological processes, including both perception and learning.

However, there are some useful things that can be said about the interdependence of perception and learning. Such is our attempt here; but as will be discussed more thoroughly in the next chapter, there are various learning theories which, to a large extent, are incompatible. This means that specific comments about interdependences of learning and perception must be conditioned by the choice of theoretical approach taken to learning. However, there appear to be several generalizations about the perceptual-learning interrelationship which can be made which fit the various learning theories.

RECIPROCATION

In contrast to making a distinction as to methodology and operation between learning and perception as noted earlier, the theoretical literature tends to emphasize, either explicitly or implicitly, the similarities in the actual processes. However, the controversy is over which of the two processes is the more encompassing or fundamental, that is, which set of basic principles is to guide the researcher in either area of investigation.

1. LEARNING INVOLVES PERCEPTION.   There is a tendency for those researchers working in *sign-gestalt* (after E. C. Tolman)[23] learning theory to emphasize the sudden acquisition of a concept or percept in both perception and learning; both tend to be conceived of as an all-or-none affair.

Perception, conceived in terms of wholes—relationships or patterns—is a necessary aspect of learning. The sensory and motor foundations of both processes are similar; "When any complex of stimuli arouses nervous activity, that activity is immediately organized and certain elements or components become dominant for reaction while others become ineffective." (K. S. Lashley, 1942.)

Both perception and learning are seen as involving changes in patterns of neural stimulation. The emphasis is, thus, on "patterns" rather than

[23] See next chapter for a description of these thories of learning.

on simple stimulus-response connections. The principles which govern the perceptual processes limit the extent to which the learning process can modify behavior; and learning becomes conceived of as persistent changes in perception.[24]

2. PERCEPTION INVOLVES LEARNING. In this approach, the processes and principles of learning are considered the more basic psychological phenomena. The following concepts, not found in sign-gestalt theory, are reduced to the basic learning concepts, including habit strength, reactional potential, synaptic connections, afferent neural interaction, fractional anticipatory goal responses, etc. In addition, the formation of percepts is considered to be another instance of learning via habit, an S-R connection in terms of contiguity and reinforcement.[25]

Conclusion

It appears that once one accepts the conceptual and empirical interdependence of perception and learning, then one is free "to pay his money and take his choice" as concerns the dominant flow of dependency. However, in order to intelligently make such a choice, one should be aware of the various theoretical and empirical approaches to the study of learning. This is the subject of the next chapter.

It should be obvious that perceptual, mediatory, and learning processes, in mutual interaction, significantly influence each of the stages of decision making described in Chapter 1. The recognition of problems, the search for causation, the generation and evaluation of alternative solutions, the choice processes involved in uncertainty absorption, and the ultimate resulting action are all conditioned by the psychological processes of the individual decision maker.

The concepts discussed in this chapter are fundamental to all that follows. Perceptual behavior results in the definition of the problem to be solved. Mediation relates in some way to the translation of the problem into choice-making alternatives. Learning is related to feedback on the results of previous choices. Such functions form the bases of much behavior elaborated upon in later chapters.

[24] The manner in which perceptual and cognitive processes are merged in this orientation is reflected in the Bruner-Postman hypothesis theory, in most of the concepts of modern social psychology, and in the directive state assumptions. In all cases, the perceptual processes are considered basic to all psychological phenomena and these phenomena can largely be interpreted in terms of these perceptual processes and principles.

[25] As we shall note in the chapter on learning, contiguity and reinforcement are not necessarily found together, according to some learning theorists.

bibliography

ALLPORT, F. H.: *Theories of Perception and the Concept of Structure* (New York: John Wiley & Sons, Inc., 1955).

BERELSON, BERNARD, and GARY A. STEINER: *Human Behavior* (New York: Harcourt, Brace & World, 1964).

BLAKE, R. R., and G. V. RAMSEY: *Perception: an Approach to Personality* (New York: The Ronald Press, 1951).

BRAYBROOKE, DAVID, and CHARLES E. LINDBLOOM: *Evaluation As a Social Process* (New York: Free Press of Glencoe, 1963).

BRUNER, J. S., and C. D. GOODMAN: "Value and Need as Organizing Factors in Perception," *Journal of Abnormal and Social Psychology*, vol. 42, 1947, pp. 33–44.

BRUNER, J. S., and D. KRECH: *Perception and Personality: a Symposium* (Durham, N.C.: Duke University Press, 1950), pp. 171–179.

CHEIN, I., R. LANE, G. MURPHY, H. PROSHANSKY, and R. SCHAFER: "Need as a Determinant of Perception," *Journal of Psychology*, vol. 31, 1951, pp. 129–136.

CHIPMAN, JOHN S.: "Stochastic Choice and Subjective Probability," in Dorothy Willner (ed.), *Decision, Values, and Groups* (New York: Pergamon Press, 1960).

COFER, C. N., and M. H. APPLEY: *Motivation: Theory and Research* (New York: John Wiley & Sons, Inc., 1964).

COHEN, MORRIS R., and ERNEST NAGEL: *An Introduction to Logic and Scientific Method* (New York: Harcourt, Brace & World, 1934).

DUBIN, ROBERT: "Business Behavior Behaviorally Viewed," in George Strother (ed.), *Social Science Approaches to Business Behavior* (Homewood, Illinois: Richard D. Irwin, Inc., 1962), pp. 11–15.

EWING, DAVID W.: "The Knowledge of an Executive," *Harvard Business Review*, vol. 42, no. 2, March–April, 1964.

GOMBERG, WILLIAM: "Entrepreneural Psychology of Facing Conflict in Organization," in George Fisk (ed.), *The Frontiers of Management Psychology* (New York: Harper & Row, 1964), pp. 50–67.

HARVEY, O. J., DAVID E. HUNT, and HAROLD M. SCHRODER: *Conceptual Systems and Personality Organization* (New York: John Wiley & Sons, Inc., 1961).

HELSON, H.: "Adaptation-level as a Basis for a Quantitative Theory of Frames of Reference," *Psychological Review*, vol. 55, 1948, pp. 297–313.

————: "Adaptation-level as a Frame of Reference for Prediction of Psychophysical Data," *American Journal of Psychology*, 1947, pp. 1–29.

———— (ed.): *Theoretical Foundations of Psychology* (New York: D. Van Nostrand Company, Inc., 1951).

HOWES, D. H., and R. L. SOLOMON: "Visual Duration Threshold as a Function of Word Probability," *Journal of Experimental Psychology*, vol. 41, 1951, pp. 401–410.

JOHNSON, DONALD M.: *The Psychology of Thought and Judgment* (New York: Harper & Brothers, 1961).

KATONA, GEORGE: "Rational Behavior and Economic Behavior," *Psychological Review*, vol. 60, 1953, pp. 307–318.

LASHLEY, K. S.: "An Examination of the 'Continuity Theory' as Applied to Discriminative Learning," *Journal of General Psychology*, vol. 26, 1942, pp. 241–265.

LONG, JOHN D.: "Problem Definition—A Prelude to Problem Solving," *Annals of Society of C.P.C.U.*, vol. 13, Fall, 1960, pp. 97–115.

MURPHY, G., and J. HOCHBERG: "Perceptual Development: Some Tentative Hypotheses," *Psychological Review*, vol. 58, 1951, pp. 332–349.

POSTMAN, L., J. S. BRUNER, and E. MCGINNIES: "Personal Values as Selective Factors in Perception," *Journal of Abnormal and Social Psychology*, vol. 43, 1948, pp. 142–154.

————, and G. LEYTHAM: "Perceptual Selectivity and Ambivalence of Stimuli," *Journal of Personality*, vol. 19, 1950–1951, pp. 360–405.

————, and B. H. SCHNEIDER: "Personal Values, Visual Recognition, and Recall," *Psychological Review*, vol. 58, 1951, pp. 271–284.

————, and R. L. SOLOMON: "Perceptual Sensitivity to Completed and Uncompleted Tasks," *Journal of Personality*, vol. 18, 1950, pp. 347–357.

RAYMOND, THOMAS C.: *Problems in Business Administration* (New York: McGraw-Hill Book Company, 1964).

ROHRER, J. H., and M. SHERIF (eds.): *Social Psychology at the Crossroads* (New York: Harper & Row, 1951), chap. 10.

ROSENTHAL, B. G.: "Attitude Toward Money, Need, and Methods of Presentation as Determinants of Perception of Coins from Six to Ten Years of Age," *American Psychology*, vol. 6, 1951, p. 317.

SCHAFER, R., and G. MURPHY: "The Role of Autism in Visual Figure-ground Relationship," *Journal of Experimental Psychology*, vol. 32, 1943, pp. 335–343.

SHULL, FREMONT A.: "Administrative Perspectives of Human Relations," *Advanced Management*, vol. 25, no. 3, March, 1960, pp. 18–22.

SIMON, HERBERT A.: "Theories of Decision Making in Economics and Behavioral Science," *The American Economic Review*, vol. XLIX, no. 3, June, 1959, pp. 255–283.

SOLOMON, R. L., and D. H. HOWES: "Word Frequency, Personal Values, and Visual Duration Thresholds," *Psychological Review*, vol. 58, 1951, pp. 256–270.

————, and L. POSTMAN: "Frequency of Usage as a Determinant of Recognition Thresholds for Words," *Journal of Experimental Psychology*, vol. 43, 1952, pp. 195–201.

VINACKE, W. E.: *The Psychology of Thinking* (New York: McGraw-Hill Book Company, 1952), p. 188.

WHITNEY, FREDERICK L.: *The Elements of Research* (New York: Prentice-Hall, Inc., 1950).

WILLNER, DOROTHY (ed.): *Decisions, Values and Groups* (New York: Pergamon Press, 1960).

three

LEARNING

This chapter provides an overview of that portion
of the learning literature particularly appropriate
for an understanding of decision making in organizations. The focus is, therefore, specifically on the
learning of human beings in structured as well as
unstructured problem sets. We here attempt to
expand our discussion of the psychological bases of
decision making as initiated in Chapter 2, and
extend this discussion in the direction of *evocation*
of decision behavior and changes in this decision
behavior over time through experience (learning).
Our vehicle to accomplish this end will be a
series of comments on (1) the role of evocation and
learning in a model of "responses to problem awareness," (2) several issues and problems frequently
dealt with in the learning literature which are

relevant to our understanding of decision making in organizations, as well as several theoretical perspectives on human learning which suggest variables needing consideration in attempting to understand and improve organizational decision making, and (3) the role of perceptual and learning phenomena in heuristic problem solving and decision making.

This chapter is not intended as an exhaustive coverage of the learning literature, either in its coverage of empirical generalizations or in its treatment of theoretical positions. It is highly selective in its coverage and focused in its relevance.

Those readers familiar with the major empirical generalizations and theoretical positions found in the learning literature will find it relatively unprofitable to spend much time on the second section of this chapter. We would direct their attention primarily to our thoughts on the role of evocation, search, and learning in decision making (see Part One), as well as our discussion of heuristic problem solving (Part Three). On the other hand, those unfamiliar with this material may find it profitable to expend more effort examining the second section of the chapter.

Evocation and Learning

Psychologists tend to agree that most human behavior is learned rather than a simple development of some neurophysiological heritage. It follows, then, that understanding any aspect of human behavior, and especially decision making, is impossible without some knowledge of the learning process. This section addresses itself to certain basic aspects of learning which are fundamental to the sophisticated type of decision making performed by man. The discussion, however, is an oversimplification and the concepts are offered in their grossest sense.

Learning may be defined as some change in behavior resulting from experience. This definition implies that learning is effective because it focuses upon *change in behavior*. The definition which more fully meets our purpose is: "Learning is *change in memory content and structure*." Two important issues are implied in this definition. First, learning may be ineffective in the sense that no change in behavior results: You may, for example, from your experiences, store additional knowledge in your mind—that is, increase the content of your memory—but this additional information may not necessarily create or stimulate a change in your behavior. Second, learning may result in two types of changes in memory, a change in structure as well as a change in content. Your experiences may result in a reprogramming or a restructuring of your mental processes; and in cybernetics it is argued "that the structure of the machine or of the organism is an index of the performance that may be expected from it." (N. Weiner, 1954, p. 57.) Paralleling this, it can be said that the intelligent management of, or adaptation to, a situation is an index of the structure of the mind. Therefore, any changes in efficiency, such as reduced search, or effectiveness, that is, better choices, resulting from the restructuring of mental processes are vital to a discussion of decision making.

Berkner (1960, p. 1378), hypothesizing about the similarity between the computer and the brain, states:

> Given a supply of memory packages, the mind has perhaps a number of programs which permit association of the memory packages in different ways. Thus, combinations of memory packages can be set up in a program to solve problems. While some programs are obviously available at birth, most are acquired by experience and training. Certainly, programs of thinking are not very useful until perfected by disciplined and repetitive experience. But I would emphasize in this hypothesis the probable complete independence of the memory process from the acquisition and perfection of independent programs.

The distinction made between changes in memory content and changes in behavior is significant for two reasons. In the first place, we must not assume, merely because we have introduced an individual to learning experiences in training and educational situations, that he will call upon these new experiences, plus their associated mental and emotional responses, in dealing with a problem even where these new phenomena are relevant and significant to the given situation. He may apply to a problem, for example, approximately the same memory content that he had employed previously merely because the first experience was sufficiently rewarding as treated then. Habit may be a stronger force than the expected rewards associated with a change in behavior.

The second reason for making the distinction between changes in overt behavior and changes in memory content is that the dichotomy between structure and content permits a more lucid conceptualization of evocation. It seems reasonable to expect that only a part of total memory content is brought to bear upon a particular problem. That part of memory which is activated for that situation is the evoked set, and evocation is the activation of this memory set. The evoked set may not change merely because of some change in memory content. Continuing, Berkner (*ibid.*, p. 1379) hypothesizes:

> Man lives primarily as a tactician with a limited supply of memory units and a few well used programs to associate those units in a stereotyped and unimaginative pattern . . . . A few who develop strategic capabilities by installing additional memory units and devising new programs to employ them are known as scholars . . . . Conventional courses of education tend to emphasize tactical ability and

tell little about bandwidth, internal noise level, unusual memory capacity or storage, discipline in learning, or consequent capability for devising novel programs for creative thinking

These comments give rise to two additional considerations. On the one hand the study of decision making is essentially concerned only with the evoked set of memory, since that which has no influence upon a decision is of no immediate concern for its understanding. On the other hand, the evoked set itself can be influenced—within, naturally, the confines of total memory content. Lower types of counseling, for example, actually perform this influencing function. Therefore, as March and Simon (1958, p. 10) suggest, although behavior can be influenced by both learning and evocation, "there is no reason a priori to suppose that influence of these two kinds is subject to the same laws." Yet both are capable of producing innovative responses.

INNOVATIVE BEHAVIOR

Let us turn our attention, then, to creative thinking. Here we are not concerned with innovative behavior or change for its own sake, since we want to ignore the psychic values associated with mental processing. Mention is made of this restriction because of the notion that creative thinking is a panacea of all organizational problems.

For our purpose, the essence of creative thinking is the generation of new courses of action, or solutions. Man, however, is probably somewhat awkward and misdirected in his efforts to exploit his creative abilities. If insensitive to his potential or if he habitually clings to tradition, he sacrifices a natural inheritance. The creative person is willing to think and act differently where such is deemed worthwhile. While most of the creative process itself appears to lie at a subliminal level, it appears to depend, to a large extent, upon the nature of his conscious behavior. In this respect, creativity may require deliberate attention and the development of a proper frame of reference. An appropriate orientation involves a belief that: (1) There are alternative solutions to, for example, ways of performing a particular task; and (2) there may be a "better," or more optimal, solution, such as a more effective method of performance.

Since innovation is a matter of degree, even routine decisions often involve elements of creativity. At the level at which we view decision making, innovation is a continuum with repetitive, routine decisions at one pole and the novel decision or reprogramming at the other pole. At the lower end of the continuum, unless the decision is completely automatic and unthinking, some search does take place; and it is unlikely that behavior is completely prescribed by a set of memorized instructions—some recombination or modification of previous behavioral pattern or patterns may occur. This may result from learning or the reinstatement of some previously established frame of reference, or, in the case of complex problem situations, a conceptual reorganization during mediation.

MENTAL PROCESSING

Let us hypothesize about the mental processes involved in creativity, especially with the change or changes in the general mental processing that result from experience. Here, we are concerned with such things as the level and "chaining" of the responses, especially their sequential nature. To exemplify the involved nature and number of possibilities relating to processing, Figure 3-1 is offered. It should be observed that this diagram is subject to many of the criticisms of such presentations; for example, it does not exhaust the subject area and does present the

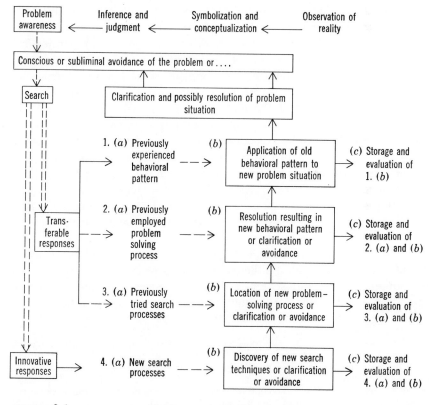

FIGURE 3-1   MENTAL RESPONSES TO PROBLEM AWARENESS

material too mechanistically. Nonetheless, Figure 3-1 does illustrate various "chaining" alternatives as well as different levels of processing.

We assume that the decision maker infers or perceives that a problem exists. He may consciously or unconsciously avoid the problem by (1) actual withdrawal, or (2) redefining the situation. On the other hand, he may be predisposed to solve the problem, but he feels that more information needs to be brought to bear upon his decision and, thus, searches for clarification. In contrast, he may search for, and apply, a previously rewarding behavioral pattern or course of action, as a tactician in the Berkner sense. Yet the decision maker may feel that the old solution and rewards do not meet the minimum requirements of the current situation, so he searches for additional clarification, or avoids the problem, or turns to some higher-order mental process.

Although a priori reasoning may support any number of particular sequences, the decision maker may conclude that no behavioral pattern in his repertoire meets the demands of a current problem. He may suspect that a previously experienced problem-solving process will apply and scans his memory for a suitable one. This search may also be unfruitful in the sense that the expectations associated with any perceived behavior from the application of an old solution technique are not sufficiently satisfying. He again has access to (1) avoidance, (2) clarification, or (3) higher-order mental processes (nontactical in the Berkner sense).

Little can be said about the development of new search techniques except that it involves reconstructed, "switching" patterns for locating relevant parts (traces) of the memory.[1] This, however, would seem to involve the search for (new) insight into the problem area with an attendant restructuring or recombination of one or more old problem-solving processes in such a way that a new process appropriate to that problem is created. It is not necessary, though, that perceptual restructuring of the problem area precede the development of a new solution technique. This relationship might be reversed—the creation of a new problem-solving process might conceivably occur independently of that particular problem.

We would be remiss to omit discussion of "storage" and "evaluation" included in our diagram. Although no one aspect of the configuration is a unique entity and separable from others, storage and evaluation provide the substance for forthcoming decisions. All transferable re-

---

[1] This is not to imply that the mind is merely a switching network plus memory, since the mind in all probability is better explained by gestalt theories than by the more mechanistic theories. This proposition finds considerable support when attention is directed to problem solving—as contrasted to search. As Bittle (1947, p. 325) concludes about gestaltists: "Perception is not the mere sum of individual 'atomistic' sensations, but the resultant of the total sensory impression."

sponses shown in the presentation are founded upon previous storage and, probably, evaluation. Note also that all parts are interdependent and fold in upon themselves and each other. The "chains" or sequences may be short-circuited and do not necessarily involve a steady progression; but the individual may, for example, move immediately from innovative responses to an earlier process.

Finally, we need to call attention to an earlier discussion on attitude and set. As previously mentioned, the decision maker must be, first, aware or sensitive to the problem and, second, predisposed to act upon it. His total orientation may restrict or enhance his ability to discover relevant and significant obstacles in his external environment. His disposition and the external circumstances must be such that sufficient tensions are aroused to move him to resolve the problem. Vinacke (1952, p. 188) concludes that: ". . . the subject's set is an important aspect of problem solving. Without an appropriate set or direction, solutions cannot be attained, except by accident, and the ease with which the individual can evolve the direction for himself varies widely."

Thus, in summary, we view the decision maker as becoming aware of his stimulus surround in the organizational as well as the external environment; that is, he *perceives* it and meditates upon it through processes as discussed in Chapter 2. There may remain an "unnoticed" remainder, as depicted in Figure 3-2. This "perception" *evokes* from

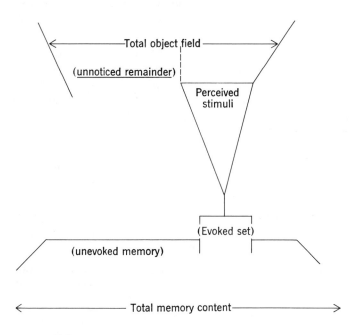

FIGURE 3-2   OBJECT FIELD AND MEMORY CONTENT

memory a subset of that memory which influences the decision-making mechanism and the eventual choice. This is conceived of as a rather static process, since it does not account for changes in memory content and decision making over time. We have introduced the construct of "learning" to facilitate our understanding of the dynamics of decision making over time. Thus, we have introduced "learning" as partially accounting for changes in memory content over time and, inferentially, for changes in decision behavior.

To the extent that learning enters our model of decision making, it will be helpful to summarize a few of the empirical generalizations and theoretical positions available regarding the antecedents and consequences (in terms of behavioral change) of learning.

An Overview of Theoretical Perspectives on Learning[2]

If memory content changes over time and thereby partially accounts for the dynamic nature of decision premises and the factual bases of decisions, it becomes relevant to consider the concepts available to the administrator as aids to understanding this dynamism.

Experimentalists and theorists in learning present us with a number of concepts which are useful in understanding and explaining changes in decision making. Selective examples would be habit formation and change, capacity of the decision maker for learning, concepts of memory and remembering, the role of practice and repetition in decision improvement over time, and the concepts of motivation and drive as these influence the rate of learning. In addition, the phenomena of understanding, insight, and creative decision making are treated in the learning literature and condition many of our ideas in the third section of this chapter.

The role of each of these phenomena in expanding and retaining memory content and evocation has been dealt with in an extensive body of experimental literature. For several of these learning concepts there exist relatively succinct empirical generalizations regarding their impact on various operational measures of learning. This means that the controversies in the literature primarily center upon varying interpretations of the same, or highly similar, sets of facts.

E. R. Hilgard (1956, pp. 486–487) has summarized what we appear to know empirically about the impact of several of these concepts upon the rate of learning as well as upon retention:

1. In deciding who should learn what, the capacities of the learner are very important. Brighter people can learn things less bright ones cannot learn; in general,

[2] This section draws heavily upon E. R. Hilgard, *Theories of Learning*, 2d ed. (New York: Appleton-Century-Crofts, Inc., 1956), by permission of Appleton-Century-Crofts, Educational Division, Meredith Corporation.

older children can learn more readily than younger ones; the decline of ability with age, in the adult years, depends upon what it is that is being learned.

2. A motivated learner acquires what he learns more readily than one who is not motivated. The relevant motives include both general and specific ones, for example, desire to learn, need for achievement (general), desire for a certain reward or to avoid a threatened punishment (specific).

3. Motivation that is too intense (especially pain, fear, anxiety) may be accompanied by distracting emotional states, so that excessive motivation may be less effective than moderate motivation for learning some kinds of tasks, especially those involving difficult discriminations.

4. Learning under the control of reward is usually preferable to learning under the control of punishment. Correspondingly, learning motivated by success is preferable to learning motivated by failure.

5. Learning under intrinsic motivation is preferable to learning under extrinsic motivation.

6. Tolerance for failure is best taught through providing a backlog of success that compensates for experienced failure.

7. Individuals need practice in setting realistic goals for themselves, goals neither so low as to elicit little effort nor so high as to foreordain failure. Realistic goal-setting leads to more satisfactory improvement than unrealistic goal-setting.

8. The personal history of the individual, for example, his reaction to authority, may hamper or enhance his ability to learn from a given teacher.

9. Active participation by a learner is preferable to passive reception when learning, for example, from a lecture or a motion picture.

10. Meaningful materials and meaningful tasks are learned more readily than nonsense materials and more readily than tasks not understood by the learner.

11. There is no substitute for repetitive practice in the overlearning of skills . . . or, in the memorization of unrelated facts that have to be automatized.

12. Information about the nature of a good performance, knowledge of his own mistakes, and knowledge of successful results aid learning.

13. Transfer to new tasks will be better if, in learning, the learner can discover relationships for himself, and if he has experience during learning of applying the principles within a variety of tasks.

14. Spaced or distributed recalls are advantageous in fixing material that is to be long retained.

As noted, the controversies among psychologists studying learning center on the theoretical interpretation of the meaning of these relatively stable findings. Theoretical perspectives on learning seem to differ in the relative weights assigned to the concepts of capacity, practice, reinforcement through motivation, insight and understanding, and transfer and forgetting. Based upon Hilgard's (1956) treatment of these differences, we have constructed Table 3-1.

Most of the perspectives represented in Table 3-1 have been developed from the empirical research on learning of relatively well-structured or programmed tasks. As we will note in the last section of this chapter, the

Table 3-1   Comparison of selected learning theories across selected dimensions

SCHOOL OF THOUGHT	DIMENSION				
	CAPACITY	PRACTICE	MOTIVATION	INSIGHT AND UNDERSTANDING	TRANSFERENCE AND FORGETTING
S-R: Skinner's (Operant conditioning)	Since "principles" (of learning) hold across species, capacity is not of central concern.	Both exercise (S-R association) and reinforced practice, e.g.: intermittent reinforcement better than continuous (results in greater resistance to extinction).	Reward and punishment not equal, e.g., (1) punishment does not remove habit from repertory, and (2) delayed punishment is relatively ineffective; (3) mild punishment may increase variability of behavior.	Conceived of as "rapid learning"—no element of originality involved.	*Transfer* both stimulus and response generalizations. *Forgetting*—not treated (implies this is slow decay), better explained as interference of incompatible responses.
Hull's (Behavior theory)	(Apparently working on variables of his model upon death.)	All improvement depends upon reinforcement.	Motivation related to arousal and reduction of drives (which provide internal stimuli that guide behavior).	". . . Fractional antedating goal response provides stimuli whose function is to guide behavior."	*Transfer*—same as above. *Forgetting*—function of time in presence of disuse.
Cognitive: Tolman's (Sign-gestalt theory)	Need for "capacity laws" (study rats so can deal at subcultural level—rat learning not strongly influenced by cultural phenomena).	Both S-R and S-R-Reward sequences are susceptible to improvement through practice.	Rewards and punishment are effective, but more as regulators, since we do have latent learning.	Heart of the process, since learning is sensible, reasonable adjustment to a situation.	*Transfer*—based on and facilitated by similarity of situations. *Forgetting*—retroactive inhibitions and repression (psychoanalytic).
Classical Gestalt (e.g., Wertheimer)	Especially important in terms of "insight."	Since learning is essentially restructuring, repetition provides the vehicle or opportunity for learning or reorganization.	"Law of effect" is accepted, but goal achievement is interpreted in terms of "closure" (not drive reduction).	Habitual learning is counterbalanced by: (1) laws of organization, e.g., similarity; (2) part-whole relationships; (3) ends-means relationships.	*Transfer*—but in terms of common patterns and relationships (understanding is more effective than rote memorization). *Forgetting*—decay in memory.
Functionalism (an eclectic learning model) (e.g., Cattell)	Individual differences are important (e.g., age, sex, etc.).	Concern with "most effective" learning curves, especially with respect to distribution of practice.	Not much different from above.	"Meaningfulness" is a function of the content and form of the subject matter—insight is an extreme case of transfer of training.	*Transfer*—similarity between old and new situations. *Forgetting*—use most of the above.

SOURCE: Adapted from E. R. Hilgard, *Theories of Learning*, 2d ed., 1956.

primary exception to this generalization has been the cognitive learning theories.

Several implications for understanding decision making in organizations emerge from a study of Table 3-1.

1. To the extent that learning influences decision making through modifying the memory content of the decision maker, several concepts serve to explain the varying effectiveness of decisions.

2. The relative weight attached to these concepts varies across theoretical perspectives; therefore,

3. Any attempts to understand and/or improve decision-making effectiveness will be conditioned by the theoretical perspective held.

4. The concepts most easily manipulated in attempts to improve decision-making effectiveness through enhanced learning would appear to be conditions of practice and conditions of motivation (particularly the reinforcement contingencies existing in the organization), and

5. The concepts of insight and understanding are of primary importance in understanding heuristic decision making on loosely structured or unstructured problems. We are now ready to turn our attention to this latter set of decision problems.

Heuristic Problem Solving

Man's decision behavior seems to be characterized by, at least, three levels of coping with his environment. We can classify these as:

1. Habit: routine and conditioned responses; performance guided by previously rewarding experiences; no, or little, effort at reevaluation.

2. Problem solving: involves a conscious assessment of the new, that is, the problem, situation, with the application of a previously successful solution strategy; may result in new behavioral patterns.

3. Creativity: related to novel situations where previous coping or reasoning responses do not suffice; such "decision" behavior is most often associated with "insight," here, heuristic decision making.

Or, as Durkin (1937) states, "one can distinguish three main types of solution, which can be considered as 'three forms' of thinking, whose characteristics are sufficiently different to warrant the application of three separable names," suggesting: Trial and Error, Gradual Analysis, and Sudden Reorganization (see Table 3-2).

Trial and error is time-consuming: For example, with a three-tiered dial, having 100 points on each tier, of which a specific point on each tier must be matched, there are 1 million possible combinations. If pure

Table 3-2   Durkin's classification of thought processes

TRIAL AND ERROR	GRADUAL ANALYSIS	SUDDEN REORGANIZATION
1. Blind groping	No groping, gradual understanding	Groping suddenly stopped
2. Hindsight	Foresight	Sudden foresight
3. Confusion cleared at last moment	Cleared step by step	Confusion suddenly cleared
4. Hopeless feeling	Satisfaction	Excitement and elation
5. Aim—molecular, inattention to solution requirements	Meet specific solution requirements	Search for structure and interrelationships
6. Attitude indefinite	Active, directed search	Passive but receptive
7. Error curve irregular, transfer poor	Error curve steplike, transfer good	Irregular with sudden drop, transfer good
8. Baffled manner	Calm, well organized	Baffled, sudden organization and efficiency

Source: Durkin, 1937, p. 83.

trial and error were relied upon for solution and the probability of solving the problem was: $1 + 1,000,000/2$, it would take approximately twenty-eight weeks to match the points on the tier, working night and day, where each choice requires only thirty seconds. Although trial and error may be the only apparent approach at times, we do not discuss it here, largely because learning is primarily ex post in this case. Further, we do not concern ourselves with habit, since such behavior appears to be a response to decisions made previously.[3] Thus it is the third level of coping which we wish to discuss here.

Mee (1956, p. 1) has defined *creativity* as: "The process of bringing a problem before one's mind clearly as by imagining, visualizing, supposing, musing, contemplating, or the like, and then originating or inventing an idea, concept, realization, or picture along new or unconventional lines. It involves study and reflection rather than action." In fact, Dewey (1933) suggested the following steps to the creative process:

1. The feeling of unease or dissatisfaction.
2. Identification of the problem.

[3] It should be acknowledged that (1) and (2) are often a part of (3), which means they will be partially attended.

3. Establishing hypotheses.
4. Logical or empirical verification.
5. Acceptance of the conclusion.

UNSTRUCTURED PROBLEMS

Problem solving can be conceived of as a broad spectrum of events. At one pole are well-structured problems, with defined goals and measurable, essential variables. As Simon (1958, p. 3) states: "Well-structured problems are those that can be formulated explicitly and quantitatively, and that can then be solved by known and feasible computational techniques."

At the other extreme are problems encompassing ill-defined goals and nonquantifiable but essential variables. For example, and without regard to goal definition, "unstructured problems" stem from such problem properties as the following: (1) multivariable relationships which do not permit establishing causalities within the system or with interdependent systems, and (2) inability to measure two or more interdependent elements at the same time, for example, Heisenberg's "uncertainty principle": that it is impossible to plot the exact position of an electron with relation to the position of the nucleus and the exact position of the electron in its own orbit while measuring the energy of the electron at the same instant of time. Either of these situations reduces the variability and appropriateness of available algorithmic techniques. Again, quoting Simon (*idem*),

> Ill-structured problems are difficult because the essential variables are not numerical at all, but symbolic or verbal . . . . (Secondly,) the objective function, the goal, is vague and nonquantitative . . . . Finally, there are many practical problems—it would be accurate to say "most practical problems"—for which computational algorithms simply are not available. Facing facts, we are forced to admit that the majority of decisions that executives face everyday—and certainly a majority of the very most important decisions—lie much closer to the ill-structured than to the well-structured end of the spectrum.

In describing such situations Valentine (1965) offers the following: "The Supervisor who has just looked through his inbasket may well doubt that there is any set of basic principles for problem-solving. The diversity and range of questions needing answers seem endless. How many years must pass before he runs through the cycle of different types of problems, and they begin to recur, so he can apply familiar solutions?" In this context, it is interesting to note that Martin (1956, p. 254) found a greater probability that behavioral alternatives possess "objective existence" at lower levels of the management hierarchy. His evidence showed that each of four levels of management can be placed on a continuum, as:

Alternatives completely objective, ready-made and enduring	Shift Foreman	Department Foreman	Division Superintendent	Works Manager	Alternatives completely subjective and constructed by the executive

If this is the case, increasingly important organizational decisions are made higher in the hierarchy with greater reliance placed upon heuristic problem solving.

INSIGHT

A manager, faced with such complexity, is forced to deal with this problem type. His remuneration may be based on his propensity to solve them successfully. Frequently one hears of such an individual who solves these problems "intuitively," or as with an ". . . immediate perception or judgment, usually with some emotional colouring, without any conscious mental steps in preparation" (Ruch, 1948, p. 333).

This explanation is not sufficient, however, for our purposes here. If progress is to be made in dealing with complex problem solving, we must perceive the process as being pursued in, at least, an illuminated black box. Indeed, Durkin, in 1937 (p. 84), contributed to our subject, concluding that:

[1.] Problem solving in human adults is never completely blind or random.

[2.] It is, except in the simplest cases, to some degree exploratory.

[3.] Seeing the relationship of the material to the goal enters at the level of so-called "insightful" thinking, but the process was there in nucleus, though but vaguely, from the beginning.

[4.] Each sudden reorganization is preceded by a short intent pause during which the subject seems to try to grasp a series of rapid, fleeting inferences and recalls which bring the reorganization to focus.

[5.] Sudden reorganization can, whenever the problem situation is beyond the subject's apprehension span, be found to be related to certain previous responses to the material . . . in form of observations, recalls, and inferences and may have occurred earlier during the solution or in previous experience.

Sudden reorganizations, according to Ruch (1963, p. 335),

. . . come suddenly and in the absence of observable trial-and-error manipulation of symbols or objects. Often there is a period in which no progress toward the solution is apparent, followed by a sudden arrival at the solution. This phenomenon has been interpreted as due to the development within the person of *insight*, by means of some sudden reorganization of the perception of the situation.[4]

However, we are unable to deal with "pure" insight. As Johnson (1955, p. 195) states, if complete insight into a problem situation is imputed, then no problem exists. He contends that ". . . insight into problematic situations changes and usually improves, with repeated tries; and that even partial insights, at various levels of complexity, limit the variation of the tries, usually reducing the errors." Thus it should not be inferred that gradual analysis is invariable, purely mechanistic, and lacking in insight.

It may be that some problem solving is of a rather mechanistic and uninterrupted nature; but evidence indicates that the decision maker often shifts and modifies his solution strategies. Where his psychological set elicits a particular mediating process, an appropriate solution may not be forthcoming. If the decision maker is unable to switch among processes or restructure the current process applied, we can speak of "fixation."

PSYCHOLOGICAL CORRELATES

The full breadth of a problem situation often presents a confusing and baffling set of stimuli to the decision maker. If reality cannot be ordered and translated into some meaningful form, avoidance or some type of neurotic behavior may result. Thus, effective decision making presupposes both perceptual categorization and abstraction. The first of these, categorizing, allows translating, ordering, and classifying elements of the real world in terms of historical experience. The second, abstracting, involves developing a simplified and only approximate representation of reality so that it becomes a "manageable" problem.[5]

In both of these activities the decision maker may go awry. Because of the limitations of his memory to store and to maintain "active" information about his experiences and because of the frailties of his sensory organs, he may create conceptual distortions of reality. The story of the five blind men and their differing descriptions of parts of the elephant is a case in point.

Moreover, the motivation and psychological "set" of the decision maker influences his problem-solving behavior. Motives can be defined as goal-directed tensions; about them, Deese (1958, p. 98) says they "provide

[4] Floyd L. Ruch, *Psychology and Life*, 6th ed. (Chicago: Scott, Foresman and Company, 1963).

[5] "Categorizing," as we have used it, is often referred to as "generalizing abstraction," while what we have called abstraction may be referred to as "isolating abstraction."

the internal impetus behind behavior (needs or drives) and the direction the behavior takes (goals)." Johnson (1955, p. 65) has defined *set* as "a readiness to make a specified response to a specified stimulus." It is a temporary unification of behavior associated with a particular stimulus surround. In this sense, motives influence the set of an individual, the former providing the long-term strategies and objectives of the individual, while the set is a translation of these in terms of his immediate state to a particular stimuli environment.

Although individual motives may be classified and examined independently for pedagogical purposes, there is a unity of them. Man is an organism embodying a constellation of drives and needs, some of which conflict with one another and some of which are reinforcing; but, while his motivational pattern is varied and complex, his behavior tends to be unified and integrated.

This does not mean that man is necessarily unchanging, however; he does learn, act innovatively, and change psychological sets on novel situations. But there does appear to be an integrity which moves with him across differing stimuli fields. His "personality" has some stability, that is, some part of his decision behavior rests upon acquired habit patterns. Yet these habits can inhibit his sensitivity and skill in dealing directly with his problems or lessen his disposition for mediation.

We are aware of the value of habitual and routine problem solving. It would be wasteful to attempt to innovate for each and every decision and, particularly, for activities that can be "programmed"—assuming that such programs are subject to periodic review. The decision maker can profitably avail himself of tested principles and practices provided by history as well as improved performance specifications. Habitual reflexes, for example, may facilitate dealing with emergency situations as well as free the mind to deal with nonrepetitive problems.

Cognitively, however, such stability manifests itself as "functional fixedness," that is, once man has ascribed a particular function to an object in the environment, he tends to associate that function with that object to the exclusion of other functions. Such a fixed association mitigates against improvisation and, where innovation is desirable, reduces the value of the solution. While traditionalism and fixedness support efficiency, both tend to preclude creativity.

SELECTIVE FOCUSING

As a problem becomes more complex the strain placed upon memory and assimilation becomes greater. Therefore, the problem solver may turn to "selective focusing," that is, he may tend to concentrate upon one or a few goals and/or variables in the problem. Since reality often encompasses a multiplicity of variables, the decision maker may focus selectively upon the problem situation. (Cf. Deese, 1958, pp. 246–248.) If this be the case, the workableness of the solution is a function of the number and importance of the elements perceived and considered. Indeed, abstracting only selected phenomena and relationships from reality suggests that certain other features are ignored. Therefore, to the extent that attention span is low, or to the extent that critical factors of the problem are ignored, the solution will be weakened.[6]

Selective focusing is true of the "quantitative" sciences, where consideration is given to only those variables and relationships which are measurable. This permits analysis by computation or algorithm. For most so-called economic problems, that is, allocation problems—those that involve a maximizing or minimizing decision—the use of an algorithmic process may be most desirable. Focusing upon profit as the decision goal, the variables capable of being quantified in monetary terms can be manipulated computationally so as to arrive at a best solution—for example, one that maximizes profits.

Let us exemplify the dilemma implied here: Suppose the decision maker desires to maximize utiles of satisfactions, but in order to make the problem manageable, he focuses upon a single factor, X, as that which he values most highly. In Table 3-3, he would choose Alternative I, since it contains 50 units of X as compared to only 25 units of X in Alternative II. Thus, he has chosen an optimal solution in maximizing X, but not the best of all possible solutions. Now, if Solution I satisfies him, no further search will be undertaken and a better solution is foregone,

---

[6] This, of course, explains the potential creativity of group problem solving, especially where the membership is heterogeneous and interacting. See Chapter 5.

Table 3-3

		ALTERNATIVE I		ALTERNATIVE II	
FACTOR	UTILES/UNIT	QUANTITY	TOTAL UTILES	QUANTITY	TOTAL UTILES
X	10.0	50	500	25	250
A	0.1	20	2	0	0
B	4.0	5	20	30	120
C	2.5	10	25	40	100
D	5.0	0	0	20	100
E	2.0	15	30	50	100
Total			577		670

which could have been obtained by considering all six factors. In contrast, economies associated with selective focusing may outweigh the possible benefits foregone by choosing a less desirable solution than the theoretical best.

Therefore, where some algorithm is used, the solution is best only in the sense that a maximizing, or minimizing, solution is found for a single goal, or very few goals, and only those variables which are quantifiable. To the extent that parameters associated with one or more critical factors are inaccurate, and to the extent the critical factors are omitted from consideration, problem-solving effectiveness is reduced.

Effective decision making is a function of the solution process elicited as well as the proficiencies related to perception and abstraction. Thus, evocation is a direct determinant of the problem solution, and those people who have large, active memory spans will tend to be most proficient. But Johnson (1955, p. 82) states that "any intellectual activity is limited to consideration of only a small number of things at any one time, in most cases about five or six." He continues, saying that if more than this number are involved in the problem, they will be (1) reclassified into a smaller number of items; (2) considered sequentially; or (3) reduced in number by ignoring certain items. Such activities may require certain cues as to how to "structure" the field. This process is called "heuristic reasoning."

We have established three types of solution patterns: (1) the "most logical method" or the "brute force" approach; (2) the use of algorithms or shortcut computational methods; and (3) various heuristic reasoning processes. The first of these is an orderly examination and elimination of all possible alternatives, that is, trial and error. Moreover, when the objective is simple and the alternatives are few in number, computation may be the "best" method to adopt. When the goals are multiple or alternatives numerous, however, these two processes become cumbersome and the problem must be structured.

Heuristic problem solving has the disadvantage of being the most vacuous and the least understood of the other forms of decision making. In addition, it is not fully susceptible to mathematical presentation and refinement. Accordingly, little empirical evidence is available to validate the concept. Support or appeal stems from inferences in the way of: (1) introspection, (2) assumptions about overt behavior, or (3) simulations with mechanical analogs. However, it is very likely the most interesting and significant tool for those involved in education, and it shows great promise of providing an important contribution in coping with nonprogrammed decision making.

Heuristics pertain to activities of the mind that are judgmental in nature. Words and constructs, such as unstructured problems, insight, and solution strategies, are used to describe aspects of this mediation process. The term finds its source in antiquity, but one of its current uses is to designate a method of education in which the pupil is trained to search, experience, and learn on his own. The methodical examination of this process is, however, quite new and, in the main, follows the development of the electronic computer.

Reflecting a current state of development, authorities do not agree on a single definition of "heuristic." Polya (1957, p. 112) says that "the aim of heuristic is to study the methods and rules of discovery and invention . . . ." Thus, heuristic, ". . . as an adjective, means serving to discover." (Newell et al., 1959, (b) p. 22.) Others, including Dunker, state that the term "heuristic" is used to "denote any principle or device that contributes to the reduction in the average search to solutions."

The definition for purposes herein is that heuristic is a cue, technique, or rule that reduces search for a solution and/or offers a novel insight into the problem area. Heuristics eliminate or expose promising paths to solutions; for example, "when in doubt, punt" is a heuristic. Such a rule might aid a novice football coach, although it might cause him to pass up a more favorable play. To a large extent, heuristics lead to plausible or provisional guesses rather than a complete solution. "We need heuristic reasoning when we construct a strict proof as we need scaffolding when we erect a building." (Polya, 1957, p. 113.)

Some simple problems, such as a classification problem or one of fit, requires a single and simple judgment, that is, X does or does not belong in Y. In contrast, many real problems involve a chain or sequence of reasoning and judgments that may be modified in the light of new data. While the first type of solution is molecular in form, the latter must be viewed as processlike, involving an overall strategy for solving the problem. An analogy might be the single return of the ball versus a strategy of defense in table tennis. Therefore, while there may be some delay in arriving at a decision, this delay may permit learning to occur. All of this leads to the inference that problem solving can be interrupted and discontinuous. If so, the decision maker can switch among mediating processes or restructure a given solution strategy.

The problem solver: (1) if predisposed, looks at the configuration and structure of the problem; (2) if reasoning, prepares a new or transfers an old solution strategy; and (3) if dissatisfied, modifies this strategy in the light of evolving clues. These modifications in strategy resulting from environmental clues, necessitate a continual assessment of progress toward solution. With dissatisfaction, the quest may be in the direction of a new solution strategy or new search techniques.[7]

As yet, most electronic computers can operate only upon one set of instructions, that is, one problem-solving strategy.[8] Man, on the other hand, is characterized by flexibility. Although he may be limited in the amount of information that he can carry in his memory and by the order and logic of his reasoning, he can utilize external cues and act upon any single item in his memory. Although limited by his set and prejudices, he can employ intuition and make guesses, both of which may make for high efficiency (cf. Deese, 1958, p. 300). He can flexibly adjust to different problem configurations. Let us illustrate:

Example 1:   *Add 3 + 5 + 7*
Example 2:   *The decision maker, standing by a lake, has two containers, one of 5 gallons and the other of 9 gallons. His instructions: Obtain exactly 6 gallons of water in the 9-gallon container.*

In the first of these examples, the strategy is a simple, straightforward summation. In the second, heuristics are involved, as in locating the requirements of the solution (that is, 9-minus-3, or 5-plus-1) and, then, in the movement backward from one of these conditions. Heuristics have to do with the rules or techniques used to settle on the best method of attack and the switching technique, for example, whether to follow the path "9 minus 3" or "5 plus 1."

Initial attention in the decision-making process may be given to the nature of the problem situation. On the other hand, attention may be originally cast upon the specifications of the solution. Or there may be some combination of these two approaches—a statement of what is given and a statement of what is required. Perhaps there is a chaining activity moving forward and backward from conditions to requirements. There is also the question of the nature of the initial intellectual process chosen, as well as the changes that occur during solution or shifting among processes. Perhaps free association, conservative focusing, or direct substitution is the activity pursued or, perhaps, some combining or sequencing of these different activities.

---

[7] For an interesting experiment dealing with propensity to change "direction" during the solution process, see: Weaver and Madden, " 'Direction' in Problem Solving," *Journal of Psychology,* vol. 27, pp. 331–345.

[8] A major exception to this is a program developed by Newell, Shaw, and Simon, the "logic theorist." They state that the program, for example, can employ three different strategies: ". . . a proof by substitution, a proof by detachment, or a proof by chaining." Newell, Shaw, and Simon, "Elements of a Theory of Human Problem Solving," *Psychological Review,* vol. 65, No. 3 (1958), p. 162.

Heuristic reasoning depends largely upon changes in the evocation of the problem solver. Cues become available sequentially, to which the decision maker activates a different part of his memory—in a sense, he learns. Again quoting Newell, Shaw, and Simon (1959, (b) p. 29): "Usually the information needed to select promising paths becomes available only as the search proceeds. Examination of the paths produces clues of the 'warmer-cooler' variety that guide the further conduct of the search."

SOLUTION STRATEGIES[9]

Let us now present a problem situation graphically and discuss the operation of different styles of heuristic reasoning. A problem situation can be viewed as a maze containing alternative solution routes with "choice" consisting of finding the correct one. Heuristic reasoning, then, involves rules or devices for narrowing the search for the correct solution. The problem situation depicted in Figure 3-3 is one of transversing the maze from point Q to P. Note that this is a relatively simple problem, with only two alternatives at each choice point.

A common heuristic employed in solving new problems is means-end analysis. March and Simon (1958, p. 190) describe it as: "Starting with the general goal to be achieved, as P in Figure 3-3, (2) discovering a set of means very generally specified for accomplishing this goal, as KN, (3) taking each of these means, in turn, as a new sub-goal and

[9] This section draws heavily upon Newell, Shaw, and Simon, 1959 (b).

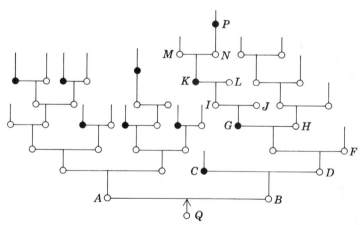

● Choice points with cues given
○ Choice points with no cues given

FIGURE 3-3   A DECISION TREE

discovering a more detailed set of means for achieving it, etc." This process is what Barnard (1938, p. 206) calls "successive approximations—constant refinement of purpose, closer discriminations of fact . . . ." If this reasoning does carry the decision maker to a feasible, concrete action and the anticipated rewards are satisfactory, he has solved the problem. This is essentially the technique that was used in solving the container problem above: (1) What was needed?—Six gallons of water. (2) How can 6 gallons be found?—Five plus 1. (3) How can 1 gallon be obtained?—Ten (or $5 + 5$) minus 9 gallons. (a) How can this be done with the available containers?—etc.

A second heuristic is planning, described as preparing a *future* course of action to accomplish a given goal. Planning is usually expressed as a set of subtasks directed toward the objective to be accomplished; for example, in Figure 3-3, the successful transversing of the maze from Q to C, from C to G, etc. Again this technique can be illustrated with a common-sense example. Suppose you are to hike through unfamiliar terrain at night and know the general direction desired. You would focus upon a prominent distant object, such as a tree or outcropping, point C. Upon reaching C, where certain cues are found (notice that C provides certain cues, so that if you were off course, you must change direction), you focus upon G, etc. Such a sequence of subtasks constitutes a plan.

Probably one of the simplest means for solving problems is using analogy. The psychologist experimenting with rats may make certain conclusions concerning human behavior. Such inferences may arrive at plausible conclusions, that is, the ad hoc problem agrees in certain respects with the referent, but the agreement, as well as the solution, must be verified by more strict evaluation and/or actual experience. The analogy, however, is one type of scaffolding for arriving at tentative solutions. This heuristic permits judgments concerning whether or not the solution fits or is satisfactory. If it is not, a new strategy may be applied to the problem.

Concluding Commentary

We have been concerned with how a problem is approached without use of brute force or tradition, particularly for unstructured problems. We feel that too much of current literature enjoins the use of the most logical method or the employment of mathematical algorithms, while, in contrast, much of man's reasoning is of a heuristic nature. In fact, Cyert et al. (1956, pp. 237–238) contend that, although "economics has provided the only considerable body of decision-making, several crucial elements are missing from the economic model (e.g., search and multiple criteria)."

We settled on heuristic problem solving as our means for focusing on certain crucial elements and, further, because the use of heuristics results in a structured subset of the problem that can be treated in an algoristic manner. Concentrating upon profit as the decision goal, for example, allows computational manipulation of values capable of being quantified in monetary terms so as to arrive at a "best" solution—one that maximizes profits. Accordingly, the computational approach may be more "economical" in terms of second-level decision costs—the costs of decision making itself—but it may not result in a "best" choice of alternatives. Thus we have focused upon a method for structuring a problem area, without the predisposition to perceive only a single dimension of the field.

Certainly, we do not contend that our exposition is a "theory of heuristics." Much research needs to be done before any such claim can be made. The major purpose of this discussion is to illustrate how complex problem solving might be structured. Further, heuristics themselves do not offer necessarily a perfect choice. As Polya (1957, p. 133) contends: "Heuristic reasoning is a reasoning not regarded as final and strict but as provisional and plausible only. We shall attain complete certainty when we shall have obtained the complete solution, but before obtaining certainty we must often be satisfied with a more or less plausible guess. We may need the provisional before we attain the final."

Although heuristics do not provide guarantees of optimal or even satisfactory solutions, their examination offers substantive contributions to the study of decision making. Such exposure is a distinct aid to academicians because heuristics are essentially related to their material of concern: man's cognitive activities as he endeavors to accommodate to and control his environment. Finally, as Polya (1957, p. 5) suggests: "A great discovery solves a great problem but there is a grain of discovery in the solution of any problem. Your problem may be modest; but if it challenges your curiosity and brings into play your inventive faculties, and if you solve it by your own means, you may experience the tension and enjoy the triumph of discovery."

bibliography

BARNARD, CHESTER I.: *The Functions of the Executive* (Cambridge, Mass: Harvard University Press, 1938).

BERKNER, L. V.: "Can the Social Sciences Be Made Exact?" *Proceedings of the IRE*, vol. 48, no. 8, August, 1960, pp. 1376–1380.

BITTLE, CELESTINE: *The Whole Man* (Milwaukee: The Bruce Publishing Company, 1947), p. 325.

CYERT, R. M., H. A. SIMON, and D. B. TROW: "Observations of a Business Decision," *Journal of Business,* vol. 29, 1956, pp. 237–248.

DEESE, JAMES: *The Psychology of Learning* (New York: McGraw-Hill Book Company, 1958).

DEWEY, JOHN: *How We Think,* rev. ed. (New York: D. C. Heath & Company, 1933).

DURKIN, H. E.: "Trial and Error, Gradual Analysis, and Sudden Reorganization," *Archives of Psychology,* no. 210, 1937, pp. 44–84.

HILGARD, E. R.: *Theories of Learning,* 2d ed. (New York: Appleton-Century-Crofts, Inc., 1956).

JOHNSON, DONALD M.: *The Psychology of Thought and Judgment* (New York: Harper & Brothers, 1955).

MARCH, JAMES G., and HERBERT A. SIMON: *Organizations* (New York: John Wiley & Sons, Inc., 1958).

MARTIN, NORMAN H.: "Differential Decisions in the Management of an Industrial Plant," *Journal of Business,* vol. 29, no. 4, October, 1956, pp. 249–260.

MEE, JOHN F.: "The Creative Thinking Process," *Indiana Business Review,* vol. 31, no. 2, February, 1956, p. 1.

NEWELL, ALLAN, J. C. SHAW, and HERBERT A. SIMON: "Elements of a Theory of Human Problem Solving," *Psychological Review,* vol. 65, no. 3, 1959 (a), pp. 151–166.

———, ———, and ———: *The Process of Creative Thinking,* The RAND Corp. (P-1320), 1959 (b).

POLYA, G.: *How to Solve It* (Garden City, N.Y.: Doubleday and Company, Inc., 1957).

RUCH, FLOYD L.: *Psychology and Life* (New York: Scott, Foresman and Company, 1963).

SIMON, HERBERT A.: *Decision Rules for Production and Inventory Controls with Probability Forecasts of Sales,* O.N.R. Research Memorandum, Carnegie Institute of Technology, Pittsbugh 13, Pa., 1958.

VALENTINE, RAYMOND F.: "Problem-Solving Doesn't Have to be a Problem," *Supervisory Management,* March, 1965.

VINACKE, W. EDGAR: *The Psychology of Thinking* (New York: McGraw-Hill Book Company, 1952), p. 188.

WEAVER, H. E., and E. H. MADDEN: "Direction in Problem Solving," *Journal of Psychology,* vol. 27, 1949, pp. 331–345.

WEINER, NORBERT: *The Human Use of Human Beings* (Garden City, N.Y.: Doubleday & Company, Inc., 1954).

part

SMALL-GROUP PERSPECTIVES

three

four

SOCIALIZATION AND NORM TRANSMISSION

Introduction

In the earlier chapters of this book, we have been primarily concerned with individual behavior and the psychological dimensions of personalized decision making. However, even while our attention was centered on the individual, it became quite clear that decision making must necessarily reflect the fact that individuals are inextricably enmeshed within an "environment" which influences the decision process. The remainder of the book following this chapter will treat the interactions between the individual and selected dimensions of the environment in detailed fashion, emphasizing in particular the small group, formal organizations, and econological technologies. The purpose of this chapter is to provide a transition between the first part of the book and subsequent chapters by setting forth the linkage between the individual and his culture in clear social-psychological terms.

Relevance of the Environment

Any complete treatment of how individuals make decisions must not only take into account "self" and "individual" psychological processes, but also recognize man is a "social being" and that he is influenced by his social environment. Much of the debate as to whether it is more fruitful to approach behavior from the focus of the individual or from a cultural-group focus is sterile: both approaches are tapping differentiated dimensions of the same reality. Indeed, the separation between the two foci is primarily a mechanism for increasing our sensitivities and for introducing a more elaborate conceptualization. At all times, common sense tells us both dimensions are relevant, and that the bifurcation between individual and group culture is artificial.

Two types of errors should be avoided in separating out the "social" dimension to protect against the "group mind" bias (Sherif and Sherif, 1956, p. 7): (1) We need to avoid treating the individual as an empty receptacle into which we pour culture. Thus, a healthy emphasis on individual differences is warranted. At the same time, (2) we need to avoid thinking of society as coercively forcing itself on an unwilling individual. Thus, an emphasis on common conditioning which provides at a point in time for a large number of individuals who possess common sensitivity to common stimuli, without which predictability is largely lost, is also warranted.[1]

When accepted in balance, the above two propositions prepare us to expect certain common-sense results. For instance, given individual differences, socialization will inevitably involve a degree of conflict where "self" rubs against "norms" in terms of discrete aspects of conformity—a basic premise of psychoanalytic theory (Hall and Lindzey, 1954). We are, consequently, not surprised by the fact that some individuals cannot accept some group norms or effectively act out some group roles because of their bioneurological makeup and of special circumstances surrounding their childhood developmental history. Nonetheless, today "self" finds needs satisfied largely through others, and thus

[1] It is this latter point which must provide the fundamental explanation, for example, of our remarkable success in predicting consumer decision making on the basis of statistical aggregates and limited economic stimuli; without this latter proposition the success of naïve models of individual behavior, which serve as useful predictors of consumer decision making in spite of untested notions of causation, would be impossible.

often actively and volitionally seeks to be an integral part of groups. Thus, most individuals are quite willing to accept group norms and activate expected group roles. Indeed, affinity for group and organizational involvement is more normal while alienation from all social involvement is viewed as pathological.

Further, it is clear that full psychological development is dependent on social stimulation from the environment. Without interaction with other persons, intelligence is grossly atypical (Hebb in Macoby, Newcomb, and Hartley, 1958; Sing and Zingg, 1942). Young animals and young children raised in isolation seem never to develop normal intelligence. Even at maturity, temporary deprivation of normal sensory inputs results in a decrease in the ability of the individual to make simple or complex decisions. The human organism requires social interaction to maintain its psychological integrity.[2]

Attention to the social environment, then, both because the normal person must develop by means of interaction with a social environment, and because the maintenance of normality is predicated upon continued interaction, must be part of our background for understanding decision making by individuals within organizations.

The Nature of Socialization

Obviously the environment encompasses a wide variety of stimuli. In this chapter we are concerned with those dimensions of the environment affecting the socialization of the individual.

When we focus on socialization, we are not focusing on the "person" aspect of individuals in interpersonal behavior, which was treated in earlier chapters, nor on the "structural aspects of groups or complex organizations," which are treated in subsequent chapters. Nor are we focusing on system relationships or institutional relationships. Rather, the specific focus of socialization is to study stimuli situations encountered by the individual which do not exist in nature but are symbolic heritages of past or current interactions. In other words, we are focusing on the transference of cultural values, sentiments, and norms—on the transfer of *concepts* which evolve out of language. When we say an individual is socialized, we imply he has internalized certain concepts endemic to a particular culture or subculture.

[2] Hebb, *op. cit.* One need not go to the rather extreme studies of isolated college students, bomb shelter studies, etc., to find evidence of the dysfunctions resulting from lack of interaction with other persons. It is very clear to each of us that being "left alone" is a painful experience if persisting over any period of time. Further, a significant aspect of the neurotic housewife syndrome reflects the relative social isolation of many suburban women no longer buttressed by an extended family.

Such a focus has several implications. First, it assumes a model of individual behavior which implies that concepts mediate between stimuli and responses; that is, a model of this type affirms the existence of:

1. A stimulus or situation which is defined or interpreted conceptually;

2. An internal response to this conceptually defined situation which includes both physiological and symbolic processes; and

3. An outward conventionalized expression which serves to indicate the nature of this response to others (Lindesmith and Strauss, 1956, pp. 117–118; Harvey, Hunt, and Schroeder, 1961, chap. 1).

This model is a conceptual orientation which posits that external responses are not merely physiological responses to raw stimuli only, but also reflect an interpretation of stimuli; that the symbolic interpretations are learned, though the physiological aspect is not; and that there is the possibility of response mimicry since a response of a conventional type does not necessarily imply the response is congruent with socialized values. (Lindesmith and Strauss, 1956, pp. 117–118.)

Thus, the fundamental premise is that symbolic (conceptual) behavior is a viable dimension of typical human functioning since individuals normally function on a conceptual level after infancy. Indeed, this is a basic premise underlying social psychology. (Sherif and Sherif, 1956, p. 9; Lindesmith and Strauss, 1956, p. 159; Piaget, 1950; Harvey, Hunt, and Schroeder, 1961, chap. 1; Scheerer, 1954.)

Before citing some examples of conceptually mediated responses in the area of organizational decision making, one can provide examples of responses conceptually mediated relative to more basic behavioral areas highly intertwined with drives or emotions:

1. Research clearly shows that sex behavior of human beings is not controlled in the same degree by physiological processes and mechanisms as is that of lower animals. In the sex practices of human beings, mental processes play a preponderant role. The possibility of engaging in sex behavior is, of course, contained in the biological structure and the intensity of the drive is physiologically conditioned. However, social influences often shape sex behavior along lines that are contrary to what might be biologically considered "natural" or even lead to a complete elimination of biological behavior. (Lindesmith & Strauss, 1956, p. 317; Seward, 1946.)

2. Emotions and their arousal reflect the social situation as well as their physiology. Thus, embarrassment is called forth by different situations in different societies. Anthropological research shows each society provides different conditions of life for its members, so that certain emotions are aroused more frequently and intensely in one society than in another; for example, in

America, keen competition gives rise to envy and resentment, emotions less frequently experienced in certain cultures. Further, the nature and context of the emotional release will differ. The individual must learn how to express an emotion in an approved fashion, and where to express or inhibit overt manifestations of emotion. Certain instrumentalities are established as appropriate for the resolution of conflicts in order to preserve social peace and individual rights. (Benedict, 1934; Rudin, 1965.)

3. Motivation reflects conceptual mediation in that a biological condition in itself has little motivational significance if it is not perceived or interpreted by the individual in whom it exists. Thus, motives which appear to the individual as peculiarly personal and private partially reflect socialization. For example, the whole "achievement motivation" syndrome is shown in recent research to be highly conditioned by a culture's literature. (McClelland, 1962.)

4. In terms of social roles, learning to take the role of the "other" is developed through rehearsing entire conversations in the imagination. This self-stimulation through language reflects the concepts of language in an inner forum through role dramatization. In this way, the concepts are applied by the individual in examining "self" behavior. (Mead in Macoby, Newcomb & Hartley, 1958.)

One can, without difficulty, overlay these four general examples of cultural socialization dealing with sexuality, emotionality, motivation, and taking of roles on organizational life and its concomitant effects on decision making. Using classical organizational models as a point of reference, the following norms are explicitly or implicitly contained within the models. (Sexuality) Decision making should be a function of role specialization and positional authority, not sexuality. An example of norm violation would be overacceptance of a beautiful female staff member. (Emotionality) Aggression must be repressed except as expressed in greater analytical rigor or acceptable task-oriented competition. Political cabals often deny the normative position. (Motivation) Success must be defined in terms of ascending the ladder of hierarchical positions with concomitant financial rewards. Rejection of the norm is evidenced by some staff specialists who find work-intrinsic rewards sufficiently seductive to refuse promotional advantages. (Roles) Staff members should restrict their role to advising and information gathering. Obviously, line-staff conflicts indicate staff dissatisfaction with this role definition.

We have, of course, deliberately chosen classical maximums which contain conflicts between normal individual propensities and organizational mores. The point is that in these circumstances where the norm calls for behavior which is in some sense "unnatural," individuals have adequately submitted to the normative mediation so that the norm has persisted, in spite of contained instances of violation. Many other norms, more congruent with behavioral realities—for example, the necessity for division of labor—may elicit much greater behavioral conformity, even though a norm such as "specialization" at times encumbers the personality of the occupant of a restricted specialized role. Finally, there is no question that organizational decision making is affected by the imposed conceptualizations of reality reflected in these norms. These are matters to which we will devote serious attention in subsequent chapters.

In order to better understand the relationship between socialization and behavior, however, we need to return to the exploration of the social-psychological dimensions of the socialization process itself and elaborate on the relationship between language and culture.

Language—The Medium for Symbolic Culture

Language represents the most general transfer mechanism for symbolic culture. An individual becomes socialized only when he has acquired the ability to communicate with others, and to influence and be influenced by them through the use of speech. (Keller, 1938; Head, 1926.) The learning of language is not merely a matter of mastering the mechanics of speech. The symbols which make up a language are concepts, and represent an abstraction of reality, that is, a way of thinking. Language thus puts the individual in touch with others in terms of a socialized perspective, so that the individual can understand his society's and group's values, sentiments, and norms. In the course of acquiring this language, the concepts contained within the word symbols take on emotional contexts, so that concepts are not intellectually neutral, but contain a mixture of sentiments and values. Further, language is necessarily related to the cultural and subcultural preoccupations and interpretations of the psychological world. Thus, as between workers and supervisors, work groups and general management, line and staff, and specialists in functional areas, differences in language as regards both word symbols and conceptual meaning are evident.

The end product of socialization is embodied in the social attitudes of the individual, and in his words and deeds reflecting these attitudes. The process of attitude formation thus reflects the total process of social influence, which is, in large part, a cognitive process deeply enmeshed in language.

Management has, of course, always shown a degree of awareness of these realities of socialization. Indoctrination programs, management and staff development programs, and concern with continuing education as integral dimensions of manpower management reflect the need for the manager to develop a language, with concomitant concepts and values, which "professionalizes" both his own behavior and his interaction with fellow managers. Further, the realities of the lack of a common technical language between functional specialties—that is, marketing, finance, and production scheduling, etc.—reinforce the conscious need for a set of "accepted" concepts, along with norms and values, to mediate interaction between organizational personnel.

Social Attitudes and Socialization

Since the end product of socialization through interpersonal relationships and conceptual education, both formal and informal, is manifested in the attitudes of the individual, we need to understand the relationship between attitudes and the varied forms of social influences which seek to "socialize" the individual manager.

Several characteristics of attitudes will make this relationship clearer. Attitudes (1) are learned, rather than innate; (2) are more or less lasting, that is, subject to social processes, as well as internal maturation, which may reinforce or modify them; (3) always imply a subject-object relationship; (4) may have as their referent a large or small number of items; and (5) have motivational-affective properties. (Sherif and Sherif, 1956, p. 494.) They are conceptual guides which influence perception.

Attitudes arise from the interaction between the individual and his environment, both the social environment which we are examining in this chapter and the physical environment which the individual has experienced. However, in keeping with our propositions set forth earlier to avoid the "group mind" error, we must be careful not to reify, that is, regard as material what are really abstract, cultural norms or to equate attitudes to norms. "Social norm" is a sociological designation referring to a product of group interaction. When an individual forms attitudes with regard to areas in which normative prescriptions exist, he does not swallow a group norm like a pill. In the process of attitude formation, his past personal history, particular temperament, intellectual formation and capacities, other personality characteristics, and position in the group or organization structure interact to make his attitude distinctive and in some sense unique to him. At the same time, the content of the attitude is derived in part from similar socialization experiences common to other individuals in the social setting, so that it usually falls within the range of acceptable beliefs or behaviors denoted by the norm. It is in this sense that we speak of internalization of social norms and the assimilation of social influences in attitude formation. (Sherif and Sherif, 1956, p. 174.)

The concrete sign that gives an individual the characteristic imprint of his groups and his culture are the attitudes he reveals in concrete situations; but his attitudes cannot be equated to cultural values and social norms in the sense of reflecting the totality or even the medium position of a particular social group.

Norms and Socialization

A useful way of summarizing our theoretical treatment of socialization is to answer the questions: What makes norms an effective form of social influence? Why are norms internalized, or, at the least, why do they so often elicit overt conformity? In answering these questions, many of the issues which we have skirted across in this chapter can be brought into focus.

To provide an answer to these questions, we need to define norms. *Norms* are generally accepted group prescriptions for or against behaviors, beliefs, or feelings, which prescriptions are reinforced by sanction. (Morris, 1956, p. 610; Bates and Cloyd, 1956, p. 29.) The important thing to notice is that this definition encompasses three dimensions: (1) a shared frame of reference, (2) social pressures, and (3) an interlocking response structure. It is the powerful combination of all three of these dimensions that makes norms an effective means of socialization and of social control.

In terms of the first dimension, a shared frame of reference, we must return to the issue of language. Norms represent summary conceptualizations about reality. As such, they serve the critical cognitive function of providing a system of ordering by means of which the environment is broken down and organized, is differentiated and integrated into its many psychologically relevant facets. Thus, norms are an important dimension of the conceptual program through which the psychologically relevant world is coded or evaluated.

There is, of course, a close relationship between the conceptual system and "self." Since the conceptual system is the medium through which the individual establishes and maintains ties with the relevant world, it is on this foundation that one's self-identity and existence are articulated and maintained. (Harvey, Hunt, and Schroeder, 1961, p. 1.) As a consequence of the integrated nature of the conceptual system and "self," affect becomes attached to dimensions of the conceptual system. Generally we talk about such ego-involvement in terms of one's system of "values," that is, judgments about the worth of entities or concepts, or "sentiments"—that is, emotional dispositions centering around the idea of an object.

In fact, we can generally say that "threat to one's conceptual map or severance with one's conceptual ties leads to a psychological mobilization aimed at maintaining or restoring the integrity of one's concepts, efforts which if unsuccessful may result in major reorientation of one's ties to the world, or more drastically, to a breakdown or destruction of the self." (Harvey, Hunt, and Schroeder, 1961, p. 11.)

Finding one's conceptual system in dissonance with group norms is one such threat. Considerable evidence indicates the propensity of the individual to bring his own perceptions into line with those of the group in order to avoid the discomfort of conceptual incongruency, sometimes achieving a readjustment of the conceptual system even at the price of conscious perceptual distortion. (Golembiewski, 1962, pp. 223–237.) Admittedly, individual differences loom large in terms of the degree of threat involved in cognitive dissonance and in terms of individual response to such dissonance. Part of the difficulty is that the relationship between cognitive dissonance and the degree of felt threat involves a complex matrix of variables—the nature of the individual's conceptual system itself in terms of its concreteness (greater absolutism, more categorical thinking, stronger reliance on external causality) versus abstractness, the dominance-dependency personality dimension, the individual's subjective evaluation of the competence of the norm source (see the later discussion of sending), the degree of ego-identification and concomitant effect attached to the threatened concept, the individual's confidence in the veracity of his concept, etc. It will be some time before all the relevant elements in the matrix are identified and related. Nonetheless, the fact remains that, generally, some degree of discomfort and threat is involved in finding one's frame of reference, or conceptual scheme out of line with that of a relevant group as articulated by the group's norm. Further, since norms arise only in those instances where the concept is of importance, it is likely that this dissonance will evidence presence of negative affect, adding emotional overtones to the intellectual discomfort. Thus, in addition, the intellectual discomfort is reinforced by the perceived irritation or anger of group members.

However, all pressure to comply with group norms does not rest in this individual, internally "felt" discomfort.[3] At the very heart of the

[3] Internalization and conformity result not only from intrinsic satisfactions, such as psychological security, and external or group sanction, but also from the fact that the sanctions have both positive (for example, share in "organized" surplus) and negative valences. Thus, we can raise an interesting experimental question: Is more to be learned from studying an individual's motives for joining a group or his reasons for conforming so as not to be expelled?

norm concept is the notion that norms are prescriptive. Therefore, they are important to the group's members, that is, generally related to their values or to important functional processes surrounding goal achievement, and the group's members will penalize deviation from these norms. Although the ultimate penalty is loss of group membership with all its benefits, even minor sanctions often involve punishment out of proportion to offense. For instance, the oft-stated proposition that "communication is directed toward the deviants" underemphasizes the diffuse source of such enforcement. Since norms are "shared frames of reference," this means the "communication," often highly critical and personalized, comes not just from a member but from members generally. Likewise, if sanctions in the form of loss of intrinsic social-emotional rewards are invoked against the deviant, the sanction becomes a generalized loss of social-emotional rewards from all members across the group.[4] If the member's status is decreased by deviation, it is decreased in the eyes of all the members. If the group withdraws resources, all members participate in the withdrawal. Likewise, the multiple sources of "grapevine" information contained within the group are withdrawn. The point is, the sanctions for norms are multiple in two senses: Generally more than one type of sanction is involved, and generally more than one source of sanction is involved. Even in the case where ritual dictates that the leader is the instrument of official sanction, unofficial sanction is diffuse, as well as reinforcing.

Finally, the norm structure is seldom independent of high affective content, since it is generally interrelated with the value and sentiment structures of conceptual systems. Therefore, group pressures are not merely dispassionate cognitive agreement and dispassionate sanctioning, but cognitive disagreement or agreement and sanction that is affect-laden.

Thus, it is a mix of this intimate relation of norms to the individual's conceptual system and thus to self, the relation of norms to the sentiment and value systems, plus the multiple sanctions involved in violation of group norms, which makes norms a multidimensional and efficacious form of social control and socialization.

Determinants of Effective Norm Transmission: A Communication Model

As seen above, a major linkage between the decision maker and his culture, organization, and/or work group is the "norm structure." Once

---

[4] It should be added that, to the degree that intrinsic satisfactions are mutual, there is a loss to the group itself.

internalized, this "norm structure" assures that the individual decision maker will intellectually mediate decisions in an "appropriate" fashion. As a conclusion to our treatment of socialization we will now concern ourselves with conditions for effective norm transmission in organizations.[5]

If norms are to provide for group maintenance and locomotion or for the psychological anchorage and conformity of the individual, they must be effectively transmitted. Since effective transmission is ultimately measured in terms of receipt, interpretation, and internalization of, or conformity to, the norm message, we will focus our attention on the gross variables that determine such measures of behavior. That is, we will examine the way a communication system operates in transmitting normative messages to facilitate collective action.

For this purpose we will assume the presence of norm patterns in an ongoing social system and concern ourselves with the effectiveness of their transference in gaining individual conformity. In doing so, however, we will attend to variables that cause disturbances in the transmission process, for example, those that create any spill-over or subtraction from the "intent" of the norm sender in transmitting the directive. In this way, we want to call attention to the fact that a norm transmission may over-evoke, under-evoke, or direct behavior in unintended ways. Such results may be attributed to the encoding, transmission, or decoding phase of the communication. Therefore, we view the communication of norms not as a single, unique event but as a process including sending, receiving, and feedback.

MAJOR VARIABLES IN COMMUNICATION

Man's ability to spread culture is partly a function of the setting in which such attempts are made. Therefore, we must look at the physical-social context as well as the translations made by the sender, known as "encoding," and the receiver, known as "decoding." We must examine the content of the message, with any attending noise, as well as the psychological processes operated by the receiver, for example, apprehension and inference. Finally, we must investigate the credibility of the sender and the sanctions implied in the message as well as the auditory and visual cues contained in the message. In total, we can frame the system as diagramed in Figure 4-1.

To illustrate the nature of this framework, we can use the concepts

[5] Much of that which follows is adapted from André L. Delbecq and Fremont A. Shull, "Norms, a Feature of Symbolic Culture," in William J. Core and J. W. Dyson (eds.), *The Making of Decisions* (New York: The Free Press of Glencoe, 1964), pp. 242–275.

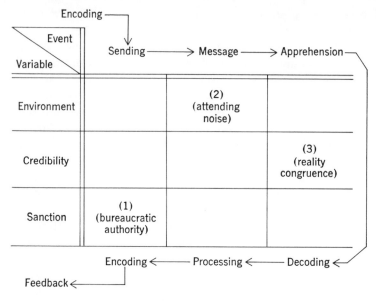

FIGURE 4-1   ELEMENTS DETERMINING COMMUNICATION EFFECTIVE-NESS

suggested by the parenthetical examples: (1) Bureaucratic authority may carry a high presumption of sanctioning ability of the sender; thus, an expectation of overt receiver conformity attends its use. (2) Transmission of norm directives under conditions of "noise" in the environment results in greater probability of communication distortion. (3) The greater the congruence of the information in a norm directive with the receiver's perceptions of reality, the higher the credibility given to the message.

The process of communication starts with the encoding of the message, that is, the translation of the intended message into normative form. Then the message must be transmitted, as part of the noisy environment, to the receiver. This transmission may require redundancy in the message or repetition through another medium to ensure receipt of the intended idea. Finally, the receiver must decode symbols into concepts meaningful and useful to himself. Yet the system is not completely open-ended; it is closed to the extent that feedback is actively sought by the sender.

The sender searches for feedback for one of two reasons. He may seek contemporary feedback during communication in order to ensure understanding, or he may seek feedback subsequent to communication in order to ensure conformity. Depending upon his perceptions of the "set" or reaction of the original receiver, he may also set in motion a secondary communication system. In this case, the same elements and problems are present as with the original message.

In feedback, however, we encounter a confounding variable. The receiver may feign either understanding or conformity. Thus, feedback can take place, in terms of the predisposition of the receiver, as (1) understand–conform or not conform; and (2) not understand–conform or not conform.[6] The receiver's feedback behavior will vary according to his perceptions of the situation. For example, while actually understanding, he may attempt to "fog" his behavior in such a way that his lack of conformity is not perceived. Accordingly, his strategy will depend upon his perceptions of the extent of the need to present an overt and conforming response. This, in turn, is a function of the receiver's perceptions of at least the following:

FACTOR	DIMENSION	JUDGMENT ON
1. Sender	Implied sanctions	Advisability of ignoring
2. Message content	Explicit sanctions	Acceptability of pleading confusion
3. Receiver	Countervailing sanctions	Ability to combat

To deal, in greater detail, with the multidimensionality of these variables, we can now examine in a detailed manner each variable of the system in the order presented, that is, sender, message, and receiver. In the main, though, our discussion will revolve about the transmission of the original norm directive and will deal only incidentally with the feedback system, since feedback can be treated similarly in most ways.

NORM TRANSMISSION MODEL: THE SENDER

In this first part of a communication model, we are concerned with the attributes of the sender, or transmitter, of the message. Therefore, we will abstract this dimension from both the content and the technical qualities of the message, as well as from conditions of its receipt.

The concept of norm implies that this sanctioned prescription is shared generally by all members of the group. That is to say, the conceptualization of the norm by each member and the degree of "affect" surrounding the normative conceptualization—and, therefore, the propensity to in-

---

[6] This is similar to the sender who transmits information which he disbelieves or for a purpose which he does not honestly intend.

voke sanctions against deviation—are congruent in some general sense across the membership. In such a situation, the locus or source of the norm is the group itself, that is, a generalized "other." Further, the locus of probable sanctions in the case of violation is diffuse, since all members are equally ego-involved and have equal sanctioning power.

We must recognize, however, that in day-to-day processes of indoctrinating, or socializing, new members as to group norms—or of enforcing member conformity—each is not equally involved. It is useful, and perhaps vital, to make the distinction between a source as the generalized "other" and a sender or senders acting as the group agent or agents who transmit the norm to the new members. The group, through role specialization, may have assigned norm enforcement to one or more particular individuals. Only in unique instances—where, for example, the norm is of significant importance to the group as a whole and in which the naïve member, or deviate, is equally exposed to all members of the group—will the senders be all members, that is, will the sender and source be the same.[7]

The distinction between the sender and source is even more important when we look at the situation where all members of the group are not equally ego-involved in its direction. In the extreme, some members may not have internalized the norm and, at best, may overtly comply with it merely for expedient purposes of avoiding sanctions: Take the case where the norm arose out of the unique value system of the charismatic founders of the group, that is, members who have been with the organization from the beginning. In such a situation, as the group matures and enlarges, norms may not be reinforced by either general cultural values, for example, eating outside the plant, or obvious connections with group function or processes, for example, wearing blue denim shirts. The reinforcement lies rather with power and, therefore, with the sanctioning ability of senior members. We may find, in such cases, that new members adhere to this norm only when under the surveillance of those "leaders."

Resulting segmentation between sender and source is more probable as we move from thinking of norms for cohesive, primary groups to a concern with larger aggregations as complex organizations. While we can quite correctly speak of organizational norms, we must realize that, for this large aggregation, two dimensions of the norm concept may not be equally applied: The power of the norm as a social influence may rest with its potential as a shared frame of reference for the majority of its members; but, in other cases, the efficacy of the norm may rest

[7] We are identifying "source" and "sender" here; however, this need not be the case. See: "Sender Sanctioning and Conformity," in Figure 4-2 on page 114.

more on a specific power structure than on congruency among the membership generally. Many norms concerned with "military protocol," for example, are violated with impunity except in the presence of officers. Consequently, we wish to examine (1) the influence of the sender on the receiver's acceptance of the norm, (2) the impact of multiple senders, and (3) the perceived sanctions surrounding the norm.

POSITIONAL ROLE AND PERSONALITY OF THE SENDER. The impact of a normative message from a sender will be related to his position and/or his role in the group structure. For instance, if the sender plays the role of leader in the group, then this role attaches a note of legitimacy to certain normative prescriptions. A leader quite legitimately prescribes behavior as the group spokesman, both in a general, normative sense and in a more specific and technical manner. Thus, a normative communication through him has special connotations of legitimacy quite independent of the content of the message.

Nonetheless, there are many types of influence roles within a group. For instance, members, on the basis of personal acquaintanceship with leaders of another group, may become that group's representative. Because of this acknowledged role, his normative prescriptions, in the presence of the other groups, carry a connotation of legitimacy.[8]

Accompanying legitimacy may also relate to the measure of competence or expertise of the sender in influencing the receiver's acceptance of the message. As an example, the social-emotional leader of a group often has no legitimacy in terms of formal position, but may have proven his expertise in social catharsis and discourse. Thus, norms prescribed by him relative to appropriate behavior in interpersonal relations have high acceptance.[9]

In addition to the sender's structural relationship in terms of role, position, and functional competence, there are his personal characteristics. One major characteristic of personality is his perceived ability or intelligence. Although intelligence is multidimensional, members of the group apparently form a generalized and holistic impression of his abil-

[8] Needless to say, if a functional role is supported by resources and prerogatives of position in the formal organization—for example, where the task-instrumental leader holds a supervisory position in the hierarchy or where the liaison member acts as formal head of a negotiating team—this legitimacy of the sender's message is reinforced.

[9] There is, of course, no necessary congruency between formal position and competence. The formal supervisor, for example, may not be considered the group expert, though the strongest support of a norm message should exist where legitimacy and competence are mutually reinforcing, that is, the legitimacy and competence of the sender, relative to the particular norm, serve to attach a certain veracity or believability to the message which he attempts to communicate.

ity. A member held to be "able" or "wise" may be capable of ascribing high veracity to a norm message even though the content of the norm is irrelevant to his area of specialization.

A second dimension of personal characteristics is "personality," that which may be called the "likableness." Again, as a composite of individual factors, for example, aggressiveness, nuturance, and so on, the individual's personality results in a certain personal attractiveness or unattractiveness to members of the group.

As a result of both ability and likableness, interpersonal attachments develop in the group. Whether one looks at this aspect of the group in terms of emotional and ego-identification between individuals or in terms of measured interpersonal ties, the fact remains that many normative messages may have high acceptance because of this personal dimension of the sender. Accordingly, one would expect highest support for a norm message to be obtained where legitimacy, competence, ability, and likableness are all mutually reinforcing.

If a norm is received from a single sender, the receiver may perceive the source of the norm to be the sender himself. Conformity to the norm would then reflect merely the perceived qualities of the single sender. However, if the norm is received from multiple senders, the receiver is more likely to perceive group consensus. The latter situation has a distinct impact, because consensus is often a test of the truth content of a concept; therefore, incongruence between that particular norm and the individual's conceptual system would constitute a greater degree of threat where the norm was reinforced by multiple senders. Transmission from multiple senders couples the qualitative characteristics of the individual senders with the strength of consensus as a reflection of relevant dimensions of reality.

From this it can be seen that a single sender can employ certain strategies in order to avoid the implication that the norm merely carries the weight of his individual influence. He can (1) make it clear he is an agent of another authority or group consensus, or (2) appeal to the logic underlying the norm and/or empirical evidence supporting its logic, that is, he can place emphasis on the content of the message itself.

SANCTIONING POWER OF THE SENDER. So far, our concern has been with the relationship between the acceptance of a norm and characteristics of the sender. An optimal combination of these attributes increases the receiver's internalization of the norm, that is, of the norm becoming part of, or affecting in some way, the receiver's conceptual system. If he does effectively internalize the norm, then we need be concerned with only one aspect of our definition of norms: a shared frame of reference. However, the definition of norms also includes the notion of "sanctioned prescriptions."

Ideally, sanctions associated with a norm merely reinforce its believ-ability and are not the sole means of obtaining group conformity. In fact, coercion through sanctions may decrease the attractiveness of the sender to the receiver. If an individual does not share the group's frame of reference, but conforms to norms merely in response to sanctions, he is likely to conform only where (1) his behavior is exposed to surveil-lance, (2) sanctions are perceived as viable, and (3) they pose a suffi-cient threat or reward to the individual.

The potential rewards or penalties, for conformity or nonconformity, associated with a norm message are often suggested by the position or role of the sender. Obviously, a supervisor who sends a norm message is perceived as possessing considerable resources for invoking sanctions against the receiver if it is violated. Likewise, he is perceived as being in a legitimate position to sanction as part of his formal role. Thus the position and role of the sender imply certain feasibility and legiti-macy for sanctioning.

Similarly, the ability and personality dimensions of the sender offer clues as to the potential power, feasibility, and affective discomfort that will accompany sanctioning. It may be considered less painful, for exam-ple, to suffer the criticism of an individual one does not respect or actually dislikes than to be criticized by an individual with whom one ego-identifies.

Finally, there is the relationship between the probability of sanction and the perceived number of norm senders. If the norm is received from a single sender, then the receiver may anticipate that the employ-ment of sanction resides primarily in that particular individual. But if the norm is received from multiple senders, then the receiver faces the probability of multiple sanctioning. Further, while the receiver may speculate that a single sender might withhold sanctions, it is less likely that among multiple senders he will entirely escape sanction. A norm transmitted from multiple senders is generally considered to be a greater threat.

There is a qualitative difference between positive rewards and nega-tive sanctions. Generally, rewards (1) increase the probability of the receiver internalizing the norm, since he wishes to comply in order to achieve continuing rewards; (2) increase the attraction of the group to the receiver, and of the sender to the receiver; and (3) decrease the necessity of surveillance in order to obtain compliance, since the receiver will want his compliance known in order to obtain rewards.

We can summarize this discussion of the sender of the norm message as follows:

FIGURE 4-2   THE SENDER OF THE NORM MESSAGE

I. Relationship between:

A. Acceptance of the norm message and the characteristics of the sender

1. Structural role and position of sender indicating:
   a. Legitimacy of sender to prescribe normative behavior;
   b. Competence of sender relative to group processes and goals.
2. Personal characteristics of sender, as:
   a. Intelligence manifested by perceived quality of sender's general conceptualizations;
   b. Personality resulting in ego-identification and interpersonal relationships facilitating acceptance.

B. Believability of the norm message and multiple norm senders

1. Single sender:
   a. Receiver may interpret sender to be norm source and therefore judge norm in terms of characteristics of sender;
   b. Sender may seek to avoid the receiver's interpretation of himself as sole source by use of strategy for influence, as:
      (1) Referral to authority;
      (2) Referral to consensus;
      (3) Reference to intrinsic logic of message and empirical support.
2. Multiple senders: Receiver may interpret source to be group consensus, thereby coupling:
   a. Characteristics of individual senders with
   b. Consensus as a test of veracity of conceptualization encompassed in norm message.

NORM TRANSMISSION MODEL: THE MESSAGE

The first part of our norm-communication model was concerned with relevant properties of the sender, or source, of norms which influence the effectiveness of their transmission. This section is concerned with: (1) the directive proper, in terms of both its technical qualities as a message, or signal, and its "content," and (2) the environmental context within which the directive is transmitted. Our concern with the directive itself reflects the fact that it is possible, at least in principle, for norma-

FIGURE 4-2 (*Continued*)

C. Sanctioning power of the sender and conformity to the norm

1. If conformity is not a function of norm internalization but merely sanctions, then conformity will be related to:
    a. Degree to which receiver perceives his behavior as subject to surveillance;
    b. Feasibility of sanctioning by sender(s);
    c. Degree of threat posed by probable sanctions.
2. Clues to probable sanctions resulting from norm violation obtained from:
    a. Structural role and position of sender, indicating:
        (1) Legitimate right of sender to sanction;
        (2) Resources available for sanctioning (feasibility);
    b. Personal characteristics of sender, indicating:
        (1) Affective discomfort of sanctions, due to
        (2) Ego-identification with sender, or
        (3) Interpersonal relationships with sender.

D. Multiplicity of norm senders and probable sanctioning

1. Generally multiple senders indicate multiple sanctions often resulting in sanctioning which will be out of proportion to seriousness of norm violation.

II. Rewards versus Negative Sanctions

1. Increase probability of internalization;
2. Decrease the necessity of surveillance; and
3. Increase attractiveness of sender and group to the receiver.

tive social control to reflect a behavioral response to the message stimulus itself, quite independent of the personal characteristics of the sender or the structural characteristics of the immediate social system. This is particularly true where the directive buttresses the value system encompassed in the conceptual system of the individual. In such a situation, the individual often "internalizes" the norm almost immediately upon receipt of the message itself, and positive reinforcement is welcomed.

However, since the message is intimately related to the stimulus surround, we must also concern ourselves with the context within which the signal is transmitted. In this light, we must consider the total symbolic culture which is the heritage of past communications to see whether or not this aspect of the environment appears congruent with the new message. Thus, we find that the directive's effectiveness is a function of the message plus or minus the support of the historical and symbolic environment.

In the main, now, we attempt to deal with the objective reality of the message itself, abstracting from the psychological implications associated with both the receiver and the sender.[10] Therefore, for example, we will talk about "information transmitted" and do not deal with "effect intended" or "information apprehended."

TECHNICAL QUALITY. The first attribute of the message with which we wish to deal has to do with the operational quality of the communication. Accordingly, we need to treat (1) the choice of symbols, (2) their manner of organization, (3) the nature of the argument contained, and (4) the presence of redundancy in and/or repetition of the message. We are especially concerned with those technical qualities of the message which support understandability and credibility of the message.

In examining these technical qualities, we can turn our attention first to the simple symbol. We are aware that words, for example, "the Civil War," and gestures singly and in isolation do not have invariant meanings to different people or to the same person at different times. This may explain the choice of a compromise accent in national broadcasting—that of the Midwestern announcer. Moreover, meaning is often as much a function of the configuration of the set of symbols encompassed in the message as it is of the particular choice of any particular symbol, for example, "to each his own" versus "each to his own." Therefore, the meaning of a message relates both to the choice and transmission of certain signals and to the manner of their organization.

Second, symbols merely represent an object, that is, they are only cognitively "real."[11] Furthermore, the historical usage of certain symbols by a subculture, that is, their symbolic "programs," may lead to misapplications of a symbol. Accordingly, to ensure accurate transmission and to hedge against misunderstanding, we may find (1) abstract normative concepts reinforced with concrete illustration, (2) substantiating arguments supporting the normative concept, or (3) colloquial words, per-

---

[10] We do admit that communication is a social phenomenon encompassing all three dimensions of sender, message, and receiver in an interrelated state, even if for the moment we do not attend the totality of the social-psychological field.

[11] Does, for example, "cow" denote the image of one grazing in a pasture or the concept of the genus, cow?

haps emotion-laden, in the message. Finally, the message content may be presented in a particular style, for example, that of the military, carrying high identification and, thus, credence.

The message may be offered without conclusions, leaving the inference to the recipient, or the argument may be presented as moving from the specific to the general or vice versa. These stylized characteristics are particularly important in holding attention and gaining acceptance of the norm message. The point is, of course, that because of the variable qualities of symbols—some dimensions of which actually create imperfections in the receipt of the message—offsetting practices may be required to reduce the possibility of communication failure. In addition to attention to style and symbolic composition, one may even use "gross" signal reinforcement methods. One practice is to increase the signal strength, for example, to shout or to underline. On the other hand, redundancy may be employed. Third, the sender may repeat his message—perhaps in another medium—to increase the probability of the transmission of a clear and accurate signal, using both oral and written communication.

It is not pedantic to comment that attempts at "normative" social control may fail because of this basic, technical aspect of communication. For example, the editors of *Fortune* magazine have indicated that many attempts of management to sell "free enterprise" to employees fails at this very remedial level. It is not just that the source is discredited—as "management propaganda"—but that the words and jargon employed have a very different connotation to the laborer from that to the authors of the "educational" material. Thus "profits" may be seen as "jobs through expansion" to the author, but may be seen by the worker as "excess return to wealth."

PRESCRIPTION AND DISCRETION. In addition to the technical qualities of the message, we must concern ourselves with the substantive content of the norm being transmitted. In the main, we need to ask whether the norm statement is offered in a positive or negative manner, and whether it deals with behavioral ends or means. The specificity of the message can be measured by both mode and manner. If the mode is negative, the message has low specificity; if positive, it has high specificity. If the manner deals with ends, it has low specificity; if with means, the communication has high specificity.

Even thus delineated, we have two possible attending constraints that need explication: (1) the message may contain certain suggestions of tolerance for nonconformity, and (2) within the message we may find the presence or absence of time constraints for specific behavior. While the individual may be willing to overtly comply with the norm, out of dependence and/or agreement, he may find that even the most highly specified norm directives are surrounded by a range of admissible deviation or enforceability of the group. Such tolerances may be implied in the message or suggested in the environment of the transmission. One technique to decrease implied tolerance that is sometimes effective in making even negative norm statements on ends more restraining is to impose detailed time specifications.

ENVIRONMENT OF THE SIGNAL. As we have said before, the environment in which the norm is transmitted affects the meaning of the message and, in turn, the recipient's accommodation to it. Actually, this environment may either attract or distract attention from the message itself, as well as give reinforcement to the normative prescription. Credibility may be enhanced, for example, by a judicious choice of medium of transmission—such as official stationery—or the norm may find reinforcement from or conflict with the total norm set, the total configuration of group norms within which the new message is exposed. Here, for example, we find administrative injunctions on consistency among organizational policies and standards.

In contrast, the environment may present noise or competing signals which distort or detract from the message content. In any case of environmental disturbances, information about the norm may be lost, accompanied by a high probability of misunderstanding and/or low conformity by the receiver. Here we may find, for example, competing signals from other norm senders, perhaps other ad hoc or reference groups. Thus, in addition to social identification, physical as well as relative psychological distances between senders and receivers must be considered, if conflict and ambiguity in the norm message are to be minimized.

THE SANCTION DIMENSION. A final dimension of the effective transference of norms, having to do with message content, relates to message clues that indicate the probability, as well as the nature, of sanctions underlying surveillance and enforcement of the norm. The message, for example, may (1) explicitly contain, or simply imply, clues as to the (2) intensity of the emotional affect associated with the sender's, or group's, belief in the norm or as to (3) the implied certainty of the strength, negative or positive, of the sanction on deviant behavior.

The general configuration of any of these properties may be heightened by the use of certain stylized appeals. First, the message may be framed in a negative way, such as a threat-arousing appeal, or in terms of the rewards accruing to the receiver for compliance. A second type of amplification has to do with the clues as to who or what endorses or gives legitimacy to the norm, such as, "scientific evidence shows . . . ." This aspect of legitimacy is different from the charismatic dimension of the sender—the personal appeal of the sender himself. A third attribute has to do with its psychological approach. The function of the norm—for example, to influence sentiment or to form a concept—may demand an appeal to fact, logic, consensus, authority, or intuition, or some combination of them. To influence sentiment, for example, it may be sufficient and most effective to use, as a persuasion technique, an appeal to intuition, as: "I know you feel that this is right." In transferring an acceptable concept of fact, however, the intuitive approach may be completely ineffective.

Finally, implied sanction in the message may be reinforced by the total context within which the message is received. Thus a message written on official stationery, in the format of a highly formalized complaint, with carbon copies sent to superordinate hierarchical officials, may well imply more than the mere "content" of the message would otherwise imply.

We can summarize this brief discussion of the norm message as shown in Figure 4-3 on page 120.

NORM TRANSMISSION MODEL: THE RECEIVER

In the last part of our communication model, we wish to examine the subjective set or frame of reference of the receiver and to do so largely through the elements developed above.

Let us begin by examining perception of the sender and reception of his message by the receiver through the operations of conceptualization. In terms of apprehension, we can ask whether or not the stimuli, both sender and message, are meaningful to the receiver. For instance, suppose the sender is the receiver's supervisor and the message is concerned with proper "presentation of self"; the receiver may subjectively ignore both concern with protocol and signals of a "fussy" supervisor.

We need to ask, now, whether the subjective set of the receiver is "receptive" to the sender and message in terms of other conceptual operations, for example, whether or not the conceptual scheme of the message is such as to evoke the intended meaning.[12] There is always the possibility that the message will over-evoke, i.e., arouse a larger cognitive set than intended, or under-evoke, i.e., elicit less of a set than intended, and consequently result in unintended responses. In addition, the concepts of the sender may be reified—considered as material— simply because of his position, resulting in rigidity and inflexibility of a type not intended.

[12] This is a familiar and perhaps hackneyed point, since it is the dimension most stressed in everyday treatments of interpersonal communication, but it is nonetheless important.

FIGURE 4-3   CONFORMITY GAINED BY MESSAGE PLUS ITS ENVIRONMENT

I. Technical Quality

A. Choice of symbols, with, e.g.:
1. The more abstract illustrated with the concrete, or
2. Colloquial wording
B. Organization of the symbols
C. Style of composition, e.g.:
1. With or without conclusions
2. Emotionality
3. Inductive versus deductive reasoning
D. Manner of emphasis:
1. Signal strength
2. Redundancy of symbols
3. Repetition of message

II. Message Content

A. Clues as to intensity of affect
B. Implied or explicit tolerances
C. Specificity of message:
1. Ends versus means
2. Positive versus negative statements
D. Presence or absence of time constraints
E. An appeal to logic, fact, or sentiment through appeal to:
1. Authority
2. Consensus
3. Intuition

III. Environment of the Signal

A. Choice of medium
B. Reinforcing or conflicting prevailing norm set
C. Presence of noise or competing signals
D. Physical and psychological distance between sender and receiver

IV. Supporting Sanction

A. Clues as to certainty and strength of sanction
B. Style of appeal
1. Threat-arousing versus positive inducement
2. Clues as to endorser of the message and/or norm
C. Clue as to ability to plead ignorance or inapplicability of the norm

Relative to inferences, we must ask whether or not those implied in the sender's message agree with the receiver's notion of reality. The receiver may feel that the sender has misinterpreted the problem field relative to the concern of the norm message. For instance, in our protocol example, the receiver may feel that the sender's norm-directive encompasses a greater degree of formality in presentation of self than is expected by others in general. Likewise, relative to processing, we may ask whether or not the reasoning process or logic of the message appears subjectively valid to the receiver.

Once again, the conceptual system is also closely tied to values and sentiments. We would therefore need to ask whether the response or conceptualization is congruent with the receiver's value system, his judgments about the worth of a particular concept or response, and therefore in some subjective sense, legitimate, and whether there will be any modification due to subjective sentiment, or affect, on the part of the receiver.

The point, here, is whether the receiver considers it important to attend to the sender and his message, and whether subsequent responses are as intended. It would be the exception rather than the rule for a sender and his message to have the same, total impact on two individuals. Even in the family, often cited as the exemplary primary group, where children are subject to largely congruent processes of socialization, the same normative message from a father may be interpreted differently and evoke quite varied responses among the individual children.

Similarly, the personality of the receiver is another intervening variable. Such an individual, with a dependent personality syndrome, may give great credence and obedience to a superordinate's normative message. An individual whose "self" is based on concrete conceptual systems, encompassing a great degree of attentiveness to duties, may quickly "obey" or "disobey" a normative prescription. An individual whose personality inherently leans toward group acceptance for self-security may give greater attention to norm messages, and so forth.

The receiver's position and role may affect his reaction to norm messages. Within a business organization, a message concerned with intergroup protocol may have a greater impact on a sales or public relations executive than on a production executive, since protocol is more central to the sales and public relations functions. Thus, the more central the norm message of the sender is to the position and role of the receiver, the greater may be the attention to the norm communication. In contrast, norm messages whose content is peripheral to the role of the receiver in other structural networks, aside from his functional position, may have an impact on norm reception. An example is Homan's famous proposition that one's position in the status hierarchy is related to his compliance with the group norms. Finally, role and position do not have to have a complementary relationship. The leader's self-defined role may be iconoclastic in the near short term; therefore, he may flout norms as a reinforcement of his independence from group tradition in order to achieve prominence among a power group seeking change.

We can summarize this discussion of the receiver as to his countervailing power:

FIGURE 4-4   THE RECEIVER OF THE NORM MESSAGE

I. Reception and perceptions of the norm message by the receiver are related to:

A. Receiver's Conceptual System:
1. Apprehension: Are the stimuli (sender and message) subjectively meaningful?
2. Conceptualization: Are the concepts encompassed by the message such as to evoke the intended response?
3. Inference: Does the conceptualization encompassed by the message concur with the receiver's notions of reality?
4. Processing: Do the logic or reasoning processes encompassed by the message appear appropriate to the receiver?
B. Receiver's Value System: Are the conceptualization and/or prescribed response subjectively legitimate?
C. Receiver's Sentiment System: Is there any effective modification of the message?
D. Receiver's Personality Profile: What are his personality characteristics, e.g., the ascendency-dependency characteristics, the concreteness-abstractness of the conceptual system, etc.?
E. Receiver's Role and Position:
1. The centrality of norm relative to functional position
2. The relationship of norm to personal role

II. Response may be relative to perception of countervailing power of receiver relative to:

A. Position and Role: Do position and role afford legitimacy and resources to oppose norm?
B. Personal Influence: Do ability and affective ties afford opportunity to oppose norms?
C. Obscurity: Does obscurity afford opportunity to avoid surveillance?

In concluding, we need to concern ourselves again with feedback, that is, with the receiver's ability to avoid, or defend himself against, prescription. We earlier made the point that if compliance is a function of the receiver's attempt to avoid sanctions, rather than the result of the receiver's internalization of the norms, then compliance will be related to the exposure of the receiver to those who sanction norm deviation. However, in addition to reliance on obscurity in avoiding sanction, there is also the possibility of the receiver exercising countervailing power. His position may provide resources and/or legitimacy for avoiding, disagreeing with, or changing the norm. Thus, while a member—for example, the leader—may comply with most norms, he may also be in a position to posit a new norm in contradiction to those currently prevailing.

This countervailing influence need not arise from position or role, but may arise also from personal competence or affective ties. The expected impact of the sanctioning power of the sender is modified by the perceptions of the receiver as to his own countervailing power.

SUMMARY OF TRANSMISSION MODEL

For administrative theory, attention to symbolism and the transfer of symbolic culture is not a mere diversion. Consequently, we have concerned ourselves in this last section with the process through which norms are transmitted. Here the "symbolic" culture is integrated with other features of the social environment, the structural characteristics of the group, organization, or society, and the characteristics of the person or persons who send or receive the norm communication.[13]

In this way, the framework provided by this final section is suggestive of important considerations for the administrator. A basic problem for him is to evoke or structure norms of individuals or to deal effectively with incompatibilities between norm sets. These two necessities (if not sufficiencies) indicate that the administrator should attend to (1) the content of the existing norm structures in their totalities and interrelatedness; (2) influence mechanisms supporting existing sets, both in influence of the sender arising from position, role, and personality and in the institutionalized symbolic heritage of the organization—for example, policies and rules; (3) the nature and content of the norm message; and (4) the elements contributing to the receptiveness or lack of it on the part of the receiver.

[13] Since, for instance, the transmission model incorporates relevant dimensions of the environment, sender, and receiver in some integrated fashion, it is hoped that the hypotheses thus generated may differ in emphasis from those which would arise from considering only the structural-functional aspects of either the rational or the natural system.

Conclusions and Implications

Any treatment of individual decision making must encompass the realization and implications generated from the fact that the individual, though a unique psychological self, is also more or less socialized, since man is dependent upon his social environment for normal psychological development. Further, the fact that man functions at the cognitive level implies he is dependent upon symbolism; thus socialization results from the intimate relations between cognition and the concepts encompassed in language symbols.

Society does not rely entirely upon the individual's absorption of culture through language, nor does it take a passive role relative to this absorption. Through education, indoctrination, and intimidation members of society, and of social groups generally, seek to influence the individual's thinking and ultimate behavior. A most pervasive form of social influence is exemplified in the treatment of group norms and the manner in which these group-sanctioned prescriptions are related to the psychological self.

When an organization hires an employee, therefore, it obtains a highly socialized individual who brings to the organization a complex frame of reference, more or less compatible with organizational norms. The history of productivity norms among workers at variance with productivity norms of the organization provides an eloquent testimony to the fact that the organization and its formal rules will often lose out to work group norms. Further, since to a large extent managers trained in different specialties are often "socialized" in subcultures with very explicit professional norms, intra-organization conflict in decision making will often result from disparate frames of reference rather than from situation-specific analysis.

Finally, organization structures and processes must reflect changing "socialization" experiences by members of a particular society. In a society which stresses egalitarianism, professional self-control, high reliance on expertise, etc., many of the traditional implications of hierarchical roles encompassed in classical organization models may no longer "fit" the socialization experiences of the individuals hired to participate in the organizational system. Current organizational experiences reflect such cleavage between organizational expectations and personal expectations. The organization seeks through this program of indoctrination and sanction to "wash out" prior socialization with but limited success. Further, there is the additional problem of the cultural gap between senior members of organizations and highly trained younger members whose expectations about professional and work-related norms reflect serious differences.

As we explore the relation between small-group and organizational models and decision making, and the implications of econological models for enhancing rationality in decision making in subsequent chapters, the "socialization" of individual organizational members must continually be a mediating variable and its implications must be either implicitly or explicitly noted.

bibliography

BATES, ALAN P., and JERRY S. CLOYD: "Toward the Development of Operations for Defining Group Norms and Member Rules," *Sociometry*, vol. 19, March, 1956.

BENEDICT, RUTH: *Patterns of Culture* (New York: Houghton Mifflin Company, 1934).

DELBECQ, ANDRÉ L., and FREMONT A. SHULL: "Norms, A Feature of Symbolic Culture: A Major Linkage Between the Individual, Small Group, and Administrative Organization," in William Gore and J. W. Dyson (eds.), *The Making of Decisions* (Glencoe, Ill.: The Free Press, 1964).

GOLEMBIEWSKI, ROBERT T.: *The Small Group* (Chicago: The University of Chicago Press, 1962).

HALL, CALVIN, and GARDNER LINDZEY: "Psychoanalytic Theory and Its Applications in the 'Social Sciences,'" in Gardner Lindzey, *Handbook of Social Psychology* (Reading, Mass.: Addison-Wesley Publishing Company, 1954).

HARVEY, O. J., DAVID E. HUNT, and HAROLD M. SCHROEDER: *Conceptual Systems and Personality Organization* (New York: John Wiley & Sons, Inc., 1961), chap. 1.

HEAD, H.: *Aphasia and Kindred Disorders of Speech* (New York: The Macmillan Company, 1926).

HEBB, D. O.: "The Mammal and His Environment," in Elenore Macoby, Theodore Newcomb, and Eugene L. Hartley, *Readings in Social Psychology* (New York: Holt, Rinehart, and Winston, 1958).

JACKSON, JAY: "The Normative Regulation of Authoritative Behavior," an expanded version of a paper presented at the Seminar in the *Social Science of Organizations*, University of Pittsburgh, June 10–22, 1962.

KELLER, HELEN: *The World I Live In* (New York: Appleton-Century-Crofts, Inc., 1938).

LINDESMITH, ALFRED, and ANSELM STRAUSS: *Social Psychology* (New York: Holt, Rinehart, and Winston, 1956).

MCCLELLAND, DAVID C.: "Business Drive and National Achievement," *Harvard Business Review*, vol. 40, July–August, 1962.

MEAD, MARGARET: "Adolescence in Primitive and Modern Society," in Elenore Macoby, Theodore Newcomb, and Eugene L. Hartley, *Readings in Social Psychology* (New York: Holt, Rinehart, and Winston, 1958).

MORRIS, RICHARD T.: "A Typology of Norms," *American Sociological Review*, vol. 30, 1956, pp. 610–613.

PARSONS, TALCOTT: "Authority, Legitimation, and Political Action," in C. J. Friedrich (ed.), *Authority* (Cambridge, Mass.: Harvard University Press, 1958).

PIAGET, JEAN: *The Psychology of Intelligence* (London: Routledge & Kegan Paul, Ltd., 1950).

RUDIN, STANLEY: "The Person Price of National Glory," *Trans-action,* September–October, 1965.

SCHEERER, MARTIN: "Cognitive Theory," in Calvin Hall and Gardner Lindzey (eds.), *Handbook of Social Psychology* (Reading, Mass.: Addison-Wesley Publishing Company, 1954).

SELZNICK, P.: "Foundations of the Theory of Organization," *American Sociological Review,* vol. 13, 1948, pp. 24–35.

SEWARD, G. H.: *Sex and Social Order* (New York: McGraw-Hill Book Company, 1946).

SHERIF, MUZAFER, and CAROLYN SHERIF: *An Outline of Social Psychology* (New York: Harper & Brothers, 1956).

SING, J. A., and R. M. ZINGG: *Wolf Children and Feral Man* (New York: Harper & Brothers, 1942).

five

THE EFFECT OF SMALL-GROUP
STRUCTURES AND PROCESSES

In the previous chapter dealing with socialization, we argued that each person is both dependent upon and influenced by his environment. In particular, the socialization chapter dealt with symbolic inputs —the world of ideas—through which man constructs a conceptual system to process and interpret the totality of his environmental stimuli.

Socialization, however, is not a random process. Rather, socialization normally takes place through interaction between individuals, often in a group setting which may be more or less formalized. Thus, in addition to understanding how decision making is influenced by socialization, one must also understand the structural properties of the groups in which the individual interacts during the socialization process.[1] This chapter, then, by pointing out how group structure and process influence and constrain individual decision making, complements the chapter dealing with socialization.

The purpose of this chapter is to show that the properties of small groups, whether formal and carefully structured or natural and spontaneous,[2] permeate the decision-making process by influencing:

1. Which problems are attended by the decision maker;

2. Which type of organizational units should be activated in the total decision process ("total process" referring to decision making, itself, as well as implementation of the decision);

3. Which group or interaction strategy is appropriate for the decision makers to follow in dealing with the problem solving;

4. Which role the individual person, caught up in the decision process, should play in the problem-solving group, which is conditioned in part by values and norms.

Since the primary focus of this book is on decision making, this chapter seeks to sensitize the reader to the pervasive influences of group structure on decision making. It does not provide an encyclopedic treatment of small-group theory.[3]

THE RELEVANCE OF THE SMALL GROUP

The chapter on socialization showed that the symbolic culture of the small group plays an important part in the process of socialization and control and in the elaboration of personality. However, a further treatment of other structural properties of the small group is warranted, since structural variables other than norms make up the social-psychological contexts of decision making. (Miller and Form, 1951, p. 72.) It is particularly appropriate, for several reasons, that those who are mostly interested in decision making within complex organizations look closely at the small group. First, the small group is an ubiquitous and inevitable element of formal organizations. "Small Groups seem to be

[1] "Interaction" is a generic term covering the totality of communication exchanges, both verbal and nonverbal, between individuals in a face-to-face meeting.

[2] By "natural" as opposed to "formal," we mean a group whose structures and processes have evolved in the course of interaction rather than having been structured according to some predetermined behavioral model such as "bureaucracy."

[3] Small-group theory consitutes a field of study in its own right, containing both sets of theoretical concepts and distinguishable methodologies significant to many concerns of administrative theory and decision making. In this sense, a comprehensive treatment of small-group theory would warrant a tome of its own.

one of the characteristics of human organization . . . that may be understood and modified, but never done away with, as their existence even in that most formal of all organizations, the military, forcefully suggests." (B. B. Gardner, 1948.) Indeed, an organic view of an organization sees the small group as the fundamental structural unit. As early as 1938, Barnard wrote that ". . . all organizations of complex character grow out of small, simple organizations." (C. R. Barnard, 1938, p. 104.) Second, the small group bears many resemblances—as a micro-system—to large-scale social systems. By studying the small group we can better understand the interaction between the structure of larger organizations and decision making within them. Finally, the small group may exercise controls obstructing or inhibiting the achievement of goals or purposes of the organization or, contrariwise, serve as linkages reinforcing, complementing, and/or supplementing the purposes of the formal organization. (R. House, 1963, p. 41.)[4]

Nonetheless, one caveat is in order: The juxtaposition of small-group theory with organizational theory, which we are about to undertake, is, at best, a tenuous affair at the present time. Small-group research has tended to center on the evolution and character of ad hoc groups. Thus, the extent to which propositions taken from these studies hold true in complex organizations of concern to the administrator is often a question of fact rather than a matter of theoretical certitude. Further, generic differences between ad hoc systems and traditional formal organizations have either remained relatively unexplored or exist in current writings in the most sketchy form. However, this problematic state of theory shall not deter us from exploring small-group theory in order to obtain the benefits of the rich insights it gives into the relation between decision making and group structure.

Before beginning, we need one last clarification: The definition of our object of study, together with an outline of this chapter.

For our purposes, a *small group* may be defined as follows: An aggregate of people, from two up to an unspecified but not-too-large number, who associate together in face-to-face relations over a period of time, who differentiate themselves in some regard from others around them, and who are mutually aware of their membership in the group (Bernard Berelson and Gary A. Steiner, 1964). Since our purpose is to obtain insight rather than to provide a complete treatment of small groups, we need not study all the elements of group structure. Rather, we will study primarily four aspects of group structure (Berelson and Steiner,

---

[4] Indeed, this review of the literature concludes emphatically that informal control is usually more effective than formal control in the accomplishment or negation of the organizational goals.

1964; Cartwright and Zander, 1960; Hare, 1962; and Golembiewski, 1962):

Pattern of interpersonal choice
Functional roles of group members
Effects of group size
Effects of group task

The first variable, pattern of interpersonal choice, is selected because it acquaints the student of decision making with the pervasiveness of subgroup structure which underlies the totality of organizational decision making. The second variable, functional roles of group members, allows us to explore the nexus between personality, group behavior, and psychological specialization in decision making without forcing us too deeply into personality theory. The third variable, group size, allows us to explore the impact of varied group size on group behavior. The final variable, group task, integrates the total structural set with differentiated situational tasks and, as such, summarizes many of the previous considerations.

The Pattern of Interpersonal Choice

Every student of management is aware that the "official" organization, or the hierarchy of positions and tasks, is constantly being modified by individual and group behavior, thus affecting the decision-making process. What often is less clear is the nature of the inexorable forces contained within the formal organizational design itself which contribute to the development of subgroups. Before talking about other specific characteristics of small-group structure, this section is concerned with how the subgroup overlay comes into being (Pfiffner and Sherwood, 1960, pp. 16–32).

FACTORS UNDERLYING INTERPERSONAL CHOICES

Attractions and repulsions occur among individual members of an organization, even under conditions of short-lived acquaintanceship. Moreover, individual sociometrically isolated choice patterns are shown in a number of studies to persist over time, and even to become more apparent. (See Hare, 1962, p. 139.) We can therefore talk of the configuration of such choice patterns as an element of group structure, and of such group structures as part of the "informal" organization overlay which permeates formal organizational decision making (Pfiffner and Sherwood, 1960, p. 19).

To understand that such choices are a ubiquitous aspect of organizational life and that the choice pattern remains relatively stable is not, however, sufficient. In order to relate interpersonal choice to formal organizational designs, the manager must understand the factors out of which interpersonal choices occur. A number of research studies have addressed this question (Hare, 1962, p. 127). These factors appear particularly salient:

1. Proximity
2. Similarities or attractiveness in terms of:
    a. Work activities
    b. Interests or values shared
    c. Complementary personality profiles
    d. Individual social characteristics (i.e., social class, status, rank, etc.)

While it is perilous to rank-order these variables in terms of importance, the following propositions appear defensible.

To begin with, proximity is clearly a necessary precondition for group formation and thus is the primordial variable. Unless physical distance is overcome in some manner, interaction is impossible. As should be clear from preceding chapters, it is inconceivable that a truly "human" relationship between individual group members could evolve without symbolic interaction (L. Festinger, et al., 1960, pp. 431–444, and A. P. Hare, 1962, p. 139). Thus, the feasibility (viability) of interaction must be assured by some form of proximity (either actual physical proximity or simulated proximity by means of modern communication methods) in order for other structural characteristics to evolve.

Relative to variables dealing with similarities or attractiveness, the following considerations are relevant:

1. Individuals can and do distinguish between two dimensions, alternatively conceptualized as "affectional" as opposed to "instrumental" choices (D. Moment and A. Zaleznik, 1963, pp. 41–42; F. K. Taylor, 1950), and "private" (relating to person-to-person friendships) (F. K. Taylor, 1950) as opposed to "public" choices[5] (feelings toward a person arising from the group as a whole as a result of the role of the individual in the group).

2. The degree to which task-instrumental or social-emotional considera-

[5] Obviously these alternative classifications are not conceptually equal. The first dimension (affectional-instrumental) refers to role played, and the second (public-private) to group situation or task content. Further, the correlation of all four choices often occurs, since there are some "great men" who have skills both "affectional" and "instrumental" and are seen as desirable members in both private and public groups. (See the next section of this chapter.) One of the methodological weaknesses in sociometric tests is the failure to make such distinctions.

tions pertain to individual choices differs, depending on the degree of achievement desires versus affiliation desires of individuals.

3. However, individuals, particularly in task-oriented groups, tend to make fewer choices on the basis of personality or social characteristics than on the basis of work criteria. (C. A. Gibb, 1950; Hare, 1962, p. 139; H. H. Jennings, 1947.)

4. Groups formed initially on the basis of personality or social characteristics, that is, on the basis of friendship, tend to be less stable than groups formed on the basis of shared work activities or values. (Hare, 1962, p. 139.)

5. Regardless of the basis of group formation, however, the stability of the group and the continuance of the group are secure only if shared values or interests are present or evolve. (T. M. Newcomb in Cartwright and Zander, 1960; E. O. Laumann, 1969.)[6]

Our objective is to relate these propositions to group formation in formal organizations rather than to elaborate on the theory underlying these propositions themselves. We will, therefore, move directly to the issue of formalization.

FORMAL "POSITIONS" AND INTERPERSONAL CHOICE

In classical management models, one talks about a hierarchy of positions in "groups." Indeed, as we will note in greater detail in the next section, the prescriptive classical maximum is to avoid building organizations around people and to build around positions.

At the same time, "position," as a concept, has largely been taken at face value in management literature. It has been seen as meaning an individualized, occupational role which encompasses certain tasks. It is, however, a much richer concept than this simplified notion of classical theory implies. The concept "position" encompasses technical, sociotechnical, and social dimensions.

The *technical dimension* of "position" includes: (1) all the physical artifacts which are part of the work activity, such as dictating machines, adding machines, etc.; (2) a cognitive content, (mediating programs), so that ways of thinking are built into the "expertise" or craft required

---

[6] It should be noted that sociologically oriented theory has not integrated clinical psychological orientations with group formation. In clinical psychological theory, it is proposed that group formation can be studied from the standpoint of drive relationships and emotional procedures within each member of a group, out of which the basis of group formative processes evolve. In one school of clinical thought, it is proposed that groups often polarize around a central person. Ten different roles which the central person might play are then discussed, including such roles as: the "patriarchal sovereign," the "love object," and the "central hero." (F. Redl, 1942.)

of the positional incumbent; (3) certain subcultural norms and values which arise out of the socialization which takes place in training and orientation for commitment; (4) and a degree of ecological separation according to process or function (specialization or departmentation). Notice that these technical aspects of the work situation implicit in "position" already encompass several factors by which subgroup formation is fostered: proximity of people engaged in similar work activities in the sense described above; common attitudes and values arising out of technical training and/or indoctrination; and perhaps even certain social class similarities which arise from the entrance and training requirements for acceptance into or selection for the position.

The *sociotechnical* dimension of "position" refers to the fact that the total decision-making process, encompassing both problem solving and implementation, requires interaction between individuals occupying specific positions whose work-related interaction reinforces subgrouping and interpersonal choices. Finally, barring incompatible personalities, social relations grow out of contacts flowing from technical and sociotechnical dimensions of work activity. Such social activities, again, reinforce interpersonal choice and subgroupings within the complex organization.

A brief example will make the matter clearer.

John Doe joins XYZ *Corporation as a personnel management trainee. He is assigned to an office on the sixth floor within the Personnel Department. (Proximity.) He finds that most of the other personnel people have been similarly trained in several nearby graduate schools. (Common training, leading to shared concepts, values, and attitudes.) In carrying out his early work assignments, he primarily converses with colleagues within the department. (Shared work activities and sociotechnical interaction.) In the course of several months, he is asked to play golf with several members of the department, and soon the biweekly golf game is a standard recreational item. (Social dimension of position.) These interrelated technical, sociotechnical, and social dimensions of John Doe's formal position as a personnel trainee create all the necessary conditions for viable group structure. This subgroup structure, in turn, results in behaviors and normative content which may or may not be congruent with organizational objectives and the official decision system. John Doe may, for instance become overattached to the personnel "gang," thereby tending to be overdefensive of their policy positions rather than adequately analytical. (Selective focus and/or tunnel vision.) He may tend to interact too exclusively with the personnel group, thereby limiting his exposure to other managers. This limited exposure mitigates the possibility of a promotion to a management position in an area related to but outside the Personnel Department. He may tend to oversell programs initiated inside the department and undervalue proposals originating outside the department. (Suboptimization.)*

The relevant point here is that the type of subgroup, suboptimization, just described should be viewed as the rule rather than an aberration in the typical formal organization, since all the conditions for subgroup formation are present (shared activities, facilitated interactions, and common sentiments). By inserting the positional dimensions parenthetically into classical propositions about group formation, we can see this more clearly. For example:

> The more people associate with one another under conditions of equality (positional congruency and equal organizational influence bases) the more they come to share values and norms, and the more they come to like one another. (B. Berelson and G. A. Steiner, 1964.)
>
> Interaction between persons (due to technical work requirements) leads to sentiments of liking (reinforced by shared professional norms arising out of training in a functional specialization) and this leads to new activities (social), and these in turn mean further interaction. . . . the more frequently persons interact with one another (ecological proximity and socio-technical requirements) the stronger their sentiments of friendship for one another are apt to be. . . . the more frequently persons interact with one another, the more alike in some respects both their activities and sentiments tend to become. (G. C. Homans, 1950, pp. 34–40.)

IMPLICATIONS FOR DECISION MAKING

Organizational subgroups (cliques and informal decision networks), well documented in research studies (Dalton, 1959, p. 20, or Merton in Etzioni, 1961, pp. 48–61), are not then to be seen as solely the result of political struggles for power and influence—a Machiavellian tone that permeates much discussion of informal organization. Rather, such cleavage behavior grows also out of seemingly innocuous processes of organizational life such as assignments to work positions and departmentalization. This implies that the integration of subgroups into an organization structure which is cohesive and possessive of congruent norms throughout all subgroups requires conscious restructuring of interactions away from the pattern of a bureaucratic or formal organization model in order to overcome fundamental propensities toward organizational cleavage.[7]

At the same time, political and affective dimensions are an inextricable aspect of subgroup interaction. Thus, political and affective overtones ultimately color decision-making processes of complex organizations. An organization is not, therefore, a monocratic structure acting as a corporate personality with a simple preference function based solely on

---

[7] The third section of this chapter, dealing with group size, provides further evidence supporting the propensity toward organizational cleavage. Thus, the proposition that cleavage rather than cohesiveness is the typical state of organizational affairs does not rest solely on the "interpersonal choice" dimension of group structure for theoretical justification.

econological dimensions of a rationalistic-choice situation. Attempts to reify organizations as "individual-choice mechanisms" and to ignore socialization within subgroups create an organizational model reinforcing the game of organizational charades where managers pretend to be totally, organizationally rational while actually pursuing subgroup goals.

At this point, we can conclude our treatment of "interpersonal choice" by pointing out several propositions which develop logically from and are congruent with revised organizational theories.

First, membership in organizational work groups should provide for "overlap" so that interaction between members of work groups from several functional areas and several hierarchical levels is facilitated. One theorist talks about this "overlap" as being developed primarily by the supervisors interacting in several groups. (Rensis Likert, 1961, p. 113.) Others argue that overlapping membership should encompass more than one member of a relatively autonomous subgroup in order to provide better representation both from the group to the organization and from the organization to the group. (R. L. Kahn, et al., 1964, pp. 388–392.) (We side with the latter proposition, for reasons which will be developed when we discuss group size in our third section.) In the two cases, the issue is quite similar. Unless the boundaries between the relatively autonomous subgroups are overcome through interactions with people from outside the groups, the increasing propensity for suboptimization is inevitable. Further, this need for overlapping membership is true of subgroups formed through other means than through formal departmentalization. If decision making of a college dean or a corporate vice-president is largely mediated by interaction with the same set of advisors, even though the advisors represent several functional areas, they may soon form the much criticized self-contained managerial oligarchy, relatively closed to other organizational members.

Second, given the increasing complexity of modern organizational decision making, no single expert or specialist can adequately claim total competence. Thus, joint decision making by specialists from several functional areas becomes necessary. However, if the interaction takes the form of power plays between specialist empires, then decision making is generally dysfunctional. Nonetheless, if specialists are generally self-contained within isolated subgroups and seldom interact outside these subgroups, then this pattern of power plays is to be expected. Thus, the overlapping participation, while intermittent, cannot be so infrequent that parochialism remains intact.

Third, recent studies show quite clearly that promotions are largely based on managerial acquaintanceships arising out of frequent sociotechnical interactions rather than based on a broad search process (Alfred, 1967, pp. 159–169). However, if acquaintances are largely confined to subgroup "cronies," then the possibility of adequate consideration of talented personnel from outside the very proximate subgroup is unlikely.

CONCLUSION

From these propositions, it may be concluded the organizational design which best provides for overlapping memberships, facilitating work-relevant interaction, is the task-force or project-group organizational design. Such an organizational design provides for overlapping memberships of short to intermediate duration which bring together decision-relevant groupings of specialists and administrators. Further, such groupings can be juxtaposed with departmentization for routine decision implementation, satisfying the need for overlapping group membership without artificially imposing the burden of "linking" groups solely on the departmental supervisors.

The Functional Roles of Group Members[8]

While interpersonal choices, discussed above, help us understand how individuals draw together, group structure[9] also deals with the interrelationships of the individuals once drawn together and engaged in shared group endeavors. Interaction between individuals, as the group begins to evolve, takes on what become characteristic patterns as the members work toward achievement of their goals. Individuals, for example, tend to specialize within the group, thereby differentiating their behavior from those of other members. Indeed, a collection of individuals actually becomes a group only when its members establish some predictable relationships with each other. Our concern in this section is with research indicating how the pattern or structure of interpersonal roles evolves

[8] The material in this section is adapted from: André L. Delbecq, "The Social-psychology of Executive Roles Re-examined," *Business Perspectives*, vol. 2. no. 3, Spring, 1966.
[9] "Group," as used in this discussion, is not synonymous with "work group" in the sense of a department or formal organizational unit. Rather, "group" is here used as the set of individual employees who interact with each other at a specific point in time for the purpose of sharing in a decision-making situation. Thus, the "group" might be a project team, committee, or informal management cabal whose membership might include managers from several functional areas and several levels of hierarchy.

in a group and with the implications of these findings for the decision process within complex organizations.

For our purposes, "role" may be conceived of as a set of behaviors which are related to group functions, in which the set of behavioral prescriptions are shared and/or enforced. (R. T. Golembiewski, 1962; P. A. Hare, 1962, p. 102.) "Role," thus, becomes the linkage between the individual actor, as a psychological entity, and the distinctly relevant social structure, the group. (T. Parsons, 1951.) Further, organizations consist ultimately of the patterned and concerted activities of their members. Thus considered, each individual's role in the organization consists of his part in the total pattern of interpersonal activity. (R. L. Kahn, et al., 1964, pp. 388–392.)

ROLE SPECIALIZATION AND FUSION

For any task-oriented group to operate successfully, two types of functions are immediately apparent. First, there are *task-instrumental* functions directly related to the group's task: the attainment of resources, the application of these resources to the task, and the processes which underlie both. In decision-making situations, resources consist of information, analysis (evaluation), and insight, etc. Attention to processing in decision making would include, for example, the gathering of information and the developing of solutions and acts which facilitate any problem phase, such as asking questions and providing clarification.

Second, there are *social-emotional* functions, which are concerned with maintaining the group and integrating group members into a satisfying social relationship. The content of behaviors within this area would be affective—emotionally expressive—and would relate to the congeniality and social tone of the group, as acts of courtesy, praise, agreement, joking, etc.

Considerable small-group research has been directed to the study of tendencies toward role separation within problem-solving groups, where the behaviors of individual members are differentiated over time, in terms of: (1) content, whether task-instrumental or social-emotional; (2) prominence, defined as the duration (for example, how long the member speaks); and (3) frequency of his acts[10] (how often he speaks) relating to these two functional areas. In particular, attention has been directed to the analysis of roles of "leaders," that is, of those who contributed in some exceptional way to either problem solving or group

---

[10] *Acts*, as used here, are defined as units of verbal interaction scored according to one of several standard interaction category systems.

congeniality.[11] Although hierarchies of task-instrumental and social-emotional roles may at first appear undifferentiated, there is a tendency, particularly in larger problem-solving groups, for them to separate or differentiate. The most apparent differentiation of informal roles is the gradual, but simultaneous, development of dual leadership: a task leader and a social-emotional leader. (Beene and Sheats, 1948; James, 1956; O. Grusky, 1957; R. F. Bales, in Bales, et al., 1955.) "In group problem-solving, the general picture is one of specialization and complementarity, with idea men concentrating on the task, and playing a more aggressive role, and best liked men concentrating on social-emotional problems, giving rewards and playing a more passive role." (P. E. Slater, 1959.)

In Bales's research, this separation between the three dimensions of interaction-role prominence, task-instrumental roles, and social-emotional roles was characterized as follows:

(A)   Prominence and task-instrumental roles were strongly associated;

(B)   The sociability role was weakly associated with prominence and the task-instrumental role;

(C)   Individuals who ranked highest in individual prominence tended to be ranked relatively low on "liking" and relatively high on "disliking," which suggested the development of a "task-specialist," relatively unconcerned with the "social-emotional" problems of his group; and

(D)   Individuals who were ranked second and third on individual prominence tended to be ranked relatively high on "liking" and low on "disliking" by group members, which suggested the development of a corresponding "social-emotional" specialist, whose function was to drain off antagonism created by the process of problem-solving in the groups studied. (R. F. Bales, in R. F. Bales, et al., 1955.)

Conflicting evidence exists but, in general, this role separation is a recurring theme in research concerned with interpersonal roles in problem-solving groups. (Moment and Zalenznik, 1963, or Etzioni, 1965, pp. 688–699.)

What emerges, then, from the study of ad hoc groups is that groups successful in problem solving often have dual leadership, and that this leadership is generally most effective under conditions of mutual support between these leaders. While these two kinds of leadership may be provided by a single actor, called the "great man" in small-group studies, they tend not to be. This raises serious questions concerning the emphasis on *the* leader (manager) in much of the conventional management literature.

[11] Generally, the research on "leaders" is based on the analysis of the interaction of individuals identified ex post by fellow group members as high contributors of "good ideas" or high contributors to group "congeniality." Observation and reading of the in-process group interaction have also been utilized.

Developmental propensities of groups toward fusion versus differentiation of roles seem intimately related to two variables: (1) personality,
and (2) externally derived role expectations. In terms of personality,
research identifies "great men," possessing substantial degrees of all three
qualities: task ability, individual assertiveness, and social acceptance.
(Borgatta, et al., 1954, pp. 755–759.) Thus, certain developmental sequences and personality traits can be identified which relate to role
fusion. (Moment and Zaleznik, 1963, pp. 688–699.) Recent studies of
business executives within problem-solving groups who assume "great
man" roles generally indicate an admixture of both personality propensities and "positional" influence—status or power which derives from the
holding of a significant position, as defined either hierarchically or culturally. In any given situation, it must be ascertained whether personality
or overachievement in terms of positional roles provides the major
impetus.

The point is that any understanding of managerial roles must take
into account expectations imposed from without, tendencies of personality expressed from within, and specialization of function.

ROLE FUSION AND MANAGERIAL DOMINANCE

Given this very brief introduction to behavioral roles as they evolve
in ad hoc problem-solving groups, we can now begin to examine some
implications of this research for decision making within complex organizations. In doing so, three issues deserve attention: (1) the fusion
of roles implicit in most conceptualizations of an administrator's role;
(2) the dominance of hierarchical managers in group problem solving
within complex organizations; and (3) the problem of stable versus
flexible role definitions as related to organizational structure.

The first two issues—the fact that the managerial role, as classically
conceived, is a fused role and that managers tend to dominate group
problem solving, or decision making, with subordinates—are so inextricably entwined that we can discuss them together.

Obviously, classical management does not conceptualize dual leadership, except that the holistic treatment of informal organization includes
notions of an informal leader. Rather, the supervisory role has been
described as encompassing both the responsibility for task-instrumental
facilitation and social-emotional support to the subordinate group.[12] Inap-
propriately then, this classical perspective does not develop fully the
social-psychological dimensions of required dual-role behavior of man-

[12] Albeit the emphasis on social-emotional support has been developed most
recently, particularly through the "human relations" movement.

agers or leaders,[13] but rather is based on a normative concept of a single, omniscient individual totally responsible for all aspects of work-group decision making.

Nonetheless, individuals vary in their ability to play a given role. (T. R. Sarbin and D. S. Jones, 1955.) While it is not the purpose in this section to discuss the relationship between roles and personality, it is axiomatic to say that expectations for a role are most easily met by an individual whose personality fits the role. However, there are no built-in mechanisms in formal organizations to assure congruence between formal role expectations and the abilities of the individual to play the role. Indeed, it appears entirely unlikely that every supervisory position will be occupied by a "great man" or "star" who can achieve the optimal balance between the requirements of the task-instrumental aspects of decision-group leadership and its social-emotional aspects. Thus, in formal organizational settings, the expectation of role fusion may often relate more to positional expectations than to personality propensities. Some recent research provides clues that would indicate it is easier to classify a manager by his emphasis on either task *or* group maintenance activities than to classify him as being optimally attentive to both behavioral dimensions. (James Mullen, 1965.)

Further, the emphasis in specific formal organizations tends to accentuate one aspect of the leader role at the expense of the other, although some attention to both role dimensions is generally ritually articulated. The notion of the decisive, profit-oriented, result-centered executive—which is the executive profile within many firms—gives greater credence or legitimacy to the task dimension than to the social-emotional dimension of decision groups.[14]

There is also substantial evidence that subordinates expect their supervisors to emphasize the task dimension anyway. In task-oriented small-group studies, task-instrumental effectiveness is a prerequisite for being selected as "leader," ex poste (Golembiewski, 1962, p. 106). Likewise, in studies of employee motivation, satisfaction with the supervisor's task-related supervisory capacity seems more of an issue than nurturant interpersonal relationships (Herzberg, et al., 1961). Also, in field and laboratory studies where both styles of leadership are represented, employees show remarkable adaptability even under conditions of ex-

[13] Note the classical management norm: that the supervisory role should be based on the logic of the formal organization rather than the social-psychological characteristics of the individual occupying the role position. (Victor Thompson, 1961.)

[14] This is not to say that such emphasis is intended to create a vicious, arbitrary, or thoughtless supervisor. But one should not confuse emotional hygiene, civility, a degree of personal warmth, and polite social conventions with social-emotional leadership.

treme, autocratic task leadership (Mullen, 1965, pp. 107–127, or Delbecq, 1963). While no subordinate wishes to remain with a supervisor who is pathological, it is doubtful in light of this recent research that he looks toward the supervisor for fulfillment of all social-emotional leadership needs.

Finally, the fact of the matter is that many situations provide the formal superordinate with little opportunity to compete successfully with informal leaders in the social-emotional sphere. At the extreme, in "total" institutions, such as prisons, custodial mental hospitals, and correctional institutions, the separation between the social-emotional set of the inmates and the duties of supervisors makes it impossible for supervisors to vie for social-emotional leadership. Similar conditions are approached outside "total" institutions in highly task-oriented organizations.[15]

IMPLICATIONS OF FUNCTIONAL ROLE THEORY FOR MANAGEMENT

Against this theoretical background from small-group theory, we can now indicate the central implications of "functional role theory" for the management of decision making within the organization. First, it is very clear that the classical management pattern of "unity of command," in which the managerial leader was to fuse all aspects of leadership into his position, is a social-psychological myth. As just indicated, there is no assurance that any individual manager will be able to play the "great man" role. Further, organizational norms and subordinate expectations make it much more likely that the manager will be a task-instrumental leader. Yet, effective decision making requires that both social-emotional and task-instrumental contributions be included.

Second, there is inadequate provision in classical management for varied interaction *processes* as one moves across varied problem-solving tasks. Thus, the command structure with centrality of communication and control is neither a relevant process for judgmental or creative decision making nor for compromise. (A. L. Delbecq, 1964–65.) One aspect of task-instrumental leadership—attention to appropriate and varied decision-making *processes*—was neglected in classical treatments of super-

[15] There are, of course, instances where just the opposite is true; that is, in religious organizations concerned with socialization and in some social-work occupations, the formal leader is expected to be nurturant and person-centered, despite task pressures. Further, while not developed here, there are also role restrictions on leadership prominence itself. Certain managers may be expected to assume non-leader roles and play a modest part in interaction. Staff officers, junior executives, and student nurses will often find their roles defined in such a way that limited task-instrumental contributions are welcomed, but social-emotional comments may be perceived as out of place and prominence in interaction considered boorish.

visory leadership, which emphasized only ends (profit-related accomplishment) and a single means (centralized control and leadership, which was not a process adequate for all types of organizational decision making). Nor was the "staff" concept a satisfactory modification, since it called upon highly trained organizational members to play a restricted role in organizational decision making quite outside that which would be natural for managers with such broad, potential influence bases. Functional role theory, then, very early provided a theoretical basis for suggesting important modifications of classical management which were necessary if effective decision making within formal organizations was to be adequately facilitated.

Much of the wisdom contained in the early "group dynamics" movement was intended to develop not so much the point that the formal leader of a problem-solving group should be solely responsible for nurturing group members, but, rather, to emphasize that he should be responsible for reorganizing group relationships as the group faced different decision tasks. Thus, employee "participation" and "democratic leadership" were not originally based on the logic of nurturance and happy employees, but on the logic of differentiated task-instrumental processes.[16] What was needed for effective decision making was not a manager who provided for social-emotional needs solely through his own actions, but a manager who facilitated appropriate involvement of subordinates where the logic of the decision-making task demanded their involvement; who was able, on occasions calling for a different type of decision making, to centralize and coordinate communication where it needed centrality and focus for efficient decision implementation; and who was sufficiently mature and free from anxieties to see more active subordinate roles as appropriate for selected phases of decision-making processes rather than as a threat to his own status. A corollary benefit to this pattern of greater subordinate involvement in decision making is the opportunity for other members of the "management team" to play an active social-emotional leader role, mutually supportive of the task leader. This duality of leadership would be impossible given total dominance of the decision-making process by the superordinate manager.

This brings us to the issue of managerial dominance of organizational decision making. Absence of role differentiation may not only be a function of leadership style, but may also be resisted by members who *expect* to have a strong central leader. In one research study of high-level

---

[16] Unfortunately, later careless generalizations and chauvinistic group dynamics practitioners lumped together emotional support and leadership, psychotherapeutic aspects of free and shared communication, etc., with the concept of formal group leadership—errors not currently being made in small-group theory. This point is not sufficiently clear, however, in management literature.

decision-making conferences in business, industry, and government, leadership was shared only when the group had an urgent problem to solve and leadership was weak. Otherwise, the expectation was that the formal superordinate manager or administrator would be the sole, dominant behavioral actor. (L. Berkowitz, 1953.)

Similar propensities toward total supervisory dominance in management decision conferences were obtained in a laboratory study of organizations (Delbecq, 1963). In this latter research, such dominance not only stood in the way of social-emotional leadership roles emerging within the group under conditions of stress and anxiety where they were badly needed, but it also precluded adequate assumption of facilitative task-instrumental roles on the part of subordinates, so that they were unable to contribute viably to creative problem solving. Obviously, a number of factors can contribute to such role expectations: management ideology, personality traits of a dominant leader, and a halo effect gained from programmed or routine task situations where focused leadership is appropriate.

ROLE FLEXIBILITY WITHIN GROUP DECISIONS

Mature individuals are shown by research to be capable of assuming a variety of roles for decision-making purposes. While it is true that certain roles will be more natural to certain personality types, and likewise that fixated personality types can assume only a single role, nonetheless, for the mature adult whose personality profile is not characterized by extremes, it is possible to play a variety of roles in a variety of decision-making situations. (L. Berkowitz, 1956.) He can be a "great man" in certain situations and a non-prominent task-instrumental contributor in other situations, and he can provide social-emotional support in still other situations. Ideally, organization structures should provide opportunity for the assumption of a variety of roles relative to differentiated problem-solving situations. (F. E. Fiedler, 1967, Part IV.)

To assume that the occupant of any particular administrative position will optimally balance both aspects of functional leadership—that is, task-instrumental and social-emotional—seems a dangerous assumption for an empirically based concept of managerial leadership. Likewise, to assume that a leadership style characterized by total dominance by the supervisor is an appropriate decision-making process for all organizational problem solving seems equally foolish.

What is needed in a conceptualization of both managerial leadership and organizational structure is: to admit it is possible both that the process can be flexible and that the role can be varied in order to facilitate adequate decision making, and to provide viable opportunities for shared prominence, so that social-emotional leadership and shared task-instrumental facilitation may arise in problem-solving conferences. It would seem that the task-force concept of organization, or matrix organization, provides a conceptualization of organizational roles and structure congruent with the discussion of managerial leader roles necessary for decision making as developed here (Mee, 1964; Shull, 1965; and Bennis, 1965). Essential to this theory of organization is the opportunity for an individual manager to play a variety of roles in a variety of group processes, across differentiated decision-making situations. While such role playing requires greater maturity, it also seems more congruent with the need for role separation and psychological specialization and the realities involved. A major implication, however, is that the "decisive manager" will reconceive his task-instrumental function so that it involves not merely the making of decisions, but also the management of the decision-making processes.

Finally, once again the logic of this group variable indicates that the task-force organization should provide the opportunity for the less flexible, but nonetheless valuable, "pure" task-instrumental or social-emotional specialist, enabling him to contribute his unique skills to problem solving without the dysfunctions present when he is forced into administrative or coordinative positions which require boundary responsibilities for full-fledged acceptance, advancement, and growth.[17]

Thus, the logic of functional roles as developed in small-group theory becomes one more stream of logic supportive of the need for new concepts of both managerial roles and organizational structure in the direction of the more organic models of the task-force or matrix organization. It further indicates that the student of decision making who relies on classical conceptions of managerial leadership as a guide for structuring all decision processes in the firm does so with considerable peril.

The Effects of Group Size on Decision Making

In the preceding section we were concerned with the impact of individual differences in role-taking on small-group functioning and, therefore, on decision making within organizations. To analyze this *individual*-group relationship, we examined how individual role differences affect the group and its decision making. We now want to look at the other side of the relationship and demonstrate how the group acts on the individual and his decision making. To demonstrate this *group*-individual relationship we can take a most obvious and parsimonious aspect

---

[17] The implications of these concepts for formal reward systems and concepts of hierarchy are significant, but they will not be elaborated here.

of group structure, namely, group size, and examine the implications of size for decision making.

Small-group theory has been concerned with size as a mediating variable affecting: (1) the distribution of interaction, (2) the content of interaction, and (3) affectional, that is, emotional and expressive, overtones of the interaction. These small-group theoretical concerns have a direct bearing on the "nature" of relationships between personnel *within* organizations. (Delbecq, 1968.)

GROUP SIZE AND THE SOCIAL-PSYCHOLOGICAL COMPLEXITY OF INTERACTIONS

Fundamental to the issue of group size is the mathematical principle set forth by Graicunas (A. Graicunas, in Gulick and Urwick, 1937, pp. 181–188): that as the number of group members increases arithmetically, the number of possible interrelationships increases geometrically. This relationship is given by the formula: $C = N(2N/2 + N - 1)$. Here C is the total number of possible interrelationships. It is clear from the mathematics of group size, as set forth by Graicunas, that size *is* a limiting condition on the amount and quality of communication that can take place among group members. Hence, group size tends to affect the character of interpersonal orientations that members develop toward each other.

Research clearly indicates that as group size increases, it becomes more difficult for each member of a group to keep every other member in mind as a separate, differentiated person. The ability to attend to each member as an individual falls beyond the number of six or seven. In groups larger than six or seven, individuals tend to be thought of as members of subgroups, "camps," or factions. (A. P. Hare, 1962, p. 228.) The reason is quite apparent.

Time "available" to each member during a meeting of fixed length decreases as size increases. The result is that each group member is forced to maintain a more complicated social relationship, but has less time in which to do so. Consequently, group members resort to a fundamental psychological defense mechanism: They simplify the situation. Rather than pay attention to each of the other group members as individual persons, they lump the group members into classifications. Such classifications for other group members develop spontaneously from either the particular problem-solving situation in progress or from the group's composition, for example, oldtimers and newcomers, conservatives and liberals, or supporters of the issues and opponents of the issues. Thus, by paying attention to selective aspects of group communications, such as supporting viewpoints, or to selective spokesmen, for example, the dominant conservative spokesman, rather than attending the unique characteristics of each of the other group members as individuals, the complex field of stimuli engendered by the enlarged-group membership and increased communication is reduced to manageable proportions.

A further mechanism for simplification of the potentially complex relationships is to rely on a "leader." The appearance of a dominant individual who becomes *the* focal point of interaction can permit a reduction in the psychological complexity of the group by reducing the pattern of interaction to a series of paired relationships between the leader and each member of the group. (A. P. Hare, 1962, p. 230.) Research supports this tendency for communication to become centralized in a "leader" as size increases. Further, as size increases, the demands on leadership become more numerous and exacting and member tolerance for increasing leader-centered direction of group activity becomes greater. (J. K. Hemphill, 1950.)

This tendency toward leader centrality in both communication and direction is also related to the emotional context of the interaction. As the size of the group increases, the strength of affectional ties (congenial, emotional feelings) and the intimacy of interaction decreases. (G. L. Coyle, 1930; E. E. Kinney, 1953.) This lack of warmth is generated at the same point that personal anxiety develops. For, as size increases, an increasing proportion of members report feelings of threat and inhibitions of impulses to participate. This is due both to the complexity of the situation and to the increasing possibility of negative feedback related to the enlarged number of "evaluators." (J. R. Gibb, 1951.) Directive leadership places the responsibility for mitigating complexity and absorbing criticisms upon the most active participant and allows other members to withdraw into passive roles. Indeed, research shows that only the more forceful members attempt to express and articulate ideas in larger groups (Bales and Borgatta, in Hare, et al., 1955; Carter, in Guetzkow, 1951).

Relative to distribution of interaction, then, as size increases, the most active participator—the leader—tends to become increasingly differentiated from other group members, in terms of initiating and receiving the majority of verbal-communication acts. Other members become increasingly undifferentiated in the same terms, and the tendency toward factionalism and dissatisfaction increases. (A. P. Hare, 1952; B. M. Bass and M. Fay-Tyler Norton, 1951.)

GROUP SIZE AND THE CONTENT OF COMMUNICATION

Naturally, the above-mentioned reactions to group complexity affect the *content* of communication as well as its distribution among members. For example, the frequency of certain categories of communication acts appears to vary with group size. In groups of sizes two to seven, the rate of giving information and suggestions increases as size increases, while the rate of asking for opinion, giving opinion, and showing agreement decreases. Thus, as size increases, there is a tendency toward a more mechanical method of introducing information, for example, by round-robin procedures, as well as evidence of a less sensitive exploration of the point of view of others. Further, as size increases, there are more direct attempts to control others and reach a solution regardless of whether or not all group members indicate agreement. Part of this lack of sensitivity to the viewpoint of other members in larger groups relates to time constraints. However, even more salient, careful attention to the multiple viewpoints in larger groups calls for considerable computational ability, great psychological concentration, and empathy—in each case to a degree beyond the capacities of most individuals.

Consequently, unresolved differences of opinion appear more tolerable in larger groups. Consensus appears as a decreasing function of group size. Differences of opinion that would be resolved through clarification, patient discussion, and analysis in smaller groups are resolved through political pressure and coalition formation in larger groups. Nor do members of larger groups expect that differences will be "ironed out." As size increases, rates of showing tension due to disagreement may decrease, being displaced by humor or some other means of reacting to lack of consensus—rather than conflict being reduced by resolution of differences of opinion. (R. F. Bales and E. F. Borgatta, 1955; A. P. Hare, 1962.)

At this point, we may summarize the relationship of size to the distribution and content of interaction developed above as follows:

1. The frequency and duration of member interaction are decreasing functions of group size. (P. H. Fisher, 1953.)

2. Affective (emotional) ties are a decreasing function of group size. (G. L. Coyle, 1930; E. E. Kinney, 1953.)

3. Leader centrality and domination are increasing functions of group size.

4. Relative to problem solving, increasing group size, *ceteris paribus*, seems to be inversely related to the degree of intricate interpersonal feedback; that is, an increase in group size decreases the possibility of mutual transmission of cognitive clues between members. (H. J. Leavitt and R. A. H. Mueller, 1951.) Consequently, political rather than analytical solutions to disagreement increase with enlarged group size.

5. As a consequence of the above, there is a tendency for "natural-state" groups to approach size two (J. James, 1951), although increased experience in larger groups or increased socialization within fluid groups does seem to increase the tolerance for slightly larger groups.[18]

[18] Thus, individuals from rural backgrounds form smaller groups than individuals from urban areas; and younger individuals form smaller groups than older individuals (A. B. Hollingshead, 1941; J. Piaget, 1932).

The above discussion of the effects of size on group processes leaves the impression that there are inexorable tendencies toward the reduction of group size. While these tendencies are real, countervailing pressures for group enlargement are also experienced. Benefits can be achieved by increasing the size of the group, since such enlargement increases the ability and resources to be brought to bear on group tasks. These benefits can be tersely summarized as follows:

1. Benefits resulting from summated resources:
   a. An increase in technical skills,
   b. An increase in energy.
2. Benefits derived from increased cognitive resources for problem solving:
   a. An increase in the number of items of information that can be absorbed and recalled,
   b. An increase in the number of critical judgments available to correct errors in inference and analysis,
   c. An increase in the number of suggested solution strategies,
   d. An increase in the range of values brought to bear on the problem,
   e. An increase in psychological attention due to social facilitation.[19]
3. Benefits resulting from organizational surplus:
   a. An increase in group size may allow for division of labor and specialization.

However, these potential benefits may be mitigated by diminishing returns due to:

1. Increased problems of coordination,
2. Increased feelings of threat, or inhibition of impulses to participate, due to the larger-size group and the increased complexity of relationships,
3. Distraction from attention to problem solving, due to attention toward social-emotional relationships, and
4. Increased problems in reaching consensus.

Potential benefits may also be mitigated by other structural properties of the organizational environment, such as inadequate subordinate status. For example, research indicates that the potential benefits of increased group size may not materialize as a result of intimidation by the supervisor or role definitions calling for subordinates to respond passively to the superior. Thus, the status relationships existing in formal organiza-

---

[19] "Social facilitation" refers to the observed tendency for individuals to apply themselves more diligently to the task given the presence of others in the immediate situation.

tions may result in creativity of the group failing to exceed the boundaries of the conceptual capacity of the formal leader. (A. L. Delbecq, 1964–1965, pp. 255–268, 32–43.)

We shall suggest shortly some practical implications of these considerations for the management of decision processes within complex organizations. However, before doing so, the question of the behavior of individuals within small groups of specified size needs to be considered.

BEHAVIOR IN SMALL GROUPS OF SPECIFIED SIZES

THE DYAD.[20] Groups of size two are shown in research to possess the following characteristics:

1. High rates of tension and anxiety;

2. High rates of disagreement and antagonism, or, contrariwise, deliberate attempts to avoid disagreement and antagonism;

3. High rates of asking for opinion;

4. Low rates of giving opinion; and

5. Concentration on exchange of information and agreement. (R. F. Bales and E. F. Borgatta, 1955; H. Becker and R. H. Useem, 1942.)

These interaction characteristics evidence the delicate balance of power and the intricacy of the relationship within a two-person group. Each person in the dyad is under pressure to behave in a manner so as not to cause the other to withdraw. Unlike groups of any other size, there are no "group norms" except those which develop between the two individuals. There is no public opinion or majority to which to appeal for validation of a position. Nor are there any other members available to mediate in seeking solutions to disagreement. Further, each person in the dyad possesses a potential veto (withdrawal), which, if exercised, can preclude task completion. All of these considerations make problem solving within the dyad a tenuous matter.

As if these difficulties were not sufficiently problematic, there is the further difficulty that interaction in two-person groups is highly personalized. While one can speak for and be identified with a "position" in a larger group, thus separating "self" from an intellectual point of view, in two-person groups rare is the member of a dyad who separates the position spoken for from the person speaking. This lack of separation between the individual group member and any position or opinion which he might hold leads to a highly charged emotional atmosphere in two-

---

[20] The "dyad" is defined as a pair of individuals maintaining psychologically significant relationships.

person groups, where the social-emotional tone is inextricably related to the verbal communications of each actor.

Consequently, as a result of all these pressures, the members of a dyad tend to deliberately avoid emotionally charged disagreement. They restrict communication to areas where a cautious exploration of the members' viewpoints, or asking for opinions, indicates probable consensus. Where the members of a dyad do find themselves in disagreement, however, they display high rates of tension and inability to develop alternative analytical frameworks or compromise strategies to resolve their disagreement.

Thus, in the smallest of groups, favorable and intimate social-emotional relations are conspicuous by both their presence and their absence. In the long run, the dyad's members must either develop a shared frame of reference or repress disagreement by a mutually respected truce, while still maintaining respect and affection for the individual person involved.

THE TRIAD. The balance of power in the three-person group is equally pronounced, but of a different nature. The power of the majority over the minority is especially marked in the triad, since in this sized group, any minority must be that of a single person, who is thus left isolated without the support of any other group member. Further, the basic strategy for the solution of conflict is not sensitive analysis, but rather one of coalition formation—divide and conquer—isolating and intimidating the minority member. The problem of reconciling the needs of the third person in triads of long duration is handled by means of shifting coalitions differing from one disagreement to another, so as to protect any one member from becoming a permanent isolate. However, it is obviously difficult to achieve a pattern where active support versus disagreement will occur with equal frequency, in order to make the triad equally supportive of each member.

ODD- VERSUS EVEN-SIZED GROUPS. Groups of even size (four or six) are shown in research to have higher rates of disagreement and antagonism and lower rates of asking for suggestion—evidence of lack of openness to conflict resolution through compromise or analysis—than do groups of odd size (three, five, or seven). These effects are attributed to the fact that in even sizes, a division of the group into two subparts of equal size (an extended dyad) is possible. Therefore, of course, these effects are less marked as size increases, since the possibility of an even opinion split decreases. (R. F. Bales and E. F. Borgatta, 1955.)

Having looked at both the problem of psychological complexity of large groups and the problem of restrictive behavioral patterns in small groups of specified size, we can now begin to suggest some implications for the management of decision processes within organizations and provide some reflections relative to the classical "span of control" thesis.

OPTIMAL SIZE FOR PROBLEM SOLVING. The implication of the above discussion relative to optimal group size for problem-solving purposes, where inter-member social facilitation and careful analytical or evaluative feedback are desired, shows small-group research to be quite supportive of the classical span-of-control hypothesis. In groups of less than five participants, satisfaction drops off, as a result of strains of face-to-face relationships implicit in the special characteristics of dyadic and triadic interaction, odd-even effects, and overexposure—the fact that the participant cannot withdraw quietly from a position, let alone speak for a position, without group attention being prominently focused upon him. (P. E. Slater, 1959.) In groups larger in size than five, satisfaction tends to drop off, as a result of restrictions on participation caused largely by time constraints; increased aggressiveness, impulsiveness, and competitiveness on the part of more dominant members; withdrawal by more passive members; increased tendencies toward leader centralization; and the increased probability of clique formation. Therefore, groups of five—and, to a lesser extent, seven—seem to possess these special advantages:

1. A strict deadlock is not possible, given the odd number of members;

2. The group tends to split into a majority of three and a minority of two, so that a minority position does not isolate an individual member;

3. The group appears large enough for members to shift roles, withdraw from embarrassing positions, and shift coalitions, thus minimizing problems of smaller groups, but

4. Is small enough to allow even more reticent members to play an active role in the discussion.

This is not, of course, an endorsement of narrow spans of control for purposes of implementation and control of predetermined action plans nor a rule of thumb for the design of formal organizational structures.[21] It is, rather, an endorsement of the need for smaller groups in the decision-making processes which underlie many action plans, where a single manager does not possess sufficient competence to unilaterally "decide" or "solve" the problem and a managerial group, task

[21] We have deliberately not addressed the issue of formal organization structure, which is a broader issue beyond the scope of this treatment.

force, conference, or committee is consequently to be involved in the decision-making process. In this restricted sense, the span-of-control thesis seems quite congruent with social-psychological characteristics of five- and seven-man groups. There are, of course, other implications for the management of decision-making situations contained in our discussion of small-group theory aside from this notion of optimal group size for problem solving.

We shall focus on some of these implications by discussing interpersonal and intra-group conflict as it relates to the above propositions concerning the dynamics of group size.

ORGANIZATIONAL CONFLICT AND GROUP SIZE. Management theory has been much castigated for failing to develop an adequate frame of reference for dealing with conflict within organizations (Krupp, 1961). In general, where conflict has been confronted in management literature, it has been dealt with largely through theory which leaves much of the social psychology of conflict resolution to the intuitions of the artful manager. It would seem appropriate, therefore, to conclude this discussion by suggesting some implications for the management of conflict within decision-making structures inside organizations.

THE OPEN-DOOR POLICY. One notorious method of dealing with organizational conflict is for the superordinate to suggest that disagreement with policy, procedures, or objectives can be "dealt with directly by coming to my office—my door is always open." However sincere the manager might be, and however comforting his philosophy might be to him personally, our earlier discussion would suggest that this approach is most inadequate.

The characteristics of dyadic interaction, as shown above, such as high tension, inability to deal viably with conflict, etc., make the two-person group a poor vehicle for the honest resolution of differences of opinion. When we add to these difficulties of natural-state dyads the hierarchical implications of superordination, the problems are significantly compounded. The senior manager possesses greater information, greater status, and control over formal rewards and sanctions important to the subordinate. Any one of the above influence variables is usually sufficient to propel a superior into a dominant role in dyadic interaction. This unequal power, coupled with all the other difficulties of dyadic communication, makes it doubtful that serious disagreement will be openly aired by the subordinate.[22]

[22] Indeed, even in larger-group settings, research shows subordinates have great difficulty in articulating honest disagreement with superiors. (Chris Argyris, 1966; André L. Delbecq, 1963.)

PARLIAMENTARY DEMOCRACY. Similarly, general staff meetings, like faculty meetings, large board meetings, etc., tend to be equally ineffective and intimidating in the handling of conflict. To begin with, if the meeting is formally organized, a "proposal" or "motion" by a committee chairman, high-status officer, or the executive who calls the meeting often opens the discussion of the issue. This is an ineffective way of dealing with disagreement in general, since it begins with a conclusion rather than a sensitive exploration of the problem. (N. R. F. Maier, 1963.)

More pertinent to our discussion of group size, however, is the evaluation of probable subordinate-manager response. Suppose twelve executives are present. (If the group is larger, the difficulties are compounded.) We can expect, from our previous discussion, that only the more aggressive and vocal executives will speak. However, if the proponent of the original proposal or motion has conferred with colleagues, as is usually the case, several other executives will have been involved in the development of the proposal. Consequently, our dissenting executive who opposes the proposal faces not merely a single proponent, but a coalition of colleagues who have already ego-identified with the conclusion which they have presented in "proposal" or "motion" form. Although several other members of the group may privately agree with the objection to the proposal voiced by the dissenter, they are likely to be doubly intimidated and remain silent for two reasons. First, the size of the group will make them hesitant to speak, as shown earlier. Second, the rapid and articulate responses of the colleagues of the individual who proposed the motion, who rise rapidly to provide support, will give the appearance of consensus, since only a few people speak in large meetings, and the several persons who shared in developing the proposal and who do speak provide support for the motion. It is unlikely, therefore, that the vocal opponent will receive much support from other hesitant group members.

The superordinate can later, in an "open door" dyadic consultation, point out to the hesitant or recalcitrant dissenter that "we discussed the matter openly before the entire staff, and majority opinion obviously supported our conclusion. Surely, you believe in democratic processes!" Even a novice, "Machiavellian" executive can thus use large-group meetings to present a façade of participation, but can count on the dynamics of larger-group size and coalitions supporting carefully planned proposals to weigh in favor of his ability to impose his motion or proposal on the group.

GROUP SIZE AND CONFLICT. In general, then, neither heart-to-heart dyadic talks nor large "democratic" assemblies provide a satisfactory group vehicle for dealing viably with disagreement within the organization, since both size situations create power dynamics repressing dissent. Disagreement is more viable when the factions are represented in a meeting where no faction is an isolated minority, but where the minority interacts within a group size that is small enough for each minority spokesman to speak comfortably. In terms of size alone, a group of five to seven, where the minority consists of more than an isolated single person, seems favorable for honest dealing with disagreement. Obviously, other group inputs to facilitate creative disagreement are necessary, too—a definition of roles that legitimates disagreement, the right of the minority to veto premature decisions until some satisfactory compromise arises, assurances of a sufficient status and influence base for the minority faction, etc. Relative to the size variable, however, it is clear that neither large nor very small groups are satisfactory vehicles for bringing disagreement into the open, however democratic the philosophy and rationale for the inappropriate group size.

CONCLUSION

Clearly size is but one structural variable which the successful manager must manipulate as he administers the decision-making processes within his organization. Group behavior cannot be determined on the basis of this single variable. Nonetheless, the number of individuals who are involved in the decision-making process at any point of time is a critical dimension of group structure and will affect the nature of the interaction processes between managerial decision makers. Since the invitation list for most meetings is usually a matter for the manager to determine, size is generally within the control of the manager calling a meeting, conference, or consultation. Unless the manager is aware of the dynamics of group size, as they affect the emotional tone, distribution, and content of interaction, he may inadvertently invite too few or too many participants into the decision-making web, and afterward complain: "Committees just don't work!"

The Effects of Group Task on Group Behavior

Having talked about group formation, group roles, and the effects of group size on decision making, we are now ready to sketch out the direct relationship between group structure and group process and decision tasks within the firm.

Recent theory concerned with group problem solving suggests that different types of decision making require different group structures and processes. The administrator who "manages" the decision-making process must, therefore, organize the executive team in different ways as he deals with the variety of decision-making situations within the firm. (Delbecq, 1967.)

Every practicing administrator is well aware of these qualitative differences in the problem-solving situations which he and his management team face. Further, even without conscious effort on his part, the management group will often change its pattern of communication, and individual managers will adjust their roles, as the management team faces different tasks. Research evidence shows that, over time, problem-solving groups tend to adjust their behavior in keeping with changes in the nature of group problem solving. (H. Guetzkow and H. Simon, 1955; Carzo, 1963.)

On the other hand, the process of adjustment to new decision-making situations is often slow, usually incomplete, and occasionally nonexistent. Managers develop expectations about appropriate behavior in decision-making meetings with their superiors, so that their behavior falls into a pattern with limited variability, which may be appropriate for some types of decision making but highly inappropriate for other decision-making situations. (L. Berkowitz, 1953; A. Delbecq, 1964.) However, if the manager is highly sensitive to differences in the decision-making tasks faced by the management team and can verbally redefine both his own and his subordinates' roles in a fashion congruent with the new decision-making situation, research indicates that the management group can much more readily change its behavior as the result of such role redefinition in order to adjust to a new decision-making situation. (A. Delbecq, 1965.)

The purpose of this section is to set forth three decision-making strategies, each of which is tailored to a different type of problem-solving situation encountered within the firm. Further, each strategy will be examined to determine the degree to which it differs from the logic of classical organization models. It is hoped that this examination of the three different strategies will fulfill the following purposes:

1. The administrator will become more sensitive to the kind of group structure and process which each of the three problem-solving tasks demands.
2. The problems of implementing the strategies within a traditional formal organization culture will be clearer.
3. The implications for the redesign of traditional formal organization models to facilitate greater flexibility for problem solving can be suggested.

THE RELEVANCE OF "TASK" FOR GROUP STRUCTURE

Since the body of this chapter proposes that managers should reorganize group structure and process as they face different types of decision tasks, a word about the relevance of task as a variable around which to construct "organization" is appropriate.

It is axiomatic to say that individual behavior is goal directed (H. J. Leavitt and R. A. H. Mueller, 1964, pp. 8–9); likewise, that group behavior is purposeful or goal directed as well. (R. T. Golembiewski, 1962, p. 181.)

The task of a group is normally thought of, however, only in terms of the stated goal of the group's activity. Thus, there are familiar typologies of groups based on stated goals. For example, Wolman classifies groups as being: Instrumental Groups, which individuals join for the satisfaction of "to take" needs, for example, business associations; Mutual Acceptance Groups, in which "give" and "take" motives are important, for example, friendship relations; and Vectorial Groups, which people join for the purpose of serving a lofty goal. (B. Wolman, 1953.)

Another typology dealing with organizations as macro groups is that of Scott and Blau, who speak of: Mutual Benefit Associations, where the prime beneficiary is the membership; Business Concerns, where the owner is the prime beneficiary; Service Organizations, where the client group is the prime beneficiary; and Commonweal Organizations, where the prime beneficiary is the public at large. (P. Blau and W. Scott, 1962.)

What is not immediately apparent in each of these descriptive typologies is that task, as a variable, affects several dimensions of the system, regardless of whether one is referring to a small group or a large organization, including:

1. Group structure: In terms of the relationship between the individual members.

2. Group roles: In terms of the behavior required of individual group members which is necessary to facilitate task accomplishment.

3. Group process: In terms of the manner of proceeding toward goal accomplishment.

4. Group style: In terms of the social-emotional tone of interpersonal relationships, for example, the amount of stress of individual members, the congeniality of interpersonal relations, and the perceived consequences of individual and group success or failure.

5. Group norms: Relative to each of the preceding four dimensions.

Thus, in treating task as merely the end goal, many of the theoretical as well as the practical implications of the group's or organization's tasks are not made explicit.

For example, when mutual benefit organizations are compared with business concerns, one would expect the former to be characterized by greater dispersion of power (structure), broader membership participation in goal setting (roles and process), greater emotional support of individual members (style), and stronger egalitarianism (norms).

In a similar fashion, the problem-solving "task" faced by a particular managerial team, within a particular organization, at a particular point of time likewise must affect the structure, roles, process, style, and norms of the management team if the group is to optimally organize itself to deal with its task (W. C. Schultz, 1952).

STRATEGIES FOR GROUP PROBLEM SOLVING

Against this background, we can now proceed directly to classify decision situations as found in groups and organizations, and to specify group strategies implied in behaviorally oriented group and organization studies appropriate for dealing with each of the situations.[23]

STRATEGY ONE: ROUTINE DECISION MAKING. (This strategy is directly related to "cell 1" organizational strategy in Chapter 6.) The first decision situation with which we will deal is the routine decision-making situation. In Simon's terminology, this is the "programmed" decision situation; in Thompson's terminology, the "computational" decision (J. Thompson and A. Tuden, 1959; H. Simon, 1960). Here the organization or group agrees upon the desired goal, and technologies exist to achieve the goal. In such a situation, the following strategy can be specified as consistent with behavioral models:

1. Group structure: The group is composed of specialists, with a co-ordinator (leader).

2. Group roles: Behavior is characterized by independent effort, with each specialist contributing expertise relative to his own specialty, including the coordinator (leader), who specializes in coordination across task phases.

3. Group process: At the beginning of the planning period, specialists, together with the coordinator, jointly discuss the productivity objectives. Subsequently, excepting occasional joint meetings to review progress, coordination of specialist endeavors is generally obtained by means of dyadic (two-person) communication between individual specialists and their coordinator, or through horizontal communication between specialists.

4. Group style: Relatively high stress is characteristic, which stress is

---

[23] The reader should be clearly forewarned that each of the strategies is the author's own conceptualization. While an extensive review of the literature, both theoretical and empirical, underlies each strategy, it is not meant to be implied that the strategy represents a model about which scholars universally agree. Rather, the strategies represent the theoretical position of the author, which is consistent with much of the literature but is admittedly open to question and refinement.

achieved through quality and quantity commitments and time constraints, agreed upon in joint consultation at the beginning of the planning period. Responsibility is decentralized within areas of specialization, but coordination is centralized in the coordinator.

5. Group norms: Norms are characterized by professionalism, or high sense of individual responsibility and craftsmanship; commitment to shared team objectives relative to quantity and quality of output; and economy and efficiency.

The above strategy evidences both similarity and dissimilarity when compared with classical organizational models. It is similar in that there is a clear division of labor, functional and structural specialization—specialization in work, and between work and coordination—and centralized coordination.

On the other hand, this "optimal" model is dissimilar in several significant ways. To begin with, responsibility is obtained primarily through team commitments to group objectives, dealing with both the quantity and quality of the output. This commitment, elicited through joint discussion between the specialists and the coordinator at the beginning of the planning period, places responsibility on both the team members and the coordinator, rather than locating responsibility solely in the coordinator.

Control is obtained in two ways. First, the coordinator provides the feedback mechanism for the team by monitoring the progress of individual specialists to assure conformity to shared productivity and time objectives. Situations where actual performance deviated from prior commitments are brought to the shared attention of the team, who institute appropriate correction measures. Thus, discipline rests upon joint commitments rather than upon superordinate sanctions.[24] Second, because motivation is task intrinsic, specialists are "normatively" expected to be "self-controlled" through professional, reference-group standards. Authority is likewise decentralized, based upon specialist expertise and shared norms.

Since responsibility, authority, and discipline are shared within the management team, there is less status disparity between the coordinator and the specialist than is the case between supervisor and subordinates in traditional organization models. Indeed, coordination is seen as a type of specialization, rather than as a function of superior personal attributes or positional status. As a consequence, there is a propensity for fluid changes in group personnel; different task experts bring to bear their differentiated competences at different points of time as the

---

[24] For a treatment of the manner in which group norms control individual behavior, see Chapter 4.

group encounters various phases of decision making in the completion of a project. Further, the role of the coordinator may shift between the specialists on occasions, as the coordination requirements demand different admixtures of skills at various phases of project management.

Admittedly, the strategy assumes high-quality personnel in terms of both task skills and interpersonal skills. Further, it requires a degree of autonomy for both individual specialists and each specialist team, which autonomy must be predicated on personal and organizational maturity. It also assumes that the objectives of the organization and each group can be integrated into a meaningful, internally consistent ends-means chain, where, at each level and between individual areas, objectives can be translated in terms of appropriate technologies.

Nonetheless, although a "pure" strategy—best approximated in project management, matrix management, or task-force groups—movement toward such a model for structuring groups dealing with "routine" tasks appears to be capable of avoiding many of the dysfunctions of classical organizational models while capturing the advantages of division of labor, specialization, centralized coordination, and task-intrinsic motivation.

STRATEGY TWO: CREATIVE DECISION MAKING. (This decision situation is directly related to "cell 4" organizational strategy as discussed in Chapter 6.) The second decision situation with which we will deal is the creative decision-making situation. Here we are talking about decision making which in Simon's terminology is "heuristic" and in Thompson's terminology is "judgmental" (H. Simon and A. Newell, 1958; J. Thompson and A. Tuden, *op. cit.*). The central element in the decision making is the lack of an agreed-upon method of dealing with the problem; this lack of certitude may relate to incomplete knowledge of causation or lack of an appropriate solution strategy. In such a situation, the following strategy can be specified as consistent with behavioral models (W. Scott, 1965; L. Cummings, 1965; V. Thompson, 1965; G. Steiner, 1965; N. Maier, 1963):

1. Group structure: The group is composed of heterogeneous, generally competent personnel, who bring to bear on the problem diverse frames of reference, representing channels to each relevant body of knowledge (including contact with outside resource personnel bringing to bear on the problem expertise not encompassed by the organization), with a leader who facilitates creative, or heuristic, processes.

2. Group roles: Behavior is characterized by each individual exploring with the entire group all ideas, no matter how intuitively and roughly formed, which bear on the problem.

3. Group processes: The problem-solving process is characterized by:
  a. Spontaneous communication between members, that is, not focused in the leader;
  b. Full participation by each member;
  c. Separation of idea generation from idea evaluation;
  d. Separation of problem definition from generation of solution strategies;
  e. Shifting of roles, so that interaction which mediates problem solving —particularly search activities and clarification by means of constant questioning directed to both individual members and the whole group— is not the sole responsibility of the leader;
  f. Suspension of judgment and avoidance of early concern with solutions, so that emphasis is on analysis and exploration rather than on early solution commitment.

4. Group style: The social-emotional tone of the group is characterized by:
  a. A relaxed, nonstressful environment;
  b. Ego-supportive interaction, where open give-and-take between members is at the same time courteous;
  c. Behavior which is motivated by interest in the problem rather than concern with short-run payoff;
  d. Absence of penalties attached to any espoused idea or position.

5. Group norms:
  a. Are supportive of originality and unusual ideas and allow for eccentricity;
  b. Seek behavior which separates source from content in evaluating information and ideas;
  c. Stress a nonauthoritarian view, with a relativistic view of life and independence of judgment;
  d. Support humor and undisciplined exploration of viewpoints;
  e. Seek openness in communication, where mature, self-confident individuals offer "crude" ideas to the group for mutual exploration without threat to the individual for "exposing" himself;
  f. Deliberately avoid credence to short-run results, or short-run decisiveness;
  g. Seek consensus, but accept majority rule when consensus is unobtainable.[25]

---

[25] In the development of the above model, we have consciously avoided the issue of "nominal" groups, where members work without verbal interaction in generating solution strategies, versus "interacting" groups. While evidence favors "nominal" groups in generating ideas, the question as to the appropriateness of the nominal group strategy for the total decision process, that is, evaluation as well as idea generation, remains open.

Further, the experimental tasks used in the studies may be different in kind from organizational decision making. In any event, the above model seems quite adaptable to separation into nominal and interacting processes at various phases, using modifications which do not vitiate the general tenor of the model. For a discussion of nominal versus interacting groups, see: A. H. Leader, 1967; P. Taylor, P. Berry, and C. Block, 1958; V. H. Vroom, L. D. Grant, and T. S. Cotton, 1969.

Obviously, the above prescription for a strategy to deal with creativity does not easily complement classical organization theory. Structural differentiation and status inequality (other than achieved status within the group) are de-emphasized. The decisive, energetic, action-oriented executive is a normative misfit. Decisions evolve quite outside the expected frame of reference of the "pure" task specialist. Communication is dispersed, rather than focused in a superior or even a coordinator. Motivation is mostly task-intrinsic, the pleasure being much more in the exploration than in an immediately useful outcome.

Indeed, the very personnel who thrive by excellent application and execution of complex technologies in the first strategy find the optimal decision rules for the second strategy unnatural, unrealistic, idealistic, and slow.

Nonetheless, although all members of any organization will not find both of the strategies equally comfortable, it can be expected that most organizational members can approximate the strategy, given appropriate role definitions. The point, here, is that the group structure and process which are called for to facilitate creativity are intrinsically different from our first strategy. While the first strategy called for an internally consistent team of complementary specialists who are "action"-oriented, the second strategy calls for a heterogeneous collection of generalists—or at least generically wise specialists not restricted to the boundaries of their own specialized frame of reference, and even not necessarily of the immediate group or organization—who are deliberately and diagnostically patient in remaining problem-centered. The membership, roles, processes, style, and norms of strategy 2 are more natural to the scientific community, or a small subset thereof, than to the practicing executive.

The general implications, however, must await the exposition of the third strategy.

STRATEGY THREE: NEGOTIATED DECISION MAKING. (This strategy is most closely associated with the concerns of Chapter 8.) The third decision situation with which we will deal is the negotiated decision-making strategy. In this instance, we are concerned with a strategy for dealing with opposing factions who, because of differences in norms, values, or vested interests, stand in opposition to each other, concerning either ends or means or both.[26] Organization theory has never given much attention to groups in conflict. One element was, of course, the existence of monocratic authority. At some level in the hierarchical system, authority to "decide" was to be found. Parties representing various opinions might be given a hearing, but, ultimately, Manager X was to make

[26] In this respect, we assume a position different from Thompson and Tuden in their earlier model, who posit that "Compromise" decision making is predicated on disagreement about ends. (Thompson and Tuden, op. cit.)

the decision. Another element in classical thought which precluded open conflict was the conviction, however utopian, that conflict was merely symptomatic of inadequate analysis. Adequate problem solving would surely show that the conflict was artificial, and that an integrative decision could be reached. Thus, the study of mechanisms for negotiation between groups in conflict was left to the student of political science and social conflict and excluded from organizational models.

Nonetheless, the realities of conflict have been ubiquitous. Present models encourage the sublimation of conflict, veiling it in portended rationality. As one wag expressed the matter, "If people don't agree with me, it isn't that I am wrong, or that they are right, but merely that I haven't been clear." In spite of Trojan efforts at "clear communication," the elimination of all conflict through analysis is, indeed, a utopian desire. There have been, and will be, instances where the organization finds itself encompassing two "camps," each supported by acceptable values and logic, and each committed to a different course of action, relative to either means or ends or both. The question remains, then, What would be an appropriate strategy in those cases where "analysis" cannot provide an acceptable solution to both parties, since the disparate opinion or positions are based on assumptions and premises not subject to total decision integration?

The following strategy can be specified:

1. Group structure: The group is composed of proportional representation of each faction (but with the minority never represented by less than two persons), with an impartial formal chairman.[27]

2. Group roles: Each individual conceives of himself as a representative of his faction, seeking to articulate and protect dominant concerns of the group he represents, while at the same time negotiating for an acceptable compromise solution.

3. Group processes: The problem-solving process is characterized by:
   a. Orderly communication mediated by the chairman, providing opportunity for each faction to speak, but avoidance of factional domination;
   b. Formalized procedures providing for an orderly handling of disputation;
   c. Formalized voting procedure;
   d. Possession of veto power by each faction;
   e. Analytical approaches to seeking compromise, rather than mere reliance on power attempts.

4. Group style: Group style is characterized by:
   a. Frankness and candor in presenting opposing viewpoints;
   b. Acceptance of due process in seeking resolution to conflicts;

[27] The justification for the minority never being represented by less than two persons is that it is difficult for one person to represent his group across the boundary, and that a minority of one is easy prey for a majority coalition of two members, let alone more than two.

    c. Openness to rethinking, and to mediation attempts;

    d. Avoidance of emotional hostility and aggression.

5. Group norms: Group norms are characterized by:

    a. Desire on the part of all factions to reach agreement;

    b. The perception of conflict and disagreement as healthy and natural, rather than pathological;

    c. Acceptance of individual freedom and group freedom to disagree;

    d. Openness to new analytical approaches in seeking acceptable compromise;

    e. Acceptance of the necessity for partial agreement as an acceptable, legitimate, and realistic basis for decision making.

There is, obviously, no parallel in either structure or norms to the above strategy in classical organizational models. The acceptance of open conflict; provision for due process between conflicting groups; openness to compromise; evolution of policy and objectives through negotiation; and "representative groups," while found in the "underworld" in most organizations, are outside the general organizational model. Indeed, managers involved in "negotiations," either in the personnel or labor relations area or the marketing or customer relations area, find it difficult to articulate the legitimacy of many of their decisions except through rationalizations.

CONCLUSIONS AND IMPLICATIONS

Both the propensities for groups to change the nature of their interaction as they change task and/or task phases, and the prescriptions for group strategies dealing with differentiated decision situations as set forth above, indicate that the structure and processes of groups must be related to changes in the characteristics of the decision-making tasks. Whether one agrees with each proposition in each of the decision-strategy models set forth in this section or not, the fact that each of the decision-making situations is endemically different is difficult to refute.

On the other hand, formal organizations, as conceived in present organizational models, are presumably structured in terms of the predominant type of task encountered by the system. Thus, the "bureaucratic" model is based on facilitating "routine" decision making; the labor union council is structured to deal with negotiated decision making; etc. Since task is, in the most pertinent sense, what members of the organization subjectively define it to be as they respond to the situation in which they find themselves, the internal features of a decision group within the organization will, thus, generally be influenced by the predominant structured roles created to deal with the "typical" decisions encountered in day-to-day organizational tasks. As a result, role expectations and behaviors molded in the central organizational system—the formal organization—may inhibit the decision-task performance in the subsystem—that is, the decision-making committee, conference, or task force.

Since there are several types of decisions to be made within complex organizations, with each general type calling for a different group structure and process, a major role of the manager in such a system is the evoking of appropriate changes in behaviors on the part of the decision team, as they move across task types, by means of role redefinition. This concept assumes that the manager can classify decision tasks according to the models presented here, or some other conceptual scheme, and that the managerial team can respond with congruent role flexibility. Earlier pilot research by the author indicates that such flexibility seems to be within the capacities of a large portion of the population, given appropriate role redefinition by the superior.[28] (Cf. Delbecq, 1965.)

In a real sense, then, management of the decision-making process is management of the structure and functioning of decision groups so that these decision-making processes become congruent with changes in the nature of the decision-making task being undertaken at a particular point of time within the organization.

Finally, we spent considerable time delineating the "task-force," "systems management," or "matrix organizational" approach,[29] as an appropriate model for strategy 1 situations since it seems to provide a mechanism for integrating various types of decision-making processes at various phases of decision making within a flexible structure. It is felt that strategy 1 avoids the structural rigidity of formal organization models such as "bureaucracy." There is no reason, for instance, why "creative" or "negotiated" strategies cannot be incorporated into the objectives- and standards-setting decision sessions at the beginning of the planning period. Further, there is no reason why personnel other than the "task specialists" cannot mediate the decision making by participation in these early decision phases. Thus, by dropping the assumption of "agreed-upon technologies" and "agreed-upon objectives," and incorporating strategies 2 and 3 into these early planning sessions, or intermittently juxtaposing these strategies with strategy 1, the incorporating of decision-making flexibility into the management context of strategy 1

---

[28] We agree that some individuals will find it impossible to assume flexible roles because of their particular developmental history which results in a fixated behavior pattern. We also agree that some roles will be more natural than others for individuals as a result of their developmental history. We disagree, however, with the notion that the normal population cannot assume at least functionally relevant roles in accordance with the various strategies, a point which appears to be the position of some theorists. A more conservative viewpoint than ours is assumed by Abraham Zaleznik, 1965.

[29] For an elaborated treatment of matrix organization, see F. Shull, 1965; J. Mee, 1964; C. Praktish, 1967.

seems not only feasible, but a desirable movement in the direction of fluid group structures and processes. Such a movement toward organizational fluidness is more congruent with the need for role flexibility as the management team moves across decision strategies at various phases of project planning and implementation. These concerns are developed further in Chapter 6.

bibliography

ALFRED, THEODORE M.: "Checkers or Choice in Manpower Management," *Harvard Business Review,* January/February, 1967, vol. 45, no. 1, pp. 157–169.

ARGYRIS, CHRIS: "Interpersonal Barriers to Decision-making," *Harvard Business Review,* March/April, 1966, vol. 44, no. 2, pp. 84–98.

BALES, ROBERT F.: "The Equilibrium Problem in Small Groups," in R. F. Bales, T. Parson, et al., *Family Socialization and Interaction Process* (Chicago: The Free Press of Glencoe, Ill., 1955).

————, and EDGAR F. BORGOTTA: "Size of Group as a Factor in the Interaction Profile," in A. Paul Hare, Edgar F. Borgotta, and Robert F. Bales, *The Small Group: Studies in Social Interaction* (New York: Alfred A. Knopf, Inc., 1955), pp. 403–405 and 411–413.

BARNARD, CHESTER R.: *The Functions of the Executive* (Cambridge, Mass.: Harvard University Press, 1938), p. 104.

BASS, BERNARD M., and M. FAY-TYLER NORTON: "Group Size and Leaderless Discussion," *Journal of Applied Psychology,* 1951, vol. 35, pp. 397–400.

BECKER, H., and R. H. USEEM: "Sociological Analysis of the Dyad," *American Sociological Review,* 1942, vol. 7, pp. 13-26.

BEENE, K. D., and P. SHEATS: "Functional Roles of Group Members," *Journal of Social Issues,* 1948, pp. 41–49.

BENNIS, WARREN G.: "Beyond Bureaucracy," *Transactions,* 1965, vol. 2, no. 5, pp. 31–36.

BERELSON, BERNARD, and GARY A. STEINER: *Human Behavior—An Inventory of Scientific Findings* (New York: Harcourt, Brace & World, Inc., 1964).

BERKOWITZ, LEONARD: "Personality and Group Position," *Sociometry,* December, 1965, vol. 19, pp. 210–222.

————: "Sharing Leadership in Small, Decision Making Groups," *Journal of Abnormal and Social Psychology,* 1953, pp. 231–238.

BLAU, PETER M., and W. RICHARD SCOTT: *Organizations, A Comparative Approach* (San Francisco: Chandler Publishing Co., 1962).

BORGOTTA, EDGAR F., A. S. COUCH, and ROBERT F. BALES: "Some Findings Relevant to the Great Man Theory of Leadership," *American Sociological Review,* 1954, vol. 19, pp. 755–759.

CARTER, L. F.: "Some Research on Leadership in Small Groups," in H. Guetzkow (ed.), *Groups, Leadership, and Men: Research in Human Relations* (Pittsburgh: Carnegie Press, Carnegie Institute of Technology, 1951), pp. 146–157.

CARTWRIGHT, DORWIN, and ALVIN ZANDER: *Group Dynamics: Research and Theory* (Evanston, Ill.: Row, Peterson & Company, 1960).

CARZO, J. ROCCO: "Organization Structure and Group Effectiveness," *Administrative Science Quarterly*, March, 1963, pp. 393–425.

COYLE, GRACE L.: *Social Process in Organized Groups* (New York: The Richard R. Smith Co., Inc., 1930).

CUMMINGS, LARRY: "Organizational Climates for Creativity," *Journal of the Academy of Management*, September, 1965.

DALTON, MELVILLE: *Men Who Manage* (New York: John Wiley & Sons, Inc., 1959), p. 20.

DELBECQ, ANDRÉ L.: *Leadership in Business Decision Conferences*, unpublished doctoral dissertation, Indiana University, 1963.

————: "Managerial Leadership Styles in Problem-solving Conferences," *Journal of the Academy of Management*, December, 1964, vol. 7, no. 4, pp. 255–268, and continued in March, 1965, vol. 8, no. 1, pp. 32–43.

————: "The Social-psychology of Executive Roles Re-examined," *Business Perspectives*, Spring, 1966, vol. 2, no. 3.

————: "The Management of Decision Making within the Firm: Three Strategies for Three Types of Decision Making," *Journal of the Academy of Management*, December, 1967, vol. 10, no. 4, pp. 324–340.

————: "The World within the Span of Control," *Business Horizons*, August, 1968.

ETZIONI, AMITAI: "Dual Leadership in Complex Organizations," *American Sociological Review*, October, 1965, vol. 30, no. 5, pp. 688–699.

FESTINGER, LEON, STANLEY SCHACHTER, and KURT BACK: *Social Pressures in Informal Groups* (New York: Harper & Row, Publishers, Incorporated, 1960), pp. 431–444.

FIEDLER, FRED E.: *A Theory of Leadership Effectiveness* (New York: McGraw-Hill Book Company, 1967), Part 4.

FISHER, P. H.: "An Analysis of the Primary Group," *Sociometry*, 1953, vol. 16, pp. 272–276.

GARDNER, BURLEIGH B.: "What Makes Successful and Unsuccessful Managers?" *Advanced Management*, September, 1948, vol. 13, no. 3, pp. 116–124.

GIBB, C. A.: "The Sociometry of Leadership in Temporary Groups," *Sociometry*, 1950, vol. 13, pp. 226–243.

GIBB, J. R.: "The Effects of Group Size and of Threat Reduction upon Creativity in a Problem-solving Situation," *American Psychology*, 1951, vol. 6, p. 324.

GOLEMBIEWSKI, ROBERT T.: *The Small Group: An Analysis of Research Concepts and Operations* (Chicago: University of Chicago Press, 1962).

GRAICUNAS, A.: "Relationship in Organization," in Luther Gulick and L. Urwick, *Papers on the Science of Administration* (New York: Institute of Public Administration, 1937), pp. 181–188.

GRUSKY, O.: "A Case for the Theory of Familiar Role Differentiation in Small Groups," *Social Forces*, 1957, pp. 209–217.

GUETZKOW, HAROLD, and HERBERT A. SIMON: "The Impact of Certain Communication Nets upon Organization and Performance in Task-oriented Groups," *Management Science*, 1955, vol. 1, pp. 233–250.

HARE, A. PAUL: *Handbook of Small Group Research* (New York: The Free Press of Glencoe, 1962).

————: "Interaction and Consensus in Different Size Groups," *American Sociological Review*, June, 1952, vol. 17, pp. 261–267.

HEMPHILL, J. K.: "Relations Between the Size of the Group and the Behavior of 'Superior' Leaders," *Journal of Social Psychology*, 1950, vol. 32, pp. 11–22.

HERZBERG, F. B., B. MAUSNER, and B. SNYDERMAN: *The Motivation to Work* (New York: John Wiley & Sons, Inc., 1961).

HOLLINGSHEAD, A. B.: *Elmstown's Youth* (New York: Reinhold Publishing Corporation, 1941).

HOMANS, GEORGE C.: *The Human Group* (New York: Harcourt, Brace & World, Inc., 1950), pp. 34–40.

HOUSE, ROBERT: *A Predictive Theory of Management Development* (Ann Arbor: University of Michigan Bureau of Industrial Relations, 1963), p. 41.

JAMES, J.: "A Preliminary Study of the Size Determinant in Small Group Interaction," *American Sociological Review,* 1951, vol. 16, pp. 474–477.

———: "Verbal Behavior in Problem-solving Small Groups Without Formally Designated Leaders," Research Study (Washington: Washington State College, 1956).

JENNINGS, HELEN H.: "Sociometric Differentiation of the Psycho-group and the Socio-group," *Sociometry,* 1947, vol. 10, pp. 71–79.

KAHN, ROBERT L., DONALD M. WOLFE, ROBERT P. QUINN, J. DIEDRICK SNOEK, and ROBERT A. ROSENTHAL: *Organizational Stress: Studies in Role Conflict and Ambiguity* (New York: John Wiley & Sons, Inc., 1964), pp. 388–392.

KINNEY, ELVA E.: "A Study of Peer Group Social Acceptability at the 5th Grade Level in a Public School," *Journal of Educational Research,* 1953, vol. 47, pp. 57–64.

KRUPP, SHERMAN: *Pattern(s) in Organizational Analysis: A Critical Examination* (Philadelphia: Chilton Book Company, 1961), pp. 140–187.

LAUMANN, EDWARD O.: "Friends of Urban Men: An Assessment of Accuracy in Reporting Their Socioeconomic Attributes, Mutual Choice, and Attitude Agreement," *Sociometry,* vol. 22, no. 1, March, 1969.

LEADER, ALAN H.: "Creativity in Management," *Proceedings of 10th Midwest Academy of Management Conference,* Business Research Bureau, Southern Illinois University, 1967.

LEAVITT, HAROLD J., and RONALD A. H. MUELLER: "Some Effects of Feedback on Communication," *Human Relations,* November, 1951, vol. 4, pp. 401–410.

LIKERT, RENSIS: *New Patterns of Management* (New York: McGraw-Hill Book Company, 1961), p. 113.

MAIER, NORMAN R. F.: *Problem-solving Discussions and Conferences* (New York: McGraw-Hill Book Company, 1963).

MEE, JOHN F.: "Ideational Items: Matrix Organization," *Business Horizons,* Summer, 1964, pp. 70–72.

MERTON, ROBERT K.: "Bureaucratic Structure and Personality," in Amitai Etzioni, *Complex Organizations* (New York: Holt, Rinehart, and Winston, Inc., 1961), pp. 48–61.

MILLER, DELBERT C., and WILLIAM H. FORM: *Industrial Sociology* (New York: Harper & Brothers, 1951), p. 72.

MOMENT, DAVID, and ABRAHAM ZALEZNIK: *Role Development and Interpersonal Competence* (Cambridge, Mass.: Harvard University Press, 1963), pp. 41–42 and 688–699.

MULLEN, JAMES: "Differential Leadership Modes and Productivity in a Large Organization," *Journal of the Academy of Management,* June, 1965, vol. 8, no. 2, pp. 107–127.

NEWCOMB, T. M.: "The Prediction of Interpersonal Attraction," *American Psychologist,* 1956, vol. 11, pp. 575–586.

————: "Varieties of Interpersonal Attraction," in Dorwin Cartwright and Alvin Zander, *Group Dynamics* (Evanston, Ill.: Row, Peterson & Company, 1960).

PARSONS, T.: *The Social System* (Glencoe, Ill.: The Free Press, 1951).

PFIFFNER, JOHN M., and FRANK P. SHERWOOD: *Administrative Organization* (Englewood Cliffs, N.J.: Prentice-Hall, Inc., 1960), pp. 16–32.

PIAGET, J.: *The Moral Judgment of the Child* (New York: Harcourt, Brace and Company, Inc., 1932).

PRAKTISH, CARL R.: "Evolution of Project Management," *Proceedings of 10th Midwest Academy of Management Conference,* Business Research Bureau, Southern Illinois University, 1967.

REDL, FRITZ: "Group Emotion and Leadership," *Psychiatry,* vol. 5, 1942, pp. 575–584.

SARBIN, T. R., and D. S. JONES: "An Experimental Analysis of Role Behavior," *Journal of Abnormal and Social Psychology,* 1955, pp. 236–241.

SCHULTZ, W. C.: "Some Theoretical Considerations for Group Behavior," Symposium for the Measurement of Group Performance (Washington, D.C.: U.S. Government Research and Development Board, 1952), pp. 27–36.

SCOTT, WILLIAM E.: "The Creative Individual," *Journal of the Academy of Management,* September, 1965.

SHULL, FREMONT A.: *Matrix Structure and Project Authority for Optimizing Organizational Capacity,* Business Science Monograph No. 1, Business Research Bureau, Southern Illinois University, Carbondale, Ill., 1965.

SIMON, HERBERT: *The New Science of Management Decisions* (New York: Harper & Brothers, 1960), chaps. 2 and 3.

————, and ALLEN NEWELL: "Heuristic Problem Solving: The Next Advance in Operations Research," *Operations Research Journal,* January-February, 1958.

SLATER, PHILIP E.: "Contrasting Correlates of Group Size," *Sociometry,* vol. 21, June, 1959, pp. 129–139.

STEINER, GARY: *The Creative Organization* (Chicago: University of Chicago Press, 1965).

TAYLOR, F. KROUPL: "The Therapeutic Factors of Group-analytical Treatments," *Journal of Mental Science,* vol. 96, October, 1950, pp. 967–997.

TAYLOR, P. W., P. C. BERRY, and C. H. BLOCK: "Does Group Participation When Using Brainstorming Facilitate or Inhibit Creative Thinking?" *Administrative Science Quarterly,* vol. 3, 1958, pp. 23–47.

THOMPSON, JAMES, and ARTHUR TUDEN: "Strategies, Structures, and Processes of Organizational Decision," in Thompson, et al., *Comparative Studies in Administration* (Pittsburgh: University of Pittsburgh Press, 1959).

THOMPSON, VICTOR: "Bureaucracy and Innovation," *Administrative Science Quarterly,* June, 1965.

————: *Modern Organization* (New York: Alfred A. Knopf, Inc., 1961).

VROOM, VICTOR H., LESTER D. GRANT, and TIMOTHY S. COTTON: "The Consequences of Social Interaction in Group Problem Solving," *Organization Behavior and Human Performance,* vol. 4, 1969, pp. 17–95.

ZALEZNIK, ABRAHAM: *Human Dilemmas of Leadership* (New York: Harper & Row, Publishers, Incorporated, 1965).

part

ORGANIZATIONAL PERSPECTIVES

four

six

ALTERNATIVE STRATEGIES FOR ORGANIZATIONAL DESIGN

In the first section of this book, the concern was with the individual as he perceives and processes information, while making choices. This focus largely abstracted from the containing environment in which he operates. In the second section, we dealt with social aspects of decision making, particularly in two ways: (1) the socialization of the individual, and (2) the impact of the immediate social environment—especially, small-group influences on his decision behavior. There, symbiotic relationships were more or less important, with direct social trade-offs as relevant dimensions of his decisions.

Now, we wish to locate the decision maker in an organizational context and study his choices therein. Accordingly, we can deal with "organizational" decisions because a structured social setting is contrived by man to guide the decisions of its constituents. In order to do this, however, we must first look at collective behavior, per se; second, examine traditional structural arrangements, that is, bureaucracy; third, develop evolving organizational designs, such as matrix; and, fourth, propose linkage systems, especially control, for these modern forms of organizations while noting their impact upon incumbent decision making. It should be emphasized that the model discussed here, matrix design, is an integrated one based upon cursory field observations, specific and diverse empirical findings, and theoretical deductions. To date, as an integrated conceptualization, it has supported only limited research. One test of all first-line supervisors of projects and departments from eighteen plants of a major electronics firm found that the "empirical test is (generally) supportive of the theories" generated by matrix design, dealing with "autonomy, control, and influence." (Grimes, Klein, and Shull, 1965, p. 14; as tested on a major dimension of the Apollo project (NASA), see Anna and Frederickson, 1969.)

Organization Behavior

The artifact which is called an organization is not the whole of our culture, but it is a prevalent and dominating microcosm, and Peter Drucker contends that the corporation is the representative organizational form of contemporary America. Moreover, "conglomerate" organizations are sweeping the economic system and multinational corporations greatly influence political states. Adolf Berle has asserted that corporate powers rival those of sovereign nations. Thus, we would be remiss not to study "organizational decisions."

One means for understanding organizations is to analyze administrative decisions. Indeed, Simon (1947, p. 1) contends that "a general theory of administration must include principles of organization that will insure effective action."[1] And Griffiths (1958, p. 122) states that

[1] Both the structural and the process approaches to management are insightful. Loosely, they are: (1) organization and (2) decision theories. For the former, organization structure is seen as the primary, if not the single, agent constraining and influencing decision making. This approach concentrates upon environmental determinants of choice, "the institutional bases of events." In this regard, Thompson (1961, p. 7) states: "An organization is not merely the chance result of a number of decisions made by a number of rational decision makers. Only decisions of decision makers already *in* the organization, and only their *organizational* decisions, are relevant. The organization, therefore, must first be accounted for, or decision-making theory never gets beyond individual psychology." Yet, in Part I, we hold rather firmly to an individualistic point of view. For certain purposes, individualism is a most fruitful perspective. However, in Part IV, especially this chapter, we

decision making is the central function of administration, that "it is not only central in the sense that it is more important than other functions . . . but it is central in that all other functions of administration can best be interpreted in terms of the decision-making process." Therefore, understanding organizations will add insight into administrative as well as individual decision making.

ORGANIZATIONAL CHARACTERISTICS

Organizations can be conceived as a specific social environment that offers the individual his conditions of choice, giving order to interacting choices. Without reference to these conditions, he could not explain order and could not predict individual behavior. With such conditions specified, the organization has been described and these statements have explained the system of order which is the organization. But looked at from this point of view, the organization is symbolism. A set of signs have been published to which the incumbent responds as though they were physical and tangible properties of the real world—which they are not.

These signs can be of two types: function and structure. On the one hand, *function* can be defined intrinsically or extrinsically; it can be highly formalized or informally held; and it can be authoritatively decreed or democratically derived. In all cases, there will be some common notion of purpose. On the other hand, *structural* characteristics are ". . . those elements in the total picture of the organization's functioning that (*a*) remain unchanged over a sufficiently long period of time to be described and (*b*) influence or constrain important aspects of the organization's total behavior" (Haberstroh, 1966, p. 117). Thus, these enduring and constraining artifacts offer some explanation for the participative decisions of its members.

Stogdill (1953, p. 40) defines an *organization* as "a social group in which the members are differentiated as to their responsibilities for the task of achieving a common goal." But, within these parameters, many kinds of organizations may exist, each imposing different constraints on its members. The organization of our concern, then, has such features as:

1. It is sufficiently large that social interactions are not totally primary in nature. Some relationships are secondary; the benefits of social participation are not exhaustive of the reward system.

---

examine formally patterned structure. In a sense, then, we think of decision making as a *causal* force, in and of organizations, as well as a consequence elicited by organizations (cf. Gore, 1962, p. 50).

2. There are differentiated roles within the group, especially between administration and operations, that is, there is vertical specialization, or hierarchy.

3. There is an external instrumental goal—the genotype function—toward which the organization attempts to move, utilizing resources in addition to those of its membership in exploiting this goal.

4. Work roles are rationally understood in terms of this instrumental goal, and some control system monitors individual performance.

5. Membership is, at least, conceptually differentiated from clientele so that some payoff to the organization is derived from meeting the instrumental goal.

6. Membership is perceived as based on some freedom of choice and not conscripted (whether or not real alternatives exist is irrelevant) and some scarcity of resources pertains.

COOPERATIVE ENDEAVORS[2]

An organization is formed to offer satisfaction to its members and to accomplish tasks that could not be obtained, or could not be accomplished as well, on an individual basis: "Organized effort enables a social group to produce more of the means of want satisfaction than it could by working as individuals" (Knight, 1933, p. 14). In short, people join a group in order to receive something from that group.

It is possible to distinguish two types of benefits which members seek. On the one hand, there are various extrinsic values—benefits accruing to members which are used as means for gaining satisfactions outside the group.[3] On the other hand, there are certain intrinsic satisfactions, called variously "fellowship," "learned dependability," and "affiliation" tendency or the gregarious "instinct." The incentive of these intrinsic benefits relates to social behavior as an end in itself—satisfaction derived directly from social intercourse. But it is the former, the extrinsic satisfaction, that is of concern here because of assumptions made in the bureaucratic model.

SPECIALIZATION

In order for each member of the organization to potentially hold extrinsic values equal to, or more than, that which he would receive as a product of his own individual and otherwise isolated effort, a "surplus" must

[2] Much of the following two sections is adapted from: Fremont A. Shull, *Matrix Structure and Project Authority for Optimizing Organizational Capacity,* Business Science Monographs, no. 1, Business Research Bureau, Southern Illinois University, 1965.

[3] Wages are the best example of this value in our culture. However, there may be certain extrinsic satisfactions associated with certain attributes of the organization itself, such as being a member of a group of high status within the community.

occur as a result of the collective behavior: The product of the group must be greater than the sum of the products of individualized endeavor—organizing must be creative.

The source of organizational surplus is commonly attributed to specialization of effort—the differentiation of instrumental roles among its members. Activities are differentiated according to geographic or temporal locations and physical or mental activities. Where done in some econorational fashion, specialization enhances "expertise" in manual and intelectual efforts.

Man has physical and mental limitations;[4] thus, a reduction in the scope of his operations makes possible a greater exploitation of his abilities. An optimum relationship can be established between his special but limited capacity and the complexity of his task. Moreover, the inefficiencies associated with early portions of his learning experience are thereby minimized; habits and routines tend to enhance skill proficiencies. Accordingly, Knight (1933, pp. 16–19) lists the attributes of specialization as:

1. Utilization of natural aptitudes; especially those of leaders and followers.
2. Development and utilization of acquired skill and acquired knowledge.
3. Changing pieces of work is cheaper, within limits, than changing jobs.
4. Natural advantages in the case of natural resources.
5. Artificial specialization of material agents. Division of operations leads to invention and use of machinery.

Specialization within an organization occurs both vertically and horizontally. Perhaps the foremost type of specialization that arises is that between the "leader" or decision maker and the "doer" or follower or operator.[5] History is replete with examples of this vertical division of effort, for example, tribal chiefs, kings, bosses, and presidents.[6] As Knight (1933, p. 16) argues: The most important differentiation in function ". . . between individuals is the separation between direction and execution, or the specialization of leadership. The gain from superior direction is so much more important than that from superior concrete performance

---

[4] Because of man's limitations in relation to "nature" a collectivity of mental and physical abilities in some integrated fashion provides the absolute power of coordinated effort. In this sense, the noncreative "brute force" of organized behavior is explained: Two men can move a boulder that one man could not.

[5] It is apparent that a leader cannot emerge in an organization unless the members assume differentiated responsibilities. Within this condition, then, a leader is "a person who becomes differentiated from other members in terms of the influence he exerts upon the goal setting and goal achievement activities of the organization" (Stogdill, 1948, p. 42).

[6] Such a division of labor has multiple causes; for example, the need for a ceremonial "head" and external accountability, etc.

that undoubtedly the largest single source of the increased efficiency through organization results from having work planned and directed by the exceptionally capable individuals." The English word "*supervision*" connotes this idea.

A second type of specialization, and the one most commonly recognized, is that of a horizontal division of labor at the operative level. This rationalized phenomenon has become known as Adam Smith's (1777) "parable of the pin." Babbage (1832) maintains that the division of labor was perhaps "the most important principle on which the economy of manufacture depends," contending that the lack of "principles" associated with division of labor accounted for much of the previous history of business failure.

The organizational requisite of differentiated membership suggests the existence of some type of structure or order in the system. As Kahn et al. (1964, p. 78) argue: "Control over the behavior of members is the essence of social organizations. Each member is charged with certain responsibilities and is subject to sanctions if he fails to carry them out properly."

Man apparently believes that he must impose a design on social interaction. The presumption, underlying most organizational constructs, is that an imposed strategy is required to optimize goal attainment. The appropriateness of the strategy is measured in terms of organizational efficiency. This criterion is supported by the fact that organizations are competing for scarce resources, especially those which operate in an amplified competitive situation provided by the economic system. As Gouldner (1959, p. 404) states,

> In the rational model, the organization (structure) is conceived as an instrument . . . (and these designs) are understood as tools deliberately established for the efficient realization of group purposes. Organizational behavior is thus viewed as consciously and rationally administered, and changes in organizational patterns are viewed as planned devices to improve the level of efficiency.

A second reason for imposed structure is that dependence on unplanned structures seems to reduce the permanency potential desired for administered organizations. Dependence on random, unplanned natural systems creates an inability to develop a succession of goals functionally related within the vertical hierarchy.

A third rationale, and one most central for our purposes, is that which relates to the individual incumbent. The member of a complex organization typically searches for structure within it. To the extent that membership is desirable to him, he will seek cues as to what is expected of him, the nature of his instrumental responsibilities, and norms on social decorum. In order to deal with reality, he will look to "the organization" to provide information on how to deal effectively with the relevant world or, perhaps, what the relevant world should be. Finally, the organization gives him cues on the status structure and proper interaction patterns. Therefore, whether man's need for structure is inherited or culturally acquired, the individual does expect and search for it in his decision-making processes.[7]

Bureaucracy

From all of this, we conclude that, for the incumbent, organizational structure becomes a major determinant of his decisions. In our immediate view, then, we mean by "structure" those persistent factors in the organizational environment which condition the decision behavior of members. These "organizational" properties, which exist apart from the single member, include such phenomena as: policy, communication, rules, specialization, chains of command, efficiency, responsibility, centralization, and integration. Structure, however, is a multivariant as well as a multidimensional phenomenon. As described in Chapter 5, it can be "natural" or "formal," and in this chapter, it will be described as matrix or bureaucracy. Let us deal with the latter here.

THE RATIONAL MODEL

Bureaucracy arose as a reaction against: (1) personal subjugation, (2) nepotism, and (3) cruelty, emotional vicissitudes, and capricious judgments. It offered a movement toward rationality, predictability, and technical competence.

In unspecialized societies, man is organized by kinship groups; and, where the family is the dominating social institution, ". . . the family enterprise is a simple and logical instrument of business activity. Loyalty and trust within the hierarchy are assured. The forces of tradition and religion support the essential integrity of the family dynasty" (Harbison and Myers, 1959, p. 119). However, with increasing social differentiation and division of labor, the common conscience (Jung's "collective unconscious") tends to deteriorate as a vehicle for interpersonal regulation. According to Thompson (1961, p. 25), interpreting Emile Durkheim,[8]

---

[7] For a brief summary of *anomie* and a study of individual differences so related, see McClosky and Schaar (1965), pp. 14–40.

[8] *The Division of Labor in Society*, trans. George Simpson (New York: The Macmillan Company, 1933).

"A new solidarity based upon the recognized mutual interdependence of specialists began to replace the old solidarity based on the common conscience. For this new kind of regulation to appear, artificial external obstacles to free specialization, such as caste, had to disappear." Otherwise the society would disintegrate because of lack of regulation, or normlessness, or anomie.

Durkheim and others conceived a new form of social anchor and direction, so that ". . . in the highly specialized industrial society of today, the predominant form of organization is a highly rationalized and impersonal integration of a large number of specialists co-operating to achieve some announced specific objective," that is, bureaucracy. Indeed, ". . . Saint-Simon viewed modern organization as a liberating force, emancipating men from the yoke of tradition and heightening productivity and efficiency" (Gouldner, 1959, p. 402). Thomas Hobbes, a seventeenth-century social philosopher, in his *Leviathan*, "reasoned that before men joined together to form society their life was solitary, poore, nasty, brutish, and short. To escape such horrible existence of anarchy and perpetual warfare, they renounced their natural rights and placed themselves under the protection of an absolute sovereign" (Petit, 1964, p. 48). Then came bureaucracy, about which Blau and Scott (1962, p. 3) state that the vehicle ". . . does not provide complete equality of occupational opportunities. Nevertheless, the fact that it does minimize the direct effect of status, privilege, such as noble birth, or skin color constitutes [a] democratizing influence. Democratic objectives would be impossible of attainment in modern society without bureaucratic organizations to implement them."[9]

Bureaucracy, as March and Simon (1958) see it, is an organization which is large enough to encompass an administrative agency and has both an operational system and a controlling hierarchy. The process of bureaucratizing is to: (1) define purpose—in this case, the efficiency rationale is singular because survival needs of the organization are assumed to be related and compatible over the relevant range; (2) determine and prescribe the activities required to achieve the purpose of the organization; (3) classify these activities into job units which will exploit the benefits of specialization; and (4) relate these units, by process or purpose, into "manageable" groups or departments.

"Fundamentally, the rational model implies a 'mechanical' model, in that it views the organization as a structure of manipulable parts, each

[9] Social instrumentalities help the individual to, among other things: (1) obtain and evaluate information; (2) provide acceptable accommodations to viable social norms; and (3) offer a defense against what to him is a less than benevolent environment.

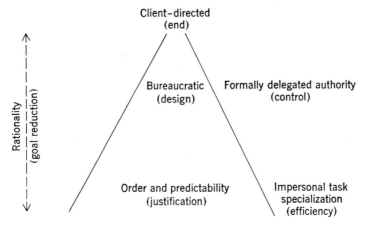

FIGURE 6-1 ELEMENTS OF BUREAUCRACY

of which is separately modifiable with a view to enhancing the efficiency of the whole. Individual organizational elements are seen as subject to successful and planned modification, enactable by deliberate decision" (Gouldner, 1959, p. 405). The overriding concerns are rationality and efficiency. Rationality is gained through the hierarchical delegation of authority; and efficiency is obtained through impersonal task specialization.

As Jennings (1959, p. 5) states, since organizations ". . . require highly precise and predictable relationships, organizational principles and procedures become worked out to the minutest detail. The effect is to create a system which constrains each member to act in ways that further the rational pursuit of organizational goals regardless of how irrational they appear to the individual himself." This frame of reference for decision making (see Figure 6-1), composed largely of the econological incumbent behaving within a "machinelike" organization, can be summarized simply as:

I. Segmentation of Work Units (to create a mechanism for achieving defined task goals)
    A. Division of labor:
        1. Functional
        2. Temporal
        3. Spatial
    B. Specialization:
        1. Simplification, to decrease training costs
        2. Rapid and detailed specification and commitment of resources

3. Increase in predictability and control and decrease in risk of improper processing

C. Expertise:
1. Instrumentally defined, task-oriented procedures
2. Participants selected for employment and promotion on basis of technical competence
3. Disciplined, impersonal relationships among members

II. Integration of Segmented Work Units

A. Departmentation:
1. Specified duties and responsibilities without overlap or duplication
2. Specified methods and technology

B. Hierarchy of authority:
1. Separation between superordinates (overseers) and subordinates (doers)
2. Unity of command, with only one point of legitimacy in any conceivable situation:
  a. Monocratic, where omniscient, "ultimate authority" at top of structure is final arbiter
  b. Downward flow of authority
    (1) Objectives and policies formulated at apex of pyramidal structure, as well as authority for initiating activity
    (2) Responsibility returned from the bottom
  c. Resolution of disputes by referral upward until the matter can be resolved by a sufficiently broad authority base
3. Limited span of control

III. Reinforcing System of Controls, Sanctions, and Norms Supporting Hierarchical Structure

A. Control systems:
1. System of detailed rules governing rights and duties of each position
2. Feedback control systems directed to operations and monitoring subordinate behavior
3. System of indoctrination to materialize an abstract hierarchical system, rules, and procedures

B. Reinforcing reward system to support hierarchical structure:
1. Reliance on extrinsic rewards of money, status, and power
2. Bartering of hierarchical positions as rewards for docility and compliance
3. Administration of rewards through superordinates

C. Reinforcing norms supporting total-system logic:
1. Legitimacy of authority
2. Economy and efficiency measures
3. Impersonality of the organization
4. Progress defined as moving upward in the power hierarchy

With bureaucracy, people had to be schooled in accepting the idea of impersonal authority. When the theories of Locke were followed, allegiance shifted from a personal loyalty to the chiefdom to an impersonal loyalty to the system. In turn, the member of the system could be viewed in terms of rationally defined and impersonally specialized roles. This resulted in a two-way fragmentation of man: (1) It abstracted from the emotive and social potential of man's creativity, and (2) it focused rather singularly upon a narrow set of his technical and conceptual abilities.

NEGATIVE ENTROPY

In addition to treating organizational members as automatons, bureaucracy conceives of the organization as a machine, especially as a closed system. But a human organization is an open system. Not only does the system itself learn, but it also receives and stores resources. Through government subsidy, economic monopoly, or political influence, the organization may obtain resources which exceed its transformational and maintenance costs. Through storage or slack, it need not die; it can survive and grow.

Yet, as with biological organisms, there is the possibility that an organization will stagnate and die. Evans (1956), using the history of coal mining as his case, sets forth the proposition that imperatives of union organizations change during the period from their origin to their maturity. This change is characterized by a three-stage emphasis on primary union objectives: (1) recruiting union membership, (2) strengthening the union's position as an organization, and (3) personal ambitions and objectives of union leaders. The hypothesis, then, can be developed that the leaders will solidify their power position through bureaucratization, and, because of the dysfunctions thus emanating, the organization will decline.

According to Katz and Kahn (1966, p. 68), "The general law of entropy states that any system will tend to run down, lose its differentiated structure, and become one with its environment." Within a human system, entropy may be reflected in the amount of "slippage" in performance, especially in the way of "ignorance, chaos, and randomness in the system" (Pfiffner and Sherwood, 1960, p. 297), resulting in loss of its differentiation from general culture.

It is a conundrum why organizations with subsidy or monopolistic controls have the greatest ability to overcome entropy. As Katz and Kahn (1966, p. 68) contend: the "death forces" of entropy ". . . are countered in the most direct and simple manner in social systems by taking over and exploiting natural resources and by taking away the possessions and even the labor power of other groups—whether by persuasion, guile, or force." Perhaps only instrumental performance, that is, serving client needs, provides for survival and growth in the short run; but, in the long run, legitimization of goals—and market control—and developing organization slack may be most fruitful.

Cyert and March (1963) describe "slack" as surplus benefits to (that is, inducements greater than contributions) organizational members. About the possibility of slack, Parsons (1951, p. 166), commenting on selecting specialized motivational energy, states that this ". . . dimensional scheme assumes that energy must either be stored up in the reservoir or it must be 'expended' through transformation into gratification (satisfactions)." The latter, according to Cyert and March (*idem.*), may be related rather directly to the innovative ability of the organization. Thus, organizational "heat"—that is, inducements designed to hold members—(negative entropy) appears to be related to the organization's sanction system ("gratification feedback") and its allocative and control networks. But these phenomena are housed in the mentality of the individual incumbent.

What, indeed, happens is that the decision maker in the organization learns through his interactions with the structure and, thereby, creates noise and distortion in the system. Further, he carries culture into the organization, and such inputs create organizational "friction." Recently, cultural evolvements have been introduced into the system which seem to operate against certain dimensions of the bureaucratic conceptualization; some are cited below:

1. The Western tradition of countervailing power (democracy, labor and management, professional power group, etc.)

2. The collapse of a class structure based upon position and ascribed status and the rise of one related to expertise and achieved status

3. The "scientific" ethic, with its propensity toward evolution and change, including the restructuring of conservative social institutions

4. Complex technologies and the knowledge explosion, which make omniscience anachronistic, creating an imbalance between authority and competence

5. The impact of educated participants in social systems
    a. Positive correlation between a person's education and his need for autonomy within his sphere of expertise and collaboration in decisions affecting the work environment
    b. Job mobility caused by professionalism placing the educated in positions of greater influence in the system

Students of organization design are readily familiar with the artificiality, limitations, and dysfunctions of bureaucracy in practice and theory. In particular, we wish to modify this machine theory in two ways: (1) the manner in which an organization contains its members and the legitimation of authority; and (2) the assumption of singularity of organizational goals and the notion of a closed system. Finally, in that which follows, we describe elements of *matrix* organization.

Classical organization theory, whether conceived of in terms of bureaucracy or of administrative organization models, is generally charged with being theoretically dysfunctional or empirically vacuous. In contrast to artifactual designs, there is the view that natural systems are functional—that "immanent order" is found in natural systems. The argument follows that ". . . there are various regularities in our experience that cannot be accounted for solely in terms of peculiarities and limitations of our human instruments of sensation and thought" (Bennett, 1963, p. 6). While certain regularities may be imputed where they, in fact, might not exist merely because of our desire for order and structure in the universe, we do suppose that certain universals exist, ". . . that there is some universal order or principles, (if not) caprice would reign. Anything and everything would be possible and nothing could be known or foreseen" (*loc. cit.*). Our desire to understand these regularities and to practice foresight, thus, gains credence; however, we attempt not only to understand and adapt to these regularities, but also to control or to amplify them. In turn, the impact of our understanding and the experiencing of regularity feeds back on our desire to find such regularity.

It is not too much to suppose that certain regularities do exist in a functioning social system. Much of this order may be culturally directed, for example, through historical conditioning, or may be consciously imposed. Nonetheless, the assumption can be made that there may be some natural, uncultivated social regularity. Here, for example, Beer (1960, p. 13) contends: "An existing system of human relationships in a large and complex society is to be regarded as self-organizing, as ordered already . . . (and that) many people dimly realize that this is a fair description."

A second premise of bureaucracy is that organizational surplus is accounted for solely through specialization. Yet, while specialization contributes to organizational surplus, one can immediately think of other sources of such creativity: for instance, participative motivation and social facilitation. In terms of the latter, social facilitation has to do with changes in performance of the solitary individual as he is exposed to certain social forces. Studies have shown that, under certain conditions, the productivity of an individual increases when operating within an interactive social environment. (Cf. Allport, 1954, pp. 45–50.)

Gantt (1902), an associate of Frederick Taylor, recognized the importance of workers' motivation. He observed that, although the job was designed scientifically, workers ". . . found good excuses for taking more than the prescribed time on every job, and for wasting enough time to hold down the output of the shop very materially," (p. 351) and he recommended a bonus system. While he found that economic stimulation did increase performance, he felt that it was his bonus system that was incomplete. He stated that workers were only rewarded for meeting what the time-and-motion experts had pre-scribed. According to him: "The next and most obvious step is to make it to the interest of men to learn more than their (instruction) cards can teach them. So far nothing has been done in this line, not because the need for some such provision has not been felt, but for the reason that no entirely satisfactory method has suggested itself." (*Ibid.*, p. 372.)

In the mid-part of the twentieth century, a multiplicity of inducements have been offered to hold constituents and to stimulate them to levels of performance beyond that which will maintain their membership therein. This we call "heat," or negative entropy, which mitigates orga-nizational growth. The premise is that man, living at a supra-subsistence level of income, is motivated by a variety of forces. A growing body of evidence about him suggests that self-actualization can lead to optimal performance and may find its expression in at least the following two ways:

1. Variance in task requirements can actually increase performance. Fiske (1961, p. 143), for example, reports that: "In vigilance studies, performance typically declines over time, presumably because normal functioning is some-what disturbed by the continually monotonous conditions. Markedly restricted stimulation clearly disrupts normal functioning and probably impairs task per-formance to some degree."

2. Participation in decision making may favorably affect task performance. March and Simon (1958, p. 54) conclude that, ". . . the more the felt partici-pation in decisions, the less the visibility of power differences in the organi-zation, and that the latter, in turn, lessens the evocation of organizationally disapproved alternatives."

Our third contention is that empirical studies show that many con-temporary organizations manifest structures such as multiple supervisors, committee overlays, task force groups, and project management designs—dimensions of structure which are contrary to prescriptions for traditional organizational models. To this extent, classical models are of limited scientific usefulness. Many structural modifications cannot be explained or predicted from classical dogma, and much behavior takes place in an organization "underworld," variously called the "informal organization" and "organizational politics"—either of which is perceived as antithetical to the rational design.

Walton (1968, p. 148) contends that new concepts of property are evolving, of which political power and professional knowledge will be the most important bases of organizational design. Reinforcing this contention are the findings of Lawrence and Lorsch (1967) on the differentiated nature of the internal makeup of organizations. They found that differences among departments included: (1) varied orientations toward goals; (2) differing time perspectives; (3) varied emphasis on interpersonal skills; and (4) differential formalization of structure.

The absence of a standard organizational design, such as bureaucracy, as described earlier, was found in Fouraker and Stopford's (1968) study of multinational organizations. They observed three different organizational forms, only one of which conformed to notions of bureaucracy. Their "Type III," which corresponds most closely to the form that we now describe, matrix, made it possible for administrators to ". . . manage a variety of heterogeneous activities, (and) made it feasible for research and development activity to be incorporated in the structure" (p. 51). Scientists and politicians are finding berth in the modern organization.

Against these evolutions, the classical model is condemned as failing to serve as a useful guide in creating a positive social-psychological environment for successful task-facilitating behavior; it is claimed that it, for example:[10]

1. Inhibits role taking based on the realities of personality propensities, thus precluding "natural" decision behavior;

2. As a power system, is intrinsically conservative, a condition which stifles innovation and change;

3. Provides:
   a. No adequate jurisdictional process,
   b. No adequate means for resolving differences and conflict between ranks and, most particularly, between functional groups;

[10] For writers dealing explicitly with these propositions see: R. Merton, "Bureaucratic Structure and Personality," in A. Etzioni, *Complex Organizations* (New York: Holt, Rinehart and Winston, 1961); C. Argyris, "Understanding Human Behavior in Organizations: One Viewpoint," in M. Haire, *Modern Organization Theory* (New York: John Wiley & Sons, Inc., 1959); V. Thompson, *op. cit.*; W. Scott, *The Management of Conflict* (Homewood, Ill.: Richard D. Irwin, Inc., 1965); H. Shepard, "Changing Interpersonal and Intergroup Relationships in Organizations," in J. March, *Handbook of Organizations* (Chicago: Rand McNally & Co., 1965), pp. 1115–1144; W. H. Read, "Upward Communication in Industrial Hierarchies," in A. Ruberstein and C. Haberstroh, *Some Theories of Organization* (Homewood, Ill.: R. D. Irwin, Inc., 1966); R. Likert, *The Human Organization* (New York: McGraw-Hill Book Company, 1967), pp. 3–12; A. Delbecq, "The Social-psychology of Executive Roles Re-examined," *Business Perspectives,* Spring, 1966.

4. Cannot assimilate the influx of new technology or scientists entering the system;

5. Proposes systems of control and authority that are hopelessly outdated, creating:

    a. Communication distortion due to hierarchical divisions,

    b. A façade of conformity and group think,

    c. A modification of personality structure so that people become and reflect the dull, gray, conditioned "organization man,"

    d. A waste of the full human resources of organizations as a result of mistrust, fear of reprisals, etc.

Rationalized models for organization structure, such as bureaucracy, are landmarks in the evolution of collective behavior. But bureaucracy is only an evolutionary branch in the development of complex organizations and, we hypothesize, a dead branch, if not integrated appropriately with contemporary affective and conative demands of mankind. It may be that bureaucracy, evolving from what Weber called traditional and charismatic organizational forms, was at one time the most viable structure for organized endeavor. However, in the process of evolution and mutual adaptation between aggregate culture and micro collectivities, especially for industrialized societies, the original benefits of bureaucracy have been neutralized, or at least serious dysfunctions appear to accompany the bureaucratic strategy.

Restrictive role compartmentalization and personal specialization are productive of organizational surplus under certain conditions. Yet diffuse interaction across specialties is contributory as well, as is suggested by man's more heuristic and innovative endeavors. Functionalism and rigid specialization can operate with a predetermined technology only in a closed system. Thus, bureaucratic theories with derived and abstract rationalism, while powerful forces in organizational performance, are inadequate explanations of the totality of complex organizations today.

Creativity and progress depend at least partially upon nonlogical thought processes and social facilitation. Heuristic decisions are associated with ill-defined and unstructured problems; creativity finds its meaning in "eureka" and nonrationalized types of behavior. To the extent that rigid, specialized technologies are prescribed, creativity and progress are constrained. Although highly restrictive or limited, bureaucracy may be a most valid and viable conception of organizations in specific situations or for particular organizational domains. Yet new conceptions and growing evidence permit us to abstract to a higher level of generality. Accordingly, we assume a model which encompasses less restrictive parameters than does bureaucracy, that is, bureaucracy is viewed as but a subclass of the rational design which structures the variegated matrix of task units in complex organizations.[11]

Matrix Components[12]

It is the purpose of this section to set forth certain dimensions of this new model of organizations, which we temporarily call "Matrix Organization."[13] It is new in that it conceives of the aggregate organization structure and its component parts otherwise than do classical models. At the same time, it deals with many classical concerns such as authority relationships, reward structures, and work-group segmentation.

An anomaly seems to exist in prevailing criticisms of bureaucracy. On the one hand, the contention is made that it is machinelike and limiting while man is adaptive and evolving. Thus, it is posited that the machine must become less and less restrictive as man grows; otherwise, it will debilitate his interests and abilities. In this way, the organization design must be open and expansive if it is to promote the total potential of man and his learning capacities.

On the other hand, social contagion is offered as a limiting feature of bureaucracy—that constituents overreact and spread dysfunctional

[11] Nonetheless, certain propositions of classical models, for example, work-unit hierarchies, control systems, and functional and structural differentiation, are relevant dimensions of the modern complex organization. These notions persist, whether from cultural conditioning or natural imperatives. Yet, comparing contemporary organizations with classical models, it is difficult to state: (1) which dimensions reflect evolutionary and/or cultural artifacts which can be discarded as no longer relevant, as opposed to (2) those which reflect universal and/or natural responses to contemporary task situations. Until we can separate (1) from (2), it is difficult to conceive of more effective organizational structures or operate more effectively in nontraditional structures where, in fact, they now exist.

[12] Much of that which follows in this chapter was contributed to by Alan C. Filley, Andrew L. Grimes, and Andy Van de Ven.

[13] As regards this model, Professor Victor Thompson states: "It is not completely clear whether you are describing or prescribing. Have we really evolved beyond bureaucracy? Not for most people. However, interesting movements are occurring." And we do assert that our emerging model:
1. Encompasses descriptions of realities of contemporary organizations;
2. Is more "organic" than conventional bureaucracy, and thus:
   a. Is more adaptable to complexities of the environment,
   b. Posits a greater variety of interaction patterns and decision strategies,
   c. Proves superior in encompassing individual and group motivational syndromes;
3. Provides a means for organizing heretofore conflicting findings in theory and field studies;
4. Suggests dimensions of classical models which are "cultural" artifacts or "natural responses" to tasks and technology.

responses to bureaucratic norms. Thus social conformity occurs and bureaucratic myopia attends the rational system. With increasing symmetry among members' talents and aspirations, the capacity for organizational survival is limited, since it ceases to be adaptive.[14]

Contemporary organizations do evidence structural arrangements which are designed quite explicitly to cope with the above constraints. In modern organizations, we find that varied degrees of autonomy of task units from the administrative system do offer means for offsetting the limiting constraints of bureaucratic rigidity and encourage greater flexibility of role behavior. Here, we want to be clear, and we point out that the variance in task units does not relate to functional specialization in the traditional sense. Our concern is with organizational units in contemporary organizations which may be seen as relatives of the "task force." These work units are problem- or mission- rather than functionally or discipline-oriented and are different from traditional committees. This latter difference stems from the fact that such units are perceived as integral parts of structure rather than organizational overlays, as in the case with committees. Moreover, they are different from profit centers in that they are budgeted less conventionally, that is, output measures may be unrelated to fiscal periods, and joint costing plays a proportionately unimportant role; independent accounting schedules are necessary for managerial control. Our major proposition at this point is the plurality and differential nature of task, or programmatic, units within complex organizations. The issue is not to dichotomize between functional and programmatic units but rather to scale the programmatic units themselves.[15] More specifically, we plan to:

1. Identify basic types of task units within complex organizations, specifying the structure, roles, decision processes, and norms for each type of unit.

2. Indicate the specific and differentiated administrative system for "managing" each type of differentiated task unit.

---

[14] For writers dealing explicitly with these propositions see: A. Gouldner, "Cosmopolitans and Locals: Toward an Analysis of Latent Social Roles," *Administrative Science Quarterly*, vol. 2, December, 1957, pp. 281–306, March, 1958, pp. 444–480; A. Etzioni, *Modern Organizations* (Englewood Cliffs, N.J.: Prentice-Hall, Inc., 1964), p. 81; V. Thompson, "Bureaucracy and Innovation," *Administrative Science Quarterly*, June, 1965; S. H. Udy, "Technical and Institutional Factors in Production Organizations," *American Journal of Sociology*, 1961/1962, pp. 247–254; W. Bennis, "Beyond Bureaucracy," *Transactions*, July–August, 1965.

[15] We employ the small group as our unit of analysis for the following reasons:

1. There is little theoretical integration of the small group with the organization. Often the former is treated as a confounding variable, while we perceive it as more central to organizational behavior.

2. We feel that the small group is a basic linking pin between individuals and

3. Predict the appropriate as well as probable issues at the interface or boundary between the subtask units and the submanagement systems.

4. Develop a concept of an aggregate, total administrative system which specifies the linkage between subtask and management systems. In conceptualizing the aggregate organization, attention is directed to:

    a. Information systems;

    b. Evaluation and control systems;

    c. Long-term and intermediate planning systems dealing with:

        (1) Legitimation and adaptation to changes in the environment;

        (2) Organizational growth and innovation;

        (3) Flexible and balanced organizational configurations for subtask and management systems;

        (4) Optimal employment of scarce scientific personnel and technological change.

Thus, we present a taxonomy of four types of nodal designs for structuring organizational units, along with complementary administrative linkages. Such a taxonomy is seen as a central step in the construction of a revised theory of organization, away from bureaucracy.[16]

DEVELOPMENT OF THE MODEL

One pervasive, distinguishing characteristic among task units is apparent in research studies around which a classification system might be developed having to do with the degree to which a project group is relatively dependent or autonomous within the parent organization.[17] Figure 6-2 presents a diagrammatic representation of a continuum dealing with

---

the organization. It is at least a primary referent, and perhaps a more immediate one, than the "organization."

3. The small group has the power of collective action. It permits organizational synergism and carries notions associated with span of management.

4. Moreover, we are reinforced by the observed tendency to create—formally or informally—small groups, such as committees, task forces, etc. And we note their existence informally in functional departments.

5. Finally, we are encouraged by the fact that there is much research on small groups.

[16] As a conceptual map, the taxonomy allows organizational incumbents, including top executives, representatives of the submanagement systems, and those of the subtask units to identify the nature of intrinsic differences between component organizational units, and thus to clarify differentiated roles and functions as well as intra-organizational relationships. This is important if real differentiations between organizational units found in modern organizations are to be highlighted, rather than obscured by filtering each differentiated system through the stereotyped and standardized lens of conventional management principles or the bureaucratic model.

[17] For examples of differing degrees of dependency of technical project groups in the aerospace industry, see Keith Davis (1965). A contrasting picture of highly autonomous project groups is presented in the treatment of venture management groups in Peterson (1967).

TABLE 6-1   Relationships between an administrative system and project groups

DIMENSION	TASK-GROUP AFFILIATION	
	DEPENDENT (POSITION 1)	AUTONOMOUS (POSITION 4)
Source of authority	Locus of coordination lies in office of project manager via the Administrative System.	Coordination decentralized to shared commitments, monitored by colleagues, with project manager as project representative.
Division of labor	By functional depth, and sequentially determined by technical process.	By problematic breadth and heuristic potential in terms of genotype output.
Resource control	Resources allocated and controlled by Administrative System.	Resources bargained for (and perhaps generated by) the project group.
Directional control	Performance feedback to Administrative System, means control specified by the Administrative System which designs the program.	Performance feedback to the project group; controls are a function of task commitment with administrative control of global task.
Normative rewards	Career ascendency in the Administrative System.	Career ascendency in professional or craft system.

this salient variable of autonomy—dependence.[18] Table 6-1 presents exemplary characteristics for project groups at either end of the continuum, as positions 1 and 4, Figure 6-2.

Both field studies and theoretical models of other researchers suggested the following variables as crucial: (1) the reciprocation between ends, that is, objectives, and technology or intrinsic properties of the task; (2) the personality, or the norms and aspirations, and competence, or expertise, of the personnel within the unit; and (3) certain institutional and/or historical circumstances associated with the group or enterprise.

[18] This continuum of levels of autonomy can be exemplified as extending from aspects of venture management in business to assembly-line types of manufacturing, and from advanced study units to actual production operations in NASA. The nodal points also can be found in other types of organizations, for example:

A. *Correctional institutions*
  1. Custodial activities
  2. Conservation programs
  3. Remedial education
  4. Clinical rehabilitations

B. *Colleges and universities*
  1. Placement activities
  2. Data-processing center
  3. Graduate education
  4. Research institute

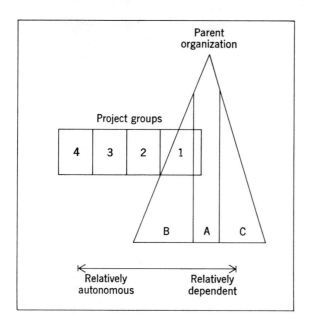

Parent
organization

Project groups

| 4 | 3 | 2 | 1 |

B   A   C

Relatively
autonomous

Relatively
dependent

Code:

A – Administrative and Support System
B and C – Functional Departmental System
1, 2, 3, and 4 – Degrees of relative autonomy
(versus dependency), with (1)
being the most dependent

FIGURE 6-2   GRAPHIC PRESENTATION OF AUTONOMY
OF TASK GROUPS FROM PARENT ORGANIZATIONS

Below, we summarize selected dimensions of these variables which
are critical as related to the nodal types of project groups:[19]

1. The nature of the technology associated with the unit in terms of:
a. Identifying function with decision process and characteristics of solution processes, particularly in terms of a continuum from programmed to
heuristic.[20]

[19] For a description of project management, see: D. Cleland, "Understanding
Project Authority Requires Study of Its Environment," in *Aerospace Management,*
vol. 2, no. 1, Spring/Summer, 1967; C. Middleton, "How to Set up a Project
Organization," *Harvard Business Review,* March/April, 1967; Keith Davis, *Role
Perceptions of the Job of Program Manager in Technical Work* (Los Angeles:
Western Management Science Institute, January, 1965).

[20] Particularly useful models dealing with the impact of decision type on structure
were those of: Thompson and Tuden (1959), pp. 198–199; Delbecq (1967),
pp. 329–341; and Simon (1960), chaps. 2 and 3.

b. Characteristics of the processing system, including task flow, as a continuum from *similar/repetitive* to *novel/unique* (cf. Perrow, 1967; and Woodward, 1965).

2. The nature of personnel, particularly in terms of a continuum from skilled to professional, relating to such variables as:[21]

a. Risk aversion and tolerance for ambiguity.

b. Intellectualism and characteristics of conceptual training, for example, degree of abstractness and differentiation of concepts.

c. Cosmopolitanism, extent of extra-organizational training, and identification.

By casting technology and personal characteristics in terms of the two continua presented in Table 6-1, alternative organizational strategies can be developed.[22] In particular, four viable nodal strategies can be identified consistent with theory and research, with position 1 in Figure 6-3 being the most dependent upon the Administrative System and position 4 being the least dependent, corresponding to positions 1 and 4 in Figure 6-2.

We must concern ourselves, however, with what the four alternative nodal strategies in Figure 6-3 represent. First, while partially derived from the study of project and task force groups, the nodal designs do not represent *merely* descriptions of structural variations between project groups. Rather, they are universal alternative strategies explaining intra-organizational structural variation. Thus, administrative, functional, control, service, research, and planning units manifest structural variation consistent with the four differentiated, characteristic strategies.[23]

[21] A. Gouldner, "Cosmopolitans and Locals: Toward an Analysis of Latent Social Roles," *Administrative Science Quarterly*, December, 1957, pp. 281–306, March, 1958, pp. 444–480; A. Etzioni, *Modern Organizations* (Englewood Cliffs, N.J.: Prentice-Hall, Inc., 1964), p. 81; V. Thompson, "Bureaucracy and Innovation," *Administrative Science Quarterly*, June, 1965; S. H. Udy, "Technical and Institutional Factors in Production Organizations," *American Journal of Sociology*, 1961/1962, pp. 247–254; W. Bennis, "Beyond Bureaucracy," *Transactions*, July–August, 1965.

[22] A third variable would include:

1. The makeup of the personnel systems, in terms of dominance by administrators, professionals or craftsmen, unskilled workers, etc.

2. The stage of organizational growth and purpose of establishing task groups, for example, the need for venture management.

3. Organizational norms relating the administrative system with the project groups, such as medical norms which place the physician in a revered position vis-à-vis the hospital administrator in routine services.

Since this variable is dependent on situational and subcultural factors quite independent of organizational theory per se, our basic model incorporates only the first two variables, namely, the nature of the technology and the competence of the personnel.

[23] While the study of project groups highlights these strategies, in that their structure and function are not expected to conform to bureaucratic standards, such

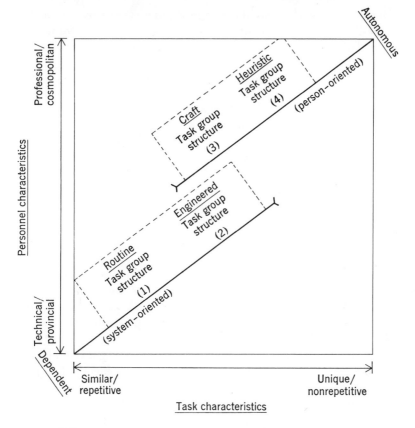

FIGURE 6-3 ALTERNATIVE, NODAL ORGANIZATIONAL UNIT STRUCTURES

The taxonomy of nodal organizational strategies is quite consistent with the position of Parsons (1964, pp. 16–59) that there is vertical specialization in organizations, that is, that some organizational units are concerned with cultural legitimation of the system and others with coordination of operational units within the system. As a consequence, different strategies are more likely to be associated with different positions within the organizational system, both horizontally and vertically. Operating Task Groups—those which deal directly, in some fashion, with clientele products or services—are the major concerns of this section. Since detailed treatment of the legitimating and coordinating units is outside the scope of this section, we lump all nonoperating task groups

---

differentiated characteristics within organization groups, and manifested differences between such groups, are demonstrably present in functional and administrative departments. The treatment of the four strategies as project-group overlays on functional departments in Figure 6-2 is merely an arbitrary illustration.

into a category that is labeled the *administrative* system in our model. In Figure 6-2, this is represented by the vertical polygon *A* within the triangle labeled "Parent Organization." The four nodal organizational designs, then, represented by the four squares in Figure 6-2, are Operating Task Groups,[24] rather than administrative units within the organization.

Finally, the nodal designs for Operating Task Groups, while partially derived from the study of project and task force groups, represent not *merely* designs for project management. Rather, they are also alternative forms to functional departmentation in the designing of operational relationships within an organization. They might, therefore, be found to be dominant operating designs of an organization, rather than overlays on traditional departmentation, as suggested in Figure 6-2.

FOUR STRATEGIES FOR OPERATING TASK UNITS

We can now describe the four nodal organizational designs presented in Figure 6-3.[25] Each of the four is "nodal" in the sense that, as one moves along the two continua, the increase in task variability and/or personnel competence results in the emergence of an organizational strategy for Operating Task Units which is different in some significant way from other points in the continuum. Thus, each design is uniquely equipped to deal with the varied nature of the task facing that part of the organization and/or with the diverse skills of its members.

One assumption must be made explicit: These nodal designs assume some congruence between personnel competence and task complexity; that is, the model assumes that an increase in task complexity normally results in the organization recruiting more highly trained or professional personnel as well as personnel with differentiated skills and interests. Thus the model deals with organizational situations where "qualified" personnel, neither underemployed nor overemployed, are available to or present within the system.

[24] Professor Victor A. Thompson raised the following question about our nodal points: "If I were asked to locate workers on this continua, I would locate them as follows: unskilled, semi-skilled, skilled engineers (including lawyers and medical doctors), and scientists, (a finer breakdown would locate the various scientists along the continua—e.g., physicists would come after political scientists)."

[25] The reader familiar with organizational literature will note parallels between this model and those of authors dealing with either decision-making strategies (Simon, 1960, Delbecq, 1967, and Thompson and Tuden, 1959) or structure strategies based on technology (Perrow, 1967, and Woodward, 1965). While we have borrowed heavily from this prior research, the present model represents both a revised position and an extension which is built on this prior work. In particular, the relationship of the Operating Task Unit to the Administrative System is more explicit in this model, requiring certain modifications of earlier works.

Each Operating Task Group strategy will be described in terms of several characteristics of the organizational unit, including:

1. Group structure: The relationships among the organizational members within the unit.

2. Group roles: The behavior required of individual group members which is necessary to facilitate task accomplishment.

3. Group process: The manner in which the unit proceeds toward goal accomplishment.

4. Group style: The emotional tone and social maintenance within the organizational unit.

5. Group norms: The values or standards to which members of the organizational unit adhere.

Finally, the relationship between the nodal Operating Task Unit and the Administrative System will be examined in terms of the locus and type of planning and control activities, the nature of the reward system within the unit, and the probable types of boundary negotiations, that is, central issues for dialog between the Operating Task Unit and the Administrative System.

CELL 1: ROUTINE STRATEGY. The first Operating Task Group structure with which we will deal is the Routine Strategy. Here the organization is dealing with a task situation requiring similar or repetitive solutions and implementation, and the organizational unit is staffed by technicians rather than "professionals." Figure 6-4 summarizes the nodal organizational strategy for dealing with this type of organizational situation.

To the extent that the "solution program" is a machine system, requiring little skills on the part of the organizational member, the following modifications will tend to occur: (1) mechanization may dilute required employee skills from those of a technician to those of an unskilled worker; (2) the unit leader may become a housekeeping coordinator, as in a troubleshooting and communication center, but having little occasion to provide task assistance; and (3) individual discretion may be largely absent, since the worker may simply be a machine appendage. At the extreme, the group structure may not possess a human input at all, but be merely a machine system.

Figure 6-5 presents characteristics of the Administrative System which are correlates of the Routine Strategy in cell 1. The two figures taken together represent an organizational strategy which is both similar and dissimilar when compared with classical organization models. The centralization of the planning function in the Administrative System is quite compatible with classical prescriptions, as is the clear division of labor between the structural units (specialization between work and coordination). On the other hand, the control and reward systems are dissimilar in important ways. To begin with, control is largely built into the program, rather than relying on the office or position of the leader as the locus of control. Further, feedback goes to the group member, allowing for self-correction. Classical prescriptions emphasize feedback primarily to the Administrative System. Assuming congruence between individual capacity and task requirements, rewards are different from classical models in that intrinsic task motivation can be emphasized. Further, career ascendency does not have to be defined in terms of movement into the administrative structure, but may be defined in terms of increased role enlargement within the task system. Thus the "nodal" strategy may be activated in a style of management which is somewhat more "organic" than classical prescriptions. Nonetheless, this particular

FIGURE 6-4   OPERATING TASK GROUP STRUCTURE CELL (1) ROUTINE STRATEGY

Group structure:
Technicians, with appointed group leader.

Group process:
Indoctrination of technicians to a "solution" program:
1. Specifying quantity and quality objectives.
2. Critical control points and sequencing.
Coordination is built into the program.
Correction achieved by:
1. Task assistance by group leader.
2. Staff assistance or reallocation of resources.
3. "Fail-safe" mechanisms operating through the "exception" principle.

Group roles:
Independent instrumental implementation by technicians.
Troubleshooting and social-emotional support by group leader.

Group style:
Relatively high stress built into program in terms of quality and quantity specifications.

Group norms:
Indoctrination of technicians to norms of economy and efficiency and individual responsibility.

FIGURE 6-5   ADMINISTRATIVE SYSTEM STRUCTURE CELL (1) ROUTINE
STRATEGY

Planning:
Ends specified by Administrative System.
Process expectations specified by programs developed in the Administrative System.

Control:
Achieved by specification of critical control points (input, output, and process) within the program, with feedback both to the group and to the Administrative System.
Individual responsibility expected of each technician within the constraints of the program (thus largely self-control monitored by program feedback, with administrative intervention only by exception).

Rewards:
Reenforcement of loyalty to aggregate organizational system in reward structure.
Performance evaluation rests within the administrative system.

Boundary negotiations:
Restricted to feedback concerning resource and personnel adequacy in meeting program standards, given existing technology.

cell most closely approximates the design set forth in the bureaucratic or "formal organization" models.[26]

CELL 2: ENGINEERED STRATEGY. The second Operating Task Group structure is the Engineered Strategy. Here the organization is dealing with a task requiring solutions to nonrepetitive situations, and the organizational unit is staffed by specialists. Figure 6-6 summarizes the nodal Operating Task Unit strategy for dealing with this type of organizational situation.

As before, situations can be specified which will shift the organizational design away from this nodal position. For example, an increase

[26] The rough congruence between "bureaucracy" and routine task strategies is pointed out in the writings of several authors. See: J. March and H. Simon, *Organizations* (New York: John Wiley & Sons, Inc., 1958), chap. 2; F. Shull and A. Delbecq, *Selected Readings in Management* (Homewood, Ill.: Richard D. Irwin, Inc., 1962), pp. 3–29; and E. Litwak, "Models of Organization Which Permit Conflict," *American Journal of Sociology,* vol. 67, 1961, pp. 177–184.

FIGURE 6-6   OPERATING TASK GROUP STRUCTURE CELL (2) ENGI-
NEERED STRATEGY

Group structure:
Specialists with designated project leader.

Group process:
Specialists with project leader jointly develop programs:
1. Specifying quantity and quality objectives.
2. Critical time path control points.
3. Periodic review of program modifications.
Coordination achieved by centralized communication and authority in project leader with feedback to the group.
Correction achieved by:
1. Task assistance from leader.
2. Remedial effort by specialist.
3. Change in resource allocation of program by group.

Group roles:
Interdependent planning project by leader and specialists.
Independent instrumental implementation by specialists.
Coordination by project leader.

Group style:
Relatively high stress achieved by quantity and quality specifications agreed upon in joint consultation at major planning phases.

Group norms:
Individual responsibility by specialists.
Shared responsibility and group loyalty through agreed-upon program bench marks.
Economy and efficiency.

in program mechanization will result in a tendency for planning and control to be transferred to a staff unit within the Administrative System, thus decreasing the level of competence needed in member and project leader positions in the Operating Task Unit.[27] Likewise, an increase in program complexity beyond the conceptual ability of specialists will result in centralization of program planning and control in the Administrative System, so that specialists become technicians. In such situations,

---

[27] A review of propositions providing the logic of movement toward mechanization is given in J. Price, *Organizational Effectiveness: An Inventory of Propositions* (Homewood, Ill.: Richard D. Irwin, Inc., 1968), chap. 2.

error correction becomes vested in the fail-safe mechanisms of the program, or in Administrative Staff units. Each of these modifications implies a movement of the engineering function toward the Administrative System, so that the Operating Task Unit becomes more like cell 1. Cells 1 and 2 must, therefore, be seen as different nodal points on our strategy continuum.

Figure 6-7 presents the structure of the Administrative System which is the correlate of the Engineered Strategy in cell 2. Figures 6-6 and 6-7 taken together represent an organizational strategy, however, which

FIGURE 6-7 ADMINISTRATIVE SYSTEM STRUCTURE CELL (2) ENGINEERED STRATEGY

Planning:
Ends specified by Administrative System.

Input and output specified by joint negotiations between engineering group and Administrative System.

Process largely determined by the engineer specialists with group leader.

Control:
Achieved by specifications of critical control points; input and output control specified by the program in terms of financial parameters carefully defined by the Administrative System; process controls largely lodged within the engineering system.

Feedback concerning input, output, and process given to both engineering group and Administrative System.

Rewards:
Performance evaluation on resource utilization and output rests in Administrative System. Process evaluation rests with project leader in engineering system.

Reenforcement of loyalty to both aggregate organization and engineering group.

Boundary negotiations:
Financial parameters in terms of resources and output negotiated between Administrative System and engineering system, with Administrative System emphasizing resource parameters and engineering system emphasizing output-feasibility dimensions.

Once program is crystallized, renegotiations must be legitimized by engineering task group on the basis of process requirements.

is considerably more decentralized and organic than classical organizational models. These differences can be summarized as follows:

1. Relative to the planning function:
   a. The locus of process decisions rests in the Engineering Task Group itself, rather than being vested in a planning group within the Administrative System.
   b. The design predicts that resources and outputs are legitimate subjects for negotiation.
2. Relative to the control function, this nodal design:
   a. Allows for self-control, once the program is established in terms of input-output standards. Further, the specialists' expertise allows for bargaining and partial self-determination of bench marks, particularly in process control.
   b. Proposes that feedback and error correction in terms of the process dimension is the responsibility of the Engineering Group itself.
3. Relative to rewards:
   a. Performance evaluation in terms of process is located in the project leader within the Engineering System.
   b. Career ascendency may be within the Engineering Specialist System, or in terms of assuming the linkage role between the Administrative and Engineering Systems as project coordinator; thus career ascendency is not restricted only to movement into the Administrative System itself.[28]

CELL 3: CRAFT STRATEGY. Cells 3 and 4 represent strategies intrinsically different from the two prior strategies. In both of the latter cells, the definition and solutions to the organizational task are seen as being encompassed in the competence of the personnel rather than in the framework of a program or system. To state it in another way, the program is "between the ears" of skilled personnel.

The Craft Strategy for an Operating Task Group is presented in Figure 6-8. Here the organization is dealing with a repetitive task situation, but is utilizing craftsmen or professionals to cope with the task, as opposed to an engineering or machine system. Figure 6-9 presents the structure of the Administrative System which is the correlate of the Craft Strategy, cell 3. Obviously, the total organizational design, resulting from juxtaposing the two figures, is significantly different from the bureaucratic model. Here planning, control, and distribution of rewards largely rest within the Professional or Craft Group. The Administrative System is no longer the command system, but is largely a support or service system for craftsmen or professionals.

---

[28] The saliency of multiple career systems, both with task-group systems and within Administrative Systems, is dealt with in: V. Thompson, *Modern Organization* (New York: Alfred A. Knopf, Inc., 1961), pp. 194–197.

Of course, several modifications can increase the relative power of the Administrative System. If the craft is generated within the organization, and no outside craft or professional reference group exists, the potential will increase for the Administrative System to be more proactive. Likewise, where contract negotiations with the organization's clients are controlled by the Administrative System, where administrative services are very central to the craftsman or professional so that he becomes dependent upon the services, and/or where resources are scarce and largely generated by the Administrative System, one can expect that the craftsman or Professional Task Group will have less dominance over the Administrative System. Nonetheless, the Craft Strategy necessarily implies that the craftsman or professional will be in a powerful position to maintain semi-independence from the Administrative System.

CELL 4: HEURISTIC STRATEGY. The final Operating Task Group structure is the Heuristic Strategy. Here the organization is dealing with a task situation which is unique or nonrepetitive, and the personnel involved include professional or highly trained personnel who possess conceptual and personality characteristics compatible with creative pro-

FIGURE 6-8   OPERATING TASK GROUP STRUCTURE CELL (3) CRAFT STRATEGY

Group structure:
   Semi-independent craftsmen or professionals with administration.
Group process and roles:
   Independent consultation, diagnosis, and task implementation by craftsmen or professionals.
   Coordination of resource services by administration.
   Consultation with peers, initiated by the craftsman or professional when difficulties are encountered.
   Peer review board to deal with charges of incompetence.
   Peer-administrative consultations regarding resource planning.
Group style:
   Moderate stress created by intragroup comparisons and achievement norms in craft or professional reference groups.
Group norms:
   Professionalism in terms of both quality standards and personnel integrity.

FIGURE 6-9   ADMINISTRATIVE SYSTEM STRUCTURE CELL (3) CRAFT
STRATEGY

Planning:
Input, output, and process requirements specified by craftsmen or professionals, modified by resource limitations reported by Administrative System.

Administrative services programmed through joint negotiations between craftsmen or professionals and Administrative System.

Control:
Resource utilization and limitation feedback given by Administrative System to craftsmen or professionals.

Input, output, and processing control is the responsibility of individual craftsmen or professionals, subject to intermittent peer review or consultation by peers upon the request of a fellow craftsman or professional.

Rewards:
Performance evaluation based on peer-group rating.

Reenforcement of loyalty is largely to profession or craft reference groups, with moderate organizational loyalty.

Boundary negotiations:
Financial parameters in terms of resources and administrative services negotiated by Administrative System, with professionals or craftsmen having allocational veto power.

cesses. Figure 6-10 presents the nodal organizational strategy and Figure 6-11 the corollary Administrative System.[29]

Obviously, the strategy lies outside conventional organizational prescriptions. Nonetheless, task situations and task groups seeking to approximate the heuristic nodal strategy are part of every complex organization.[30]

[29] For a complete rationale for the creative decision process, refer to: A. Delbecq, "The Management of Decision-making Within the Firm," *op. cit.;* W. Scott, "The Creative Individual," *Academy of Management Journal,* September, 1965; L. Cummings, "Organizational Climates for Creativity," *Academy of Management Journal,* September, 1965; V. Thompson, "Bureaucracy and Innovation," *Administrative Science Quarterly,* June, 1965; Gary Steiner, *The Creative Organization* (Chicago, Ill.: University of Chicago Press, 1965).

[30] Professor Victor A. Thompson makes the following point: "Another possibly important dimension is whether the project or task group is formally constituted or has come together informally because of felt need to solve some problem that the formal structure prevented solving. I imagine that informal organization of this type is more prevalent than is suspected."

Classical organization theories (whether the bureaucratic or formal organizational model) posited a single strategy encompassing a design both for Operating Work Units and for the Administrative System. In contrast, studies of organizations show that there is significant intrastructural variation within complex organizations, as well as interorganizational variation between organizations. One cannot use a single, stereotyped organization model and meaningfully understand the rich variety of task and administrative units within modern complex organizations.

FIGURE 6-10   OPERATING TASK GROUP STRUCTURE CELL (4) HEURISTIC STRATEGY

Group structure:
Heterogeneous administrative, professional, and technical personnel with creative capacities, who bring to bear diverse expertise with a leader who facilitates creative group processes.

Group processes:
Independent analyses and solution study; joint group evaluation of independent study with final decision by majority rule, growing out of:
1. Full participation by each member and spontaneous communication.
2. Avoidance of premature closure (i.e., deliberate treatment of problem and emphasis on analysis rather than early solution commitment).
3. Careful attention to heuristic processes by leader.

Group roles:
Careful and effective individual problem analysis followed by open communication and "hitchhiking" in joint group evaluation.

Group style:
Relaxed, nonstressful environment.
Ego-supportive interaction but open disagreement.
Absence of time constraints with emphasis on quality of analysis.

Group norms:
Support originality, allow eccentricity and communication openness.
Seeks high quality independent effort and full participation in group effort.
Seeks integrative decisions through analysis and creative compromise.

Planning:

Administrative System is not intruded into planning process except to negotiate for representation of vital administrative linkages in the group structure and contribute to the general problem definition, especially in terms of the genotype function of the organization.

Control:

As bounded by the propriety of the genotype function, within the heuristic task group itself.

Rewards:

Performance evaluation is group centered, as opposed to individual centered.

Due to time span removing outcome evaluation from group solution proposal, evaluation is often based on process measures. Process, however, can only be measured in terms of adherence to general norms concerning creativity.

Loyalty is to heuristic group and motivation is process as well as task intrinsic.

Boundary negotiations:

Heuristic group specifies amount of resources and "slack" required; generally given open-ended commitment with vague, general organizational parameters specified.

One must necessarily speak of a variety of organizational designs and a variety of administrative systems for coping with different mixes of these nodal forms.[31]

Here, we have attempted to indicate the logic and nature of variation within organizational units and systems, and the particular usefulness of explaining this variation in terms of the two continua dealing with the nature of task and personnel variability. While we recognize that we are dealing with continua which admit limitless variety in organiza-

[31] For studies dealing with intra-organizational structural variation, see: R. Hall, *op. cit.*, and D. Katz and R. Kahn, *The Social Psychology of Organizations* (New York: John Wiley & Sons, Inc., 1966), chap. 5. Yet Professor Victor A. Thompson contends that ". . . it is dangerous to overstress this. The fact is that most people, most of the time, are in a bureaucratic milieu. These departures are increasing, but they cause a lot of pain and the interesting questions are: (1) Why are they increasing? and (2) Why do they cause so much pain?"

tional forms, we feel we have successfully isolated strategic nodal strategies along the relevant continua.

Administrative Configuration of Matrix Design

As an agent of the system, an actor is constrained by the organization. Specifically, he is subject to its decision rules and regulatory activities, that is, he is subject to its controls. Before turning to such a discussion, however, we must examine the general configuration of contemporary organizations as we conceive of it, since this format provides the bases of membership control. Then, we will discuss administrative linkages between this generalized structure and the Operating Task Units.

ORGANIZATIONAL POISE

Earlier, we described the matrix design as composed as four nodal task units, with autonomy from the Administrative System varying by the characteristics of the personnel and the nature of the technology of each. The support for this contention lies in the notions that: (1) cosmo-professionals demand and justify more autonomy than local technicians, and (2) unique unspecified problems are less subject to external control and programming.[32] To the extent that it exists, autonomy has important implications for any discussion of control.[33]

Organizations within the same industry vary in their relative emphasis on this task-unit continuum. Juvenile correctional institutions, for example, emphasize the autonomous end of the continuum more than do maximum-security prisons (Street, 1965, pp. 40–45). Business firms within the same industry are characterized individually by their innovative behavior versus more routine production of standard times (cf. Fouraker and Stopford, 1968, pp. 47–56). From this we infer that controls for task units at the autonomous end of the continuum are less detailed and specific and, thus, the Administrative System is subjected to more uncertainty when prescribing for such task units. Thus, we want to comment on the hazards to the Administrative System of the various nodal cells by degree of autonomy. For this purpose, we visualize the relative emphasis across the continuum as a vector, shifting from the Administrative System.

[32] It is interesting to note that the cosmo-professional not only carries his own program with him, rather than being externally engineered, but also more readily perceives the technology associated with the local technicians as being variable and multiple-purpose than do the latter.

[33] For a discussion of differing control structures as related to local unions, see: Tannenbaum and Kahn, 1957, pp. 127–140.

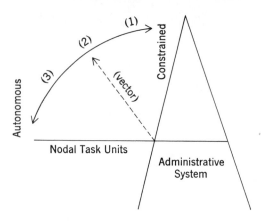

FIGURE 6-12 ORGANIZATIONAL POISE BY TASK-
UNIT EMPHASIS

As presented in Figure 6-12, vector 2 is mixed between the autonomous, or venturesome, and constrained, or dependent, dimensions, while
vector 1 would be more purely dependent and vector 3 would be more
purely autonomous.[34] If such is the case, poise 1 of the organization
contains less uncertainty than does 3 for the Administrative System.[35]
This tendency can be accounted for by at least three explanations:

1. The Administrative System is less able to program the technology of
the more autonomous units, since the program resides "between the ears" of
the professionals. This inability is compounded by the fact that such programs
may not be so available in the Administrative System, and may depend on
knowledge generated externally to the organization, perhaps at a university
or in an apprenticeship program;

2. The span of discretion (period of time between reviews) is longer for
autonomous units. This difficulty is compounded by the fact that such units
may be operationalizing the organization charter into specific output definitions,
semi-independently of the Administrative System and bargaining for resources
on the basis of their mystique; and

[34] We use the word "vector" here because distance as well as direction has relevance
in some of that which follows.

[35] Another, but more tentative, hypothesis can be described in terms of the poise
of the organization in this way: We would expect low conflict in position 1, but
higher inter-unit conflict in the mixed position, position 2. Further, we would
anticipate high intra-unit conflict in position 3, because of the differing programs
internalized by the various professionals. Organizational conflict is discussed in the
following chapter.

3. The professional has low tolerance for highly specified means or progress reviews, being inclined toward ends control. This disinclination is amplified by the fact that cosmo-professionals may not perceive it as rewarding to be promoted into the Administrative System or to be judged in terms of its norms. Further, diagnostic units, by themselves, may generate external funding, freeing them from the financial constraints normally used as leverage when the Administrative System bargains with task units relative to resource allocations and output specifications. (Cf. Hall, 1967, especially pp. 473–477.)

Increased independence tends to decrease the subjective predictability of task-unit behavior by the Administrative System. Accordingly, greater uncertainty is perceived by the latter with respect to these more autonomous units.[36]

ENVIRONMENTAL DETERMINANTS

These notions of autonomy are based partially upon the presumption that task units do have some exposure to the external environment, that is, they may not be buffered completely by the containing organization—all task units may not be wholly closed within the system. If it is closed within the system, the countervailing power of a task unit may be so weak as to cause uncertainty in dealing with external forces, that is, the environment is perceived, not only as dynamic, but also as relatively uncontrollable. (Cf. Emery and Trist, 1963, pp. 20–26.)

As McWhinney (1967, p. 1) states: "One of the functions which organizations perform is to buffer the individual member (task unit) from the impact of the chaotic interrelation of everything to everything. Organizations free the member (unit) to effectively deal with just so much of the environment as his intellect and psyche permit." In this light, matrix design would suggest that the routine task unit (cell 1) would be closely contained, while the diagnostic task unit (cell 4) would have greater exposure.

As implied above, task units vary in their ability to operationalize their individual organizational functions. To the extent that the modern complex organization conceives of its objective as broad and general-purpose, the variance across the task units on our continuum is high. For certain task units, goal reduction is possible and their objectives become rather fully operationalized in the form of methods or, perhaps, procedures. For other units, goal definition is made only in terms of a broad

[36] There may be a constant tug-of-war between the Administrative System, wanting more predictability, and the autonomous task units, desiring to maintain their relative independence. Some quarters hold that, since these units tend to ossify, a change in personnel must take place by forcing them closer to the Administrative System.

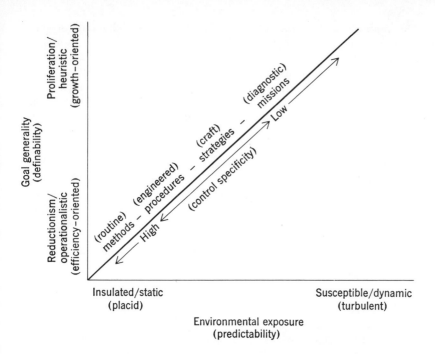

FIGURE 6-13   ENVIRONMENTAL PREDICTABILITY AND ORGANIZATIONAL DEFI-
NITION OF TASK UNITS

genotype[37] function where objectives are largely given as strategic briefings or mission orientations. Now, environmental exposure and functional universalism can be combined into a pattern of strategies, as presented in Figure 6-13.

To exemplify the application of this taxonomy, we can show that objectives for routine task units would be operational goals, or specified methods, while those for diagnostic task units would relate to the organizational charter—the genotype function. Moreover, for routine or machined units, the market would appear as closed or fixed and the technology as standardized and single-purpose. For diagnostic or innovative units, the market would be conceived as open and largely uncommitted, with the technology of the organization conceptualized as variable and general-purpose.

[37] Our meaning of "genotype function" is perhaps more limited than that of Katz and Kahn (1966, p. 111), who state: "By genotype function we refer to the type of activity in which the organization is engaged as a subsystem of the larger society. Thus we are concerned with the throughput or work that gets done in relation to its contribution to the surrounding social structure." We mean merely that AT&T is involved in the communication field and TWA in transportation.

To the extent that control systems in modern complex organizations are determinants or reinforcing of these propositions, they in turn will be multiple and varied. Certainly, alternative control systems—with their differences—are subject to description. (Cf. Miles and Vergin, 1966, esp. pp. 57–62.) Thus, we give our attention to that discussion.

Alternative Control Systems

The conception and design of an organization, especially role definitions and interaction linkages, are clearly major determinants of the nature and process of control. Organization structure and control are inextricably intertwined because either structure is the conduit of control, or the requirements of control dictate structure. Thus, any discussion of a matrix organization design must concern itself with an inherent property; related control systems. In addition, control techniques have significant social-psychological implications for administering organizational decisions. (See Tannenbaum and Kahn, 1957, pp. 127–128.)

IMPOSED CONTROL

An organization must be regulated internally for efficient goal accomplishment[38] and, to be effective, it must be assured that its diverse activities are "in control."[39] This imperative suggests that there must be some function or agency within the organization to check on whether or not the various task units are achieving their goals and/or meeting operational standards and, if they are not, to correct their behavior toward relevant performance criteria. This specialization and centralization of the function make for the imposition of, at least, the monitoring of task units by an organizational agent external to the task unit. For purposes of this discussion, we refer to that agent as the "Administrative System," although control is only one function of this system. Further, as we discuss later, certain aspects of control are performed within the task units themselves.

The most common type of regulatory system is error or feedback control.[40]

[38] Lawrence and Lorsch (1967) suggest the following means for integration of organizational parts: committees, schedules, staff departments, and unofficial activities directed toward unity.

[39] An organization is monitored by the external or containing environment. Society is concerned with the purposes for which its resources are expended and with the economy and effectiveness with which these resources are transformed.

[40] This type is presented here in its more rudimentary form. For a more detailed discussion, see Miles and Vergin (1966), pp. 57–65.

With this type of control, when performance deviates significantly from an established standard (as *CD* in Figure 6-14), the regulator sends certain instructions to direct operative performance back toward standard (as *EF* in Figure 6-14). This feature of error control holds interesting implications for the Administrative System. If only error control is practiced, actual behavior may be in continuous oscillation around the desired standard of performance. If so, it may be "normal" for performance of the task unit to deviate continuously beyond desired control limits.

Deviations from standard may be "dampened," however, either internally or externally. In terms of indigenous behavior, employees—because of conditioning or motivation—may hold to close tolerances on task standards. In addition, the Administrative System may reduce the latitude allowable for acceptable performance, including heightened inspection and penalties for deviations. But tighter controls, imposed externally on the task unit, have certain limitations. In the first place, the higher the quality requirements, the fewer the personnel who can meet standard performance. In the second place, because of the possibility of human error, the closer the tolerances, the less the viability of the "exception principle," that is, the more the exceptions from expected behavior with which the Administrative System must deal. Third, the tighter the controls, the more elaborate the inspection-monitoring system must be.

However, there are control systems which do not require temperance until errors in performance have occurred, that is, where corrective ac-

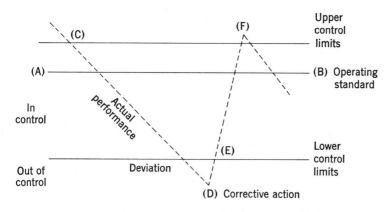

FIGURE 6-14 OPERATIONS OF A CLOSED-LOOP CONTROL SYSTEM

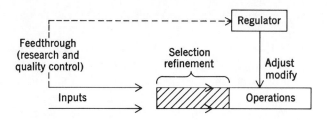

FIGURE 6-15   DIAGRAM DEPICTING INPUT CONTROL

tion is dependent upon measures of waste or scrap. One of these is called "input control" (cf. Box and Jenkins, 1966), which operates as:

> In the manufacture of rubber tires, the quality of the rubber shipped to a manufacturer may vary significantly. Apprised of this, the tire manufacturer can inspect relevant dimensions of the quality of raw material before production and adjust processing operations accordingly. For example, the length or temperature of the heat treatment given to the raw rubber might be increased. Input control can also be performed as, where the quality of copper shipped to a brass manufacturer varies so widely from standard, so that he establishes his own refinery to purify the quality of the copper before it is inventoried into operations. Personnel selection and orientation are analogous activities.

Increased attention has been given to input control in order to avoid ex post errors in operations—the attempt is to prune the input or operations for input variance before processing rather than delay until errors are observed in output. For human systems, input control can make for a high level of commonality or socialization, for example, in values, attitudes, and perceptions[41] (cf. Price, 1968, esp. chap. 2).

Nonetheless, while having many advantages, input control—like output control—cannot be relied upon solely for organizational effectiveness. Its limitations are related to two problems, measurement and predictability. On the one hand, and this is especially important where inputs become, in fact, cells of the social organism, it is difficult to isolate and measure human characteristics relevant to task requirements in today's complex organizations. On the other hand, and related to the above, problems of causality intrude themselves into the selection and

[41] The military has long recognized the necessity of input control as a supplement to output control and has established the Army War College partially for this purpose. Officers of varying backgrounds are sent to the College for training and indoctrination under the same instructors. Since these officers may be involved later in widespread battle-fronts, they are better able to predict decisions of each other on the front because of their exposure to the same strategy, values, and tactics in the War College.

placement of personnel, for example, the predictability of executive success is a case in point.

Because of limitations of both output, that is, corrective, and input, that is, preventative, controls, the administrative system often turns to "intermediate" processing control, or the specification and monitoring "how" the task unit is to perform rather than "what" it is to accomplish.[42] The practice of "means" control has its own limitations, as do the other two imposed control systems described here. In the first place, for example, the regulator can only observe and infer from acts which are suggestive of the nature of the output. Secondly, the personnel of the task units are restricted in creativity—innovation may be severely reduced where method is prescribed or monitored. Finally, mature task-oriented personnel resent the "close supervision" required by means control (cf. Mann and Dent, 1954).

ALTERNATIVES TO IMPOSED CONTROL

From the above discussion, we can see that these approaches to control are both simplistic and mechanistic. They are simplistic because of an almost exclusive focus on that which is formally imposed, especially feedback control; they are mechanistic in prescribing a set of activities that is largely denuded of the human or social context of the control sequence, that is, "establish standards, monitor performance, and correct deviations." Early management theory, for example, in an attempt to describe organizational behavior, used a mechanical analogy to exemplify regulated systems. Since this analogy was a closed system, administered social organizations were so viewed.

With human systems, as contrasted to most mechanical systems, there are forces acting for organizational rationality. Man brings to the work situation, culturally or innately, certain norms and aspirations which give him a sense of self-discipline; man can exercise self-control, and the need for external error control is reduced. In human systems, then, less reliance needs to be placed upon the regulatory function of the Administrative System because behavior can often be assumed to abide by technical, craft, or professional standards.

A second facilitator of the control of human, versus mechanical, systems is the presence of social control. A major factor, here, is the high exposure of the actor to other members of the work group. Members of work groups oftentimes have higher surveillance of one another than the Administrative System has over each of them. This surveillance,

[42] Recourse to this control type is particularly prevalent when completion of the task requires time durations longer than the fiscal period, or when the Administrative System is reviewed by its sponsoring or policy board in terms of progress reports.

reinforced by visible and immediate social disapproval by his peers, tends to curtail deviate behavior of the actor. Social control is additionally amplified with professional personnel because of their close identification with their craft or profession rather than with the Administrative System (cf. Katz and Kahn, 1966, pp. 340–350).

Any social unit transmits beliefs, norms, and customs which enhance its integrity, offer direction, and ensure its effectiveness. Complex organizations often ritualize and formally publish such regulatory directives. These become at least a minimal base for the disciplining aspects of structure; and the containing culture operates in a similar manner. Thus, the individual—as citizen and as organizational member—becomes a role actor within the organization subjected to two sets of normative prescriptions.[43]

He may find that these two roles, in terms of a specific act, are reinforcing, neutral, or conflicting. If conflicting, and he holds to the norm associated with his citizenship role, while conformity to the conflicting organizational norm is organizationally imperative, it must exercise power or influence. In this case, however, power will alienate him and he will conform only for ulterior motives. Accordingly, as Etzioni (1964, p. 51) contends: "His conformity is likely to be limited to the matters explicitly backed by power. He will be unlikely to volunteer information, show initiative, or cooperate, except when he is explicitly forced to." Indeed, if mobile, he may leave the organization or sabotage it.

In contrast, if the organizational norm is deemed legitimate, that is, reinforcing of another value which he holds for himself or one that is representative of another group to which he refers, he will be "internally" rewarded. Because of the artifactual nature of formal organizations, this psychologically sanctioned form of behavior is particularly important: such artifacts often provide few intrinsic job satisfactions; they are more likely to be structured so as to provide largely extrinsic rewards or penalities.[44] Accordingly, wherever attained, legitimacy holds deep power for organizational integrity.

This concept of legitimacy provides the base, then, of an alternative—self-discipline—to imposed control. If the organizational norm reinforces the code of his profession or craft, he will be inclined—in fact, induced—to pursue organizational standard. Assuming skill in implementation, the level of imposed control can be reduced. In this manner, we

[43] The individual plays many roles as a member of a variety of microsystems and, for any specific act, may refer to any one of them. That which is said about the citizenship role, however, is true of these specific organizations.

[44] Imposed control is a case in point: other than satisfactions obtained from conformity itself, behavior is conditioned largely from "external" sanctions, for example, wages.

propose the substitutability of social control and self-discipline for imposed control.[45]

Control Systems in Matrix Organizations

Let us discuss the emphasis on control forms relative to each cell in the earlier taxonomy of nodal task units of matrix organizations. In the exhibit that follows, Figure 6-16, we have illustrated the relative emphasis given to the various control forms by extreme ends of the autonomy continuum in the matrix design. Here, we note, as would be expected from the above, greater emphasis upon self-discipline versus imposed process control for diagnostic task units. We observe the contrary for the "routine" end of the continuum. We also note that group (collegial) control in the more heuristic units is substituted for imposed output control in the routine and engineered units.[46] In essence, our diagram suggests that, for those units reflected in the unshaded areas, control is performed proportionately more from within but, for those in shaded areas, control is imposed to considerably greater extent.

[45] For an early study illustrating the differential nature of control structures and one which graphically describes them, see: Williams, Hoffman, and Mann (1959), pp. 189–195.

[46] While an oversimplification, Figure 6-16 suggests areas of complementarity. Leadership is apparently complementary to input control. Such a relationship results from the fact that all processing adjustments usually cannot be anticipated from inspection of the inputs. Accordingly, supervision must be available for corrections of exceptional deviations in inputs.

Task Unit	Control system					
	Imposed			Social		Self-discipline
	Process	Output	Input	Leader	Group	
Routine						
Engineered						
Craft						
Diagnostic						

Code: Relative emphasis on autonomous end of continuum

Relative emphasis on adminstrative end of continuum

FIGURE 6-16   EMPHASIS ON CONTROL FORMS BY TYPE OF TASK UNIT

This distinction becomes increasingly clear as we consider the imposition of norms specifically directed toward the work environment proper, as shown in Table 6-2. This exhibit helps us to discriminate finitely among the four cells or task units where control is centered on three aspects of work environment, as:

1. *Task:* on the technical ability of the person.
2. *Process:* on the sequence of work flow.
3. *Goal:* on the end result or operating objective.[47]

Notice that, for cell 1, the Administrative System prescribes for all three work dimensions, goal, process, and task. We infer the breadth of this specification for the following reasons:

1. For the organization, the "market" has been analyzed, the product standardized, and the production system closed. The objective is operationally prescribed to obtain the benefits of routinization and specialization, that is, the efficiency norm dominates.

2. Given specified outputs, fixed technology, and optimal interrelations as constraints, the manner of task performance for the individual can be highly engineered. Scientific techniques can be brought to bear on the system for maximal solution.

3. Division of labor, with routinization, makes for a high degree of interdependence within the work unit. To gain the advantages of hierarchical perspective and specialization for dealing with coordination, planning and

[47] We wish to restrict the meaning of "objective" to that which is operationally defined. Although interacting with it, diagnostic units do operate within general constraints but most identifiably with organization charter or genotype function.

Table 6-2   Source of related control by type of task unit

| CELL | TASK UNIT TYPE | CONTROL APPLICATION TO: | | |
		GOAL	PROCESS	TASK
1	Routine	AS	AS	AS
2	Engineered	AS	AS	TU
3	Craft	AS	TU	TU
4	Diagnostic	TU	TU	TU

Code: AS = Control generated by Administrative System.
      TU = Control generated by Task Unit.

control are centralized in a staff unit. Thus, detailed controls are imposed upon the task unit via the Administrative System.

Because of needs for professional expertise and heuristic group interaction, and because of the lack of definitive objectives—in fact, goal redefinition is often its purpose—and the technological variability perceived by its personnel, imposed specifications are generally inappropriate for the diagnostic unit. Thus control, as with rewards and penalties, is internally generated in such task units, as indicated for cell 4 in Table 6-2.[48]

This presentation also aids us in discriminating between cells 2 and 3. It will be noted that the external regulator does prescribe the process for the engineering cell but does not do so for the craft unit. This difference is explained by the fact that, within engineering units, interaction is the mode, while much of the behavior in craft units is co-acting in nature. Task interaction in cell 2 suggests specialization, with administrative specification for coordination, as explained above for routine Task Units. With co-acting behavior, and with the manner of task performance intrinsic to the craftsman, as in the case of cell 3, imposed controls on process may impede more than they facilitate individual performance. Control, in this latter case, then, is largely on the operational objective rather than detailed on work flow (cf. Stinchcombe, 1959).

RESOURCE CONTROL BY TASK UNIT

There are, however, organizational controls other than those related to the work environment proper. Important among these are controls on resource utilization, chief among which are: time, personnel, and financing. Much of what we have said above, especially that relating to control of the intrinsic work situation itself, also pertains to what is described here.

Figure 6-17 presents the nature of the major linkages between the Administrative System and array of Task Units in terms of controls

[48] Professor Alan Filley suggests that Woodward's (1965, chap. 9) distinction between control forms is useful to Matrix. She distinguishes between that control which is built into the technology of the system and that exercised by the organization with the latter related to social relationships of the participants. Thus, for Matrix design, control in cells 1 and 2 is largely on technology via imposed control, with little emphasis upon social interaction because of the relatively mechanistic view of man-task behavior. For cells 3 and 4, however, little attention is given to task-process controls by the Administrative System because the Task Unit generates and maintains them. Therefore, since technological control grows out of social interaction, the latter dominates as intrinsic to the Task Unit itself. Filley, then, concludes that organizations, because of automation, may be moving away from technological control to that administered by the organization for production.

TIME SPAN:

Routine: With engineered and standardized performance, review of pace and quality is frequent; this is *intermediate fiscal* control.

Engineered: With the work system specified, processing is controlled but perhaps by project; this is *intermediate fiscal or project* control.

Craft: With processing and intermediate performance standards internalized, project termination may dominate; this is *project or fiscal* control.

Diagnostic: Heuristic operationalizing of new dimensions of the organization charter generally surpasses fiscal periods; this is *project* control.

PERSONNEL:

Routine: With task and process prescribed, personnel requirements are given; this is *total personnel* control.

Engineered: As above, but high functionalism requires that supervisors specify staff specialists; we call this *all but specialist* control.

Craft: Because of the artistic nature of craft work, only generalized attributes can be assessed; control is by *managers and subtask leaders.*

Diagnostic: As above, but with need for big mix of expertise; only control is on *managerial selection.*

FINANCE:

Routine: Within the closed system, utilization of finances predicted with high accuracy; this is *total financial* control.

Engineered: To the extent that staff specialists and the projects dominate *partial negotiations on limits* is necessitated.

Craft: With programs internalized by craftsmen and in the absence of means specification, *project negotiation* is required.

Diagnostic: Since some funding is generated internally and with difficulties in specifying output, we find *ex ante, partial* financial control.

on time, personnel, and finances. Note, again, how the characteristics of the two dimensions, technology and personnel—which we use to discriminate among the cells—dictate the appropriate linkages with the Administrative System. Note, too, that these linkages differ by kind and degree across the cells. With financial control, for example, the diagnostic unit may generate some of its own funding and hold fiscal authority for disbursements, while the craft unit may bargain with the Administrative System for project funding; but the routine unit operates only within the constraints established by the larger system. Thus, again, we observe sharp differences across the four cells of the Matrix organization.

The discussion above on the predictability of the environment and the definability of organizational goals contributes to understanding the nature of Task Unit control. If the Task Unit has exposure to a dynamic environment and its purpose is to heuristically operationalize organizational objectives, administrative control must take the form of mission briefing rather than task specification (cf. Etzioni, 1964, p. 68).

CONTROL SPECIFICITY BY TASK UNIT

This latter dimension of control further enhances understanding of these linkage systems. This dimension has to do with the specificity with which performance standards are communicated by the Administrative System, that is, with the latitude or discretionary content found in the norm statement.[49] The distinctions that we make in Figure 6-18 are crude and simplistic but illustrative of the depth of control as it relates to the various task units.

[49] Here, we wish to draw a distinction between clarity or ambiguity and the specificity or discretion with which a norm is transmitted. A norm may be clear and specific or broad and ambiguous. We are concerned with specificity, the detailedness with which action is specified.

Form of statement

		Positive	Negative
Behavioral focus	Means	(1) Routine	(2) Engineered
	Ends	(3) Craft	(4) Diagnostic

FIGURE 6-18   SPECIFICITY OF NORM STATEMENTS IN ESTABLISHING STANDARDS BY TASK UNIT

In this figure, we propose two aspects of the depth of specificity with which norm statements are transmitted: one, statements may be positive or negative in form—norms may prescribe a particular value or act, or merely make illegitimate a subset among a generic class of acts. The latter is held to offer more discretion, that is, to be less specific, than the former. Two, norms may focus upon the output, or end, of a particular act, or they may be centered on the behavior—the means— itself. The latter focus provides greater specificity than the former.

The four types of task unit can now be juxtaposed on this derived, four-celled matrix of specificity, as is done in Figure 6-18. Thus, we see the routine task unit as highly prescribed, with positive statements on means, while diagnostic units have high discretion, with negative statements on ends. As this taxonomy is studied against our full discussion of control, the fabric of administrative-task unit linkage is seen in its breadth and depth.

Conclusions and Implications

In this chapter, we have attempted: (1) through a cybernetic framework, to suggest how a general systems approach to management has disclosed new necessities for administrative decision making; and (2), through behavioral empiricism and theory, to describe personal and social realities of organizational decisions.

Our first concern was with the justification of collective behavior and its structure, especially bureaucracy, for we agree with Jennings (1959, p. 5) that, unlike the trend of democracy, the notion of bureaucracy "goes back as far as economic enterprise itself. We may even say that it goes back as far as social organization. Ever since Plato based his ideal state on specialization of effort and limitation of size to approximately 5,000 people, we have had both the beginning of bureaucracy and attempts to minimize it."

Bureaucracy, like profit maximizing, is subject to discussion; yet it does maintain itself. The controversy with this design, however, leads us to the following set of propositions on business organizations. These provided the base for the current chapter:

A. A business organization is more than an economic, decision-making unit; it is also a complex, social system.

B. For intelligent interaction in this complexity, the individual generally demands some type of structure for his behavior.

C. While certain social interactions are formally structured in the organization, some relationships and activities are not highly formalized.

D. Accordingly, formal structure is an abstraction (a crude conceptual map) of the actions of organization members and does not describe their behavior exactly.

E. In addition, the conventional design of business organizations (often called "bureaucracy") is under severe criticism today.

F. It is claimed, for example, that the business firm must pursue multiple goals and serve several publics in order to be successful.

G. If this is the case, its structure cannot be focused singly on profit opportunities from serving only one public—the customer.

H. From such logic, the business organization encompasses many instrumental, that is, processing, and maintenance or survival systems.

I. And each of these diverse, functioning systems requires its own sequence of activities and its own set of performance standards.

J. These differing operating systems crisscross the organization, and the individual manager finds himself performing in several of them.

K. Thus, the incumbent—the manager—to be most effective, must recognize the specific process to which he is contributing at any given time.

L. However, the ability to recognize and adjust to changing imperatives on individual behavior requires a high degree of role versatility.

M. Competing demands placed on a subordinate may result in an inability to make a decision known (ambivalence) and create frustrations associated with conflict.

N. The specialist feels confronted especially with the conflict between hierarchy, in the form of demands of the system, and task, in the form of requirements of the specialty.

O. If task specialization increases, managers may be chosen more for skills of support and housekeeping than for an all-knowing and authoritarian personality.

P. Deductively, the conclusion is made that promotions through the management hierarchy may be based on excellence in non-task, that is, nonoperational, assignments.[50]

These contentions led us to search for a model of organizations that appeared more viable than the bureaucratic form. From this search, Matrix structure evolved. Thus, here, we have contended that the modern complex organization contains a matrix of differentiated task units: some units involve structure and processes based upon closed-system imperatives, with performance tightly monitored and controls highly specified. Such organizations may also contain task units which are environmentally exposed, with innovation dominating and membership discretion broad. Where this variety exists, an organization can compete effectively with a standard product from one set of task units and, at

[50] For a kindred set of propositions, see: Cleland and King (1968), p. 168.

the same time, initiate endeavors for growth and adaptation in an ever-changing environment from another set.

But this variability in structure suggested differentiation of control systems, by form of control and its method of application. (Cf. Tomb, 1962.) In particular, we noted the changing emphasis in administrative control, as concern shifts toward the more organic dimension of the Matrix design, as: (1) talents of the personnel become more dominating as a resource; (2) task outputs are less subject to measurement; and (3) there is increasing inappropriateness of process control.[51]

Coinciding with this structural differentiation, the Matrix model specified nodal points which are congruent with a style of management within each cell consistent with contemporary organic theories of management. Nonetheless, we have pointed out that cells 1 and 2 have a systems orientation, while cells 3 and 4 have a person-centered orientation, which necessarily implies significantly different patterns of management in these polar positions. Thus this cleavage suggests a means of sorting between apparent conflicts in contemporary schools of management theory. At the same time, the absolute and necessary separation of all dimensions or organic styles of management from the systems-oriented cells is rejected.

Organizational structure can be treated as an independent as well as a dependent variable, and as associated with function and human resource. Early in the history of management theory, a standardized and mechanical approach was used as a stereotype to structure task units. Later concern was given to "organization management," that is, inter-departmental coordination. Coinciding with this latter evolvement, the theory of bureaucracy developed, which proposed attitudes and propositions on role behavior, especially specialization and personal expertise. Throughout these developments, the total organization was viewed as closed and fully clientele-directed. Now, however, there is evidence that organizations allocate energies to "publics" other than the product market, for example, the government, and can be viewed as an open system having attributes to offset the tendency for it to wear out.

Therefore, we observe that Matrix design provides the possibility of organizational life. If viewed as a closed system with the major input being "load"—materials operated on—the human-social processing system wears out unless its components create enough surplus, or "slack," so as to rejuvenate, or "heat," the system. The force for offsetting organizational "decay," that is, system entropy, other than perhaps certain kinds of organizational growth, is the "heat" created by the human com-

[51] For a discussion of "information gaps" of quantitative data for the Administrative System, especially that based upon accounting information, see: Roman (1962).

ponents of the system; and there are various potential sources of this heat. Among them are:

1. *Social facilitation:* Organizational creativity can be obtained from "social facilitation," which, in its simplest form, has to do with changes in performance of the solitary individual as he is exposed to social stimuli. Studies have shown that, under certain conditions, the productivity of an individual increases when operating within an interactive social environment (cf. Allport, 1954, pp. 45–48).

2. *Personal motivation:* There is a growing body of evidence to the effect that the opportunity for self-actualization of the member can lead to performance beyond minimal requirements for holding the job. Task enrichment is one means for tapping this need for self-actualization. Variation within task assignments may actually increase performance (cf. Fiske, 1961, p. 142–144).

3. *Subordinate participation:* Man is not necessarily simply hedonistic or solely passive to organizational structure. Even at the lowest levels in the organization, he is a cognitive piece of processing hardware; he can perceive problems and solve them on his own.[52] As management recognizes this ability and offers him opportunity to participate in decisions which affect him, further "heat" may be created in the organization. (Cf. March and Simon, 1958, pp. 53–55.)

While these sources of organizational rejuvenation provide little of the underpinning for current practice in bureaucratic structures, the modern manager is becoming increasingly sensitive to them for organizational development, especially in the more highly interactive task units of Matrix organizations. Equally functional, then, is the ability of Matrix design to generate negative entropy and to attract cosmo-professional members from our increasingly literate society. This latter problem is not unimportant to the modern organization. Therefore, notions of "fusion," as related to Matrix, remain to be developed.

Since control is the crucial link between member desires and organizational requirements, it is a basic determinant of individual decisions and satisfactions as well as of organizational efficiency and effectiveness. Yet all organizational constraints may not be deemed legitimate by the constituent. To this extent, then, the nature and degree of control may be viewed as a negative influence on the individual to which he responds

---

[52] Much needs to be learned about the nature and value of "participation," but empirical evidence gives support to its potential. Certainly, a managerial attitude that workers are lazy, ignorant, and contrary contributes to organization decay, especially if this attitude is manifested to the members. Predictions for the future reinforce the implication made here, particularly as the educational level of our culture rises and as the concept of democracy becomes increasingly viable within micro systems.

in various ways. Such concerns are discussed in the chapter which follows.

bibliography

ALLPORT, G. W.: "The Historical Background of Modern Social Psychology," in Gardner Lindzey (ed.), *Handbook of Social Psychology* (Cambridge, Mass.: Addison-Wesley Publishing Co., 1954).

ANNA, H. J., and H. G. FREDERICKSON: *Project Management and the Organization,* Working papers nos. 20 and 22, Syracuse NASA Project, Syracuse University, 1969 and 1970.

ARGYRIS, C.: "Understanding Human Behavior in Organizations: One Viewpoint," in Mason Haire (ed.), *Modern Organization Theory* (New York: John Wiley & Sons, Inc., 1959).

BEER, S.: "Under the Twilight Arch," *General Systems,* vol. 5, 1960, pp. 9–21.

BENNETT, J. G.: "General Systematics," *Systematics,* vol. 1, no. 1, June, 1963, pp. 5–19.

BENNIS, W.: "Beyond Bureaucracy," *Transactions,* July–August, 1965.

BLAU, P. M., and W. R. SCOTT: *Formal Organizations* (San Francisco: Chandler Publishing Co., 1962).

BOX, G., and G. M. JENKINS: "Models for Prediction and Control," Technical Report no. 72, Department of Statistics, University of Wisconsin, May, 1966. (Mimeographed.)

CLELAND, D. T.: "Understanding Project Authority Requires Study of Its Environment," *Aerospace Management,* vol. 2, no. 1, Spring–Summer, 1967, pp. 5–14.

―――, and W. R. KING: *Systems Analysis and Project Management* (New York: McGraw-Hill Book Company, 1968).

CUMMINGS, L. L.: "Organizational Climates for Creativity," *Academy of Management Journal,* vol. 8, no. 3, September, 1965, pp. 220–227.

CYERT, R. M., and J. G. MARCH: *A Behavioral Theory of the Firm* (Englewood Cliffs, N.J.: Prentice-Hall, Inc., 1963).

DAVIS, K.: *Role Perceptions of the Job of Program Manager in Technical Work* (Los Angeles: Western Management Science Institute, January, 1965).

DELBECQ, A. L.: "The Management of Decision-Making within the Firm," *Academy of Management Journal,* vol. 10, no. 4, December, 1967, pp. 329–341.

―――: "The Social Psychology of Executive Roles Re-examined," *Business Perspectives,* vol. 2, no. 3, Spring, 1966, pp. 23–28.

EMERY, F. E., and E. L. TRIST: "The Causal Texture of Organizational Environments," *Human Relations,* vol. 18, 1963, pp. 20–26.

ETZIONI, A.: *Modern Organization* (Englewood Cliffs, N.J.: Prentice-Hall, Inc., 1964).

EVAN, W. M.: "Superior-subordinate Conflict in Research Organizations," *Administrative Science Quarterly,* vol. 10, no. 1, June, 1965, pp. 52–65.

EVANS, C.: *History of the United Mine Workers of America,* vol. 1 (Indianapolis: Alligo Printing, 1956).

FISKE, D. W.: "Effects of Monotonous and Restricted Stimulation," in D. W. Fiske and S. R. Maddi (eds.), *Functions of Varied Experience* (Homewood, Ill: The Dorsey Press, Inc., 1961), pp. 106–144.

FOURAKER, L. E., and J. M. STOPFORD: "Organizational Structure and the Multinational Strategy," *Administrative Science Quarterly*, vol. 13, no. 1, June, 1968, pp. 47–56.

GANTT, H. L.: "A Bonus System of Rewarding Labor," *Trans. ASME*, vol. 23, 1902, pp. 341–372.

GORE, W. J.: "Decision-making Research: Some Prospects and Limitations," in S. Mailick and E. H. VanNess (eds.), *Concepts and Issues in Administrative Behavior* (Englewood Cliffs, N.J.: Prentice-Hall, Inc., 1962).

GOULDNER, A. W.: "Cosmopolitans and Locals: Toward an Analysis of Latent Social Roles," *Administrative Science Quarterly*, vol. 1, December, 1957, pp. 281–306, vol. 2, March, 1958, pp. 444–480.

————: "Organizational Analysis," in R. K. Merton, L. Broom, and L. S. Cottrell, Jr. (eds.), *Sociology Today* (New York: Basic Books, Inc., 1959), pp. 400–419.

GRIMES, A. J., S. M. KLEIN, and F. A. SHULL: "Matrix Model: An Empirical Test," accepted for Spring, 1970, meetings of the Midwest Academy of Management, November, 1969.

HABERSTROH, C. J.: "Control as an Organizational Process," in A. H. Rubenstein and C. J. Haberstroh (eds.), *Some Theories of Organization* (Homewood, Ill.: The Dorsey Press, Inc., 1966).

HALL, R. H.: "Some Organizational Considerations in the Professional-organizational Relationship," *Administrative Science Quarterly*, vol. 12, no. 3, December, 1967, pp. 461–478.

HARBISON, F., and C. MYERS: *Management in the Industrial World* (New York: McGraw-Hill Book Company, 1959).

JACQUES, ELLIOTT: *Equitable Payment* (London: Heineman Educational Books, Ltd., 1961).

JENNINGS, E. E.: "The Authoritarian Cultural Lag in Business," *Journal of the Academy of Management*, vol. 2, no. 2, August, 1959.

KAHN, R. L., D. M. WOLFE, R. P. QUINN, J. D. SNOEK, and R. A. ROSENTHAL: *Organizational Stress: Studies in Role Conflict and Ambiguity* (New York: John Wiley & Sons, Inc., 1964).

KATZ, D., and R. L. KAHN: *Social Psychology of Organizations* (New York: John Wiley & Sons, Inc., 1966).

KNIGHT, F. H.: *The Economic Organization* (New York: Augustus M. Kelley, Inc., 1933).

KRUPP, S.: *Pattern in Organization Analysis* (New York: Chilton Co., 1961).

LAWRENCE, P. R., and J. W. LORSCH: *Organization and Environment: Managing Differentiation and Integration* (Boston: Graduate School of Business Administration, Harvard University, 1967).

LIKERT, R.: *The Human Organization* (New York: McGraw-Hill Book Company, 1967).

LITWAK, E.: "Modes of Bureaucracy Which Permit Conflict," *The American Journal of Sociology*, vol. 67, no. 2, September, 1961, pp. 177–184.

MANN, F. C., and J. DENT: *Appraisals of Supervisors and Attitudes of Their Employees in an Electric Power Company* (Ann Arbor: Survey Research Center, University of Michigan, 1954).

MARCH, J. G., and H. A. SIMON: *Organizations* (New York: John Wiley & Sons, Inc., 1958).

MCCLOSKY, H., and J. H. SCHAAR: "Psychological Dimensions of Anomie," *American Sociological Review*, vol. 30, no. 1, February, 1965, pp. 14–40.

MCWHINNEY, WM. H.: *Organizational Form, Decision Modalities and the Environment* (Los Angeles: The Graduate School of Business Administration, University of California, 1967). (Mimeographed.)

MERTON, R. K.: "Bureaucratic Structure and Personality," *Social Forces*, vol. 17, 1940, pp. 560–568.

MIDDLETON, C. J.: "How to Set up a Project Organization," *Harvard Business Review*, March–April, 1967, pp. 73–82.

MILES, R. E., and R. C. VERGIN: "Behavioral Properties of Variance Control," *California Management Review*, vol. 8, no. 3, Spring, 1966, pp. 57–65.

PARSONS, T.: *The Social System* (Glencoe: The Free Press, 1951).

————: *Structure and Process in Modern Society* (New York: The Free Press, 1964).

PERROW, C.: "A Framework for the Comparative Analysis of Organizations," *American Sociological Review*, vol. 32, no. 2, April, 1967, pp. 194–208.

PETERSON, R. W.: "New Venture Management in a Large Company," *Harvard Business Review*, vol. 45, no. 3, May–June, 1967, pp. 68–76.

PETIT, T. A.: *Freedom in the American Economy* (Homewood, Ill.: Richard D. Irwin, Inc., 1964).

PFIFFNER, J. M., and F. P. SHERWOOD: *Administrative Organization* (Englewood Cliffs, N.J.: Prentice-Hall, Inc., 1960).

PRICE, J.: *Organization Effectiveness: An Inventory of Propositions* (Homewood, Ill.: Richard D. Irwin, Inc., 1968).

READ, W. H.: "Upward Communication in Industrial Hierarchies," in A. H. Rubenstein and C. J. Haberstroh (eds.), *Some Theories of Organization* (Homewood, Ill.: Richard D. Irwin, Inc., 1966).

ROMAN, D. D.: "Organization for Control," *Proceedings of the Academy of Management*, Pittsburgh, July, 1962.

SCOTT, WM. E.: "The Creative Individual," *Academy of Management Journal*, vol. 8, no. 3, September, 1965, pp. 212–220.

SCOTT, WM. G.: *The Management of Conflict* (Homewood, Ill.: Richard D. Irwin, Inc., 1966).

SELZNICK, P.: *TVA and the Grass Roots* (Berkeley and Los Angeles: University of California Press, 1949).

SHEPARD, H.: "Changing Interpersonal and Inter-group Relationships in Organizations," in J. March (ed.), *Handbook of Organizations* (Chicago: Rand McNally & Company, 1965), pp. 1115–1144.

SHULL, F. A.: *Matrix Structure and Project Authority for Optimizing Organizational Capacity* (Carbondale, Ill.: Business Research Bureau, Southern Illinois University, 1965).

SHULL, F. A., and A. L. DELBECQ: *Selected Readings in Management* (Homewood, Ill.: Richard D. Irwin, Inc., 1962).

SIMON, H. A.: *Administrative Behavior* (New York: The Macmillan Company, 1947).

———: *The New Science of Management Decision* (New York: Harper & Brothers, 1960).

STEINER, G.: *The Creative Organization* (Chicago: University of Chicago Press, 1965).

STINCHCOMBE, A.: "Bureaucratic and Craft Administration of Production: A Comparative Study," *Administrative Science Quarterly,* vol. 4, September, 1959, pp. 168–187.

STOGDILL, R. M.: "Leadership, Membership and Organization," in D. Cartwright and A. Zander (eds.), *Group Dynamics* (Evanston, Ill.: Row, Peterson & Company, 1953), pp. 39–51.

———: "Personnel Factors Associated with Leadership: A Survey of the Literature," *Journal of Psychology,* vol. 25, no. 1, January, 1948, pp. 35–71.

STREET, D.: "The Inmate Group in Custodial and Treatment Settings," *American Sociological Review,* vol. 30, no. 1, Feburary, 1965, pp. 40–55.

TANNENBAUM, A. S., and R. L. KAHN: "Organizational Control Structure," *Human Relations,* vol. 10, no. 2, 1957, pp. 127–140.

THOMPSON, J. D., and A. TUDEN: "Strategies, Structures, and Processes of Organizational Decision," in J. D. Thompson, P. B. Hammond, R. W. Hawkes, B. H. Junker, and A. Tuden (eds.), *Comparative Studies in Administration* (Pittsburgh: University of Pittsburgh Press, 1959).

THOMPSON, V. A.: "Bureaucracy and Innovation," *Administrative Science Quarterly,* vol. 10, no. 1, June, 1965, pp. 1–20.

———: *Modern Organization* (New York: Alfred A. Knopf, Inc., 1961).

TOMB, J. O.: "A New Way to Manage—Integrated Planning and Control," *California Management Review,* vol. V, no. 1, Fall, 1962.

UDY, S. H.: "Technical and Institutional Factors in Production Organizations," *American Journal of Sociology,* 1961–1962, pp. 247–254.

WALTON, C. C.: "Management in Retrospect," in *Management 2000* (Hamilton, N.Y.: The American Foundation for Management Research, Inc., 1968), pp. 139–150.

WILLIAMS, L. K., L. R. HOFFMAN, and F. C. MANN: "An Investigation of the Control Graph: Influence in a Staff Organization," *Social Forces,* vol. 37, no. 3, March, 1959, pp. 189–195.

WOODWARD, J.: *Industrial Organization: Theory and Practice* (London: Oxford University Press, 1965).

seven

ADMINISTRATIVE ROLE CONFLICT

In the preceding chapter, we focused on the cooperative aspects of organizational behavior. While we were concerned with perceptual fragmentation of the organization, we presupposed general concurrence among its parts with its definition. There, decisions were largely econological, with allocations of resources directed by introducing organizational constraints on the individual decision makers. In this perspective, each decision center, or managerial position, was perceived as locked into a rational structure which functionally related its decisions to the objective or objectives of the organization. The organizational body responded in logical fashion to environmental needs in such a way as to optimize survival. Our deductions were moderated by: (1) the logic of goal reduction, (2) reinforcement offered by the authority structure, and (3) the selected expertise of the incumbent, aided by (4) the formal communication system.

Certainly, a basic justification of organization lies in benefits derived from the cooperative interaction of its members. Yet the bringing together of a collectivity of people, harnessing them in terms of scarce resources, and focusing their efforts upon a limited set of objectives make for competition and conflict. Gomberg (1964, p. 50) states:

> The very concept of organization implies the existence of conflict, conflict with other individuals, conflict with the environment, conflict with other individual organizations or coalitions of organizations and, above all, conflict within the organization. If no conflict were present, there would be no need for organization, the ends of individuals would be realized without any effort.

In this chapter, therefore, we wish to change our perspective and look at managerial incumbents who make decisions within the organizational setting. We view the organization as a coalition or coalitions of individuals who are cooperating in the achievement of common objective or objectives but who are also making decisions, within the collective setting, in terms of their own private purposes, and Hayes (1955, p. 178), for example, does contend that administrators often put personal, private ends, such as security, prestige, and aggrandizement, above economic input-output relationships.

Earlier, we were most concerned with the imperatives on cooperative behavior. Now we will take a different stance and investigate aspects of "noncooperative" behavior. As Krupp (1961, p. x) has said: ". . . an interpretation of the business firm through the language of 'group cooperation' may be analogous to a description of a jungle using the theory of a farm." Thus we contend that as much, if not more, understanding and predictability can be gained by analyzing the social and egoistic needs of man as he operates within an organization as by viewing the decision behavior of man as a reflexive accommodation to economic imperatives of the organization.

Sociology of Conflict

The world would seemingly have known conflict since the formation of human groups—including the family. Early concern with the evolution of man stressed the competitive necessity for endurance. Then, from Malthus's works (especially, *Essay of the Principle of Population*, 1798), Darwin proposed the notion that struggle and conflict were essential to the process of survival. In summary, his thesis (*Origin of Species*, 1859) contends that there is competition among species and members of the same species for use of the earth's limited resources. In the competition some organisms will survive, others will not.

The British philosopher, Hobbes (especially, *Leviathan,* n.d.), conceived of man as innately competitive and that, in the pursuance of his desires, he would be in constant warfare with his fellow man. Realizing the conflictual nature of his demands, Hobbes argued that man would contract with the "state" to resolve conflicts among men. In contrast, government intervention was to Adam Smith (*Wealth of Nations,* 1776) an anathema against the "invisible hand" of the economic system. He contended that the competitive system was orderly, not a system of chaos and anarchy, and asserted that each individual, in pursuing intelligently his own selfish interest, would achieve the best for the community. While recognizing limitations to his argument, Smith felt that governmental intervention was injurious to optimal allocations of resources. In effect, Smith proposed an amplification, but direction, of the natural-struggle hypothesis through an artifact—the economic system.

Durkheim, 1858–1917 (*The Division of Labor in Society*), given his concerns with individual feelings of isolation and lack of coherence in the modern culture, introduced the term *anomie* to designate the absence of common values or norms (as Jung's "collective unconscious") and a lack of sense of rhyme or reason in life. Weber then, in his turn, conceived of a new form of social anchor and direction: bureaucracy—a highly rationalized and impersonalized structure, integrating a large number of specialists cooperating to achieve some commonly announced objective. Thus we see conflict justified in terms of survival and amplified through the economic system, with its impact mediated through the bureaucratic structure.

Pervasiveness of Conflict

Conflict is a fact of life. Indeed, Boulding (1961, p. 1) states: "Conflict is a phenomenon so omnipresent in social life that we tend too easily to take it for granted, almost like speaking prose."[1] Certainly, the literature abounds with illustrations of conflict across cultures as well as across domestic situations. Let us cite several examples:

1. Nyunt (1960, p. 2) presents the following case of a Buddhist priest:

   During the days of the Burmese kings, a presiding priest in a city wielded great influence. On one occasion, an urchin, while doing some mischief, was caught by the police. The penalty for the deviance was death. The boy, in order

---

[1] Until very recently little concern has been given to the problem of organizational conflict in studies of managerial behavior. "Twenty years ago it seemed easy to account for organization conflict by blaming the problem behavior of individuals. But the simple formula 'trouble due to trouble makers' is unfortunately inadequate in the light of our present knowledge of the social processes" (Sanford, 1961, p. 3).

to avoid punishment, told the policemen that he was the nephew of the presiding priest of the city, when in fact he was not. The police took the boy to the priest to verify the boy's statement.[2]

2. There are situations in which a person feels that he is acting against his conscience or image of himself. Leavitt (1960) describes the following:

> Salesmen seem to suffer from this conflict more than some other occupational groups. Sales managers beat the drums and wave the flag to get them to go out to sell *Ajax* iceboxes to Eskimos. But some Eskimos seem not to need iceboxes; or some other iceboxes look more useful than *Ajax;* or the salesman feels uneasy and uncomfortable about putting his foot in people's doors when he hasn't been invited.

3. Operating criteria within the same organization may conflict with each other. Grusky (1959, p. 452) found the following situation with respect to a prison camp:

> For the guards the conflict stemmed principally from the fact that objectives of quasimilieu treatment required a different set of decision-making criteria than did the custodial objectives. If an inmate violates the rules . . . , in a treatment-oriented prison organization, it complicates the guard's response and creates conflict, for he must decide whether he ought to write up a ticket or whether for treatment reasons, he ought to let the immate express his emotions.

4. Apparently, more organic forms of organizations are subject to conflict as well. Two such examples can be cited:

> *a.* Gross et al., in *Explorations in Role Analysis* (1958), state that a school superintendent may be faced with conflict when he makes salary recommendations for his teachers. The teachers and the PTA are apt to press him very strongly to increase salary levels, but he may find himself just as strongly opposed by the taxpayers' association and the town finance committee, who complain that the community cannot support higher taxes.
> *b.* Sayles and Strauss, in *The Local Union* (1953), describe the case of a business agent confronted by a group of clerks who demand that he file a grievance for full pay for a day they had been sent home early because of insufficient work in their office. Another group of clerks in the same local union argue against filing this grievance, that the first group doesn't deserve full pay—it was the second group that worked all day.

[2] In this case, it is interesting to note the resolution. The priest said: "Has anybody testified that the boy is not my nephew?" Thereby he was able to satisfy the requirements of the priesthood by not permitting himself to tell a lie and, at the same time, to save the youth's life (*ibid.*).

5. Staff and service units in the business firm appear to be particularly subject to conflict, as the following findings suggest:

> The purchasing agent is a focal point for conflict: as the manager of a service function, he finds himself serving multiple masters whose requirements may not be in agreement; because he is measured in terms of his internal budget as well as meeting external demands from other functional areas; and as a result of differing job concerns on the part of the firm and the professional organization of which he is a member (Leader, 1960, p. 10).

While no census data exist on conflict, these examples indicate its pervasiveness. Katz and Kahn (1966, p. 186) report: "In a nationwide study of male wage and salary workers, Kahn and his colleagues (1964) found nearly half to be working under conditions of noticeable conflict. Forty-eight percent reported that from time to time they were caught between two sets of people who wanted different things from them, and 15 percent reported this to be a frequent and serious problem." Moreover, Miller and Shull (1962), in a study of training directors, found that all twenty respondents had encountered at least one type of conflict situation in their organizational position. The conflict incidents, selected from a prepared list, with the frequency of responses, were:

CONFLICT INCIDENT	RESPONSE
1. Expectation that training will be done by company line officers versus expectation that training will be conducted by training department personnel.	20
2. Expectation that the trainer will develop his own material for the program, reflecting specific company problems, versus expectation that he will use a standard, more generalized program.	13
3. Expectation that the trainer will visit widely and participate in professional activities versus expectation that the trainer will stay at the plant and keep his attention in the work place.	8

Let us admit, then, to conflict as a feature of organizational life and turn our attention to its nature and source in collective behavior.

Organizational Containment

Structural forces influence the choices that a positional incumbent makes. The process of organizing, for example, brings about changes in him which would not otherwise occur. Through this process, social relationships are developed and his behavior is restricted by the necessity for coordinated and directed effort. The formal organization, however, should not be considered an all-powerful force to which he completely succumbs. As Dubin (1949, p. 294) has stated: "The individual is able to exercise some choice in achieving his private goals as a member of an organization."

The individual is only partially contained in any organization, partly because he lives in a pluralistic society where no one institution provides for his full array of needs or is the sole focus of his attention. In this regard, Pollak (1964, p. 30) concludes that: "It is the pride and the tragedy of our national character that we operate under the impact of a plurality of often conflicting values." The plurality of our society does create continuing conflict for the decision maker as a result of the disparity among norms of his varied referent groups.[3]

"Machine theory" of organization[4] does not admit to conflict generated from the partial containment of its members. "The traditional concept of organization presupposed cooperation, harmony, and the absence of conflict. In this view, the formal goals of an organization were also the goals of the participants" (Rico, 1964, p. 68).[5] But the fact of partial containment does exist and results in conflict for the individual manager.

OWNER-MANAGER DICHOTOMY

An entrepreneur who closely identifies his private success with that of the enterprise, or vice versa, may substitute his personal value structure for that of the formal purpose of the firm. Yet, where the owner-manager identity has been splintered, personal and private motives of a manager may dominate at the expense of formal purpose.

With the advent of the corporate form of organization, it is no longer necessarily true that "where lies the risk also lies the control." Broad responsibilities and authority have been passed on to nonowner man-

---

[3] In this cultured network, Strauss (1964) suggests three major types of conformity for a manager: "conformity to accepted middle-class standards," "organizational loyalty or conformity to organizational objectives," and "group cohesion or conformity to the values of one's own work group."

[4] "Machine theory" of organization is a term first applied to organization theory by James C. Worthy in his writings about Sears, Roebuck and Company. Within this context, machine theory can be used to designate the type of organization that does not regard the human input to be a variable in the functioning of the system. This human input is considered to be a relatively inefficient and passive, if not accommodating, factor in the system.

[5] It is interesting to note Thompson's (1961, p. 21) comments in this regard: "Since a monocratic institution cannot admit the legitimacy of conflicts, the legitimacy of divergent goals and interests, much effort is spent securing the appearance of consensus and agreement—securing a 'smooth-running organization.' The modern organization wants converts as much as it wants workers."

agers. The locus of operating decisions, at the very least, may be transferred from owners to hired professional managers. The identification of institutional purpose with personal ends may become debilitated through this splintering of the owner-manager identity. Further, the expertise and special knowledge of the manager may result in his ability to largely dominate even in the case of the definition of objectives and other strategies, as opposed to mere tactical decisions. Indeed, Galbraith (1967) argues that the technocrats, that is, managers, do so dominate.

Economists have long recognized the dichotomy of the entrepreneur-managerial relationship and have speculated upon its effects. Early views attributed to human nature a lack of responsibility toward property where such property was not owned. John Stuart Mill stated: "The intensity of interest in the subject that is necessary to the successful conduct of a great business is seldom to be expected (in a man), conducting a business as the hired servant and for the profit of another" (1948, p. 168). In Adam Smith's view, ". . . the directors of such companies . . . being the managers rather of other people's money than their own, it cannot be expected, that they should watch over it with the same anxious vigilance with which the partners in a private co-partnery frequently watch over their own" (1937, p. 700).[6]

Much study has been made of the lack of operative employees' identification with the firm. On the other hand, relatively little had been done with respect to management—a major exception being the work done by Gordon (1945, p. 317). In most cases, labor has been viewed as having a basic conflict with management, where the latter attempts to integrate and direct workers' interests toward organizational ends. In fact, many employee studies give the impression that management is essentially logical and completely bounded by the formal structure and objectives of the organization. Finally, Buchanan (1940, pp. 448–449) concludes that the owner-manager dichotomy is not particularly significant; and, if such is the case, management can be treated as intending organizational rationality. Miller and Form (1951, pp. 217–218), however, contend the contrary.

The extent of the deviation of the nonowner-manager's behavior from the formal purpose of the firm is determined by several factors: (1) the restraints imposed by the employment contract and its application; (2) the inducements offered for conformity; (3) the direction and strength

[6] However, risk bearers, or owners, do exercise some control over management decisions, particularly in the long run, and the interests of stockholders and nonowner managers do partially coincide, since ". . . both parties derive benefits from successful operations. Profitable operations enhance the prestige, secure the position, and probably increase the monetary rewards to management" (Weston, 1949, p. 143). The nonowner manager, therefore, may find inducements in a strong allegiance with ownership interests.

of the individual's own volition and perceived self-interest; (4) the actual existence of a stated organizational purpose; (5) the group affiliations of the official, and (6) his cultural norm and value commitments.

DETERMINANTS OF MANAGERIAL IDENTIFICATION

The extent and nature of the employment contract is indefinite in most cases. Although corporate bylaws customarily specify the powers of the board of directors, many of whom are professional managers, the board itself often has the power to amend these codifications. These formal limitations, however, usually affect not the type of action that may be taken, but its purpose and intent. Apathy and lack of organization among stockholders, together with vague delegation of legal authority, have resulted in the accumulation of operating authority in the hands of management. According to Purdy et al. (1949, p. 95), the specific conditions which expand management's real discretion are: (1) dispersion of ownership, (2) docility and apathy of shareholders, (3) costs of organization and opposing management, (4) strategic position of management with respect to machinery of vote-gathering, and (5) changes in corporation laws and their application which have diluted stockholder strength. In fact, Chamberlain (1948, p. 13) states that, although certain legal restrictions apply, "(managerial) authority . . . is profound. Indeed, so singular, so undivided, is the power of management . . . that it has been held to exist independently of the stockholders themselves."

Accepting differential efficacy of its limits, however, organization contributions elicited by the employment contract are a function of the inducements offered the members for conformity. But for the nonowner manager we must distinguish between organizational returns and individual reward. First of all, organizational gains, such as profit, do not return directly to the participant; profits are translated into salaries and wages before being distributed among the membership. Second, the complex organization provides a set of operational standards across functions and levels against which rewards to individual performance are made. Third, incumbents make their choices in terms of these standards in some optimal way for themselves. Thus, where decision makers are torn between organizational and private pressures, in the absence of compulsory identification, they may tend to satisfy personal needs at variance with those of the organization.

In the first instance, if salary is not representative of the manager's goal, he may not strive to maximize profits even where the two are directly related. According to Katz and Kahn (1966, p. 658): "The connection between the formal reward system of the organization and the behavior of the individual is often indirect and is mediated by processes which in themselves may be more significant than the formal reward system." In the second instance, regular executive compensation ". . . could be cited as an incentive to make executives stay at their job. But it is not a direct incentive to sound judgments and wise decisions—in short to efficiency on their jobs—since rarely does premium or penalty attach to executive performance" (Maurer, 1955, p. 79). Since executive compensation may not be related directly to profits, the manager may turn his attention to those variables which most directly and immediately affect his salary. It is to this latter contention which we now wish to turn.

INDUCEMENT-PARTICIPATION MODEL

In an organization of our concern, the membership is joined together around a common objective or set of objectives. In fact, an important organizational bond is consensus on function (cf. Bakke, 1950). Thus, to the extent that the individual subscribes to this consensus, he incurs a personal cost. To the extent that this commonly held, but limited, consensual end constrains his behavior, he loses individual freedom.

The "cost of membership" varies with the restrictions inherent in the design of the means for attaining the goal and with the perceived disutility of conforming to this design. But the organization, to hold its constituents—to survive—must offer inducement for membership participation, whether the personal costs of conforming are large or small. March and Simon (1958, p. 84) present this relationship as: each participant ". . . receives *from* the organization *inducements* in return for which he makes *to* the organization *contributions* (and he will) . . . continue his participation in an organization only so long as the inducements offered him are as great or greater (measured in terms of *his* values and in terms of the alternatives open to him) than the contributions he is asked to make."

Our assumption, like that of March and Simon, is that the member will leave the organization when he is dissatisfied with the rewards of membership, that is, when the cost of his contributions outweighs membership inducements. This relationship can be diagramed as in Figure 7-1. In this figure, we should note that the relationship may rise or fall. For example, it will fall:

1. If search is not fruitful and aspirations diminish, so that the dissatisfaction falls in the short run; or

2. If alternatives discovered are poorer than expected, the contribution utility falls.

From all of this, we contend that the individual is confronted with plural, and often conflicting, values; and he has some organizational

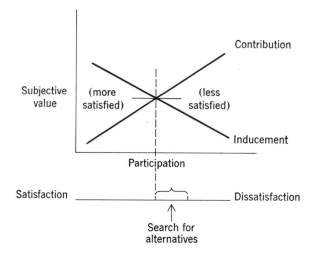

FIGURE 7-1   INDUCEMENT-PARTICIPATION MODEL

leniency in his choice among them. It now remains for us to examine (1) the significance and relevance with which organizational values are communicated to him as a participating member and (2) the level of his performance induced by its formal reward system. The former we discuss in the next section, while motivation to contribute is examined here.

MORALE AND PERFORMANCE

Thus far we have implied that membership motivation and performance motivation are the same; that is, if the individual wishes to remain a member, he will also perform at some optimal level. Since this may not be the case, we need to distinguish between membership satisfaction, or morale, and organizational contribution, or performance.

Without covert subversion, the organizational member will meet minimal performance standards or leave the organization, but successful organization may be characterized by performance above that prescribed as minimal for constituents who wish to maintain their membership. On the other hand, organizational slack, where inducements exceed contributions, may exist. The nature of short-run competition for resources may permit organizational rewards to exceed membership performance.

Organizational slack, while a necessary condition, is not a sufficient empirical explanation for differences between reward and contribution, especially where the reward is extrinsic to the task itself. Yet classical theory of organization assumes a positive and direct relationship between these two variables, where morale is the independent and performance the dependent variable. To this thesis, however, Brayfield and Crockett (1955, p. 421) in summarizing evidence to that date contend that:

> . . . it is time to question the strategic and ethical merits of selling to industrial concerns an assumed relationship between employee attitudes and employee performance.[7] In the absence of more convincing evidence than is at hand with regard to the beneficial effects on job performance of high morale, we are led to the conclusion that we might better forego publicizing these alleged efforts.

As March and Simon (1958, p. 53) contend: "Motivation to produce (the organizational fit of the decision) is a function of the character of the evoked set of alternatives, the perceived consequences of evoked alternatives, and the individual goals." Accordingly, the observer must be careful in making conclusions about the relationship between membership morale and organizational productivity. For example, Porter and Lawler (1968, p. 153), in a very particular way, hypothesize that: "Where organizations provide pay in relation to performance, and where an individual's perception of equitable pay is not influenced by the organization's performance evaluations, high levels of effort and performance will be related to high levels of satisfaction with pay." This relationship appears to be both bilateral and confounded by organizational practice.

The absence of singular causality between these two variables may be explained in various ways. We suggest the following as possible explanations; for example, the inducements may:

1. Not be perceived by the member as related to performance. He may not perceive variations in organizational inducements or not anticipate a viable relationship between rewards accruing to him and his own performance.

2. Be insufficient to induce desired performance. The rewards for meeting organizational optimal standards of productivity may not be objectively sufficient or subjectively stimulating to induce performance at the level desired.

3. Not be representative of the value system of the member. A potential increase in wages, for example, may not be important to the member and elicit no change in his productivity or contribution to the organization.

The discussion above is not a denial of organizational contributions. Although the psychological basis of organizational identification and its nature are obscure, the imposition of its aims upon an individual's value structure cannot be denied—consensus is basic to cooperative effort (cf. Barnard 1938, p. 86). Yet Simon (1947, p. 18) describes three

[7] The reader should note that we have used "attitudes" and "performance" in a very special sense.

sets of variables which may fulfill such socialization or identification: "First, personal success often depends upon organizational success. . . . Second, loyalty seems based partly on . . . the spirit of competition which is characteristic of private enterprise. Third, the human mind is limited in the number of diverse considerations which can occupy the area of attention at one time . . . ," but, as a result, job preservation may take precedence over improving the firm's position—the desire for a clean record can have stultifying effects. The actualization of ego-centered, nonconforming motives may prove irrational in terms of the formal purpose of the organization: a manager, for example, may spend more time preparing a highly detailed budget that is justified by its extrinsic value, merely because he likes to do a "good" job. Nonetheless, a manager is influenced by his employing organization; he does respond to the social stimuli which it provides.

Thus far, we have observed that the organizational member has opportunity to exercise private choice and that he may perceive this behavior to be in conflict with collective purpose. Now we want to set forth propositions on structural sources of conflict, those forces internal to the functioning organization; that is, we want to examine bases of conflict created by the formal process of organizing.

Intra-organizational Bases of Conflict

For this purpose an organization can be defined as ". . . a group of persons deciding about different variables on the basis of different information (that is, each having different facts and perceptions of the action field), but agreeing to obey a set of rules and directives (statements concerning formal enterprise purpose, competitive strategies, etc.) and rules of information about the state of nature in pursuing their respective goals" (Marschak, 1955). Identification with the firm's objective and cooperation among members do not occur at random, however. Individual efforts must be directed and coordinated, and this involves organization.

The "organization" strives for predictability and consonance among its disparate parts. Accordingly, it employs some of its resources for these ends.[8] Berwitz (1957), for example, contends that uniformity in

---

[8] The energy of an organization can be expended in two ways: (1) maintenance energy, that which is used in the internal machinery, keeping the group in being; and (2) effective energy, that residue used to carry out the purposes for which the group explicitly exists (cf. Cartwright, 1949). Concern with problems of internal equilibrium is not separate from, or unrelated to, those of attaining the objectives of the enterprise, since ". . . the success with which the concern maintains external

decisions ". . . will only result where there has been a conscientious, planned effort to achieve them. But, following the bureaucratic rationale, they can be achieved throughout an organization by permeating each decision-center with the purpose, objectives, policies, and procedures of his company."

Nonetheless, and important to us, the modern complex organization is fractionated. As an organization grows in size and scope, there is tendency for each of the original functional areas to become subdivided into several more highly specialized task units. In 1931, Robinson (p. 49) stated that ". . . no one individual can effectively control more than four or five subordinate department heads. If he attempts to manage more he must either cause endless delays or else become no more than a rubber stamp." If such is the case, the executive must assign responsibility, and the organization is coordinated through the progressive devolution of authority to successive tiers of subordinate executives. The executive organization becomes a series of decision centers, operating throughout the hierarchy.

Tiers or layers of performing units, more and more distant from the overall objective, are created. As these units evolve, measures of their performance must be devised. Where, for example, profit maximization may be the end toward which the business firm strives, this more general criterion is no longer appropriate to the individually operating units contained therein. More operational standards of performance must be developed in relation to the ends of the next higher, containing system.

The "levels" concept of organizations implies seriality of decision making. Authority for decision making may be delegated and decisions reviewed, or tentative decisions may originate at lower levels and then pass upward in the hierarchy. In effect, an organization can be viewed as a value system or hierarchy of standards, composed of differing yet related levels of criteria. The hierarchical structure of an organization, then, can be conceived of as a means-end chain with trade-offs between operating units (as between public relations and advertising), or as a decision tree. Accordingly, formal organizational communication is a necessity, and its manner and completeness influence the nature of resultant decisions. Formal structure does propose the definition of policies, rules, and standards for the components of the organization. These defined and explicated, institutionalized and legitimated expectations make for a cohesive and deliberately planned artifact. Where such ex-

---

(or economic) balance is directly related to (the effectiveness of) its internal organization" (Rothlisberger and Dickson, 1950, p. 552).

plication of norms does not occur or they are not internalized by the incumbent, we can hypothesize the following:

1. If value premises are not formally specified and communicated, the incumbent develops his own. Such informal standards may be based on the specific, isolated, or expedient. Resultant choices may not contribute to realization of the firm's goal, and decisions based upon them may only haphazardly coincide with organizational purpose.

2. In the treatment of information, there is a tendency for " . . . the relay point (decision center) to de-emphasize data inconsistent with the information with which it is primarily concerned" (Cyert and March, 1955, p. 134). The communication center may distort information that it believes will reflect unfavorably upon it.

Furthermore, a decision unit may miscalculate or learn. He may perceive inappropriate cues about organizational purpose or he may over-conform. In terms of the latter, Berelson and Steiner (1964, p. 367) say that: "The day-to-day decisions of an organization tend to be taken as commitments and precedents, often beyond the scope for which they were initially intended, and thus come to affect the character of the organization." Thus, side effects, including dysfunctions, attend organizational communication. Selznick (1949) contends that increasing spans of control result in delegation and concentration upon increasing specialization of effort, or "bifurcation." Increasing bifurcation results in internalized standards of departmental performance, which are defined in terms of narrow specialties and create conflict within the organization.

Likewise, Merton (1940) contends that behavior is controlled in order to increase reliability and efficiency; but, with increased predictability, relationships are de-personalized and individual search and innovation are reduced. (See Figure 7-2.) Increased demands for control follow which, in turn, lead to an increase in rules; thereby existing controls are amplified. Further, as unintended responses are encountered, for example, difficulties with the customers and market losses from lack of discrimination, the organization becomes more rigid and less flexible—all of which feeds back upon itself.

Even where the incumbent's behavior is functionally related to organizational purpose, formal structuring may fail, as March and Simon (1958, p. 35) contend:

1. A stimulus may have unanticipated consequences because it evokes (1) a *larger* set than was expected, or because the set evoked is (2) *different* from that expected.

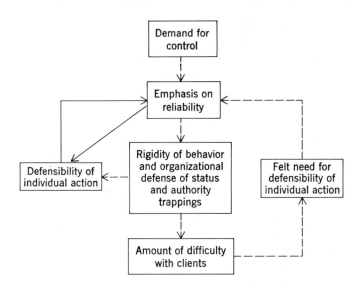

——— Intended results
– – – – Unintended results

FIGURE 7-2 MERTON'S ORGANIZATIONAL CONSEQUENCES OF
BUREAUCRACY (*Source: James G. March and Herbert A. Simon,
Organizations, John Wiley & Sons, Inc., 1958, p. 41*)

2. . . . The stimulus itself may include elements not intended by the organization
hierarchy when providing it.
3. . . . The individual who is supposed to respond to a stimulus mistakes it for
another . . . or simply does not respond at all because the stimulus does not
define the situation for him completely.

Thus, while the previous section discussed the semi-independent, incumbent manager faced with conflicting norms for his behavior, now
we admit to the possibility that the decision maker may misread structural cues and, thus, create organizational dysfunction and conflict. In
the next section, we wish to examine how organizational segmentation—
especially horizontal segmentation, occurring through departmentation—establishes the bases for intra-organizational conflict.

SUBOPTIMIZATION

When organizational growth generates complexity beyond the manipulative ability of a single executive, the result is some type of segmentation,
typically departmentalization. Thus, a horizontal pattern of relationships

develops. A major executive delegates responsibility for routine and detailed tasks to a group of subordinates and, thereby, creates formalized subunits in the organization. In order to fix accountability, a supervisor is assigned to manage these subsections. Then an executive organization evolves which knits together these department heads. But the executive is a member, or representative, of a work unit as well as of this management, or command, group. Since his primary responsibility is measured in terms of his work unit, his decisions may be dictated by the needs of his department. Since his performance is judged largely by the contribution of his work unit, he may value this far more than cooperation with other units. In fact, Simon (1947, p. 18) has contended that departmental loyalties may result in ". . . incapacitating almost any department head for the task of balancing the financial needs of his department against the financial needs of other departments . . . ." If each department is judged by different standards, divergent and conflicting value premises will exist among departments, resulting in differing considerations and evaluations. Intra-organizational conflict is, therefore, partially explained by the complexity of the typical organization and a subordinate manager's inability to perceive it in its entirety and define his relationship to it. "Unless he can attain a vision of the whole, he is forced to try to obtain the optimum for a partial area regardless of the effect on the whole" (Drucker, 1955, p. 120). This reaction, called "suboptimization," may permeate many of his decisions.[9]

"The major characteristic of modern management organization is its diversity rather than its universality. The variety, complexity, and dynamic nature of the environment of a modern organization require a selective rather than a unitary managerial response" (Rico, 1964, p. 70). Therefore, we would anticipate disagreement among the organizational segments.[10] In fact, Maier and his associates (1961), in a study of communication, found considerable disagreement between superiors and subordinates about the latter's job content (see Table 7-1). Certainly differ-

---

[9] Suboptimizing stems in part from the strength of membership allegiance within the subunit. A natural cleavage develops between the various subunits as a result of departmentalization. Work units tend to become socially isolated, particularly if departments have been established on a functional basis. Since all groups tend to regard themselves as somewhat separate and superior to all other groups, the schism between suborganizations perpetuates itself. "One of the most difficult conundrums of organization teamwork, then, is how to fix responsibility . . . and yet ensure cross-departmental cooperation at the same time" (Learned, 1956, p. 72).

[10] We restrict our attention to "rational" (rather than irrational) conflict. The former relates to a situation which ". . . exists whenever two or more value systems, apparent to both parties, are in juxtaposition. The emotions which this state of affairs gives rise to, however, do not necessarily find expression in open hostility" (Sanford, 1961, p. 34).

Table 7-1   Comparative agreement between superior-subordinate pairs on four basic areas of the subordinate's job
(Percentages based on study of 58 pairs in patterned interviews)

LEVEL OF AGREEMENT

BASIC ASPECT OF JOB	ALMOST NO AGREEMENT ON TOPICS	AGREEMENT ON LESS THAN HALF THE TOPICS	AGREEMENT ON ABOUT HALF THE TOPICS	AGREEMENT ON MORE THAN HALF THE TOPICS	AGREEMENT ON ALL OR ALMOST ALL TOPICS
Job duties	3.4 %	11.6 %	39.1 %	37.8 %	8.1 %
Job requirements (subordinate's qualifications)	7.0	29.3	40.9	20.5	2.3
Future changes in subordinate's job	35.4	14.3	18.3	16.3	15.7
Obstacles in the way of subordinate's performance	38.4	29.8	23.6	6.4	1.7

Source: Norman R. F. Maier et al., *Superior-subordinate Communication in Management,* AMA Research Study (New York: American Management Association, 1961), p. 10. (Reprinted by permission of author and publisher.)

ing expectations about the appropriate content of subordinates' jobs would create stress and conflict as between the two highly related interactors. The presence of this disagreement on job performance is highlighted by the condition that was found where functionalism would be anticipated as most viable, between superior and subordinates.

A logic about selective focusing in organizations can be summarized as follows:

1. The organization can be viewed as a decision network, especially as related to the managerial hierarchy (Pfiffner and Sherwood, 1960, pp. 22–23);

2. To increase the capacity attributable to collective behavior, decision making in the organization becomes specialized (Barnard, 1938, p. 111); but

3. Specialization by subprogram increases the need for interdependencies among departmental units (March and Simon, 1958, p. 159);

4. While performance standards applicable to subunits are merely translated, and often tangential to organizational goals, they tend to become terminal values to the decision makers (Merton, 1940, pp. 563–565);

5. These values—as decision premises—tend to dominate, with selective perception practiced at each decision center in the hierarchy (Dearborn and Simon, 1958, pp. 140–143);

6. Therefore, interdependence and selective focus in decision making create a situation conducive to role conflict (Haire, 1956, p. 166).

Differing expectations about job performance do give rise to conflict within the organization. As well, however, varied perceptions of personal attributes, specialties, and values among incumbents can provoke conflict. In this respect, Best (1963) found that engineers were able to contrast sharply the qualities held by themselves and those which they attributed to management, for example, in the way of teaching versus manipulating people and in the relative depth penetrated in pursuing a problem.

As suggested earlier in a reference to partial containment, the incumbent of any one organization may maintain multiple sociological attachments, both within and outside that environment. Those groups with which an individual identifies are his "reference groups." The effect of reference groups on a decision maker's orientation varies with the organization and among individuals. Since membership in reference groups is for the most part "voluntary," the affinity for such associations is strong. Therefore, such referents must be included in our concern with the decision making of organizational members.

Because of formal departmentalizing and specialization of tasks, "work-contact" groups tend to develop that have the usual characteristics of primary groups. Each work group has a peculiar and identifiable psychological environment, quite apart from that of the formal organization. The nature of these formal or informal groups determines the directional affinity of the member.[11] Relevant phenomena reflecting the informal aspects of an organization include decisions which are based partially upon the sentiments and values of an informal group or upon information transmitted by the "grapevine" and decision making that is allocated to, or assumed by, "unauthorized" individuals.

Moreover, as discussed in Chapter 4, social learning results in the acceptance of positional roles and relative status. Forced by various factors to join groups, the individual eventually is acculturated to a point where membership sanction becomes so important that he is willing to limit other motives to attain it—some part of the individual's

---

[11] The relationships established by ". . . the formal organization in general are more logically explicit and articulate than those of the informal organization, but they are not for that reason more powerful in their effects than those of the informal organizations" (Roethlisberger and Dickson, 1950, p. 562). In fact, the effectiveness of the formal organization is dependent upon its relationships with the informal, and the informal group may be indifferent or attracted or opposed to the formal purpose of the organization.

"ego-ideal" requires satisfaction in terms of group acceptance. Countering this desire for social proximity, however, is some aspect of a "competitive spirit"—that which sets up a barrier to undifferentiated association with those of lesser ability, those holding inferior resources, or those performing less significant tasks. The intrinsic value of social approval rests upon differentiated acceptance.

In any ad hoc organization, then, where people have continuing contacts, or exposure, a process of social evaluation is constantly taking place. And, as socializing is effective, it increases an individual's awareness of status attributes and they become desirable to him. Whyte (1954, p. 145) says that many managers have the mistaken belief that status and "all that sort of stuff" are an extremely minor incentive; but, in fact, privileged stratification "seems to be as much an accepted thing as salary differentials . . . . It has become a larger section of the carrot a corporation man chases."

The desire for status leads to rationalizations about its necessity and its use, particularly with respect to the exercise of authority. The executive may attempt to influence decisions outside his purview or, in order to maintain status, may isolate himself from subordinates who have superior knowledge in task dimensions. Further, status may be related to the specialty associated with an executive's position. And, if a budget is a symbol of organizational status, the executive may act in his organizational capacity irrationally to attain an inordinately large one (cf. Hughes, 1951).

These perceived differences among incumbents, their varied role expectations, and the divergences in value systems manifest the potential sources of conflict within an organization. Subunits become attached to their own subgoals with often an inversion of means and ends. Various external forces, in addition, reinforce this identification with subgoals, "particularly the fact that communication within the unit, and between it and the rest of the organization is heavily concerned with the subgoal" (Thompson, 1961, p. 16).

In fact, there is some evidence supporting the claim that perception in an organization is not vertical but horizontal (cf. Scott, 1956). It is not surprising that there is conflict among managers within the same organization when they do not share similar premises about each other's role (cf. Gore and Silander, 1959, p. 97). As Boulding (1961, p. 53) contends: "Every group which has been together for any length of time has certain *conflict traps,* or patterned ways, into which all new problems tend to fall. These conflict traps are in fact old unresolved and long hidden problems and issues which unconsciously arise whenever new issues are introduced."

Within this framework, then, the analysis of conflict and conflict resolution seems to hold much promise for understanding decision making in managing administered organizations. Thus, it will be useful to study in some detail how conflict situations are resolved and what organizational and personal phenomena attend their resolution.

A Model of Role-conflict Resolution

"Organizational" conflict, whether diffuse or concentrated and whether functional or dysfunctional, is ultimately housed in the roles of the organization's active members. Thus, a useful perspective for conflict resolution is in terms of organization roles—or role conflict. Accordingly, we must examine the process of role definition and role taking.

ROLE DEFINITION

If social disorganization is not to be the result of internal conflict, the diverse actors involved in the coalition must be coordinated. This requires predictability of membership behavior. In this regard, Merton (1957) has contended that the reliability of role behavior is essential to the effective functioning of all human organizations. To state this requirement differently, every organization faces the task of reducing the variability, instability, and spontaneity of individual human decisions. Apart from its "common purpose" orientation, Scott (1962) describes a fruitful way of viewing an organization by treating it as a mechanism to offset conflict by lessening the significance of individual behavior. He notes the increase in stability in human relationships and a reduction of uncertainty by human roles inherent in the structure.[12]

For intelligent and foresightful interaction, or effective coordination and for purposeful instrumental behavior, a group at least partially defines the role that an incumbent is to play. In this way, we can identify formal groups as having some form of structure, that is, a normative set that prescribes to some degree the role conduct of its members. If the individual does not accept the minimal prescription inherent to the organization, he may be ostracized. In essence, by remaining in a formal group over time, the individual accepts and may internalize some aspects of the organization's role prescriptions.

[12] A more precise description of the control forces for reducing the variability of human actions to the uniform and dependable patterns of a social system has been suggested by Thelen. His model distinguishes between three types of control pressures: (1) environmental or task requirements in relation to needs, (2) demands arising from shared expectations and values, and (3) the enforcement of rule" (Katz and Kahn, 1966, p. 39).

The concept of role[13] refers primarily to the organizationally specified nature of behavior for an incumbent, which is intended to govern the individual's actions within the organization. In the process of role taking, norms or standards constrain and/or govern how persons should act in specific situations (cf. Moment and Zeleznik, 1964, p. 43). In fact, Katz and Kahn (1966, p. 195) contend that the individual's manner of role taking is more a function of the social settings of an organization than that of an individual's own personality characteristics, and that it becomes for the individual a basic determinant for acceptability in the group. To a considerable extent, then, the role expectations held by a person are determined by the broader organizational context. The technology of the organization, its structured subsystems, its formal policies, and its sanctions and reward systems specify in large degree the role of a given position. In this sense, roles become demands upon the incumbent which prescribe certain acts and forbid others. In an organization, furthermore, roles become the linkages for the individual as a psychologically behaving entity to the organization as a distinctly social structure (Delbecq, 1966, p. 3).

But, given our earlier assumptions of multiple survival needs and functional specialization, we must admit that conflicting demands may be made upon any single organizational role.

CONFLICT RESOLUTION AS DECISION MAKING

Role conflict is a situation in which the administrative incumbent, acting in his organizational role, is confronted with conflicting expectations as concerns a particular behavioral event. Conflict, here, denotes incompatible expectations, a dilemma or a choice-making situation (cf. Gross, expectation results in a lesser allocation to the opposing expectation. Mason, and McEachern, 1958, p. 5). Some degree of conformity to one For this concept, Katz and Kahn (1966, p. 184) elaborate as follows: "We define role conflict as the simultaneous occurrence of two (or more) role sendings such that compliance with one would make more difficult compliance with the other. In the extreme case, compliance with one expectation as sent would exclude completely the possibility of compliance

---

[13] Thibaut and Kelley (1959, p. 144) suggest various meanings of the term *role:* (1) a *prescribed role:* those specified norms existing in the social world surrounding the individual; (2) *subjective role:* how an individual wants to play (believes that he plays) the role; (3) *enacted role:* some objective definition of the actual behavior of an individual; and (4) *functionally requisite role:* those norms which should govern the individual if the group is to deal successfully with the tasks confronting it.

with the other; the two expectations are mutually contradictory." This situation does provide the substance of an effective decision—a situation demanding choice. And although we do not argue that role-conflict resolution encompasses all of decision making, we do contend that it is a significant feature of administrative behavior.[14]

Decision making, in a crude way, can be viewed as a settling or termination of a controversy or debate by giving a judgment or decree upon an issue (Griffiths, 1958, p. 122) which, according to Bross (1953, p. 28), would involve a rational and intelligent calculation of:

1. A set of alternative actions,
2. An array of outcomes for each action,
3. Probabilities associated with the outcome,
4. Values resulting from each outcome.

Bross then suggests that, when these data are available, a course of action is selected through the application of a decision criterion or choice mechanism. This refers to a generalized action principle utilized by the decision maker, who sorts out a particular strategy from his own psychological "set" to process these data in order to make a specific choice.

Accepting this general decision model, one can make certain assumptions:

1. That the gross features of decision problems may vary widely. The variables in the problem may be predominantly social or predominantly economic in nature.

2. That varying features of the problem evoke different elements from the decision maker's value system and a different decision criterion. He may, for example, *maximize* a discounted stream of expected profits or *minimize* some set of negative sanctions, or penalties.

3. That the personality of the decision maker carries some influence in the choice as it is made. His own orientation or predilections are involved in the assignment of priorities to the relevent variables. He may, for example, assign the greatest weight to the "rightness" of the act or to the "cooperativeness" of his behavior (cf. Cartwright and Festinger, 1943, pp. 595–621).

The typical decision model does not offer much insight for dealing with role conflict. Lundberg (1962, p. 167) expressed our position, here, very well as: ". . . (traditional) decision theories do not let us predict

---

[14] Since we are basically concerned with pre-decisional behavior, we have focused upon conflict analysis rather than cognitive dissonance, which is primarily a post-decisional effect. Yet anticipated dissonance may take place and influence the decision before the fact. (See: Braden and Walster, 1964, pp. 145–155.)

decision behavior accurately. . . . Such rational normative devices are either too gross in their conception and/or do not give realistic recognition to the influence of personal, social, and cultural factors." What is needed is not a normative model for an econological decision function, but a descriptive model to predict managerial behavior in an organized setting. We need a model for decision making postulated by Diesing (1955):

> It is the type of decision-making which occurs in the solutions of problems characterized by conflicts of cultural values. . . . Instead of economic factors, this type of decision-making entails factors such as duties, values and beliefs, and ceremonies functioning as symbols of the group. There are no predetermined goals to consider and the approach is basically one where there are no limiting alternatives.

RESOLUTION MODEL

Accordingly, we will examine a theory of decision making proposed by Gross et al., in *Explorations in Role Analysis* (1958). This theory states that an incumbent faced with conflict will make one of four choices: (1) Follow the course of one specified action, A; (2) follow the counterproposal, B; (3) compromise the opposing demands in some manner, C; or (4) avoid any action at all, D. These alternative choices are illustrated in an example by Bass (1960, p. 320) of how a platoon sergeant can "resolve" his conflict problems:

> (A) A sergeant can force his platoon to carry out orders from above, much against the men's wishes, on the basis that his position is endangered unless he carries out the official orders of his superiors.
> (B) He can lead the men in disobeying the superior's orders. "It's hot . . . you take the men out, making everyone else think you are going to do the job. Then you don't. You lay quiet for awhile. This way the men are on your side."
> (C) He can compromise the interests of the colonel and his platoon. "On reconnaissance you get several ideas, but you only tell part of them. In case the colonel wants more, you lay in the weeds and then report the rest of them."
> (D) The sergeant can avoid taking any stand. During classroom instructions, when asked by one of the platoon if they can smoke in the classroom, he can answer that he doesn't know whether or not the "no smoking" rule applies.

Given these alternatives, the model presents three major variables which account for the actor's choice: legitimacy, sanctions, and personal orientation. "Legitimacy" refers to whether or not an expectation is perceived as "right," that is, whether or not the incumbent believes that either of the individuals or groups making the claim has a right to expect him to conform to the expectation. "Sanctions" refer to penalties perceived as a consequence of following either of the conflicting role expectations. Gross asked his respondents to indicate how those who expected him to conform to expectation A and to expectation B would react if he did not do what each expected of him.

According to the model, then, there are two types of sanctions from which the decision maker withdraws: (1) those penalties which others can impose for lack of compliance, and (2) the internal, psychological pain for violating one's own sense of rightness, that is, legitimacy. Where these two "costs" reinforce each other, as the judgments do in the following example, the choice is fairly definitive:

A Training Director was instructed to prepare a supervisory training program and administer it according to the best known practices. (He believes that these instructions call for a compulsory program on company time.) The general plant superintendent, now operating under a heavy production schedule, insists that the training program be voluntary and off company time.

To this incident, some respondents said that:

(1) The President's (A's) expectation was right and reasonable,

(2) The Superintendent's (B's) desires were unreasonable and improper,

(3) Penalties for failing to produce a good program under the President's expectations would be slight,

(4) Penalties for failing while following the Superintendent's wishes, on the other hand, would be high.

All of these forces operate so that the Training Director would follow the President's expectations. It is helpful to present this in diagrammatic form. Figure 7-3 shows the courses of action predicted for different evaluations of a conflict situation where the decision maker weighs both penalty and legitimacy. This tree illustrates a general array of solutions to the problem situations. Given the evaluations described above, the tree can be followed as: The President's (A's) expectations were right and reasonable ("*Yes*" in column I), and thwart pressures (sanctions for nonconforming and failure) from not following the President's demands would be low (in column III). At the same time, the Superintendent's (B's) demands are unreasonable ("*No*" in column II) but the penalties would be high for failing if following the Superintendent's wishes (in column IV). For these evaluations, it is predicted that the incumbent will follow the President's (A's) wishes. (Note: Alternative 7.) As stated above, all forces operate so that the decision maker would, in avoiding both internal and external penalties, follow A's expectation.

Yet, in other instances, the decision maker may feel that claim A is illegitimate, that is, the request is judged improper and/or unreasonable, and stems from the source of high potential penalty, while feeling that claim B is right and reasonable but also associated with high penalty

Column I	Column II	Column III	Column IV	Column V	
A's claim is right and reasonable	B's claim is right and reasonable	Thwart penalty from failure of action A	Thwart penalty from failure of action B	The action predicted	
Yes	Yes	High	High	Compromise or avoidance	1
			Low	Action B	2
		Low	High	Action A	3
			Low	Compromise	4
	No	High	High	Action A or compromise or avoidance	5
			Low	Action B	6
		Low	High	Action A	7
			Low	Action A	8
No	Yes	High	High	Action B or compromise or avoidance	9
			Low	Action B	10
		Low	High	Action A	11
			Low	Action B	12
	No	High	High	Compromise or avoidance	13
			Low	Action B	14
		Low	High	Action A	15
			Low	Compromise	16

FIGURE 7-3 PREDICTED DECISION TREE FOR THE "MAN-IN-THE-MIDDLE"

for failure. (See alternative 2.) In this situation, whether the manager compromises or follows the demands of B depends upon the personality of the decision maker. If he weighs legitimacy heavier than sanction, he would follow course of action B. Some persons react differently to the moral aspects of a situation as well as to the varying pressures that either promise to reward them or threaten to penalize them.[15] Thus,

[15] This accounts for the alternative choices in Fig. 7-3. See, for example, Nos. 1, 5, 9, and 13.

the third factor in the Gross theory is the orientation of the incumbent as he brings his own values to bear upon a decision.[16]

"Personal orientation" refers to three possible evaluations of legitimacy and sanctions which the incumbent may make. The *moral* person places more weight on legitimacy than upon sanctions. The *moral-expedient* person weighs both dimensions relatively equally. The *expedient* person weighs sanction more heavily than legitimacy. Correspondingly, Gross constructed alternative-choice models, each with sixteen predicted actions, to represent the behavior of incumbents with these three different personal orientations. To illustrate, assume in Figure 7-3 the following subjective evaluations of an incumbent: legitimate expectations associated with A and a weak penalty for failure to conform to A, illegitimate expectations associated with B but a strong penalty for failure to conform to B, as:

INCUMBENT'S EVALUATION	EXPECTATION	
	A	B
Legitimate	Yes	No
Negative sanctions	Weak	Strong

If the incumbent acts in terms of a moral orientation, that is, if he weighs legitimacy exclusively or most heavily, it is apparent that he would choose to follow expectation A; on the other hand, if the incumbent acts expediently, he would choose to follow expectation B; if a moral-expedient choice is made, he would weigh a positive legitimacy against a strong opposing penalty and would choose to compromise (C) or to avoid (D) a decision. A generalized model, then, would predict the choices as:

PERSONALITY	DECISION RULE	CHOICE
1. Expedient	Sanction > Legitimacy	A
2. Moral	Legitimacy > Penalty	B
3. Moral-expedient	Legitimacy = Penalty	C or D

[16] The decision rule depends upon an evaluation complex composed of (1) difference between the relative weights assigned sanction and legitimacy, (2) relative difference between the two sanctions as well as the total or combined weight of the sanctions associated with A and B, (3) the degree of polarity of either the legitimacy or illegitimacy judgment.

Although rarely discussed, when choice involves conflicting demands about the same issue and where both sources have the ability to severely penalize the actor, he may avoid or compromise. Nonetheless, in high-pressure situations, some managers may take the course of action which they view as legitimate without weighing penalty. Although avoidance may lessen his internal conflict, this course is not necessarily the one dictated by his supervisor, unless he views his superior's expectation as legitimate. But examination of empirical findings suggests that avoidance is not a common practice. This may be accounted for by the fact that a manager, in a responsible position, must do something; he cannot avoid taking some action. Thus, we can present the Gross model as in Figure 7-4.

OPERATIONAL TEST OF THE MODEL[17]

To study role conflict and its resolution, the Gross model was applied to four different populations. Each of the four populations was exposed to the same decision factors as presented in the theory.[18] The design permitted a comparison of the success of the predictions found for our different populations to those of the school superintendents who were used in the original study (Gross et al., 1958).

The instrument for collecting the data was a questionnaire, as follows:

A. *Legitimacy Assessments*

1. Assuming that you are the training director, do you think it was right and reasonable for the President to expect you to present a successful program under the conditions just described?

☐ Yes   ☐ No

2. Do you think it was right and reasonable for the Plant Superintendent to expect you to present a successful program which was to be voluntary and off company time?

☐ Yes   ☐ No

---

[17] Delbert C. Miller and Fremont A. Shull, "The Prediction of Administrative Role Conflict Resolutions," *Administrative Science Quarterly*, vol. 7, no. 2, September, 1962, pp. 143–170.

[18] Gross and associates primarily concerned themselves with thwart pressure (penalties for not conforming), while in ours, we added "failure" sanction: that which becomes effective if the decision maker *fails* in implementing his choice of one of the suggested courses of action. Further, we assumed that reliable predictions of role-conflict resolution could be made by ascertaining only two variables, legitimacy and sanctions. The concept of personal orientation, as a stable personality trait, was replaced with a concept of variable choice. We held that the same individual may make different choices in role-conflict situations according to the nature of the situation; that is, he is moral, moral-expedient, or expedient in his choice depending on his personal and organizational goals, group support, values at stake, and so on.

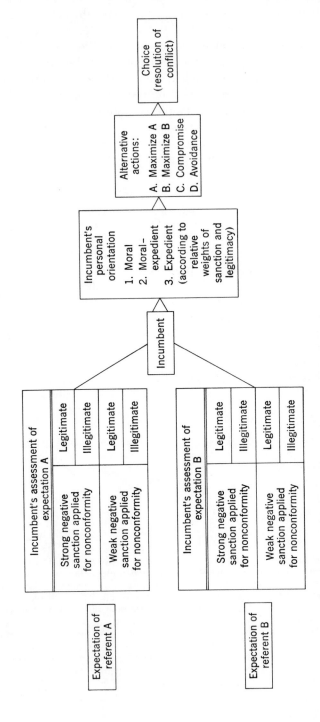

FIGURE 7-4 MODEL OF ALTERNATIVES FOR ROLE-CONFLICT RESOLUTION

B. *Assessments of Negative Sanctions*

3. What do you anticipate will happen to you if you do not follow the wishes of the Plant Superintendent and proceed with compulsory meetings on company time, invoking the authority of the President, and then fail to produce good results? (——————).

4. What do you anticipate will happen to you, if you fail to produce a successful program under the conditions that you go ahead with voluntary meetings, off company time, violating what you feel to be the prerequisites of a good training program? (——————).

No Dis-approval	Mild Dis-approval	Strong Disapproval, No Formal Action	Salary Decrease or Demotion	Loss in Status or Discharged
0	1	2	3	4

C. *Choice of Action*

5. What would you do in the situation described above:

a. Request Presidential order to plant superintendent and establish a compulsory program on company time. (Maximize A),

b. Conduct program according to Plant Superintendent's demands. (Maximize B),

c. Conduct program off company time but insist that it be compulsory. (Compromise),

d. Conduct program on company time but agree that it be voluntary. (Compromise), or

e. Postpone program (Avoidance).

Table 7-2 makes a comparison of the proportion of correct predictions obtained as the predicted actions are summated across the moral-expedient orientation models. The final prediction for the inclusive moral-expedient model is based upon 117 cases for which respondents have designated a particular action.

In the table the difference between the proportions expected in each situation according to chance expectancy and the proportion actually obtained on the basis of the inclusive moral-expediency model in each case is shown to be at the 0.01 level of significance. The overall predictive accuracy is shown to be 71 percent. We may conclude that the hypothesis may be accepted; there is convincing evidence that the role-conflict resolutions of business and labor leaders in the populations studied can be predicted with a high degree of accuracy. Seven situations sampled have provided high proportions of successful predictions. These predictions fall slightly below the best results which Gross and his associates obtained, but they used tightly structured, uniform case situations while we used many open-end and loosely structured case situations. However, both studies show that high predictability of role-conflict resolution is possible when legitimacy and sanction dimensions are known and the criterion is accurate.

Table 7-2   A comparison of correct prediction for seven situation samples of business, training director, and labor-leader populations within the inclusive moral-expedient model

SITUATION SAMPLES OF THE TEST POPULATIONS	NUM-BER OF CASES	COR-RECT PREDIC-TIONS	PROPOR-TION OF CORRECT PREDIC-TIONS	PROPORTION OF CORRECT PREDICTIONS EXPECTED BY CHANCE*	t**	PROBA-BILITY LESS THAN
Structured Situations						
1. Business Managers 2	21	14	0.67	0.36	5.2	0.01
2. Training Directors	20	14	0.70	0.36	5.3	0.01
3. Labor Leaders	20	14	0.70	0.36	5.3	0.01
Open-end situations						
4. Business Managers 2	15	11	0.73	0.36	5.9	0.01
5. Business Managers 1	18	13	0.72	0.36	5.7	0.01
6. Training Directors	13	11	0.85	0.36	8.6	0.01
7. Labor Leaders	10	6	0.60	0.36	3.7	0.01
TOTAL	117	83	0.71	0.36	8.5	0.01

*Since, in some instances, more than one action for each sanction-legitimacy choice point was predicted, the likelihood of chance expectancy varied with the addition of alternative predictions. Thus, chance expectancy was computed in the following manner:

	NO. OF INSTANCES	METHOD OF COMPUTATION	NO. OF CORRECT PREDICTIONS BY CHANCE
Expectancy for actions specified in type MME, singular predictions	100	0.25×100	25
Expectancy in instances involving two possible actions	26	0.50×28	14
Expectancy in instances involving three possible actions	18	0.75×18	13.5
Total	144		52.5

Proportion of total correct predictions by chance = 0.36.
** $t = 2.601$ at 0.01 level of significance, d.f. = 215.

Additional Selected Findings on Role Conflict

In a nationwide study, 39 percent of the respondents from employing organizations ". . . reported being bothered by their inability to satisfy the conflicting demands of their various role senders" (Katz and Kahn, 1966, p. 186). Because of the plurality and interdependence of our society and subunits within it, the individual will find himself in an interlocking network of role prescriptions and, for our purposes, becomes a "star" (actor) in this network. Kahn and Wolf exemplify this situation in their "starnet" (see Figure 7-5).

We hypothesize, therefore, that: (1) The hierarchical position of the star in the organization would influence his exposure to conflicting demands; (2) the strength of the opposing forces would affect his performance and satisfaction; and (3) certain of his personality characteristics would determine his method of resolving conflict. Let us, then, turn to selected empirical evidence bearing directly on these hypotheses.

ORGANIZATIONAL CHARACTERISTICS

The characteristics of the formal organization and the positioning of the incumbent within it appear to affect perceptions and tensions relating

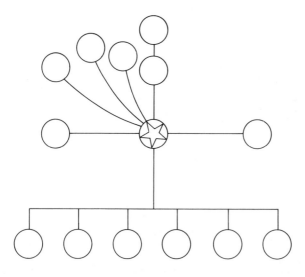

FIGURE 7-5 THE STARNET OF AN ORGANIZATIONAL INCUMBENT (*Source: Robert Kahn and Donald Wolfe, "Empirical Research," in Conflict Management in Organizations, The Foundation for Research on Human Behavior, Ann Arbor, Michigan, 1961, p. 22.*)

to conflict. As concerns level of position in the hierarchy, Porter and Lawler (1965, p. 29), in reviewing the work by Triandis (1959), state that: ". . . managers made finer discriminations among their job perceptions than did workers. . . ." Coates and Pellegrin (1957) reported that: ". . . the 'top-level' executives emphasized the intrinsic features of their jobs, whereas the 'first-level' supervisors viewed their jobs more as means to off-job rewards." Thus, we find perceptual and motivational factors related to levels in management which would seem to bear on "felt" conflict.

This, in fact, is what one study has shown. Katz and Kahn (1966, p. 193), summarizing Kahn et al. (1964), state: "The often heard assertion that the lowest levels of supervision are subjected to the greatest conflict is not borne out; rather there is a curvilinear relationship in which the maximum of conflict occurs at the upper middle levels of management."[19] They (ibid., p. 192) report further from the same study that: ". . . the location of positions within the organization was found to be related to the degree of objective conflict to which the occupant of the position was subjected. In general, positions contained deep within the organizational structure were relatively conflict-free; positions located near the skin or boundary of the organization were likely to be conflict-ridden." In fact, Shull and Van de Ven[20] found that civil service managers, supervising other managers, anticipated higher negative sanction for nonconformity than did those managers supervising operative employees.

Size of the organization would seem to be an additional variable. Social or geographic proximity may vary the intensity of interaction or shared frames of reference. Gross and his associates (1958) found less consensus in larger systems. Lack of consensus makes for greater ambiguity in role prescriptions and, thus, greater frustration and conflict.[21]

As suggested earlier, functional interdependence is related to perceived conflict. The findings of Kahn and his associates (1964) bear this out. They (ibid., p. 215) conclude that: "When functional dependence of role senders is of lesser magnitude, the focal person is more free to cope (via avoidance) with the conflicting pressures they impose,

[19] Kahn and Wolfe (1961, p. 30) commented on the same relationship: "Since upper management operates at a high tension level at all times, it is likely that there are other (perhaps internalized) sources of pressure more powerful than the sent role pressure at work. Lower management's tension level seems to be a more direct response to amount of sent pressure." There is probably a selection effect in the promotion systems of most organizations; thus, personality factors might be studied in this respect.

[20] Unpublished.

[21] Shull and Van de Ven (1968) found a significant tendency for civil service managers faced with ambiguity to anticipate higher negative sanctions than did those who perceived less ambiguity.

thereby escaping some of the strains that he would otherwise experience."

We should expect the strength of the bonds operating among incumbents to be a function of interaction patterns, in the sense of both formal and informal relationships and functional interdependence. Kahn et al. (1964, p. 209) hypothesize: ". . . such bonds to be strongest where the parties talk to each other frequently," and suggest that "increased liking" between two people leads to higher rates of interaction between them; and Triandis (1959) contends that: ". . . cognitive similarity affects the process of interpersonal communication," and finds that they ". . . are related to perceived effectiveness of communication and liking between two people."[22]

Accordingly, we might expect emotion and social incompatibilities to have a bearing on conflict perception and resolution. Shull (1965, p. 21), in a study of middle managers in business organizations, found that the decision maker who was confronted with conflict tended to conform more to a congenial role sender than he would to those with whom he was dissident. In testing whether or not social affinities also related to perceived sanctions, he (ibid.) found that where the business manager was dissident with his organizational claimant, the anticipated negative sanction was higher than where he perceived the relationship as congenial.[23]

Thus, we see a multiplicity of social and organizational variables at play on the decision maker who is faced with conflict. Nonetheless, we do hypothesize individual differences in behavior within the more generalized organizational setting.

Few historical or biographical data have been related to role conflict. But Shull (1965) found that public administrators who had some college education expected higher penalties, that is, greater total negative sanctions resulting from nonconformity, than did those who had had no college training. This relationship may be explained by the self-selection of the population or the effect of college education. Whatever the case, Shull and Van de Ven (1968) found that civil servants who felt organizationally compelled to violate their conscience anticipated lower penalty for nonconformity than did those not feeling such compulsion.

[22] Triandis (ibid.) contends that: "Increased liking leads to higher rates of interaction between A and B and this, in turn, permits greater cognitive similarity thus starting the cyle all over again."

[23] Shull and Van de Ven (1968) found the same relationship for civil service managers at the 0.01 significance level.

As hypothesized earlier, environmental conditioning affects the perception and resolution of role conflict. In effect, the actor "learns" the organization. Shull (*ibid.*) tested the assumption that the length of time that an incumbent was a member of a particular organization would relate to his anticipations about the sanctioning power of that setting. He found that the longer the seniority of the incumbent, the higher the anticipated penalties for nonconformity.

A further finding by Shull and Van de Ven seems to be related to the observations of Porter and Henry (1964). The latter reported on the perceptions of managers in terms of the type of behavior that each level believed was most important for jobs at their particular level. According to them, each higher level of management placed increasing emphasis on "inner-directed," as opposed to "other-directed," personality traits. This probably relates directly to the finding of Shull and Van de Ven that public administrators, feeling responsible more for operational tasks than for supervisory tasks, anticipated lower penalties for not conforming.[24]

Finally, the results of Leader's study (1960) suggest that perceived conflict, as influenced by functional interdependence and social affinities, may be moderated by biographical factors themselves. He found that relationships between purchasing agents and other functional areas of the firm varied by biographical factors of the agents, for example, by education and tenure with the company (see Table 7-3).

---

[24] The assumption is made that the operation-supervisory dichotomy is related to level in hierarchy, with the operational tasks at a lower level in the organization.

Table 7-3   Relationships between purchasing agents and functional departments, by selected biographical data on the agents

BIOGRAPHICAL ITEM	FUNCTIONAL AREA			
	MARKETING	PRODUCTION	ENGINEERING	FINANCE
Education	+ +	+	+ +	0
Tenure with company	−	0	−	0
Length of service	+ +	+ +	0	+ +

Code: + + Strong positive relation   0 No relation
    + Weak positive relation   − Negative relation
Source: Alan H. Leader, *A Study of the Purchasing Agent Members of the Purchasing Agents Association of Rochester*, unpublished master's dissertation, University of Rochester, 1960.

Summary and Conclusions

Conflict and its resolution are a function of three major variables: (1) formal impediments to consistency among subunits, (2) lack of personal affinities among incumbents, and (3) individual propensities that preclude adjustment to organizational necessities and social conformity. All of these are interrelated; but most insight may be gained from focusing upon the perceptions of the incumbent. The degree of perceived role conflict, for example, is related to: (1) the requirements of the position and its exposure, (2) the nature and specificities of the incompatible expectations and associated activity, and (3) the orientation and sensitivity of the incumbent.

Exposure, in turn, is probably a function of level in the hierarchy, range of personal influence, and technical importance of position. Formal requirements of the position, for example, are related to the level in the hierarchy, degree of centralization, bifurcation of the organization, and the nature of tasks supervised by the incumbent.

It is generally impossible for a responsible manager to escape from concern with conflict resolution. In the first place, the administrator is concerned with budgeting scarce resources, usually effort and funds, among the various units under his responsibility. Secondly, he is dealing with, and accountable for, people with different backgrounds, perspectives, and values. He may supervise researchers who are dedicated to the collection of information for its own sake and report to men of affairs who are responsible to financial interests. Finally, the very difference in time perspectives among decision makers will create opposing points of view.

There are many alternatives available to the individual confronted with conflict. Leavitt and Bass (1964, pp. 378–379) suggest the following supervisory behaviors:

(a) Identify with superiors and organizational demands . . .

(b) Identify with subordinates . . .

(c) Successfully initiate structure for their subordinates, at the same time maintaining considerate, friendly awareness of their needs . . .

(d) Acquiesce to their superiors and rationalize their position to their subordinates . . .

(e) Are hypocritical, practicing duplicity in order to avoid disapproval from above or below . . .

(f) Develop blind spots, refusing to accept the existence of conflicts . . .

(g) Withdraw from conflict, wearing a "mask" of seeming neutrality and objectivity . . .

(h) Employ other defense mechanisms—displacing aggression or introjecting.

Whatever the case, the response may be generally productive, personally and organizationally, or destructive. As Kubly (1964, p. 8) states:

> Organizational conflicts take two general forms. The first is destructive and wasteful. It has its origin in the "frailties of human nature" and thus it is hard to eradicate . . . . The second form of conflict is basically constructive. It is the clash of opinions of men of good will. It is the warfare of viewpoints carefully prepared, capably stated, and stoutly defended. Its value lies in bringing differences out into the light of day where there is a chance for sober evaluation.

bibliography

ARGYRIS, CHRIS: "Human Problems With Budgets," *Harvard Business Review,* vol. 31, January-February, 1953, pp. 97–110.

BAKKE, E. WRIGHT: *Bonds of Organization* (New York: Harper & Brothers, 1950).

BARNARD, CHESTER I.: *The Functions of the Executive* (Cambridge, Mass.: Harvard University Press, 1938).

BASS, BERNARD M.: *Leadership, Psychology, and Organizational Behavior* (New York: Harper & Brothers, 1960).

BERELSON, BERNARD, and GARY A. STEINER: *Human Behavior* (New York: Harcourt, Brace & World, Inc., 1964), p. 367.

BERWITZ, C. J.: "Securing Uniform Decisions in Similar Judgmental Situations," *Advanced Management,* January, 1957, pp. 10–14.

BEST, ROBERT D.: "The Scientific Mind versus the Management Mind," *Industrial Research,* October, 1963.

BOULDING, KENNETH: "A Pure Theory of Conflict Applied to Organizations," in *Conflict Management in Organizations* (Ann Arbor, Mich.: The Foundation for Research on Human Behavior, Oct. 20, 1961).

BRADEN, MARCIA, and ELAINE WALSTER: "The Effect of Anticipated Dissonance on Pre-Decision Behavior," in L. Festinger (ed.), *Conflict, Decision and Dissonance* (Stanford, Calif.: Stanford University Press, 1964), pp. 145–151.

BRAYFIELD, ARTHUR H., and WALTER H. CROCKETT: "Employee Attitudes and Employee Performance," *Psychological Bulletin,* vol. 52, no. 5, September, 1955.

BROSS, IRWIN D. F.: *Design for Decision* (New York: The Macmillan Company, 1953).

BUCHANAN, NORMAN S.: *The Economics of Corporate Enterprise* (New York: Henry Holt and Company, 1940).

CARTWRIGHT, DORWIN: "Some Principles of Mass Persuasion," *Human Relations,* vol. 2, no. 3, 1949, pp. 253–267.

———, and LEON FESTINGER: "Quantitative Theory of Decisions," *Psychological Review,* vol. 50, November, 1943, pp. 595–621.

CHAMBERLAIN, NEIL W.: *The Union Challenge to Management Control* (New York: Harper & Brothers, 1948).

COATES, C. H., and R. J. PELLEGRIN: "Executives and Supervisors: Contrasting Self-conceptions and Conceptions of Each Other," *American Sociological Review,* vol. 22, 1957, pp. 217–220.

COFER, C. N., and M. H. APPLEY: *Motivation: Theory and Research* (New York: John Wiley & Sons, Inc., 1964).

CYERT, RICHARD M., and J. G. MARCH: "Organizational Structure and Pricing Behavior in an Oligopolistic Market," *The American Economic Review*, vol. 45, no. 1, March, 1955, pp. 129–139.

————, HERBERT A. SIMON, and DONALD B. TROW: "Observation of a Business Decision," *Journal of Business*, vol. 29, 1956, pp. 237–248.

DAHRENDORF, R.: "Toward a Theory of Social Conflict," *Journal of Conflict Resolution*, vol. 2, 1958, pp. 170–183.

DALE, ERNEST: "New Perspective in Managerial Decision Making," *Journal of Business*, vol. 26, no. 1, January, 1953, pp. 1–8.

DALTON, MELVILLE: "The Role of Supervision," *Industrial Conflict*, Institute of Industrial Relations, University of California, Reprint No. 39, 1954.

DEARBORN, DEWITT C., and HERBERT A. SIMON: "Selective Perception: A Note on the Departmental Identifications of Executives," *Sociometry*, vol. 21, no. 2, June, 1958, p. 140.

DELBECQ, ANDRÉ L.: "The Social Psychology of Executive Roles, Re-examined," *Business Perspectives*, Spring, 1966, pp. 23–27.

DIESING, PAUL: "Noneconomic Decision-Making," *Ethics*, vol. 66, 1955, pp. 18–35.

DRUCKER, PETER F.: "Management Science and the Manager," *Management Science*, vol. 1, January, 1955, p. 120.

DUBIN, ROBERT: "Decision-Making by Management in Industrial Relations," *American Journal of Sociology*, vol. 54, no. 4, January, 1949, pp. 292–297.

EPSTEIN, SEYMOUR, and WALTER D. FENZ: "Theory and Experiment on the Measurement of Approach-avoidance Conflict," *Journal of Abnormal and Social Psychology*, vol. 64, no. 2, 1962, pp. 101–102.

GALBRAITH, JOHN KENNETH: *The New Industrial State* (Boston: Houghton Mifflin Company, 1967).

GOMBERG, WILLIAM: "Entrepreneurial Psychology of Facing Conflict in Organizations," in George Fisk (ed.), *The Frontiers of Management Psychology* (New York: Harper & Row, Publishers, Incorporated, 1964), pp. 50–67.

GORDON, ROBERT A.: *Business Leadership in the Large Corporation* (Washington, D.C.: The Brookings Institution, 1945).

GORE, WILLIAM J., and F. S. SILANDER: "A Bibliographical Essay on Decision Making," *Administrative Science Quarterly*, vol. 4, no. 1, June, 1959, p. 97.

GRIFFITHS, DANIEL E.: "Administration as Decision-Making," in Andrew W. Halpin (ed.), *Administrative Theory in Education* (Chicago: The Midwest Administrative Center, 1958).

GROSS, NEAL, W. S. MASON, and A. W. MCEACHERN: *Explorations of Role Analysis* (New York: John Wiley & Sons, Inc., 1958).

GRUSKY, OSCAR: "Role Conflict in Organization: A Study of Prison Camp Officials," *Administrative Science Quarterly*, vol. 3, no. 4, March, 1959, pp. 452–472.

HAIRE, MASON: *Psychology in Management* (New York: McGraw-Hill Book Company, 1956).

HARVEY, O. J., DAVID E. HUNT, and HAROLD M. SCHRODER: *Conceptual Systems and Personality Organization* (New York: John Wiley & Sons, Inc., 1961).

HAYES, SAMUEL P., JR.: "Behavior Management Science," *Management Science*, vol. 1, no. 2, January, 1955, pp. 177–179.

HUGHES, EVERETT C.: "Status and Informal Relations," in Robert Dubin (ed.), *Human Relations in Administration* (New York: Prentice-Hall, Inc., 1951), pp. 268–270.

KAHN, ROBERT, and DONALD WOLFE: "Empirical Research," *Conflict Management in Organizations* (Ann Arbor, Mich.: The Foundation for Research on Human Behavior, Oct. 20, 1961).

———, DONALD M. WOLFE, ROBERT P. QUINN, J. DIEDRICK SNOEK, and ROBERT A. ROSENTHAL: *Organizational Stress: Studies in Role Conflict and Ambiguity* (New York: John Wiley & Sons, Inc., 1964).

KAMANP, D. K.: "Relationship of Ego Disjunction and Manifest Anxiety to Conflict Resolution," *Journal of Abnormal and Social Psychology*, vol. 66, 1963, pp. 281–284.

KATZ, DANIEL: "Approaches to Managing Conflict," *Conflict Management in Organizations* (Ann Arbor, Mich.: The Foundation for Research on Human Behavior, Oct. 20, 1961), p. 19.

———, and ROBERT L. KAHN: *Social Psychology of Organizations* (New York: John Wiley & Sons, Inc., 1966).

KRUPP, SHERMAN: *Pattern in Organization Analysis* (New York: Chilton Company, 1961).

KUBLY, HAROLD E.: *One Way to Resolve Organizational Conflict*, Wisconsin Project Reports, vol. 1, no. 6, Bureau of Business Research and Services, University of Wisconsin, 1964.

LEADER, A. H.: *A Study of the Purchasing Agent Members of the Purchasing Agents Association of Rochester*, unpublished master's dissertation, University of Rochester, 1960.

LEARNED, EDMUND P.: "Getting the Organization to Work Effectively as a Team," in Edward C. Bursk and Dan H. Fenn, Jr. (eds.), *Planning the Future Strategy of Your Business* (New York: McGraw-Hill Book Company, 1956), pp. 71–84.

LEAVITT, HAROLD J.: *Managerial Psychology* (Chicago: University of Chicago Press, 1958).

———: "Recent Concepts in Administration," *Personnel Psychology*, vol. 13, no. 3, Autumn, 1960, pp. 287–294.

———, and BERNARD M. BASS: "Organizational Psychology," in Paul R. Farnsworth, Olga McNemar, and Quinn McNemar (eds.), *Annual Review of Psychology* (Palo Alto, Calif.: Annual Reviews, Inc., 1964), pp. 371–398.

LUNDBERG, CRAIG C.: "Admiinistrative Decisions: A Scheme for Analysis," *Journal of the Academy of Management*, vol. 5, 1962, pp. 165–178.

MAIER, NORMAN R. F., et al.: "Superior-Subordinate Communication: A Statistical Research Project," AMA Research Study 52, *Superior-Subordinate Communication in Management* (New York: American Management Association, 1961).

MARCH, JAMES G., and HERBERT A. SIMON: *Organizations* (New York: John Wiley & Sons, Inc., 1953).

MARSCHAK, J.: "Elements for a Theory of Teams," *Management Science*, The Institute of Management Sciences, vol. 1, no. 2, January, 1955, pp. 127–137.

MAURER, HERRYMON: *Great Enterprise* (New York: The Macmillan Company, 1955).

MERTON, ROBERT K.: "Bureaucratic Structure and Personality," *Social Forces*, vol. 17, 1940, pp. 560–568.

———: *Social Theory and Social Structure* (New York: Free Press, 1957).

MILL, J. S.: *Principles of Political Economy* (Boston: Charles C. Little and James Brown, 1948).

MILLER, DELBERT C., and WILLIAM H. FORM: *Industrial Sociology* (New York: Harper & Brothers, 1951).

————, and FREMONT A. SHULL: "The Prediction of Administrative Role Conflict Resolutions," *Administrative Science Quarterly*, vol. 7, no. 2, September, 1962, pp. 143–170.

MISHLER, ELLIOT G.: "Personality Characteristics and the Resolution of Role Conflicts," *The Public Opinion Quarterly*, vol. 17, no. 1, Spring, 1953, pp. 115–135.

MOMENT, DAVID, and ABRAHAM ZALEZNIK: *The Dynamics of Interpersonal Behavior* (New York: John Wiley & Sons, Inc., 1964).

NAFTALIN, ARTHUR, BENJAMIN N. NELSON, MULFORD Q. SIBLEY, DONALD W. CALHOUN, and ANDREAS G. PAPANDREOU (eds.): *An Introduction to Social Science* (Philadelphia: J. B. Lippincott Company, 1953).

NYUNT, U. T.: "A Study in Role-Conflict," unpublished manuscript, Indiana University, August, 1960.

PFIFFNER, JOHN M., and FRANK P. SHERWOOD: *Administrative Organization* (Englewood Cliffs, N.J.: Prentice-Hall, Inc., 1960).

POLLACK, OTTO: "The Protestant Ethic and the Values of Middle Management," in George Fisk (ed.), *The Frontiers of Management Psychology* (New York: Harper & Row, Publishers, Incorporated, 1964).

PORTER, L. W., and MILDRED M. HENRY: "Job Attitudes in Management: V. Perceptions of the Importance of Certain Personality Traits as Function of Job Level," *Journal of Applied Psychology*, 1964, p. 48.

PORTER, LYMAN W., and EDWARD E. LAWLER III: *Managerial Attitudes and Performance* (Homewood, Ill.: Richard D. Irwin, Inc., 1968).

———— and ————: "Properties of Organization Structure in Relation to Job Attitudes and Job Behavior," *Psychological Bulletin*, vol. 64, no. 1, 1965, pp. 23–51.

PURDY, HARRY L., MARTIN L. LINDAHL, and WILLIAM A. CARTER: *Corporate Concentration and Public Policy* (New York: Prentice-Hall, Inc., 1949).

RICO, LEONARD: "Organizational Conflict: A Framework for Reappraisal," *Industrial Management Review*, vol. 6, no. 1, Fall, 1964, pp. 67–80.

ROBBINS, LESLIE F.: "Remarks on the Relationship between Economics and Psychology," *Manchester School*, vol. 5, 1934, pp. 89–101.

ROBINSON, E. A. G.: *The Structure of Competitive Industry* (London: James Nisbet & Co., Ltd., 1931).

ROETHLISBERGER, FRITZ J., and WILLIAM J. DICKSON: *Management and the Worker* (Cambridge, Mass.: Harvard University Press, 1950).

SAMUELSON, PAUL A.: *Foundations of Economic Analysis* (Cambridge, Mass.; Harvard University Press, 1951).

SANFORD, R. NEVITT: "Individual Conflict and Organizational Interaction," in *Conflict Management in Organization* (Ann Arbor, Mich.: The Foundation for Research on Human Behavior, Oct. 20, 1961).

SAYLES, LEONARD R., and GEORGE STRAUSS: *The Local Union: Its Place in the Industrial Plant* (New York: Harper & Brothers, 1953).

SCOTT, ELLIS L.: *Leadership and Perceptions of Organization*, Bureau of Business Research Monograph No. 82 (Columbus, Ohio: Ohio State University, 1956).

SCOTT, WILLIAM G.: *Human Relations in Management* (Homewood, Ill.: Richard D. Irwin, Inc., 1962).

SELZNICK, PHILIP: *TVA and the Grass Roots* (Berkeley and Los Angeles: University of California Press, 1949).

SHEPARD, HERBERT A.: "Responses to Situations of Competition and Conflict," in *Conflict Management in Organizations* (Ann Arbor, Mich.: The Foundation for Research on Human Behavior, Oct. 20, 1961).

SHULL, FREMONT A., JR.: "Managerial Conflict in Administered Organizations," *Proceedings of the 8th Annual Midwest Management Conference* (Carbondale, Ill.: Business Research Bureau, Southern Illinois University, 1965), pp. 11–26.

———, and DELBERT C. MILLER: "Decisions of the Man-in-the-Middle," *Nation's Business,* vol. 7, no. 1, April, 1961.

———, and A. VAN DE VEN: "Role Conflict of Civil Service Managers," unpublished manuscript, University of Wisconsin, 1968.

SIMON, HERBERT A.: *Administrative Behavior* (New York: The Macmillan Company, 1947).

SMITH, ADAM: *The Wealth of Nations,* ed. Cannan (New York: Random House, Inc., 1937).

STRAUSS, GEORGE: "Organization Man—Prospect for the Future," *California Management Review,* vol. 6, no. 3, Spring, 1964, pp. 5–16.

THIBAUT, J. W., and H. H. KELLEY: *Social Psychology of Groups* (New York: John Wiley & Sons, Inc., 1959).

THOMPSON, VICTOR A.: *Modern Organization* (New York: Alfred A. Knopf, Inc., 1961).

TRIANDIS, HARRY C.: "Categories of Thought of Managers, Clerks, and Workers about Jobs and People in an Industry," *Journal of Applied Psychology,* vol. 45, 1959, pp. 338–344.

WESTON, J. FRED: "Enterprise and Profit," *The Journal of Business,* vol. 22, no. 3, July, 1949, pp. 141–159.

WHYTE, WILLIAM H., JR.: "How Hard Do Executives Work?" *Fortune,* vol. 49, no. 1, January, 1954, pp. 108–112, 147–152.

part

ECONOLOGICAL PERSPECTIVE

five

eight

COMPETITIVE SYSTEMS AND BARGAINING

Assuming scarce resources and multiple uses, any social unit requires some allocative or distributive mechanism among its functioning systems. This can be of two types: (1) an econological or financial structure, as a market or budgetary system; and (2) an administrative or political organization, as an authority or power network within which members interact (cf. Dunlop, 1958).

As Bernard (1952, p. 42) has said: "All people at all times have had to evolve ways of meeting the problem of scarcity. Competition is one way . . . ." And competition, according to Webster, is the act of striving for something that is sought by another at the same time; or rivalry, as between aspirants for honors or for advantage in business. Yet Bernard (*ibid.*) adds: "It is not the problem of scarcity alone that has to be met." Problems also arise because the community is multivalued; and, from this plurality, its members are pulled in different directions. Communal people ". . . want not only different things but seemingly incompatible things. Their wishes are in conflict."

It was this latter characteristic of community life with which the preceding chapter concerned itself, that is, with decisions of an actor in a system which confronts him with trade-offs and compromises among internalized values. In this chapter, we are primarily concerned with the decision process among parties competing for scarce resources and the individual actor responding appropriately in such situations.[1] In economic systems, where the fortune of one individual is coupled with the fortunes of others, there is "bargaining." Thus, here, we want to examine the competitive system, wherein bargaining is the dominating mode of interaction.

Interdependence

Economic models contain the essence of a competitive situation. In this province, it is in the mutual interest of the participants in the system to come to some agreement; this provides a cooperative rationale to the internal, cohesive behavior. Nonetheless, while agreement may be achieved, the interests of the participants are opposed, and this is the basis for rivalry. Thus, we are concerned with a mixed-motive game structure, as with interdependence among competitors within the economic system.[2]

When the decision maker finds his interests linked to the behavior of others in the system, we can speak of "joint fortunes." These may be related in two ways: (1) through functional interdependence, where two units are linked, as between sales and production in a business firm, or as between wholesaler and retailer in a trade channel; or (2) through conjectural interdependence, as between partners bidding in a bridge game (cf. Chamberlain, 1955).

For our analysis, joint fortune is a necessary but not a sufficient condi-

---

[1] Most of this chapter is normative in form and econological in nature. The theory and technologies come largely from the science of economics, with its assumptions and abstractions. (Cf. Fouraker and Siegel, 1963, pp. 3–4.)

[2] Utilities, other than economic, are allocated in a social system, for example, status, security, and friendship. We, however, will treat these "other" variables as independent of the strategy which the competitor composes. Our discussion of the value, utility, or end to be attained will be limited to those generally considered "economic."

tion. Also necessary are states of scarcity and conflicting aspirations. First, the environment is not fully benevolent: The sharing of benefits can result in some loss to one or both parties—a fully integrated solution is not possible. Secondly, the parties are not willing or are unable to cooperate fully with one another. With conflicting aspirations, where each wants to maintain what he has or to gain more, one party can achieve his goal only at a partial cost to the other. These are the basic conditions underlying our discussion of competition and bargaining.

JOINT FORTUNES EXEMPLIFIED

To illustrate these conditions, let us start our discussion with an example of competition in advertising.

The advertisers in our example are not independent or autonomous, for the number of firms in the industry is limited. Where "fewness" is a characteristic of an industry, whatever variation is presumed on the part of any is relevant and, given joint fortunes, the actions or reactions of other members of the system become germane and must be included in the decision function of any one member. For a decision maker to include "reaction" variables of competitors in his decision function,[3] he must anticipate the skills of competing firms in dealing with the factors under their control, as well as forecast the form and degree of their probable retaliation.

Suppose that advertising (A_1) of firm 1 affects the quantity demanded, q_2, of the product of firm 2, that is, $q_2 = f(A_1, A_2)$. Firm 2 must partially adjust its advertising, A_2, to the various advertising outlays of firm 1. Also suppose that $q_1 = g(A_1, A_2)$, where q_1 is the quantity demanded of the product of firm 1. Thus, an equilibrium position must be found for firm 1 in the light of various advertising outlays of firm 2.

In Figure 8-1, contour I shows the optimum adjustments of firm 2 to the efforts of firm 1.[4] If firm 1 expends OU dollars for advertising, the optimum expenditure by firm 2 is OT. Consider contour II, which shows for firm 1 what contour I does for firm 2. Assume that I has a greater slope than II, so that the two contours intersect at some point

---

[3] A seller's concern with retaliation is aroused if complete homogeneity (or differentiation) of product is absent, and if both he and his opponents are large enough to affect the fortunes of each other. (Cf. Fellner, 1949, pp. 71–77.)

[4] As drawn in Figure 8-1, the optimal condition for firm 2 requires that an increase in advertising by firm 1 be met by an increase by firm 2. This is shown by the positive slope of contour I. A similar condition is shown for firm 1 by contour II. Such a situation may not necessarily be true, since a substitution of price or product quality may be made for advertising in the combative programs.

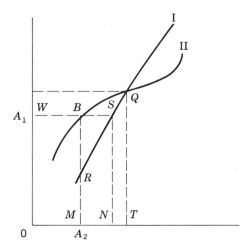

FIGURE 8-1   EQUILIBRIUM ADJUSTMENTS OF
TWO PARTIES WITH INTERDEPENDENT OUT-
COMES (*Adapted from Kenneth Boulding,
Economic Analysis, 2d ed., New York:
Harper & Brothers, 1948, p. 508*)

Q and that their individual actions and joint outcomes are tending to
place them in equilibrium.

Let firm 1 increase its advertising expenditures from *MR* to *MB*.
Firm 2 must increase its appropriation by *BH* to compensate for the
coming competitive increase. Then firm 1 must increase its expenditures
by *HS* to offset the advantage gained by firm 2. From these successive
increases the firms will tend toward equilibrium.[5] At point Q, advertising
efforts of the firms are in equilibrium. However, stability is not necessarily forthcoming at Q, nor are the firms necessarily maximizing joint
profits.

Alternative to Bargaining

Because of these latter possibilities, "competing" firms may collude.
Moreover, our conditions above notwithstanding, one competitor may
attempt to eliminate the other, as through war. Bernard (1952) presents
such an array of possibilities as a continuum from assimilation to elimina-

---

[5] If consecutive increases become larger in order to be equally effective, the
efforts of one or both firms are tending away from equilibrium.

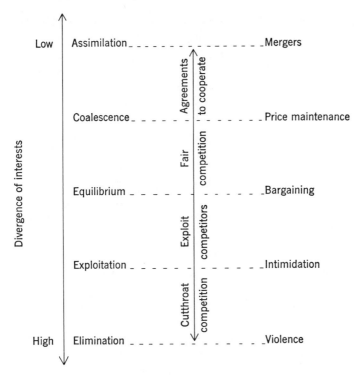

FIGURE 8-2 BERNARD'S CONFLICT-ACCOMMODATION CONTINUUM
(*Adapted from Jessie Bernard, American Community Behavior,
New York: The Dryden Press, 1952, p. 48*)

tion. (See Figure 8-2.) She (*ibid.*, p. 4) contends that points on the
continuum suggest degrees of divergence in the interests of the two
parties, ranging from small disparities (coalescence-assimilation) to great
disparities (exploitation-elimination) between them.[6]

NONNEGOTIATED BEHAVIOR

It may be that the two parties, with joint fortunes, do not bargain
under the conditions that we assumed above. They may not accept
the rules of the game that we have laid down; they may be antagonists

---

[6] However, she (*idem.*) suggests: "Perhaps the lower part of the figure is as
much a measure of relative power of the opposing parties as it is of degree of
divergence of interests. Or perhaps the lower zone selects out those whose interests
are utterly irreconcilable. Or perhaps the recognition of relative power relationships
modifies interests so that the continuum is fundamentally true."

in a more primitive sense and not perceive sufficient value to playing the game within more "civilized" constraints.[7]

This value of entering into negotiation relates to the perceived payoff of the field itself—for example, the topology defined by the alternative values in our advertising example—which includes perceptions of each party's ability to influence the game favorably to himself. This we can refer to as relative bargaining power, similar to what Chamberlain (1955, p. 80) describes as "inducements to agree"—that which is obtainable from the game in order to induce the player to remain in the game and meet eventually the general terms of his opponent. He defines *bargain influence* as: "The influence of X is the importance of X *to* Y of Y cooperating with X, that is, X's power to withhold (potential) gains of cooperating." Thus, for Y, inducement to agree is equal to:

$$\frac{\text{Cost of disagreeing on X's terms}}{\text{Cost of cooperating on X's terms}} \quad \begin{array}{l}(=\text{gains lost by cooperating})\\(=\text{risks from agreeing})\end{array}$$

The "cost of agreeing" is, in some way, an opportunity cost of Y's aspirations. It can include the possibility that the cooperative endeavor will fail or that X will not fulfill his obligations. If the numerator and denominator are equal, Y will be "on the bind" and X may have to supply a side payment. If the numerator is smaller than the denominator, Y is induced; he will cooperate in the game. This may occur, especially, where Y has a cooperative attitude or has a high aversion to risk.

If the fraction in the equation is larger than 1, Y is under-induced; he will not cooperate. This case, we can portray as a bilateral-monopoly situation where we do not find negotiated equilibrium. In Figure 8-3, the curve EF depicts X's perceptions of Y's marginal value of agreement, and AB, the same for Y. In this case AB and EF do not intersect: Negotiations, under our conditions of "bargaining," cannot commence.

Of course, if X does provide a side payment, or if Y develops a higher aversion to risk, as depicted by AB', an equilibrium may be found, as Q. In contrast, if the situation remains as AB, equilibrium can be

[7] Shepard (1961, p. 33) suggests the following modes of conflict:

PRIMITIVE METHODS (DESTRUCTIVE)		MODERN METHODS (PARTIALLY DESTRUCTIVE)		CIVILIZED METHODS (NOT YET ATTAINED)
Suppression	Total war	Limited war	Bargaining	Problem solving

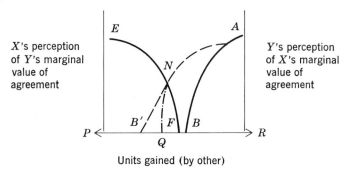

X's perception of Y's marginal value of agreement

Y's perception of X's marginal value of agreement

Units gained (by other)

FIGURE 8-3 BARGAINERS' PERCEPTIONS OF MARGINAL VALUES TO NEGOTIATION (*Adapted from Neil W. Chamberlain, A General Theory of Economic Process, New York: Harper & Brothers, 1955, p. 80*).

obtained only by changes in the parameters of the field, for example, by:

1. Authoritative coercion from the containing environment, or
2. Force by one party through a coalition with an external public.

JOINT PROFIT MAXIMIZATION

If the environment has "slack," that is, if the fortunes of the field can be increased, the firms may enter collusion, which is the agreement or cooperation among two or more competing segments of a system. These competing interests, whose fortunes are linked, arrive at joint policies in order to further collective welfare and, thereby, their individual gains.

Here, we hypothesize a situation that ". . . exists when the nature of a problem permits solutions which benefit both parties, or at least when the gains of one party do not represent equal sacrifices by the other" (Walton and McKersie, 1965, p. 4). This can be shown by what Boulding (1961, p. 46) calls a "trading move." In Figure 8-4, he designates X_1, X_2, X_3, X_4, and X_5 as points in a conflict field. For each of these points in the field he supposes that each party allocates a number which is a measure of preference for that position. He also supposes that, the higher the number assigned, the more preferable the position will be to the party.

According to Boulding, a trading move is a movement within the field which improves the fortunes of both parties. "The move from X_2 to X_3 or the move from X_4 to X_5 moves both parties from a lower to a higher number, indicating that both parties are *better off*" (*idem.*). Suppose, however, that the players perceive or control individ-

FIGURE 8-4   CHOICES FOR PARTIES TO A CONFLICT

PROTAGONISTS	ALTERNATIVES				
	X_1	X_2	X_3	X_4	X_5
Party A	1	2	3	4	5
Party B	5	3	4	1	2

Source: Kenneth Boulding, "Further Reflections on Conflict Management: Summary of Group Discussion," *Conflict Management in Organizations* (Ann Arbor, Mich.: Foundation for Research on Human Behavior, 1961).

ually only alternatives X_2 and X_4—that, without collusion, alternatives X_3 and X_5 cannot be perceived or controlled. Under such circumstances they may act in cooperation rather than in competition.

Cooperation, however, requires group restrictions of some sort. They may be only a loose system of consultation among themselves or in the form of an informal ". . . body of practices which progressively win the support and approval of the majority as being practicably workable and equitable to the parties concerned" (Nourse, 1938, p. 135). On the other hand, the agreement may be accomplished in a more formalized fashion through the medium of a trade association. Finally, collusion may occur from other members passively adjusting to certain leaders in the system. These leaders tend to stylize policies followed by the others.

However accomplished, rules and customs will be established in order to conserve the values or to protect existing rights of group members. Distribution of opportunity will be controlled, and the members will support those rules and practices that tend to perpetuate the relative advantage which they have been enjoying.

Nevertheless, cooperative efforts do not necessarily result in joint profit maximization. First, the group is vulnerable to vicissitudes of other segments of the economy. Singly, and in total, members must deal with other interest groups—for example, labor and government. Second, the direction, effectiveness, and timing of the individual or collective action is difficult to measure. Therefore, the group must control the actions of its members. Where changes are unpredictable, ". . . it is not advisable to disarm in relation to one's rivals" (Fellner, 1949, p. 199).

From all of this, the spirit of competition may dominate the motive to cooperate for any one member. He may believe that he can contribute to his own fortunes more by individual than by collective action; he may resort to competition. In our advertising example, firm 2 may not desire to react passively to dictates of firm 1; it may be that firm 2 wants to be a leader or "influencer." If such is the case, he may attempt to anticipate the actions of firm 1 and, thus, force a particular type of reaction upon the latter.

Distributive Bargaining

Nonetheless, given our concern with "fair competition," we now assume that the choice of firm 1 lies within the field of acceptable negotiation of firm 2. Accordingly we follow Shephard's (1961, p. 43) assumption that a solution will not be satisfactory to one party unless it is satisfactory to the other party—that bargaining is a process which leads to the attainment of objectives not fundamentally outside the preference field of those of the other party and, therefore, capable of being juxtaposed to some degree: The two parties are agreeable to bargaining.

We are brought, then, to a concern with "distributive bargaining." Within the area of mutually acceptable preference fields, we want to examine what Walton and McKersie (1965, p. 4) describe as a complex system of activities instrumental to the attainment of one's party's goals when they are in particular conflict with those of the other party. But, more specifically, "What game theorists refer to as fixed-sum games are the situations we have in mind: one person's gain is a loss to the other" (*idem.*).

GAME THEORY[8]

Mathematicians and economists have developed a method of analysis, known as "game theory," for dealing with this type of decision making. "It was anticipated in early 1920's by the French mathematician, Emile Borel, but it was the 1944 publication of *Theory of Games and Economic Behavior,* by von Neumann and Morgenstern, that created a tremendous stir in economic circles. Since then game theory has also been applied to competitive situations in business, warfare, and politics." (Gardner, 1967, p. 127.)

However, before examining this analytic technique, let us review our position. Bargaining and negotiations presuppose a strategic situation. The decision maker in such a situation is confronted with others in a competitive situation. He has little or no control over the actions of other decision makers, but the action of any one of them affects the well-being of the rest. A second aspect of strategic behavior is that

[8] The authors wish to thank Mr. Jay Dalal, Ph.D. candidate in industrial engineering, University of Wisconsin, for his contribution to this section.

the decision maker must select his action without being able to calculate the exact risks involved. These are the basic presuppositions of a game theory model. Let us now examine its operative elements.

In game theory terms, decision makers are called "players." A set of behavioral patterns which specifies a player's action in light of every conceivable action of competing players is known as *strategies*. The outcome of the game varies according to the strategies employed by the players and is called the *payoff* of the game. It is assumed that each player tries to maximize his gain, that is, to minimize his loss, and is aware of the conflicting desires of others. A game theory solution indicates the optimal strategy for a given player. Common terms are defined below:

1. *Player*—autonomous decision-making unit—not limited to the individual, but could include a firm, a country, or a group of individuals.

2. *Rules of the game*—Each player has resources available to him. These resources can be in various forms—capital, labor, materials, etc. The rules of the game specify the methods by which these resources can be utilized.

3. *Payoffs*—assigned values of the outcome of the game.

4. *Strategy*—set of instructions which states ex ante how a player intends to select his actions under various circumstances until the game is over.

TWO-PERSON, ZERO-SUM GAME. Most of the exercises in game theory have been done on what are called "two-person, zero-sum" games. This implies that the conflict is between two players and what one player wins the other player loses.

Consider the following example: The game is played by two players, A and B. A has three choices—P, Q, and R—available to him, and B has two choices—S and T. The corresponding payoff matrix is given below. The positive elements are payoffs received by A and the negative ones are the payoffs received by B.

		B	
		S	T
	P	-2	2
A	Q	-1	1
	R	3	2

The payoff matrix is interpreted as follows. If A selects action Q, and B chooses T, then A receives $1. On the other hand, if B chooses S, then A loses $1. The objective of either player is to maximize his gain or minimize his loss. The strategy which guarantees the maximum gain is known as the "optimal strategy."

The optimal strategy for A can be determined as follows: Suppose he selects P. Inspecting the payoff matrix, we immediately know that the most he can lose is $2—when B selects S. Similarly, if A selects Q, the most he can lose is $1, and if he selects R, he will win at least $2 irrespective of B's choice. Since the action R offers the best payoffs ($2 gain) under unfavorable circumstances, the optimal strategy for A is to always select R. These criteria of selecting a policy are known as "maximin" criteria. We first determined the minimum payoff for each action (the payoff corresponding to the most unfavorable choice of policy by the opponent). Then we compared these minimums and selected the policy corresponding to the maximum among them.

Now let us consider B's optimal strategy. If he selects S, the most he can lose is $3 when A selects R. When B selects T, he can lose no more than $2. Hence, his optimal strategy is T. Note that T minimizes his maximum loss. The criterion used in selecting B's optimal policy is known as the "minimax" criterion.

Observe that if both A and B follow their optimal policies, the gain of A equals the loss of B ($2), and that the deviation from the optimal policy by any player can only hurt him. In game theory terms, the payoff which corresponds to both the maximum choice of one player and the minimax choice of the other is known as the "saddle point." For our game, the element of the matrix corresponding to R and T is the saddle point.

The games where such a saddle point exists are known as *strictly deterministic* and are the easiest to solve. The optimal strategy for each player is to choose a strategy associated with the row or the column of the saddle point. The payoff corresponding to the saddle point is known as the *value of the game*.

Not all the games, however, are strictly determined. For such games, a saddle point does not exist. Take, for example, a coin-matching game played by A and B. A shows his coin, and if B matches it, A pays him $1; otherwise, he collects $1 from B. The payoff matrix for this game is shown below.

		B	
		H	T
A	H	−1	1
	T	1	−1

Assuming that this game is played more than once, there is no optimal pure strategy for either player. (A pure strategy is one which can be followed repeatedly as an optimal choice.) If A shows, say, heads repeatedly, then B can take advantage of this and ruin A. In this case the best choice of actions will prevent his opponent from guessing the selected action and taking advantage of it. When a player selects his strategies at random, in game theory terms he is said to use "mixed strategies."

If the game does not have a saddle point, then the optimal strategy of at least one player will be mixed. The following example will illustrate a procedure to determine the optimal strategies for a game which is not strictly deterministic—a game for which there is no saddle point.

		B		
		S	T	V
	P	−3	7	8
A	Q	6	1	2
	R	5	−4	−3

The payoffs for this game are as shown in the above payoff matrix. Before analyzing the game, let us study the payoff matrix carefully. As far as A is concerned, he is better off selecting Q rather than R under all circumstances. When such a situation exists, we say that Q "dominates" over R, and then we can eliminate R from further analysis. Similarly for B, the policy T dominates over V, and we can drop V from further considerations. The resultant payoff matrix is as shown.

		B	
		S	T
	P	−3	7
A	Q	6	1

The maximin payoff for A is $1—corresponding to his choice of Q and the choice of T by B. The minimax payoff for B is $6—corresponding to his choice of S and A's choice of Q. The maximum payoff of A does not equal the minimax payoff of B; hence there is no saddle point for the game. Therefore, the players cannot use pure strategies, and they will have to use mixed strategies.

Since the strategies are selected at random, we would like to determine how often each policy should be selected by the players.

Suppose A selects P with probability Pa. Then the probability with which he selects Q is $(1 - Pa)$. His expected earnings when B selects S are:

$$g(A,S) = Pa(-3) + (1 - Pa)(6) = 6 - 9(Pa)$$

similarly,

$$g(A,T) = Pa(7) + (1 - Pa)(1) = 1 + 6(Pa)$$

The optimal choice for A in this case is to select Pa such that his expected earnings are independent of the policy selected by B. The value of such a Pa is obtained by equating $g(A,S)$ and $g(A,T)$ and solving for Pa.

$$g(A,S) = g(A,T)$$
$$6 - 9(Pa) = 1 + 6(Pa)$$
$$Pa = \tfrac{1}{3}$$

Following the same procedure, if Pb is the probability with which B selects S, then:

$$g(B,P) = Pb(-3) + (1 - Pb)(7) = 7 - 10(Pb)$$
$$g(B,Q) = Pb(6) + (1 - Pb)(1) = 1 + 5(Pb)$$

but for optimal strategy,

$$g(B,P) = g(B,Q)$$
$$Pb = \tfrac{2}{5}$$

The optimal strategy for the game can be expressed as follows:

For A: Select P—1 out of 3 times;
       Select Q—2 out of 3 times
For B: Select S—2 out of 3 times;
       Select T—3 out of 5 times

Knowing the optimal strategy, we can now compute the expected gain of each player.

$$g(A: \tfrac{1}{3}, \tfrac{2}{3}) = Pb[\tfrac{1}{3}(-3) + \tfrac{2}{3}(6)] + (1 - Pb)[\tfrac{1}{3}(7) + \tfrac{2}{3}(1)] = 3$$

and

$$g(B: \tfrac{2}{5}, \tfrac{3}{5}) = Pa(\tfrac{2}{5}, \tfrac{3}{5}) = Pa[\tfrac{2}{5}(-3) + \tfrac{3}{5}(7)] + (1 - Pa)[\tfrac{2}{5}(6) + \tfrac{3}{5}(1)] = 3$$

Once again we see that the expected gain of A equals the expected loss of B, and the value of the game is $3.

Thus, we have analyzed the bargaining process associated with optimal decision making in two-person, zero-sum games. For non-zero sum games, the method of simulation can be used, but the analytic methods are more complicated and are not presented here. When more than two persons are involved, the analysis is further complicated by the possibilities of coalition formation.[9] Yet the procedure for analyzing a two-person, zero-sum game can be summarized as follows:

1. Search the payoff matrix for dominating policies. Eliminate all the policies which are dominated by other policies.

2. Check for the saddle point. If the saddle point exists, then the element in the payoff matrix corresponding to the saddle point yields the value of the game. The policies corresponding to the row and the column containing the saddle point are optimal policies, and both the players follow pure strategies.

3. If there is no saddle point, compute the optimal frequency with which each policy should be selected and the value of the game. At least one player will have to use mixed strategy.

Thus far, however, we have been treating alternative strategies as known and without analyzing the components of the decision variables. The question of information will be investigated in the next section, but here we want to analyze major considerations of a player involved in a bargaining situation. To do so, we will study "bidding" behavior.

A SPECIAL CASE: BIDDING[10]

One of the most difficult areas in which models for decision making have been attempted is that of competitive bidding. Here, all other competitors can be treated as "other," and we have a situation where two "sellers" are competing for the bid of a single buyer—the triad. From such a study, we amplify the major dimensions of strategic bargaining. The complexity of the bidding relationship is high; consider the major strategic considerations in such a situation:

1. Potentially, an indeterminate number of competitors;
2. Varied cost structures among bidders;

[9] For presentation of analytic techniques appropriate to these advanced problems, we suggest that the interested reader refer to more complete works in game theory, e.g., R. D. Luce and H. Raiffa, *Games and Decisions* (New York: John Wiley & Sons, Inc., 1957).

[10] Much of this section was adapted from a contribution by Professor Richard G. Newman, University of Missouri at Kansas City. Selected portions are reprinted by permission of author and publisher, "A Note on Competitive Bidding," *Journal of Purchasing*, vol. 3, no. 2, May, 1967, pp. 69–83.

3. Differences between estimated and real costs;

4. Varying attitudes toward bargaining in the bid.[11]

Initially, a series of assumptions must be made—not so much to simplify the problem, but to establish parameters of the model to be developed. Typically, in the bidding operation, some uncertainty of the competition exists; but this uncertainty is somewhat removed by the fact that only firms in an "industry" are ordinarily allowed to bid on a contract and usually transport limitations are imposed. While this assumes nonabsorption of freight rates, the limitation of a geographical distance of x miles can be accepted as a constraint. What does become problematic, however, is the rationale for bidding, as previously listed. Consequently, we can assume:

1. Knowledge of the competition, that is, of those firms which bid on the relevant contracts;

2. Availability of information on the financial structures and (physical) locations of competition;

3. Existing data on costs of raw materials, labor, overhead, etc., of the competing firms.

From these assumptions, we can develop our model, focusing on two major dimensions: (1) evaluation of the probability that the bidder's cost will exceed his estimated bid: "the internal evaluation"; and (2) analysis of competition to determine the depth with which it may be encountered: the "mapping process."[12]

Our first problem is that of determining the probability that actual costs will exceed the estimated costs of the bidder. We can establish a histogram, if dealing with discrete cases, of the past bidding history.

After this internal evaluation, the problem lies in determining the probability of winning the contract against competition. This may be performed by mapping the competition which one may expect to meet in the bid situation. Suppose that $p(L)$ equals the probability that the

---

[11] Differences in bargaining attitudes reflect varied psychological bases of strategy. For example, we will discuss later attitudes toward risk taking. Moreover, bidding behavior can be identified with different objective rationale. The latter includes attempts to:

1. Gain profits resulting from the difference between bid price and actual cost;

2. Break even so as to develop a reputation for future bids; or

3. Utilize available capacity, even though only a portion of the costs of that capacity are covered.

[12] An insightful approach to these problems is that of Wilfred Brown, *Product Analysis Pricing* (London: Heinemann Educational Books, Ltd., 1958).

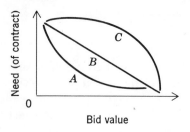

FIGURE 8-5 HYPOTHESIZED AL-
TERNATIVE BIDDING POSTURES OF
COMPETITORS

ratio of true cost to estimated cost lies between L and L + ΔL. Let
x equal the amount bid for the contract. If x wins, then profit = x — LC,
where C is the estimated cost of fulfilling the contract. If profit is not
sufficiently large, or if loss is too great, as extrapolated from historical
data, the negotiator will not offer a bid. The essence of this approach
is to determine the need of the compeititon to secure the bid. Hypotheti-
cally, the greater the need for the contract, the lower the negotiator
will bid; and, inversely, the less the need, that is the greater the desire
to secure profits for the company, the higher the bid will be.[13]

We may construct curves based upon these suppositions. In Figure
8-5, our curves are meant to approximate maps of alternative bidding
behavior. We assume that the shapes may take three possible forms,
as: curve A, representing an extreme sensitivity to the need for the
contract; curve B, portraying a bidder whose need is linear—it varies
directly with the expected value of the bid; and curve C, showing
marked insensitivity to the need for the contract.[14]

From such analyses, the bidder can define the field of competition
and, once he has stereotyped his competition, he can "fit" his pattern
and estimate his bid, using "value of contract" as an index. If A is
a firm which attaches high priority to need, and if he follows this pattern

[13] In actual practice, firms may submit bids realizing that they will be too high.
The rationale is to keep their "names" on the bid list, knowing that they will not
receive the bid. In effect, they are hedging against some future need to bid more
competitively.

[14] Using past data on bids, we can develop the ratios of competitor A's bids to
our estimated costs over previous bid situations, thus developing a series of bidding-behavior curves. The bidding-behavior curves can then be used to develop
needed data; that is, if A's bid is consistently lower, *cetirus paribus,* we can assume
that A has a relatively high need value. Consequently, we may stereotype his
pattern.

consistently, we can expect him to follow a path as defined by curve A. If B equates need and value equally, he will follow the path defined by curve B.

While firm A may accept the field of negotiation—may cooperate on this set of bidding postures—he may become aggressive within it: He may not accept stereotypes of the others as given. It may be within his province and desire to form a coalition with other bidders or to practice secrecy and bluff. Boulding (1961, p. 46) deals with the possibility of changing "conflict" to "trading" moves within such a context.

If the reader will refer to Figure 8-4, the process of coalition formation can be demonstrated; with side payments, conflict moves may be transformed into trading moves. "If the system is at X_2, B would like to go to X_1 but A would not. If B's gain in going to X_1 is large enough, however, B may be able to bribe A to move to X_1 as well. The bribe thus changes the conflict into a trading move . . ." (Boulding, 1961, p. 46.)

In addition, firm A may exercise secrecy or bluff. McDonald (1952, p. 196) states that the ". . . incompleteness of information in markets is not altogether accounted for by disabilities of observation and elements of chance. The incompleteness is in part created by the free rational decision to withhold information for strategical purposes." This further reduces the ability of other members of the competitive field to predict his intentions accurately; his use of competitively random acts may confound his competitors. The actor may undertake strategic maneuvering and deception in his bargaining behavior. The accumulation of accurate data about the competitive system, in turn, becomes paramount.

Thus, in the following parts of this chapter, we want to examine: (1) the state of knowledge about the field of negotiation, especially relating to the certainty with which its payoff matrix is perceived; and (2) the posture which the actor assumes in bargaining, especially his aggressiveness in accepting risk. Let us discuss these two phenomena in reverse order.

Bargaining Propensities

When dealing with uncertainty, a decision maker must choose a rule or strategy for acting in spite of the unknowns facing him. The choice of this decision rule will reflect his own attitude toward risk, for example, pessimism versus optimism, as well as the "nature" of the game that he is playing—that is, the structure of competitor interaction as determined by the relative control of resources, including information.

We have held a tacit assumption about the nature of the bargaining field, notably that the negotiators are equal in strength—we have ignored, generally, the question of relative bargaining power. Here, we want to posit that the competitors may not be equal in their relative influence. They may have differential advantages.

Attitudes toward risk taking appear to be related to, for example, the relative or absolute financial position of an actor. The stronger this position, the less the need—not necessarily, desire—for greater conservatism. Felt influence may be related, also, to recent changes in income or profit. As the decision maker becomes adjusted to greater income, he may attach less importance to the possibility of loss. In contrast, he may desire to spend a higher proportion of his income on security (cf. Bradford and Johnson, 1963, p. 371).

Historically, most economic analyses of competition have assumed "equal-strength" relationships, following Pareto (1909). However, Fouraker and Siegel (1963) studied the unequal case. These researchers, employing the Bowley (1928) model, describe the situation wherein ". . . one of the parties has the power to establish the price at which the exchange will take place; the other party has the power to choose the quantity which will be exchanged at the established price" (ibid., p. 13). In regard to the structure of the field, then, the Fouraker and Siegel study is worthy of examination.

Largely within a simulated situation, and with student bargainers, Fouraker and Siegel found that "the Bowley price is the optimum choice for the seller, and the Bowley quantity is the optimum choice for the buyer, given the seller's price," and where the negotiators are motivated solely by their own profits (ibid., p. 204). This position did not maximize joint profits, but they found that by manipulating the experimental conditions, that is, the amount of information, form of bidding, and location of the equal-profit contract, they could induce the Pareto type of solution for an appreciable number of subjects.

From this, we would assume that the structure of the field influences the bargaining process as well as the final or contract position of the negotiators. In fact, Miller (1959) concludes from his study that outcomes within a bargaining field are as much a function of the interactions of the parties as they are of the attitudes and dispositions of the players. Yet attributes of the individual negotiators cannot be ignored. Fouraker and Siegel (1963, p. 66) suggest that there may be several different bargaining types. With incomplete information, "some subjects appear to be concerned only with their own rewards, as assumed by Bowley;

they seem indifferent to the fortunes of their opponents. Such a subject might be called a simple maximizer."[15]

To predict behavior, then, we need to know the disposition and attitudes of the bargainer. Decision theory calls this psychological construct a "decision rule," and offers several alternatives.

These decision rules can be characterized as more or less conservative. For example, a complete optimist would follow the "maximax" criterion. He is gambling-oriented and, ignoring intermediate outcomes, would choose alternative A in the matrix below, because it has the highest possible outcome (100). He strives for maximum possible outcomes.

ALTERNATIVE CHOICE	POSSIBLE STATES OF NATURE		
	X	Y	Z
A	100	2	1
B	99	98	0

A slightly less optimistic strategy is the one proposed by Hurwicz. This is derived from a weighted average of the minimum and maximum outcomes. The Hurwicz "coefficient of optimism" is a number between 0 and 1 which is the weight assigned to the best possible payoff, such as $\frac{3}{4}$. Then $1 - \frac{3}{4}$ ($= \frac{1}{4}$) is the weight assigned to the worst possible payoff (cf. Shuchman, 1963, p. 328). This proposition directs the decision maker to choose alternative A, as:

$$
\begin{array}{lll}
 & \text{WORST (PLUS) BEST} & = & \begin{array}{c}\text{AVERAGE}\\\text{VALUE}\end{array} \\
\text{Alternative A:} & 1 \cdot \frac{1}{4} + \frac{3}{4}(100) & = & 75.25 \\
\text{B:} & 0 \cdot \frac{1}{4} + \frac{3}{4}(99) & = & 74.25
\end{array}
$$

[15] Fouraker and Siegel (1963, p. 208) also found that "complete-information conditions induced a variety of 'non-simple' maximizing rules." They classified such behavior as: "rivalistic (a decision which reduces a player's profits, but generally reduces his opponent's profits by a larger margin); cooperative (a decision which increases a player's profits, but generally increases his opponent's profits even more); and simple maximizing (an optimal individual decision)."

A more conservative rule is the "maximin," which states that the decision maker will choose the maximum of the minimum alternatives. In the matrix above, he would choose alternative A. Since the minimum outcomes are 0 and 1 (in state Z), the "maximiner" will take the largest of these minimum possible outcomes (cf. Wald, 1950). This reflects a conservative point of view by ignoring other possible states of nature and focusing only on the worst possible outcomes. Such a disposition may reflect a situation of very scarce resources where the decision maker cannot afford to lose much.

Luce and Raiffa (1957, p. 316) contend that the maximin rule and the Hurwicz rule go counter to intuition. Their major criticism is that these rules ". . . focus so strongly on the best and worst states of nature that often they do not permit one to gather negative information about the plausibility of such states." Thus, we can suggest the Bayesian criterion, which focuses not on only the best and worst states of nature, but on all. Here, the decision maker makes the following calculation: "Multiplies for a specific act the probability of each state of nature by the consequences of that act and state, and sums these products for all the possible states. This is the expected value of the act" (Bierman et al., 1961, pp. 7–8). The alternative with the highest expected value is the Bayes solution.

Let us assume, for each state of nature, the following (subjective) probabilities:

$$
\begin{array}{ccc}
X & Y & Z \\
\frac{2}{10} & \frac{3}{10} & \frac{5}{10}
\end{array}
$$

From the matrix above, we can find the expected value for each alternative as:

		EXPECTED VALUE
A	$0.2(100) + 0.3(2) + 0.5(1) =$	21.1
B	$0.2(99) + 0.3(98) + 0.5(0) =$	49.2

Accepting the Bayesian criterion the decision maker would choose alternative B, the larger of the two expected values.

If, however, he does not know the relevant probabilities, he may employ the Laplace criterion. This decision rule is based upon the assumption that each state of nature has an equiprobability of occurrence and is weighted accordingly. From above, each of the three states of

nature have one-third likelihood of occurring, and their expected values
would be:

EXPECTED
VALUE

Alternative A: $\frac{1}{3}(100) + \frac{1}{3}(2) + \frac{1}{3}(1) = 34.2$

B: $\frac{1}{3}(99) + \frac{1}{3}(98) + \frac{1}{3}(0) = 65.7$

and alternative B would, again, be chosen.

A major criticism of the Laplace criterion, however, is its association
with what is called the "principle of insufficient reason." According to
this principle, if there is no reason for something, then it will not happen.
Thus, Buridan's ass ". . . would starve to death if exactly equidistant
from two equally attractive bales of hay. Since the ass would have no
reason to move to one bale in preference to the other, he could not
move, and hence, must starve to death" (Shuchman, 1963, p. 329). Nonetheless, it seems most unlikely that the decision maker is completely
ignorant of the various states of the world and, if so, the Laplace theorem
seems a reasonable way to fill that void.

The last decision criterion presented here is the "minimax regret function." Essentially this measures the ex post opportunity cost of a less
than most desirable choice. Savage (1954) contends that, after an alternative has been chosen and the relevant state of nature has occurred,
the decision maker experiences regret, if he received less than the highest
payoff from that state.

We can calculate regret values from the matrix above. Let alternative
B be chosen by the decision maker, but X by nature. This would result
in a regret value of 1 for cell BX, since the payoff for BX of 99 is
1 less than the payoff in AX (of 100), which would have resulted if
alternative A had been chosen, etc.

ALTERNATIVE CHOICES	REGRET STATES OF NATURE		
	X	Y	Z
A	0	96	0
B	1	0	1

Then, applying the minimax criterion, the decision maker will want to
keep his regret as small as possible and choose alternative B. This cri-

terion, while ex post in nature, relates to much of the work in cognitive dissonance, and Shuchman contends that this is the only criterion which would be optimal as a hedging strategy. "Since hedging is a very frequently occurring phenomenon in the business world, it seems that . . . (the minimax regret) criterion is more realistic than the other criteria in this regard" (*ibid.* p. 331).

While descriptions of these decision criteria are important in themselves, we must remind the reader that an equally important assumption is the fact that the negotiator is willing to bargain with good faith in the system. Let us examine the process whereby the bargainers reach a definition of the acceptable field of negotiation, and we can do this through viewing the purchasing activity.

NEGOTIATION IN PURCHASING[16]

Negotiation is "process-like" wherein the parties have opportunity to search for information on the potential of the contract as they bargain, that is, they can discuss their joint interests with a view to reaching an agreement. But these bargainers are operating without full knowledge, and information may become available during negotiations or the utilities of the parties may change during interaction. Therefore, let us extend bargaining into a set of sequential activities where the parties may search for commonality.

Harsanyi (1962) presents two interesting mechanisms for dealing with the problem of ignorance of opponents' utility functions—"stereotyping utility functions" and "mutual adjustment." For the former, he states: "We may assume that at least persons of a given sex, age, social position, education, etc. are expected to have similar utility functions of a specified sort. Any utility function (u) attributed by public opinion to persons of a given description we shall call a stereotype utility function."

He contends that the stereotype utility function is recognized by each of the participants as they enter the bargaining situation. ". . . party 1 will know that party 2 will expect him to display a certain stereotype utility function u_1, and party 2 will know that party 1 will expect party 2 to entertain this particular expectation, etc." (*ibid.*, p. 33). His second mechanism is one that develops during the bargaining process through mutual adjustments by both parties in terms of their respective expectations. While these expectations may have been highly dissimilar prior to negotiations, convergence on mutually agreeable concession points is a function of the bargaining process itself. It becomes less viable, however, if bluffing is present on the part of either participant.

---

[16] Major portions of this section are based upon: Richard G. Newman, "Some Comments on Negotiation," *Journal of Purchasing*, May, 1966, pp. 52–56, by permission of author and publisher.

Bluffing, Harsanyi defines as gross misrepresentations of final demand. If no penalty is attached to bluffing, mutual adjustment cannot bring about compatible concession points, if the initial concession points were not compatible.

Ikle and Leites (1962) approach the problem of instability and unknown preferences in a different manner. They apply a concept related to political negotiations in order to shed light on the problem. Stressing the need for a construct which accounts for changes in preference, an important concept for them is the "minimum disposition." This is considered to be the least favorable terms which a negotiator will accept in preference to no agreement, at a given point in time.

The use of this model requires one simplifying, but very critical, assumption: conflict of interest occurs over only one set of mutually exclusive alternatives, and A's preference over these alternatives is the reverse of that of B. Briefly, Ikle and Leites deal with the situation where each side estimates the real bargaining range for his opponent, including minimum-disposition estimates of the "others." Consequently, the bargaining range for A would be his own minimum disposition defined through estimates of his opponent's minimum disposition. Any demand upon the part of the opponent in excess of this range is defined as a *sham* bargaining position, that is, it lies outside the relevant bargaining range. Next, they define "concessions," which are considered movements from more favored positions to less favored ones. Consequently, the objective of the negotiator is to modify the opponent's estimate of the probable outcome of the negotiation (the minimum disposition of his opponent and the latter's estimate of his own minimum disposition). This may be accomplished by:

1. Altering the actual situation on which minimum dispositions are based.

2. Illustrating advantages and minimizing disadvantages of proposed terms to opponents.

3. Convincing opponents that *proper conduct* is essential in negotiation, i.e., rules of "fair play."

4. Refusing proposals and threatening to break off negotiations. (Cf. *ibid.,* pp. 23–24.)

Such tactics are used to move an opponent's offer closer to the actor's minimum disposition. In reality, such attempts may be made across various factors of the issue, as: price, service, quality, etc.

Presented in Figure 8-6 is a set of ranges in terms of the attitudes of the negotiators toward the situation, what the seller and buyer are willing to accept and pay.

These, as seen in Figure 8-6, consist of five ranges: The first, for

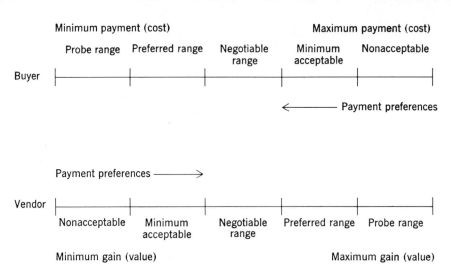

FIGURE 8-6 DEFINING STRATEGIC RANGES IN NEGOTIATION PROCESS

the buyer (the last for the vendor), is labeled the "probe range." This range, for the buyer, is a value which obviously would be below any expectations of the vendor. The rationale for employing this probe might be to test for knowledge of the vendor's costs, to establish himself as an able opponent, or specifically to force the vendor "to play in his league" by establishing dominance early. Undoubtedly, the probe range would be considered unacceptable by the vendor (assuming a level of competence on the part of both opponents and that "negotiation" has meaning).

The buyer must decide how long to remain in his probe range—if at all. A precise answer to this question is difficult. If, for example, the initial probe meets with resistance, the buyer is given an indication that the vendor is knowledgeable regarding costs and values in the negotiation. Then the continued use of the probe will result in no legitimate gain for the buyer and may substantially hinder him. The hindrance can come about by presenting an attitude which may be interpreted by the vendor as "horse trading" (consequently, sacrificing other variables for the sake of price).

The vendor's operation in the probe range may be viewed in much the same manner. Prolonged operation in that range, however, may convey three possible images of the vendor to the buyer, that the vendor:

1. Is unwilling to assume responsibility of taking on the contract;

2. Is unsure of his costs, probing at relatively high prices to transfer risk and uncertainty to the buyer;

3. Assesses the buyer as a weak opponent.

If it becomes apparent that both parties have definite ideas in terms of costs and values, this preliminary "jockeying" will quickly end. One party may terminate probing by revealing a piece of information, such as estimated value of the item under negotiation. Should the buyer release this information, he immediately excludes or minimizes (3) above. Should such a condition exist as stated in (2), the buyer places himself in a stronger and, perhaps, dominant role. Continued high probe by the vendor can signal the possibility of a condition as existing in (1), and the negotiations may be discontinued.

With movements from the probe range toward a mutually acceptable range, the process of negotiation takes on increased meaning. If both vendor and buyer begin to operate in the "preferred range," by releasing information on both product and process, not only is a healthy respect fostered by both sides, but it may cause both vendor and buyer to move into the "negotiable range." The final solution lies in the "negotiable range," at which point an agreement between the vendor and buyer is reached, but it is impossible to define that range for every situation.[17]

Within our extension of bargaining behavior, then, we see a concern with not only subjective evaluations but also perceptions of these subjective evaluations, that is, perceived risk as well as perceptions of value assessments that opponents are making. And here, for example, if A underestimates B's subjective value of cooperating or aversion to risk, A may modify his terms more than necessary to complete the negotiation. In effect, the actor establishes tentative hypotheses, which he then "tests" against the hypotheses of others. In the process, he may reject his own original hypothesis, modify it to weight variables differently, or influence others to support his hypothesis. He searches for information about the problem field.

We see, therefore, that the accuracy of perceptions is vital to a negotiator and that information is a highly valued, economic commodity, itself. This includes an impact on both perceptions and attitudes toward uncertain states. Therefore, let us turn our attention briefly to uncertainty.

Information and Uncertainty

Where the possibility of error or contingency is perceived in risk taking, the decision maker may recognize that his probability judgments are inexact. The advertiser may think that, nine times out of ten, a unit

[17] Professor Victor A. Thompson states that he has never understood whether this sort of theory is considered to be an empirical description or a *post hoc,* logical reconstruction. We, at this state of development, hold to the latter.

of advertising will return an expected value. But he may believe that the total of his experiences does not permit him to place 100 percent confidence in that expectation. When such a state exists, uncertainty is present.[18]

We can note differences in an actor's willingness to accept risk. Some actors are noted for their willingness to act in the face of uncertainty; others, for their conservatism. Varying preferences exist even for the extremes—where risk is undertaken for its own sake or where subjective certainty is a prerequisite to action. (Cf. Friedman, 1953, pp. 303–304.) Whatever the case, we assume that actors cannot be neutral toward risk; as Hart (1951, pp. 72–73) states, "they will have risk aversion because of . . . the principle of diminishing utility; and, the obvious emotional halo surrounding danger and security." One entrepreneur may hesitate, for example, to increase advertising, since advertising itself causes change. Another may create change as a strategic or intrinsically rewarding experience.

Although the actors may vary in their behavior when confronted with uncertainty, generally greater unwillingness to act is encountered with greater uncertainty of expectation. Thus, an allowance for uncertainty will tend to reduce the magnitude of an expected value; and the allowance will have a positive relationship with the degree of uncertainty. (Cf. Lange, 1952, p. 33.) Moreover, the more remote the execution date from the decision date, the less predictable the outcome of an action; and the more remote the action, the greater the uncertainty allowance. Accordingly, expected values discounted by uncertainty allowances are termed "effective expected values" and can be treated as any other unique value.

BAYES' THEOREM[19]

Fellner (1949, p. 80) objects to this simplistic method of treating uncertainty on the grounds that it ". . . comes rather close to making the problem of uncertainty disappear completely." Moreover, a technology is available to analyze the process of incoming information as it becomes available to the bargainer during negotiation. This is known as "Bayes' theorem."

Holding to the "degree of belief" assumption of the probability of

[18] The actor is partly ignorant of the parameters of the universe of possible outcomes. But he may be able to determine an interval within which the parameter will fall: thus the standard deviation or coefficient of variation may be used as a measure of uncertainty (cf. Lange, 1952, p. 29).

[19] Much of this section was prepared by Mr. Jay Dalal, Ph.D. candidate in industrial engineering, University of Wisconsin.

an event—that is, stronger beliefs give rise to larger probabilities, while weaker beliefs result in smaller probabilities—the decision maker assigns probabilities which reflect his degree of belief in the occurrence of an event. With time he receives more information about the situation and revises his estimates. The theorem, then, can be stated as:

Modified probability = (prior probability)

x(information) ÷ (normalizing constant)

In mathematical terms the theorem can be stated as follows:

$$p(x/y) = \frac{p(x) \cdot p(y/x)}{p(y)}$$

where p(x) = prior degree of belief about unknown parameter, x.

p(y/x) = conditional distribution of observations.

p(x/y) = posterior probability of x, given the observations.

Consider two boxes, marked A and B, respectively, each containing four balls:

Box A: 3 white; 1 red

Box B: 2 white; 2 red

A box is selected at random at the beginning of the game. The object of the game is to guess which box it is.

Before we draw a ball from the selected box, since the box is selected at random, it is reasonable to use $p(A) = p(B) = \frac{1}{2}$ as our prior degree of belief [p(A) probability that box A is selected; p(B) probability that box B is selected].

Let
W = white ball

R = red ball

Then the conditional probabilities are:

$$p(W/A) = \tfrac{3}{4}; p(R/A) = \tfrac{1}{4}$$
$$p(W/B) = \tfrac{1}{2}; p(R/B) = \tfrac{1}{2}$$

Now suppose we are allowed to draw one ball from the selected box. Say we draw a white ball. We use Bayes' theorem to modify our prior degree of belief about the selected box, on the bases of new information (draw of a white ball).

$$\text{Prior belief: } p(A) = p(B) = \tfrac{1}{2}$$

Information: draw of a white ball

$$p(A/W) = \frac{p(A) \cdot p(W/A)}{P(W)} = \frac{\tfrac{1}{2} \cdot \tfrac{3}{4}}{P(W)} = \frac{\tfrac{3}{8}}{P(W)}$$

$$P(B/W) = \frac{p(B) \cdot p(W/B)}{P(W)} = \frac{\tfrac{1}{2} \cdot \tfrac{1}{2}}{P(W)} = \frac{\tfrac{1}{4}}{P(W)}$$

$$p(A/W) + p(B/W) = 1$$

$$\therefore \ \frac{\tfrac{3}{8}}{p(W)} + \frac{\tfrac{1}{4}}{p(W)} = 1$$

or

$$p(W) = \tfrac{5}{8}$$

Substituting for $p(W)$, we get the modified probabilities as follows:

$$p(A/W) = \tfrac{3}{5}; \ p(B/W) = \tfrac{2}{5}$$

Suppose we put the white ball back into the selected box and once more we are allowed to draw a ball. Let us assume that we draw a white ball again. Bayes' theorem can be used again to modify our degree of belief.

$$\text{Prior: } p(A/W) = \tfrac{3}{5} : p(B/W) = \tfrac{2}{5}$$

Information: draw of a white ball

$$p(A/WW) = \frac{p(A/W) \cdot p(W/A)}{P(W)} = \frac{\tfrac{3}{5} \cdot \tfrac{3}{4}}{P(W)} = \frac{\tfrac{9}{20}}{P(W)}$$

$$P(B/WW) = \frac{p(B/W) \cdot p(W/B)}{P(W)} = \frac{\tfrac{2}{5} \cdot \tfrac{1}{2}}{P(W)} = \frac{\tfrac{1}{5}}{P(W)}$$

Once again,

$$p(A/WW) + p(B/WW) = 1$$

$$\therefore \ 1 = \frac{\tfrac{9}{20}}{P(W)} + \frac{\tfrac{1}{5}}{P(W)} \quad \text{or} \quad p(W) = \frac{13}{20}$$

Substituting for $p(W)$, we get

$$p(A/WW) = \tfrac{9}{13}; \ p(B/WW) = \tfrac{4}{13}$$

The following diagram illustrates the sequential nature of Bayes' theorem and its use in decision making under certainty.

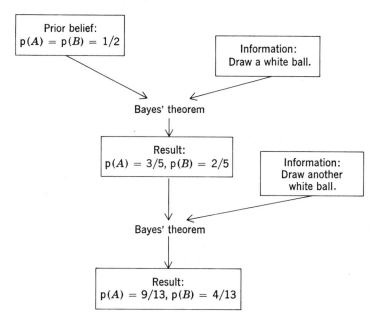

FIGURE 8-7 DIAGRAMMATIC PRESENTATION OF THE BAYESIAN CONCEPT

AN EXPERIMENTAL STUDY

Thus far, we have gone to some length in analyzing decision criteria (posture of the bargainer) and information flows (knowledgeability of the decision maker). Now, let us provide some empirical evidence pertaining to these elements of negotiation. These data are taken from a single study, and the reader should be careful of generalization.[20]

Interest, here, is centered on the twofold bilateral relationship in which each participant can only buy (or sell) to another member of the channel. Thus, in effect, we have two bilateral monopoly relationships, one between the manufacturer and the wholesaler and the other between the wholesaler and the retailer.

One "solution" to a bilateral monopoly problem suggests that "rational" players, if they behave in their respective self-interests, should always

[20] This section is based upon Donald L. Harnett, Larry L. Cummings, and G. David Hughes, "Bargaining Behavior and Risk-taking Propensity," *Behavioral Science,* vol. 13, no. 2, March, 1968, pp. 91–101.

negotiate a contract at the quantity (Qm) where joint profits are a maximum. The prices associated with Qm between the retailer's average revenue curve and the manufacturer's average cost curve therefore represent the players' welfare frontier and correspond to Pareto's optima.

If this interpretation is assumed correct, and quantity *is* determinate at Qm, the establishment of buying and selling prices and the resulting division of profits are of major importance. Schelling (1957) specifies an even division of maximum joint profits as the apparent solution, but stipulates that the "value" of the game be known to the participants. This stipulation is usually bypassed in bilateral monopoly theories, since most solutions imply complete information. However, it may be unrealistic in many markets to assume complete knowledge of the cost and revenue functions of all firms. For example, it may be more appropriate to assume that the seller is aware of his cost function and the buyer aware of his revenue function but that neither has knowledge of the other's information.

Studies conducted by Fouraker and Siegel (1963) indicate that assumptions involving the amount of knowledge possessed by participants are a critical determinant of the bargaining outcome. At first glance it appears obvious that the more information a member of the channel possesses, the greater would be his bargaining power. The suggestion of other studies, however, is that this is not always the case and that Schelling's hypothesis may hold. In essence, this hypothesis states that a bargainer with less information receives a greater share of any joint payoff than his bargaining position would indicate because his lack of knowledge of what constitutes a "fair" or "reasonable" solution places him at some advantage.

THE EXPERIMENT. In order to test specific hypotheses concerning a channel model, seventy-eight subjects (twenty-six groups of three) acted as monopolistic sellers and monopsonistic buyers in experimental situations simulating a manufacturer-wholesaler-retailer relationship. The experiments consisted of a series of negotiations concerning the price and quantity of a fictitious product to be exchanged among the actors. As a result of these negotiations, and depending upon price and quantity agreements of the participants, a profit was earned by each subject. This profit provided incentive and assured seriousness among participants because a cash payoff, corresponding to the amount of profit gained during the bargaining, was given to each subject.

Subjects were tested in the model under complete, partial, or incomplete information. Under conditions of complete information, all members of the bargaining group were fully informed as to the payoffs associated with every possible quantity and price negotiated in the channel. Participants under incomplete information knew their own payoff for any negotiated price and quantity, but did not know their counterparts' payoff. Under partial information, the wholesaler was informed while the manufacturer and retailer operated under incomplete information.

HYPOTHESES. The general hypotheses of the experiment concerned the relative profits earned and the effects of information on bargaining. It was hypothesized that the behavior of each participant, and his resulting monetary reward in the channel, was a function of the level of information afforded him as well as of established institutional arrangements and economic forces.

DISCUSSION AND GENERAL CONCLUSIONS. The findings indicate that the amount of profit earned was a function of the knowledge each subject possessed about the payoff structure as well as his bargaining role. In addition, the wholesaler was shown to have a particularly unique bargaining advantage or disadvantage depending on his bargaining skill and the amount of personal and strategic information furnished him.

Under incomplete information, participants' lack of knowledge on the reasonableness of their demands added uncertainty to the situation, emphasizing individual differences, such as level of aspiration and bargaining ability. The wholesaler, on the whole, suffered the most because of these differences, probably because he was forced not only to negotiate with two bargainers, but also to coordinate quantity demands as well. A few presumably skilled wholesalers were able to take advantage of their position and play one opponent against the other for a large gain. Although the average quantity negotiated in a channel did not differ significantly from the joint-maximizing quantity, the wide range in agreements suggests that participants were not able to approximate such a solution.

Under partial information, however, seven of nine quantity agreements were closely correlated with Q_m. Thus, while the wholesaler under this condition was unable to earn, on the average, more than his counterpart earned under incomplete information, he was at least able to negotiate quantity terms close to the optimal. Additional information appeared to eliminate some of the variability resulting from the wholesaler role, as the variance of profit earned was substantially reduced. This fact lends support to the suggestion that individual differences will play a smaller and smaller part in the negotiation process as information is increased.

Consistent with the above were the results reported under complete information. For the wholesaler role, where this effect was most noticeable, there was a significant decrease in profit variance when compared to partial information. Such a reduction in variance did not result in equality of earnings across conditions, however, as the wholesaler was found to turn his role to his own advantage. That is, by giving the manufacturer and retailer additional information, their profits were decreased while the wholesaler's position was improved. This clearly supports the Fellner hypothesis that additional information may actually be harmful in a bargaining situation.

One of the most surprising facts was that total profits, under complete information, showed a decrease. The most logical explanation for this tendency seemed to be that participants were more interested in assuring themselves of their "fair" share of the profits rather than seeking an optimal solution.

RISK IN BARGAINING BEHAVIOR. So much for the situational and structural determinants of bargaining results, that is, information conditions and bargaining position. It is probable that much of the variability around the predicted outcomes can be attributed to individual differences in such factors as level of aspiration and willingness to yield. Suggestive of such factors are those posited by Fellner (1949) as influencing bargaining ability: the long-run consequence of "faring too well," the ability of parties to take and inflict loss in a "stalemate," and the unwillingness to yield in a range in which other parties are expected to yield.

Only a few works have been published actually identifying individual differences associated with bargaining ability. Deutsch [1949 (a) and 1949 (b)] identified differences in bargaining ability attributed to motivational set—either cooperative or competitive. As noted earlier, Fouraker and Siegel (1963) used the categories proposed by Deutsch and isolated three "bargaining types:" (1) a "simple maximizer," who wants only to maximize his own profits, (2) a "cooperator," who is concerned with maximizing the joint profits of the group, and (3) a "rivalist," who desires to maximize the difference in profits between his rivals and himself. In addition, Siegel and Fouraker (1960) have identified level of aspiration as a major determinant of the differential payoffs to the subjects in bargaining contracts negotiated under incomplete information.

One identifiable personality characteristic, more than any other, seems to thread through the work of Deutsch and Fouraker and Siegel as well as the analysis by Fellner—the propensity to take *risk*.

RISK-TAKING PROPENSITY AND RESULTS.[21] First, the relationship between risk-taking propensity (RTP) and the profit earned by all Ss investi-

---

[21] The instrument used in the present study to assess risk-taking propensity was that developed by Nathan Kogan and Michael A. Wallach, *Risk Taking: A Study in Cognition and Personality* (New York: Holt, Rinehart and Winston, 1964), Appendix E, pp. 250–261.

gated—summing across all information conditions and role positions—suggests a positive relationship between RTP and amount of profit earned. Further reflection and data ($r = -.069$) suggest that individual differences (in, for example, level of aspiration) emerging in the play of the bargaining game under conditions of *incomplete* information would be likely to operate in such a fashion as to negate our initial hypothesis.

The next logical analysis seemed to be to relate RTP and profit earned, restricting our sample to those Ss bargaining under *complete* information conditions. If it is true that the effect of individual differences in level of aspiration that might influence initial bid levels are "washed out" under the complete information condition (where each participant in the channel can calculate the profit earned by any other participant, given a specific contract), we would expect RTP to exert its greatest impact on bargaining results under this condition. In other words, complete information is assumed to lessen or even eliminate the effect of initial bidding levels, thereby increasing the likelihood of RTP exerting some influence on bargaining. Therefore one can hypothesize a positive relation between RTP and amount of profit earned; the resulting r equaled $+.341$ ($p < .10$). Thus, although the relationship is positive, other factors appear to be operating under the *complete information* condition. This is consistent with hypotheses suggested previously concerning the factors assumed to influence bargaining behavior under complete information, that is, "equalizing" behavior in which the participants are assumed to desire an even distribution of profits.

So, RTP would seem to play a central role, if it ever will, under incomplete information. This would suggest a positive relation between RTP and amount of profit earned for those Ss operating under incomplete information. The hypothesis was not supported: $r = -.176$. These results of this study suggest that a reexamination of the logic relating the concept of RTP, as a personality characteristic, to bargaining behavior would prove fruitful.

RTP AND BARGAINING PROCESSES. In an attempt to relate RTP, level of aspiration, and bargaining processes, the following interpretation of the bargaining dynamics facing a typical participant is offered. Assume that after having read the instructions to the bargaining game, the participant develops a subjective estimate of the amount of profit he desires to earn, that is, he establishes a level of aspiration. Secondly, assume that the S's initial bid offered to another member of his bargaining channel is an exploratory bid which does not reflect his level of aspiration. Indeed, data indicate that most participants offer initial bids at levels very advantageous to themselves. Assume then that the S's second bid reflects his initial asking level or initial level of aspiration. The difference between this second bid and his final bid can be taken as an operational measure of the S's bargaining ability. The greater the difference between the second bid and the final bid, the less the bargaining ability of the subject; the less the difference, the greater his bargaining ability.

This interpretation of the bargaining process led to hypothesizing new relationships between RTP and bargaining behavior. Subjects possessing high RTP will tend to exhibit greater bargaining ability, that is, will tend to yield less from their initial level of aspiration, than subjects low in RTP. Subjects possessing low RTP will tend to exhibit less bargaining ability—will tend to yield more from their initial level of aspiration—than subjects high in RTP. In other words, high risk takers will tend to "give in" less from their initial bargaining positions.

In addition, as indicated previously, one can hypothesize that individual differences in bargaining behavior are more likely to emerge as the information conditions becomes less complete. It was, therefore, hypothesized that the relationship between RTP and bargaining ability would tend to increase as we move from the complete to the incomplete information conditions of the bargaining game. In other words, RTP, as a personality characteristic, will exert its strongest influence on bargaining ability under conditions of information scarcity.

EMPIRICAL RESULTS AND INTERPRETATIONS. If the hypotheses hold, the results should indicate (1) a positive relationship between RTP and bargaining ability and (2) that this relationship increases in magnitude as the amount of information available in the bargaining channel decreases. The results in the following table indicate strong support for both hypotheses.

Table 8-1   Relationship between information and RTP and bargaining ability

INFORMATION CONDITION: FROM MORE TO LESS INFORMATION IN THE BARGAINING CHANNEL	PEARSON PRODUCT MOMENT CORRELATION BETWEEN RTP AND BARGAINING ABILITY
1. Manufacturers and retailers under partial and incomplete information	1. $r = +.3532$ ($p < .05$)
2. Ms and Rs under partial information plus Ms, Ws, and Rs under incomplete information	2. $r = +.4501$ ($p < .01$)
3. Ms and Rs under incomplete information	3. $r = +.6439$ ($p < .01$)
4. Ms, Ws, and Rs under incomplete information	4. $r = +.6951$ ($p < .01$)

In each of the four variations of the information variable, there is a relationship in the predicted direction between RTP and bargaining ability. The greater the RTP (the lower the score on the Wallach-Kogan instrument), the less the tendency for the S to yield in his bargaining behavior. As hypothesized, this relationship increases as the amount of information available in the total bargaining channel decreases. The strongest relationship between RTP and bargaining ability emerges under that condition wherein all participants in the channel are operating under the incomplete information condition.

Thus, it would appear that risk taking as a general personality characteristic has little impact on the bargaining *results attained,* that is, the amount of profit earned by a participant, in the bargaining context studied in this research. On the other hand, risk taking does appear to emerge as an important determinant of bargaining behavior or *process.* So, under partial and incomplete information conditions, risk-taking propensity is significantly associated, in an inverse direction, with the participant's willingness to yield or "give in" from his initial level of aspiration.

Summary

In this chapter we began with a general description of the nature of competition in organized settings. We then examined bargaining as exemplified through bidding, followed by an attempt to elaborate a typology of bargaining relationships and introduced the notion of inequality among bargainers. This led to a discussion of relevant decision criteria, theoretically possible under varied conditions.

An examination of bargaining under uncertainty led us into a discussion of informational search processes in bargaining strategies. We then illustrated these notions concerning bargaining by reporting a study investigating the effects of information and personal orientation toward risk on bargaining behavior.

Postscript

As we want to conclude this work, we find that we cannot. We are unable to conclude for several reasons: (1) this study is dated; fundamental conceptualizations are historically based, while new empirical evidence is generated daily; (2) our discussions of the concerns presented here have been highly selective, and biases are explained by our own experiences and personalized evaluations of available research; and thus (3) because our model is eclectic and not integrative, the presentation does not offer a representative or full isomorphism of organizational incumbents in their decisional processes.

We might comment, however, on the circularity of this overall presentation.

Commencing with an overview—albeit a mechanistic approach—in Chapter I, we immediately examined psychological postulates relating to "individualized" decision making in Chapters 2 and 3. Here we discussed both (1) the constructs of perception and learning as they bear on decision making; and (2) scientifically and deductively based propositions as empirical operationalisms of learning and speculations on heuristic problem solving.

Through theories devoted to aspects of decision making pertaining to social impacts on choice (Chapters 4 and 5) and expanding on what may be characterized as an egoistic point of view, from what may be a reductionist posture, we elaborated in the way of (1) the impact of socialization on individual decision making, especially that of normative prescriptions as they become internalized and provide value premises in choice; and (2) small group decision making, particularly as a phenomenon in ongoing organizations and as related to managerial concerns, for example, style and span of control.

Through propositions stemming from theories of organizational design, organizational decision making, while still viewed as "individualized," was seen to have unique features. Here, we (1) looked first at structure as a conflict-resolving mechanism (Chapter 6) and, second, at structuring as a conflict-generating phenomenon (Chapter 7); and (2) examined both privately held values and those more public to the organization. Although the "group mind" thesis was not held, some commonality of decision premises was an essential feature of organized behavior.

To, finally, this last presentation on bargaining and negotiation, our econological focus limited, in some ways, the treatment of decision making in a bargaining situation. However, we did come full circle in that we again treated certain psychological constructs as risk propensity and willingness to conform to a generalized social field.

bibliography

BERNARD, JESSIE: *American Community Behavior* (New York: The Dryden Press, 1952).

BIERMAN, HAROLD, LAWRENCE FOURAKER, and ROBERT JAEDICKE: *Quantitative Analysis for Business Decisions* (Homewood, Ill.: Richard D. Irwin, Inc., 1961), pp. 307–316.

BOULDING, KENNETH: *Economic Analysis,* 2nd ed. (New York: Harper & Brothers, 1948), p. 508.

————: "A Pure Theory of Conflict Applied to Organizations," in *Conflict Management in Organizations* (Ann Arbor, Mich.: Foundation for Research on Human Behavior, 1961).

BOWLEY, A. L.: "On Bilateral Monopoly," *The Economic Journal,* vol. 38, 1928, pp. 651–659.

BRADFORD, LAWRENCE A., and GLEN L. JOHNSON: *Farm Management Analysis* (New York: John Wiley & Sons, Inc., 1963).

BROWN, WILFRED: *Product Analysis Pricing* (London: Hienemann Educational Books, Ltd., 1958).

CHAMBERLIN, EDWARD H.: *The Theory of Monopolistic Competition,* 6th ed. (Cambridge, Mass.: Harvard University Press, 1950).

CHAMBERLAIN, NEIL W.: *A General Theory of Economic Process* (New York: Harper & Brothers, 1955).

DEUTSCH, M.: "A Theory of Cooperation and Competition," *Human Relations,* vol. 30, 1949, University of Michigan Press, Ann Arbor, Mich.

DUNLOP, JOHN T.: *Industrial Relations Systems* (New York: Holt, Rinehart, and Winston, Inc., 1958).

FELLNER, WILLIAM: *Competition Among the Few* (New York: Alfred A. Knopf, Inc., 1949).

FOURAKER, LAWRENCE E., and SIDNEY SIEGEL: *Bargaining Behavior* (New York: McGraw-Hill Book Company, 1963).

FRIEDMAN, MILTON: *Essays in Positive Economics* (Chicago: University of Chicago Press, 1953).

GARDNER, MARTIN: "Mathematical Games," *Scientific American,* December, 1967.

HARNETT, DONALD L., LARRY L. CUMMINGS, and G. DAVID HUGHES: "Bargaining Behavior and Risk-taking Propensity," *Behavioral Science,* vol. 13, no. 2, March, 1968, pp. 91–101.

HARSANYI, JOHN C.: "Bargaining in Ignorance of the Opponent's Utility Function," *The Journal of Conflict Resolution,* vol. 6, March, 1962, pp. 29–38.

HART, ABERT GAILORD: *Anticipations, Uncertainty, and Dynamic Planning* (New York: Augustus M. Kelley, Publishers, 1951).

IKLE, FRED C., in collaboration with NATHAN LEITES: "Political Negotiations as a Process of Modifying Utilities," *The Journal of Conflict Resolution,* vol. 6, March, 1962, p. 21.

KEMENY, JOHN G., et al.: *Finite Mathematics with Business Applications* (Englewood Cliffs, N.J.: Prentice-Hall, Inc., 1962).

KOGAN, NATHAN, and MICHAEL A. WALLACH: *Risk Taking: A Study in Cognition and Personality* (New York: Holt, Rinehart, and Winston, Inc., 1964).

LANGE, OSCAR: *Price Flexibility and Employment* (Evanston, Ill.: The Principia Press, Inc., 1952).

LUCE, R. DUNCAN, and HOWARD RAIFFA: *Games and Decisions* (New York: John Wiley & Sons, Inc., 1957).

MCDONALD, JOHN: "Strategy of the Seller—or What Businessmen Won't Tell," *Fortune,* vol. 44, December, 1952.

MILLER, DELBERT C.: "The Application of Social System Analysis to a Labor-management Conflict: A Consultant's Case Study," *Conflict Resolution,* vol. 3, no. 2, June, 1959, pp. 146–152.

MORRIS, WILLIAM T.: *The Analysis of Management Decisions* (Homewood, Ill.: Richard D. Irwin, Inc., 1964).

NEMHAUSER, GEORGE L.: *Introduction to Dynamic Programming* (New York: John Wiley & Sons, Inc., 1966).

NEWMAN, RICHARD G.: "Some Comments on Negotiation," *Journal of Purchasing,* vol. 2, no. 2, May, 1966, pp. 52–66.

———, "A Note on Competitive Bidding," *Journal of Purchasing,* vol. 3, no. 2, May, 1967, pp. 69–83.

NOURSE, E. G.: *Industrial Price Policies and Economic Progress* (Washington, D.C.: The Brookings Institution, 1938).

PARETO, V.: *Manuel d'Economie Politique* (Paris: M. Giard, 1909).

RICHMOND, SAMUEL R.: *Statistical Analysis,* 2nd ed. (New York: The Ronald Press Company, 1964).

SAVAGE, LEONARD: *The Foundations of Statistics* (New York: John Wiley & Sons, Inc., 1954).

SCHELLING, T. C.: "Bargaining, Communication, and Limited War," *Conflict Resolution,* vol. 1, 1957, pp. 19–36.

SCHUCHMAN, ABE: *Scientific Decision Making in Business* (New York: Holt, Rinehart and Winston, Inc., 1963), pp. 329–330.

SHEPARD, HERBERT: "Responses to Situations of Competition and Conflict," *Conflict Management in Organizations* (Ann Arbor, Mich.: Foundation for Research on Human Behavior, 1961).

SIEGEL, S., and L. E. FOURAKER: *Bargaining and Group Decision Making* (New York: McGraw-Hill Book Company, 1960).

STONE, RICHARD: "The Theory of Games," *Economic Journal,* vol. 58, no. 2, June, 1948, pp. 185–201.

THOMPSON, JAMES D.: "Games and Decision Strategies," Administrative Science Center, University of Pittsburgh, October, 1960, 3 pp. (Working paper, mimeographed.)

———, and ARTHUR TUDEN: "Strategies and Processes of Organizational Decision," in Thompson et al., *Comparative Studies in Administration* (Pittsburgh: University of Pittsburgh Press, 1959).

VON NEUMAN, JOHN, and OSCAR MORGENSTERN: *Theory of Games and Economic Behavior* (Princeton: Princeton University Press, 1947).

WALD, ABRAHAM: *Statistical Decision Functions* (New York: John Wiley & Sons, Inc., 1950).

WALTON, RICHARD E., and ROBERT B. MCKERSIE: *A Behavioral Theory of Labor Negotiations* (New York: McGraw-Hill Book Company, 1965), p. 4.

index

index

Anomie, 177n., 178
Anticipatory behavior, 20–21
Aspirations and perceptions, 45
Attitude change, 4
Attitudes, 103
  and socialization, 102–104
Authority:
  impersonal, 180
  structure, 228

Bargaining, 269–272
  alternatives to, 272–277
  and aspiration, 300
  and Bayes' theorem, 294–300
  and Bayesian criteria, 288
  and decision rules, 287
  definition, 277
  distributive, 277–285
    bidding, 282–285
    game theory, 277–282
      nonzero sum, 282
      two-person, zero-sum,
        278–281
  and economic equilibrium, 271,
    272
  and information, 293–300
  and motivational set, 300
  and personality, 300
  power structure, 276, 277
  propensities, 285
  and risk taking, 286, 300–304
  and uncertainty, 285
Bayes' theorem, 294
Behavior:
  anticipatory, 20, 21
  decision, 23
  innovative, 74
  managerial, 5
  nonnegotiated, 273
  organizational, 4, 173

Behavior:
  symbolic, 100
  task-facilitating, 185
Behavioral decision theory and
    perception, 11
Behavioralism approaches to per-
    ception, 42–47
  adaptation level theory, 43–46
  motivational theory, 43, 46, 47
Bidding, 282
Bluffing, 290, 291
Bounded discretion, 18–21
  legitimacy of, 18
  and social control, 18
Bureaucracy, 7, 177, 178, 186
  alternatives to, 183–187
  and culture, 8n., 182
  definition, 7n.
  dysfunctions of, 182
Business concern groups, 156

Characteristics:
  organizational, 173
  structural, 173
Classical model (see Rational
    model)
Classical organizational theory, 203
Coalitions in groups, 150, 153
Coefficient of optimism, 287
Cognition:
  behavioral decision theory, 11
  definition, 30
Cognitive dissonance, 105, 106, 190
Collusion, 276
Commonweal Organization groups,
    156
Communications:
  content, 117, 118
    and group size, 146, 147